POINTS *of* DEPARTURE

THE BIBLE
AS/IN LITERATURE

SECOND EDITION

JAMES S. ACKERMAN

THAYER S. WARSHAW

JOHN SWEET
(Editorial Consultant)

ScottForesman

A Division of HarperCollins*Publishers*

EDITORIAL OFFICES: Glenview, Illinois
REGIONAL OFFICES: Sunnyvale, California · Tucker, Georgia
· Glenview, Illinois · Oakland, New Jersey · Dallas, Texas

ACKNOWLEDGMENTS

Bible Passages

Units 1 and 8 From *The Oxford Study Bible, Revised English Bible with the Apocrypha* edited by M. Jack Suggs, Katharine Doob Sakenfeld and James R. Mueller. Copyright © 1989 by Oxford University and Cambridge University Press. Reprinted by permission of Cambridge University Press.

Unit 2 From *Tanakh the Holy Scriptures: The New JPS Translation According to the Traditional Hebrew Text.* Copyright © 1985 by The Jewish Publication Society. Reprinted by permission of The Jewish Publication Society.

Units 3 and 5 From *The Revised Standard Version of the Bible.* Copyright 1946, 1952, © 1971 by the Division of Christian Education of the National Council of the Churches of Christ in the USA. Used by permission.

Unit 4 From *The Holy Bible, New International Version®.* NIV® Copyright © 1973, 1978, 1984 by International Bible Society. Used by permission of Zondervan Publishing House. All rights reserved.

Units 6, 7, and 12 From *The New Revised Standard Version of the Bible.* Copyright © 1989 by the Division of Christian Education of the National Council of the Churches of Christ in the USA. Used by permission. All rights reserved.

Unit 9 From *The New Jerusalem Bible.* Copyright © 1985 by Doubleday, a division of Bantam Doubleday Dell Publishing Group, Inc. and Darton, Longman & Todd, Ltd. Used by permission of Doubleday, a division of Bantam Doubleday Dell Publishing Group, Inc. and Darton, Longman & Todd, Ltd.

Units 10 and 11 From *The Holy Bible, The New King James Version.* Copyright © 1979, 1980, 1982, Thomas Nelson, Inc. Reprinted by permission of Thomas Nelson, Inc., Publishers.
(Acknowledgments continue on page 467.)

Front cover: Eliza Schulte
Back cover: Photograph of James Ackerman by Paul Riley.
Photograph of Thayer Warshaw by Leon Somers.

Contents

11 Jesus: Teachings, Death, and Resurrection

12 In the End of Days

Appendix

Introduction

As its title suggests, *The Bible as/in Literature* has a two-fold purpose: to study the literary craftsmanship of passages from the Bible (the Bible *as* literature) and to explore the relationship of a variety of other stories, poems, and plays to the Bible (the Bible *in* literature). Some of these latter selections are directly influenced by the Bible, openly retelling or quietly alluding to specific biblical passages. Other nonbiblical selections, while not connected explicitly to a Bible passage, have a similar theme or situation.

This second edition of *The Bible as/in Literature* builds on the foundation and experiences of the first. We offer more Bible passages, including portions of the story of Jacob, Ecclesiastes 3, and 1 Corinthians 13. To acknowledge diverse traditions and to showcase some of the many excellent translations available, the Bible passages are now taken from a variety of sources. We have added more marginal notes and refined the text questions— *(a)* **For Close Reading**, factual questions that help the student focus upon and grasp important or subtle details; and *(b)* **For Thought and Discussion**, open-ended questions, the answers to which may be judged "more appropriate" or "less appropriate" rather than "right" or "wrong." **Responding** activities, both verbal and nonverbal, have a stronger emphasis on group projects and include a new focus on multicultural and humanities connections. An **Appendix**, new to this edition, contains a brief history of the Bible; a sampler of Bible translations; a review of people, events, and key expressions in the Bible; as well as maps and timelines.

All of these elements, old and new, are only initial stimuli to the imaginations and resources of teacher and student. Interests and abilities will, we hope, lead still further out from, or more deeply into, the text.

A few words about the Bible *as* literature. First, craftsmanship is only one aspect of a piece of literature. The relationship between craftsmanship and ideas, how well the manner and matter support each other, is basic to the study of literature. The question is which of these two aspects should be the focus in using the Bible in a public school literature class. We start with the craftsmanship and only then move to the ideas it expresses.

Second, the literary approach to the Bible focuses on only one aspect of a book that has had an immeasurable influence on the western world and is sacred to three of the world's major religions. Concentration on the literary aspects of the Bible does not imply any intent to ignore or diminish its cultural, historical, moral, and religious content. Rather, focus on the Bible as literature provides a common ground for people of all traditions and attitudes to examine and appreciate the Bible in the same classroom. (For example, at the outset, different religious traditions vary as to what constitutes "the Bible.")

Third, an understanding of any piece of literature may lead to a consideration of its relevance to the reader's own experiences and values. In this respect biblical and Bible-related literature, more than most, can present problems for a multicultural society. Such problems are not barriers, however; they are instead welcome reminders that teachers and students must be aware of the sensibilities of other people.

We hope you will read and enjoy and think and learn.

James S. Ackerman
Thayer S. Warshaw

POINTS *of* DEPARTURE

THE BIBLE

AS/IN LITERATURE

SECOND EDITION

1

Stories from the Beginning

Creation: Heaven and Earth

In the beginning God created the heavens and the earth. The earth was a vast waste, darkness covered the deep, and the spirit of God hovered over the surface of the water. God said, "Let there be light," and there was light; and God saw the light was good, and he separated light from darkness. He called the light day, and the darkness night. So evening came, and morning came; it was the first day.

God said, "Let there be a vault between the waters, to separate water from water." So God made the vault, and separated the water under the vault from the water above it, and so it was; and God called the vault the heavens. Evening came, and morning came, the second day.

vault: arched roof of heaven; sky.

God said, "Let the water under the heavens be gathered into one place, so that dry land may appear"; and so it was. God called the dry land earth, and God saw that it was good. Then God said, "Let the earth produce growing things; let there be on the earth plants that bear seed, and trees bearing fruit each with its own kind of seed." So it was; the earth produced growing things: plants bearing their own kind of seed and trees bearing fruit, each with its own kind of seed; and God saw that it was good. Evening came, and morning came, the third day.

God said, "Let there be lights in the vault of the heavens to separate day from night, and let them serve as signs both for festivals and for seasons and

Genesis 1:1–2:4a (Revised English Bible).
LEFT: *Ancient of Days* by William Blake (1794). The Pierpont Morgan Library.

years. Let them also shine in the heavens to give light on earth." So it was; God made two great lights, the greater to govern the day and the lesser to govern the night; he also made the stars. God put these lights in the vault of the heavens to give light on earth, to govern day and night, and to separate light from darkness; and God saw that it was good. Evening came, and morning came, the fourth day.

God said, "Let the water teem with living creatures, and let birds fly above the earth across the vault of the heavens." God then created the great sea-beasts and all living creatures that move and swarm in the water, according to their various kinds, and every kind of bird; and God saw that it was good. He blessed them and said, "Be fruitful and increase; fill the water of the sea, and let birds increase on the land." Evening came, and morning came, the fifth day.

God said, "Let the earth bring forth living creatures, according to their various kinds: cattle, creeping things, and wild animals, all according to their various kinds." So it was; God made wild animals, cattle, and every creeping thing, all according to their various kinds; and he saw that it was good. Then God said, "Let us make human beings in our image, after our likeness, to have dominion over the fish in the sea, the birds of the air, the cattle, all wild animals on land, and everything that creeps on the earth."

us . . . our: may refer to lesser beings in God's heavenly court.

have dominion: rule.

> God created human beings in his own image;
> in the image of God he created them;
> male and female he created them.

God blessed them and said to them, "Be fruitful and increase, fill the earth and subdue it, have dominion over the fish in the sea, the birds of the air, and every living thing that moves on earth." God also said, "Throughout the earth I give you all plants that bear seed, and every tree that bears fruit with seed: they shall be yours for food. All green plants I give for food to the wild animals, to all the birds of the air, and to everything that creeps on the earth, every living creature." So it was; and God saw all that he had made, and it was very good. Evening came, and morning came, the sixth day.

Thus the heavens and the earth and everything in them were completed. On the sixth day God brought to an end all the work he had been doing; on the seventh day, having finished all his work, God blessed the day and made it holy, because it was the day he finished all his work of creation.

This is the story of the heavens and the earth after their creation.

FOR CLOSE READING

1. Make a list of what is created on each of the first six days. What are the main differences between the seventh day and the first six?

2. What kinds of food does God feel that the creatures will need?

3. Certain phrases are repeated for almost every day and every created act. What are they?

4. Make a list of the verbs that describe what God does.

FOR THOUGHT AND DISCUSSION

5. Look at your list of each day's creations. Can you see any logic to the order? Explain. Why do you think human beings are created last?

6. Consider the verbs describing God's actions. What sense of the personality or character of God do you get from these words and other details? What seems to be God's relation to the world and its creatures? Use specific phrases from the passage to show how God's personal qualities are revealed.

7. Certain phrases in this passage call up vivid images or emotions for many readers. What words or phrases have a special interest or attractiveness for you? Why?

8. According to this passage, human beings are created "in the image of God." What do you think this means?

RESPONDING

1. **Activity** With a group of classmates create something—pictures, diagrams, models, and so on—that will help you explain one or more stages of the biblical creation story to a small child. If possible, make your presentation to a group of children and report to the class how the children reacted.

2. **Activity** Each person in the class takes a piece of clay to shape into anything he or she wishes. You are all "creating." Now try to decide which is the most "creative" creation. How did you decide? What criteria did you agree upon?

3. **Humanities Connection** Examine five or six paintings (in art books, prints, or museums) that show God creating the world. Identify the one that you feel most clearly represents the biblical account.

Creation: In the Garden

When the Lord God made the earth and the heavens, there was neither shrub nor plant growing on the earth, because the Lord God had sent no rain; nor was there anyone to till the ground. Moisture used to well up out of the earth and water all the surface of the ground.

The Lord God formed a human being from the dust of the ground and breathed into his nostrils the breath of life, so that he became a living creature. The Lord God planted a garden in Eden away to the east, and in it he put the man he had formed. The Lord God made trees grow up from the ground, every kind of tree pleasing to the eye and good for food; and in the middle of the garden he set the tree of life and the tree of the knowledge of good and evil.

> **human, ground:** In the original Hebrew, the word for ground is *adamah* and the word for humankind is *adam*.

> **tree of life:** its fruit was believed to bring eternal life.

There was a river flowing from Eden to water the garden, and from there it branched into four streams. The name of the first is Pishon; it is the river which skirts the whole land of Havilah, where gold is found. The gold of that land is good; gum resin and cornelians are also to be found there. The name of the second river is Gihon; this is the one which skirts the whole land of Cush. The name of the third is Tigris; this is the river which flows east of Asshur. The fourth river is the Euphrates.

> **gum resin:** a fragrant plant resin that dries to a stonelike hardness.

> **cornelians:** precious stones; gems.

The Lord God took the man and put him in the garden of Eden to till it and look after it. "You may eat from any tree in the garden," he told the man, "except from the tree of the knowledge of good and evil; the day you eat from that, you are surely doomed to die." Then the Lord God said, "It is not good for the man to be alone; I shall make a partner suited to him." So from the earth he formed all the

Genesis 2:4b–25 (Revised English Bible).

wild animals and all the birds of the air, and brought them to the man to see what he would call them; whatever the man called each living creature, that would be its name. The man gave names to all cattle, to the birds of the air, and to every wild animal; but for the man himself no suitable partner was found. The Lord God then put the man into a deep sleep and, while he slept, he took one of the man's ribs and closed up the flesh over the place. The rib he had taken out of the man the Lord God built up into a woman, and he brought her to the man. The man said:

man, woman: The Hebrew words are *ish* and *ishshah*.

> "This one at last
> is bone from my bones,
> flesh from my flesh!
> She shall be called woman,
> for from man was she taken."

That is why a man leaves his father and mother and attaches himself to his wife, and the two become one. Both were naked, the man and his wife, but they had no feeling of shame.

FOR CLOSE READING

1. According to the opening sentence, what two things were lacking for shrubs and plants to grow? Of these two things, which did God create first?

2. According to this part of the Bible story, what is the order of creation of the world? Why, and from what, did God create the wild animals and birds? the woman?

3. God gives man two instructions. What must he not do? What is the first job he is given to do?

4. According to the story, why do people get married?

5. Make a list of new verbs, not used in the previous creation passage, that describe God's actions in this passage.

FOR THOUGHT AND DISCUSSION

6. The tree of the knowledge of good and evil is forbidden to Adam and Eve. What danger might God have seen in their having this knowledge? In what ways is knowledge a good thing? a bad thing?

7. The roles of men and women in society, and of husbands and wives in marriage, are continually being discussed today. What does this story seem to suggest about the roles of men and women? husbands and wives?

8. Look at your list of new verbs describing God's actions. What sense of the personality or character of God do you get from these words and other details of the story? What new relation does God seem to have to the world and its creatures? Give examples from the story to support your opinion.

9. As you compare and contrast this part of the creation story with the preceding passage on page 3, what variations do you notice? How might one explain these variations?

RESPONDING

1. Writing Suppose that you can overhear Adam and Eve thinking as well as speaking. Write what you learn in one of the following instances: (*a*) What goes on in Adam's mind between the time he is created and the time he discovers his "partner." (*b*) What goes on in Eve's mind from the time she is created until Adam wakes from his deep sleep.

2. Activity This story suggests that naming things is a very early human practice. As a class, make a list of 10–15 animals, places, and objects to be renamed. Work in small groups to devise new, "better" names for these things. When you're done, share and compare the new names with the whole class.

The Creation

And God stepped out on space,
And He looked around and said,
"I'm lonely—
I'll make me a world."

5 And as far as the eye of God could see
Darkness covered everything,
Blacker than a hundred midnights
Down in a cypress swamp.

Then God smiled,
10 And the light broke,
And the darkness rolled up on one side,
And the light stood shining on the other,
And God said, *"That's good!"*

Then God reached out and took the light
   in His hands,
15 And God rolled the light around in His hands,
Until He made the sun;
And He set that sun a-blazing in the heavens.
And the light that was left from making the
   sun
God gathered up in a shining ball
20 And flung against the darkness,
Spangling the night with the moon and stars.
Then down between
The darkness and the light
He hurled the world;
25 And God said, *"That's good!"*

Then God himself stepped down—
And the sun was on His right hand,
And the moon was on His left;
The stars were clustered about His head,
30 and the earth was under His feet.

And God walked, and where He trod
His footsteps hollowed the valleys out
And bulged the mountains up.

35 Then He stopped and looked and saw
That the earth was hot and barren.
So God stepped over to the edge of the world
And He spat out the seven seas;
He batted His eyes, and the lightnings flashed;
He clapped His hands, and the thunders rolled;
40 And the waters above the earth came down,
The cooling waters came down.

Then the green grass sprouted,
And the little red flowers blossomed,
The pine-tree pointed his finger to the sky,
45 And the oak spread out his arms;
The lakes cuddled down in the hollows of the
    ground,
And the rivers ran down to the sea;
And God smiled again,
And the rainbow appeared,
50 And curled itself around His shoulder.

Then God raised His arm and He waved His hand
Over the sea and over the land,
And He said, *"Bring forth! Bring forth!"*
And quicker than God could drop His hand,
55 Fishes and fowls
And beast and birds
Swam the rivers and the seas,
Roamed the forests and the woods,
And split the air with their wings,
60 And God said, *"That's good!"*

Then God walked around
And God looked around
On all that He had made.
He looked at His sun,
65 And He looked at His moon,
And He looked at His little stars;
He looked on His world
With all its living things,
And God said, *"I'm lonely still."*

70 Then God sat down

On the side of a hill where He could think;
By a deep, wide river He sat down;
With His head in His hands,
God thought and thought,
75   Till He thought, *"I'll make me a man!"*

Up from the bed of the river
God scooped the clay;
And by the bank of the river
He kneeled Him down;
80   And there the great God Almighty,
Who lit the sun and fixed it in the sky,
Who flung the stars to the most far corner of
    the night,
Who rounded the earth in the middle of His
    hand—
This Great God,
85   Like a mammy bending over her baby,
Kneeled down in the dust
Toiling over a lump of clay
Till He shaped it in His own image;

Then into it He blew the breath of life,
90   And man became a living soul.
Amen. Amen.

FOR CLOSE READING

1. List the verbs used in the poem to describe God's actions.

2. According to this poem, why did God create the world?

FOR THOUGHT AND DISCUSSION

3. Compare and contrast the descriptions of God's actions in this poem with the verbs used in the two passages of the biblical creation. What differences do you see?

4. The Bible passages do not say why God created the world; this poem does. How persuasive would you say is the reason the poem gives?

Heaven and Earth in Jest

A couple of summers ago I was walking along the edge of the island to see what I could see in the water, and mainly to scare frogs. Frogs have an inelegant way of taking off from invisible positions on the bank just ahead of your feet, in dire panic, emitting a froggy "Yike!" and splashing into the water. Incredibly, this amused me, and, incredibly, it amuses me still. As I walked along the grassy edge of the island, I got better and better at seeing frogs both in and out of the water. I learned to recognize, slowing down, the difference in texture of the light reflected from mudbank, water, grass, or frog. Frogs were flying all around me. At the end of the island I noticed a small green frog. He was exactly half in and half out of the water, looking like a schematic diagram of an amphibian, and he didn't jump.

He didn't jump; I crept closer. At last I knelt on the island's winterkilled grass, lost, dumbstruck, staring at the frog in the creek just four feet away. He was a very small frog with wide, dull eyes. And just as I looked at him, he slowly crumpled and began to sag. The spirit vanished from his eyes as if snuffed. His skin emptied and dropped; his very skull seemed to collapse and settle like a kicked tent. He was shrinking before my eyes like a deflating football. I watched the taut, glistening skin on his shoulders ruck, and rumple, and fall. Soon, part of his skin, formless as a pricked balloon, lay in floating folds like bright scum on top of the water; it was a monstrous and terrifying thing. I gaped bewildered, appalled. An oval shadow hung in the water behind the drained frog; then the shadow glided away. The frog skin bag started to sink.

I had read about the giant water bug, but never seen one. "Giant water bug" is really the name of the creature, which is an enormous, heavy-bodied brown beetle. It eats insects, tadpoles, fish, and frogs. Its grasping forelegs are mighty and hooked inward. It seizes a victim with these legs, hugs it tight, and paralyzes it with enzymes injected during a vicious bite. That one bite is the only bite it ever takes. Through the puncture shoot the poisons that dissolve the victim's muscles and bones and organs—all but the skin—and through it the giant water bug sucks out the victim's body, reduced to a juice. This event is quite common in warm fresh water. The frog I saw was being sucked by a giant water bug. I had been kneeling on the island grass; when the unrecognizable flap of frog skin settled on the creek bottom, swaying, I stood up and brushed the knees of my pants. I couldn't catch my breath.

Of course, many carnivorous animals devour their prey alive. The usual method seems to be to subdue the victim by downing or grasping it so it can't flee, then eating it whole or in a series of bloody bites. Frogs eat everything whole, stuffing prey into their mouths with their thumbs. People have seen frogs with their wide jaws so full of live dragonflies they couldn't close them. Ants don't even have to catch their prey: in spring they swarm over newly hatched, featherless birds in the nest and eat them tiny bite by bite.

That it's rough out there and chancy is no surprise. Every live thing is a survivor on a kind of extended emergency bivouac. But at the same time we are also created. In the Koran, Allah asks, "The heaven and the earth and all in between, thinkest thou I made them *in jest?*" It's a good question. What do we think of the created universe, spanning an unthinkable void with an unthinkable profusion of forms? Or what do we think of nothingness, those sickening reaches of time in either direction? If the giant water bug was not made in jest, was it then made in earnest? Pascal uses a nice term to describe the notion of the creator's, once having called forth the universe, turning his back to it: *Deus Absconditus.* Is this what we think happened? Was the sense of it there, and God absconded with it, ate it, like a wolf

enzymes: substances that help in digesting food.

bivouac (biv'wak): temporary outdoor camp.

Koran: the sacred book of Islam. Allah is the Muslim name of God.

profusion: great number.

Deus Absconditus: (Latin) the hidden or departed God.

absconded: left quickly.

who disappears round the edge of the house with the Thanksgiving turkey? "God is subtle," Einstein said, "but not malicious." Again, Einstein said that "nature conceals her mystery by means of her essential grandeur, not by her cunning." It could be that God has not absconded but spread, as our vision and understanding of the universe have spread, to a fabric of spirit and sense so grand and subtle, so powerful in a new way, that we can only feel blindly of its hem. In making the thick darkness a swaddling band for the sea, God "set bars and doors," and said, "Hitherto shalt thou come, but no further." But have we come even that far? Have we rowed out to the thick darkness, or are we all playing pinochle in the bottom of the boat?

Cruelty is a mystery, and the waste of pain. But if we describe a world to compass these things, a world that is a long, brute game, then we bump against another mystery: the inrush of power and light, the canary that sings on the skull. Unless all ages and races of men have been deluded by the same mass hypnotist (who?), there seems to be such a thing as beauty, a grace wholly gratuitous. About five years ago I saw a mockingbird make a straight vertical descent from the roof gutter of a four-story building. It was an act as careless and spontaneous as the curl of a stem or the kindling of a star.

gratuitous: without reason or cause.

The mockingbird took a single step into the air and dropped. His wings were still folded against his sides as though he were singing from a limb and not falling, accelerating thirty-two feet per second per second, through empty air. Just a breath before he would have been dashed to the ground, he unfurled his wings with exact, deliberate care, revealing the broad bars of white, spread his elegant, white-banded tail, and so floated onto the grass. I had just rounded a corner when his insouciant step caught my eye; there was no one else in sight. The fact of his free fall was like the old philosophical conundrum about the tree that falls in the forest. The answer must be, I think, that beauty and grace are performed whether or not we will or sense them. The least we can do is try to be there.

insouciant: (in sü′sē ənt): carefree.

conundrum: puzzle; i.e., if nobody hears it, does the tree make a sound?

Another time I saw another wonder: sharks off the Atlantic coast of Florida. There is a way a wave rises above the ocean horizon, a triangular wedge against the sky. If you stand where the ocean breaks on a shallow beach, you see the raised water in a wave is translucent, shot with lights. One late afternoon at low tide a hundred big sharks passed the beach near the mouth of a tidal river in a feeding frenzy. As each green wave rose from the churning water, it illuminated within itself the six- or eight-foot-long bodies of twisting sharks. The sharks disappeared as each wave rolled toward me; then a new wave would swell above the horizon, containing in it, like scorpions in amber, sharks that roiled and heaved. The sight held awesome wonders: power and beauty, grace tangled in a rapture with violence.

We don't know what's going on here. If these tremendous events are random combinations of matter run amok, the yield of millions of monkeys at millions of typewriters, then what is it in us, hammered out of those same typewriters, that they ignite? We don't know. Our life is a faint tracing on the surface of mystery, like the idle, curved tunnels of leaf miners on the face of a leaf. We must somehow take a wider view, look at the whole landscape, really see it, and describe what's going on here. Then we can at least wail the right question into the swaddling band of darkness, or, if it comes to that, choir the proper praise.

At the time of Lewis and Clark, setting the prairies on fire was a well-known signal that meant, "Come down to the water." It was an extravagant gesture, but we can't do less. If the landscape reveals one certainty, it is that the extravagant gesture is the very stuff of creation. After the one extravagant gesture of creation in the first place, the universe has continued to deal exclusively in extravagances, flinging intricacies and colossi down aeons of emptiness, heaping profusions on profligacies with ever-fresh vigor. The whole show has been on fire from the word go. I come down to the water to cool my eyes. But everywhere I look I see fire; that which isn't flint is tinder, and the whole world sparks and flames.

run amok: behaving wildly.

millions of monkeys: a reference to the speculation that millions of monkeys at typewriters for millions of years could type all the great literary works ever written—by sheer chance.

leaf miners: insect larvae that feed on leaves.

FOR CLOSE READING

1. The author focuses on frogs, a water bug, a mockingbird, and sharks. How does she respond to each?

2. This passage includes many vivid comparisons; for instance, "his very skull seemed to collapse and settle like a kicked tent." Find several other vivid comparisons.

FOR THOUGHT AND DISCUSSION

3. What part of this selection most affected you? Why?

4. From your own knowledge and experience of nature, describe one or two things that suggest (*a*) the harshness and (*b*) the beauty of something in the universe.

5. How do you think the author feels about the purpose of the universe and the possibility of knowing why it is the way it is?

Forbidden Fruit

The serpent, which was the most cunning of all the creatures the Lord God had made, asked the woman, "Is it true that God has forbidden you to eat from any tree in the garden?" She replied, "We may eat the fruit of any tree in the garden, except for the tree in the middle of the garden. God has forbidden us to eat the fruit of that tree or even to touch it; if we do, we shall die." "Of course you will not die," said the serpent; for God knows that, as soon as you eat it, your eyes will be opened and you will be like God himself, knowing both good and evil." The woman looked at the tree: the fruit would be good to eat; it was pleasing to the eye and desirable for the knowledge it could give. So she took some and ate it; she also gave some to her husband, and he ate it. Then the eyes of both of them were opened, and they knew that they were naked; so they stitched fig-leaves together and made themselves loincloths.

The man and his wife heard the sound of the Lord God walking about in the garden at the time of the evening breeze, and they hid from him among the trees. The Lord God called to the man, "Where are you?" He replied, "I heard the sound of you in the garden and I was afraid because I was naked, so I hid." God said, "Who told you that you were naked? Have you eaten from the tree which I forbade you to eat from?" The man replied, "It was the woman you gave to be with me who gave me fruit from the tree, and I ate it." The Lord God said to the woman, "What have you done?" The woman answered, "It was the serpent who deceived me into eating it." The Lord God said to the serpent:

deceived: tricked.

Genesis 3:1–24 (Revised English Bible).

"Because you have done this you are cursed alone of all cattle and the creatures of the wild.

> "On your belly you will crawl,
> and dust you will eat
> all the days of your life.
> I shall put enmity between you and the woman,
> between your brood and hers,
> They will strike at your head,
> and you will strike at their heel."

To the woman he said:

> "I shall give you great labor in childbearing;
> with labor you will bear children.
> You will desire your husband,
> but he will be your master."

And to the man he said: "Because you have listened to your wife and have eaten from the tree which I forbade you,

> on your account the earth will be cursed.
> You will get your food from it only by labor
> all the days of your life;
> it will yield thorns and thistles for you.
> You will eat of the produce of the field,
> and only by the sweat of your brow will you win
>   your bread
> until you return to the earth;
> for from it you were taken
> Dust you are, to dust you will return."

The man named his wife Eve because she was the mother of all living beings. The Lord God made coverings from skins for the man and his wife and clothed them. But he said, "The man has become like one of us, knowing good and evil; what if he now reaches out and takes fruit from the tree of life also, and eats it and lives for ever?" So the Lord God banished him from the garden of Eden to till the ground from which he had been taken. When he drove him out, God settled him to the east of the garden of Eden, and he stationed the cherubim and a sword whirling and flashing to guard the way to the tree of life.

cattle: domesticated animals.

brood: offspring.

Eve: very close to the Hebrew word for "living."

cherubim (cher′ə bim): winged angels.

FOR CLOSE READING

1. For what three reasons does Eve eat the fruit?

2. What do Adam and Even "learn" from eating the fruit?

3. What punishments are given to the serpent? to Eve? to Adam?

4. Some parts of the Bible explain why certain aspects of life are hard or painful. What aspects of life can you find explained in this passage?

FOR THOUGHT AND DISCUSSION

5. Eve's answer to the serpent includes an addition to God's original command. Where do you suppose she got that additional information? Why do you think it is added at this point?

6. Who do you think receives the harshest punishment? Why?

7. Earlier we are told that Adam and Eve were naked but "had no feeling of shame." How does this attitude compare with Adam and Eve's behavior after they have eaten the forbidden fruit? How does it compare with contemporary attitudes about nakedness and sexuality?

8. Some have argued that it was unfair of God to place a tempting but forbidden tree in the Garden before Adam and Eve knew about good and evil. Others feel that without the presence of the tree and the possibility of disobeying God, Adam and Eve would not have had free choice, would not have been fully human. What is your opinion? Give some modern examples to support your opinion.

9. Note the phrase "the earth will be cursed." How would you explain its meaning? Originally, God had told humans to "fill the earth and subdue it." How might these and other phrases in the creation story relate to ecology problems in our own time?

10. Ever since Adam and Eve left Eden, it seems that human beings have wished to return to a paradise, to a place of beauty, peace, and innocence. What do you think people would gain or lose if this were possible?

RESPONDING

1. **Writing** What is your notion of a perfect place? Write a detailed description under the title "My Personal Garden of Eden."

2. **Writing** Retell this story from the point of view of the serpent.

3. **Activity** With a group of classmates, construct a model of the Garden of Eden as a small stage set; or create a detailed map of the Garden; or construct a mobile that includes elements of the story.

4. **Activity** By yourself or with a classmate, design a theater poster for a play titled *The Forbidden Fruit*.

5. **Humanities Connection** This Bible story has inspired many paintings throughout history. Examine at least six of these paintings (in art books, prints, or museums) and report the similarities and differences you find. What figures are most common? What colors? What moods or emotions are expressed?

Original Sequence

Time was the apple Adam ate
Eve bit, gave seconds to his mouth,
and then they had no minute left
to lose. Eyes opened in mid-kiss,
5   they saw, for once, raw nakedness,
and hid that sudden consequence
behind an hour's stripped leaves.

This is one sequence in the plot,
the garden where God came, that time,
10   to call. Hands behind him, walking
to and fro, he counted how
the fruit fell, bruised on frozen sod.
This was his orchard, his to pace;
the day was cool, and he was God.

15   Old Adam heard him humming, talking
to himself: *Winesap, King,*
                    ripen in the sun,
                    McIntosh and
                    Northern Spy
20   *fall one by one,*
                    ripen to die.

Adam heard him call his name,
but Adam, no old philosopher,
was not sure what he was after.

25   *We're naked, Lord, and can't come out.*
Eve nudged him with the bitter fruit.
God paused. *How do you know? Where is*
that woman that I sprung from you?

Winesap . . . Spy:
kinds of apples.

Eve held the twisted stem, the pulp;
30 she heard the low snake hiss, and let fly
blindly with a woman arm, careless
where her new-won anger struck.
The fodder for that two-fold flock

fodder: food for
domesticated animals.

fell, an old brown core, at God's
35 stopped feet. He reached, and wound the clock.

FOR THOUGHT AND DISCUSSION

1. What do you think the first line means? Remember
that God expelled Adam and Eve before they could
eat of the tree of life and live forever.

2. What impression do you get of God when he talks
to himself? when he talks to Adam?

3. Why do you think Eve is angry?

4. Review lines 1, 16–21, 26, 29, 33–34. What different
impressions of apples are created throughout
this poem? How do these changing impressions
contribute to the poem?

EMILY DICKINSON

Eden is that old-fashioned House

Eden is that old-fashioned House
We dwell in every day
Without suspecting our abode
Until we drive away.

5 How fair on looking back, the Day
We sauntered from the Door—
Unconscious our returning,
But discover it no more.

abode: place where one lives

sauntered: walked slowly and happily; strolled.

FOR THOUGHT AND DISCUSSION

1. Why do you think the words *House, Day,* and *Door* are capitalized?

2. Line 4 states "we drive away," in contrast to the fact that Adam and Ever were "driven" from Eden. What does this different wording suggest?

3. What does the poem say about people's attitudes toward what they have? When do these attitudes change?

ABOVE: *God Creating Adam*, color print, watercolor by William Blake, 1795. The Tate Gallery, London.

PAGE 25: *The Hand of God*, Romanesque fresco from St. Climent de Taull. Museo de Arte de Catalũna, Barcelona.

RIGHT: *The Tree of Life*, cut-out gouache maquette for a window in the Vence chapel by Henri Matisse, 1949. Paris, private collection. Photo Studio Adrion, Paris/ZIOLO. © SPADEM, Paris, 1975.

PAGE 28: *Adam and Eve Driven from the Garden of Eden*, detail from a tapestry, Brussels, sixteenth century. Galeria della Accademia, Florence.

BELOW: *Adam and Eve in Paradise*, detail from an oil painting by Peter Paul Rubens. Mauritshuis, The Hague, The Netherlands.

Extracts from Adam's Diary

Monday. This new creature with the long hair is a good deal in the way. It is always hanging around and following me about. I don't like this; I am not used to company. I wish it would stay with the other animals. . . . Cloudy today, wind in the east; think we shall have rain. . . . *We?* Where did I get that word?—I remember now—the new creature uses it.

Tuesday. Been examining the great waterfall. It is the finest thing on the estate, I think. The new creature calls it Niagara Falls—why, I am sure I do not know. Says it *looks* like Niagara Falls. That is not a reason, it is mere waywardness and imbecility. I get no chance to name anything myself. The new creature names everything that comes along, before I can get in a protest. And always that same pretext is offered—it *looks* like the thing. There is the dodo, for instance. Says the moment one looks at it one sees at a glance that it "looks like a dodo." It will have to keep that name, no doubt. It wearies me to fret about it, and it does no good, anyway. Dodo! It looks no more like a dodo than I do.

Wednesday. Built me a shelter against the rain, but could not have it to myself in peace. The new creature intruded. When I tried to put it out it shed water out of the holes it looks with, and wiped it away with the back of its paws, and made a noise such as some of the other animals make when they are in distress. I wish it would not talk; it is always talking. That sounds like a cheap fling at the poor creature, a slur; but I do not mean it so. I have never heard the human voice before, and any new and strange sound intruding itself here upon the solemn hush of these dreaming solitudes offends my ear and seems a false

imbecility: stupidity.

pretext: excuse.
dodo: an extinct bird that is commonly used as a symbol for stupidity.

note. And this new sound is so close to me; it is right at my shoulder, right at my ear, first on one side and then on the other, and I am used only to sounds that are more or less distant from me.

Friday. The naming goes recklessly on, in spite of anything I can do. I had a very good name for the estate, and it was musical and pretty—GARDEN OF EDEN. Privately, I continue to call it that, but not any longer publicly. The new creature says it is all woods and rocks and scenery, and therefore has no resemblance to a garden. Says it *looks* like a park, and does not look like anything *but* a park. Consequently, without consulting me, it has been new-named—NIAGARA FALLS PARK. This is sufficiently high-handed, it seems to me. And already there is a sign up:

KEEP OFF
THE GRASS

My life is not as happy as it was.

Saturday. The new creature eats too much fruit. We are going to run short, most likely. "We" again—that is *its* word; mine, too, now, from hearing it so much. Good deal of fog this morning. I do not go out in the fog myself. The new creature does. It goes out in all weathers, and stumps right in with its muddy feet. And talks. It used to be so pleasant and quiet here.

Sunday. Pulled through. This day is getting to be more and more trying. It was selected and set apart last November as a day of rest. I had already six of them per week before. This morning found the new creature trying to clod apples of that forbidden tree.

Monday. The new creature says its name is Eve. That is all right, I have no objections. Says it is to call it by, when I want it to come. I said it was superfluous, then. The word evidently raised me in its respect; and indeed it is a large good word and will bear repetition. It says it is not an It, it is a She. This is probably doubtful; yet it is all one to me; what she is were nothing to me if she would but go by herself and not talk.

Tuesday. She has littered the whole estate with execrable names and offensive signs:

clod: knock down with lumps of earth.

superfluous: unnecessary.

execrable: detestable.

THIS WAY TO THE WHIRLPOOL
THIS WAY TO GOAT ISLAND
CAVE OF THE WINDS THIS WAY

She says this park would make a tidy summer resort if there was any custom for it. Summer resort—another invention of hers—just words, without any meaning. What is a summer resort? But it is best not to ask her, she has such a rage for explaining.

Friday. She has taken to beseeching me to stop going over the Falls. What harm does it do? Says it makes her shudder. I wonder why; I have always done it—always liked the plunge, and coolness. I supposed it was what the Falls were for. They have no other use that I can see, and they must have been made for something. She says they were only made for scenery—like the rhinoceros and the mastodon.

custom: i.e., customers.

I went over the Falls in a barrel—not satisfactory to her. Went over in a tub—still not satisfactory. Swam the Whirlpool and the Rapids in a fig-leaf suit. It got much damaged. Hence, tedious complaints about my extravagance. I am too much hampered here. What I need is change of scene.

Saturday. I escaped last Tuesday night, and traveled two days, and built me another shelter in a secluded place, and obliterated my tracks as well as I could, but she hunted me out by means of a beast which she has named and calls a wolf, and came making that pitiful noise again, and shedding that water out of the places she looks with. I was obliged to return with her, but will presently emigrate again when occasion offers. She engages herself in many foolish things: among others, to study out why the animals called lions and tigers live on grass and flowers, when, as she says, the sort of teeth they wear would indicate that they were intended to eat each other. This is foolish, because to do that would be to kill each other, and that would introduce what, as I understand it, is called "death"; and death, as I have been told, has not yet entered the Park. Which is a pity, on some accounts.

obliterated: rubbed out.

Sunday. Pulled through.

Monday. I believe I see what the week is for; it is to give time to rest up from the weariness of Sunday. It seems a good idea. . . . She has been climbing that tree again. Clodded her out of it. She said nobody was looking. Seems to consider that a sufficient justification for chancing any dangerous thing. Told her that. The word justification moved her admiration—and envy, too, I thought. It is a good word.

Tuesday. She told me she was made out of a rib taken from my body. This is at least doubtful, if not more than that. I have not missed any rib. . . . She is in much trouble about the buzzard; says grass does not agree with it; is afraid she can't raise it; thinks it was intended to live on decayed flesh. The buzzard must get along the best it can with what is provided. We cannot overturn the whole scheme to accommodate the buzzard.

Saturday. She fell in the pond yesterday when she was looking at herself in it, which she is always doing. She nearly strangled, and said it was most uncomfortable. This made her sorry for the creatures which live in there, which she calls fish, for she continues to fasten names on to things that don't need them and don't come when they are called by them, which is a matter of no consequence to her, she is such a numskull, anyway; so she got a lot of them out and brought them in last night and put them in my bed to keep warm, but I have noticed them now and then all day and I don't see that they are any happier there than they were before, only quieter. When night comes I shall throw them outdoors. I will not sleep with them again, for I find them clammy and unpleasant to lie among when a person hasn't anything on.

Sunday. Pulled through.

Tuesday. She has taken up with a snake now. The other animals are glad, for she was always experimenting with them and bothering them; and I am glad because the snake talks, and this enables me to get a rest.

Friday. She says the snake advises her to try the fruit of that tree, and says the result will be a great and fine and noble education. I told her there would be another result, too—it would introduce death into the world. That was a mistake—it had been better to keep the remark to myself; it only gave her an idea—she could save the sick buzzard, and furnish fresh

justification: reason.

meat to the despondent lions and tigers. I advised her to keep away from the tree. She said she wouldn't. I foresee trouble. Will emigrate.

Wednesday. I have had a variegated time. I escaped last night, and rode a horse all night as fast as he could go, hoping to get clear out of the Park and hide in some other country before the trouble should begin; but it was not to be. About an hour after sun-up, as I was riding through a flower plain where thousands of animals were grazing, slumbering, or playing with each other, according to their wont, all of a sudden they broke into a tempest of frightful noises, and in one moment the plain was a frantic commotion and every beast was destroying its neighbor. I knew what it meant—Eve had eaten that fruit, and death was come into the world. . . . The tigers ate my horse, paying no attention when I ordered them to desist, and they would have eaten me if I had stayed—which I didn't, but went away in much haste. . . . I found this place, outside the Park, and was fairly comfortable for a few days, but she has found me out. Found me out, and has named the place Tonawanda—says it *looks* like that. In fact I was not sorry she came, for there are but meager pickings here, and she brought some of those apples. I was obliged to eat them, I was so hungry. It was against my principles, but I find that principles have no real force except when one is well fed. . . . She came curtained in boughs and bunches of leaves, and when I asked her what she meant by such nonsense, and snatched them away and threw them down, she tittered and blushed. I had never seen a person titter and blush before, and to me it seemed unbecoming and idiotic. She said I would soon know how it was myself. This was correct. Hungry as I was, I laid down the apple half-eaten—certainly the best one I ever saw, considering the lateness of the season—and arrayed myself in the discarded boughs and branches, and then spoke to her with some severity and ordered her to go and get some more and not make such a spectacle of herself. She did it, and after this we crept down to where the wild-beast battle had been, and collected some skins, and I made her patch together a couple of suits proper for public occasions. They are uncomfortable, it is true, but stylish, and that is the

variegated: varied; diverse.

wont: habit.

Tonawanda: a town in western New York, not far from Niagara Falls.

main point about clothes. . . . I find she is a good deal of a companion. I see I should be lonesome and depressed without her, now that I have lost my property. Another thing, she says it is ordered that we work for our living hereafter. She will be useful. I will superintend.

Ten days later. She accuses *me* of being the cause of our disaster! She says, with apparent sincerity and truth, that the Serpent assured her that the forbidden fruit was not apples, it was chestnuts. I said I was innocent, then, for I had not eaten any chestnuts. She said the Serpent informed her that "chestnut" was a figurative term meaning an aged and moldy joke. I turned pale at that, for I have made many jokes to pass the weary time, and some of them could have been of that sort, though I had honestly supposed that they were new when I made them. She asked me if I had made one just at the time of the catastrophe. I was obliged to admit that I had made one to myself, though not aloud. It was this. I was thinking about the Falls, and I said to myself, "How wonderful it is to see that vast body of water tumble down there!" Then in an instant a bright thought flashed into my head, and I let it fly, saying, "It would be a deal more wonderful to see it tumble *up* there!"—and I was just about to kill myself with laughing at it when all nature broke loose in war and death and I had to flee for my life. "There," she said, with triumph, "that is just it; the Serpent mentioned that very jest, and called it the First Chestnut, and said it was coeval with the creation." Alas, I am indeed to blame. Would that I were not witty; oh, that I had never had that radiant thought!

Next year. We have named it Cain. She caught it while I was up country trapping on the north shore of the Erie; caught it in the timber a couple of miles from our dug-out—or it might have been four, she isn't certain which. It resembles us in some ways, and may be a relation. That is what she thinks, but this is an error, in my judgment. The difference in size warrants the conclusion that it is a different and new kind of animal—a fish, perhaps, though when I put it in the water to see, it sank, and she plunged in and snatched it out before there was opportunity for the experiment to determine the matter. I still think it is a fish, but she is indifferent about what it is, and will not let me have it to try. I do not understand this. The coming of the creature seems to have changed her whole nature and made her unreasonable about experiments. She thinks more of it than she does of any of the other animals, but is not able to explain why. Her mind is disordered—everything shows it. Sometimes she carries the fish in her arms half the night when it complains and wants to get to the water. At such times the water comes out of the places in her face that she looks out of, and she pats the fish on the back and makes soft sounds with her mouth to soothe it, and betrays sorrow and solicitude in a hundred ways. I have never seen her do like this with any other fish, and it troubles me greatly. She used to carry the young tigers around so, and play with them, before we lost our property, but it was only play; she never took on about them like this when their dinner disagreed with them.

solicitude: concern.

Sunday. She doesn't work, Sundays, but lies around all tired out, and likes to have the fish wallow over her; and she makes fool noises to amuse it, and pretends to chew its paws, and that makes it laugh. I have not seen a fish before that could laugh. This makes me doubt. . . . I have come to like Sunday myself. Superintending all the week tires a body so. There ought to be more Sundays. In the old days they were tough, but now they come handy. . . .

FOR THOUGHT AND DISCUSSION

1. A number of things seem out of place in this account—the first one being that Adam is setting down his thoughts in English, presumably with pen and paper. What are some other oddities? Why do you think the author included them?

2. What kind of person is Adam? Describe him in two sentences.

3. What stereotypes of masculinity and femininity are presented in Adam's diary?

4. In what ways might this diary be different if it were written by Eve? (Twain later wrote "Eve's Diary"; you may wish to find and read it.)

DEREK WALCOTT

New World

Then after Eden,
was there one surprise?
O yes, the awe of Adam
at the first bead of sweat

5   Thenceforth, all flesh
had to be sown with salt,
to feel the edge of seasons,
fear and harvest,
joy that was difficult,
10   but was, at least, his own.

The snake? It would not rust
on its forked tree.
The snake admired labor,
it would not leave him alone.

15   And both would watch the leaves
silver the alder,
oaks yellowing October,
everything turning money.

So when Adam was exiled
20   to our New Eden, in the ark's gut,
the coined snake coiled there for good
fellowship also; that was willed.

Adam had an idea.
He and the snake would share
25   the loss of Eden for a profit.
So both made the New World. And it looked good.

FOR THOUGHT AND DISCUSSION

1. What emotions do humans experience "after Eden"?

2. What does the term "New World" mean to you? To what does "New World" refer in this poem?

3. According to the speaker, who made the New World? What seems to be the reason for doing so?

4. Some people today are still trying to make a new world. What would you say are some of their motives for doing so?

5. Review all references to the snake in this poem. What is the effect of describing the snake as "coined"? How would you describe the relationship between Adam and the snake in this poem?

6. The last four words resemble a phrase from the biblical creation story. How is this line different? What is the effect of these last four words?

The First Murder

Cain: related to
an early Hebrew word
for "created."

fruits: produce.

glowered: stared
sullenly, angrily.

keeper: i.e., always
responsible for knowing
where he is.

The man lay with his wife Eve, and she conceived and gave birth to Cain. She said, "With the help of the Lord I have brought into being a male child." Afterwards she had another child, Abel. He tended the flock, and Cain worked the land. In due season Cain brought some of the fruits of the earth as an offering to the Lord, while Abel brought the choicest of the firstborn of his flock. The Lord regarded Abel and his offering with favor, but not Cain and his offering. Cain was furious and he glowered. The Lord said to Cain,

> "Why are you angry? Why are you scowling?
> If you do well, you hold your head up;
> if not, sin is a demon crouching at the door;
> its desire is for you, but you must master it."

Cain said to his brother Abel, "Let us go out into the country." Once there, Cain attacked and murdered his brother. The Lord asked Cain, "Where is your brother Abel?" "I do not know," Cain answered. "Am I my brother's keeper?" The Lord said, "What have you done? Your brother's blood is crying out to me from the ground. Now you are accursed and will be banished from the very ground which has opened its mouth to receive the blood you have shed. When you till the ground, it will no longer yield you its produce. You shall be a wanderer, a fugitive on the earth." Cain said to the Lord, "My punishment is heavier than I can bear; now you are driving me off the land, and I must hide myself from your presence. I shall be a wanderer, a fugitive on the earth, and I can be killed at sight by anyone." The Lord answered him, "No: if anyone kills Cain, sevenfold vengeance will be

Genesis 4:1–16 (Revised English Bible).

exacted from him." The Lord put a mark on Cain, so that anyone happening to meet him should not kill him. Cain went out from the Lord's presence and settled in the land of Nod to the east of Eden.

mark: according to tradition, on his forehead.

Nod: the Hebrew word for "wandering."

FOR CLOSE READING

1. Brothers sometimes compete with each other; they have certain responsibilities for each other; and there are limits to what they may do to each other. Where are these three themes dealt with in the story?

2. What is Cain told about his future?

3. What protection does the Lord offer Cain after his crime?

FOR THOUGHT AND DISCUSSION

4. This story suggests a competition between two ways of living: herding (Abel) and farming (Cain). Can you think of other examples where people are set against each other because of their different livelihoods? Explain.

5. The Bible story gives no reasons for God's rejection of Cain's offering. What possible reasons can you suggest?

6. When do you think Cain made his decision to kill Abel? Explain. Which do you think is worse, a planned act of revenge or an angry, thoughtless attack? Why?

7. Why do you think the Lord gives Cain a guarantee of protection? If you committed a crime, would you prefer to have a mark that would protect you from others, or to have no mark at all? Explain.

RESPONDING

1. **Writing** The most famous line in the story is Cain's question, "Am I my brother's keeper?" As a rule, how should that question be answered? Can you offer any exceptions? Write a single paragraph under the title: "I Am —or Am Not— My Brother's Keeper."

2. **Writing** Tell this story from the point of view of Adam or Eve.

3. **Writing** You are Cain, wondering "Why was my offering rejected? Was it the time I . . ." Using your imagination, complete Cain's thought with something that might make sense to Cain.

4. **Activity** With a group of classmates, imagine what the mark of Cain might look like, then create a portrait of "the marked man."

5. **Activity** Stage a classroom trial of Cain, with prosecutors, defense attorneys, witnesses, and a jury.

Cain

(*A field at the edge of a forest. Two altars, or fireplaces anyhow, one blackened and smoking, the other clean stone. To the second altar, enter* CAIN *carrying vegetables.*)

CAIN. The corn is coming along,
    Tomatoes ripening up nicely, in a week
    There should be melons. The apples
    Are still green, but, then, after what happened
5   It might be as well if apples were not mentioned.
    There is a good deal I don't understand
    About that story, often as I've heard it told.
    Mother doesn't like to discuss it, of course.
    And I suspect that Adam my father
10   Is not entirely clear himself as to what happened
    Though he wears a very wise expression.
(*Enter* ABEL.)
ABEL. Well! My sacrifices accepted for the day, I see.
    And nothing more to be done for the moment.
    Not bad. But you, brother,
15   I don't see any flames at your offering.
    It's blood and meat the Lord likes,
    Charred on the outside, red and juicy inside;
    There's something unmanly about vegetables,
    I always say. That's probably your trouble.
20 **CAIN.** Go on, amuse yourself at my expense,
    I guess you have the right, for certainly
    God favors your offerings of meat,
    And leaves my vegetables alone. He leaves
    The flowers too, that I bring
25   Because they are lovely, a something extra
    To ornament the altar, and do Him honor
    These lilies that are blooming now.
ABEL (*laughing*). You can't imagine the mighty
    God of All
    Eating a lily! What God wants

30   Is strength. Strong men want strong meat.
      CAIN. If He made All, He made the lilies too.
          And he can't be like a man.
      ABEL. I'm not arguing, I'm telling you,
          It's simply a matter of fact.
35   The Lord has put His blessing on blood and meat.
          Therefore He prefers me before you,
          And I prosper greatly, and sit on the hillside
          Watching my flocks, while you
          Sweat in your vegetable patch.
40   **CAIN.** You have to kill those poor little lambs.
      ABEL. Well, it's a man's work anyhow.
      CAIN. It's horrible. I've heard them bleat
          Before you cut the throat, and I've seen
          The fear dumb in their eyes. What must it be
              like,
45   I wonder, to die?
      ABEL. We can't tell, till one of us does.
          I expect you'll be the first.
      CAIN. Me? Why me?
      ABEL. It's perfectly simple. Death is a punishment.
50   In dying we are punished for our sin.
      CAIN. *Our* sin? I haven't sinned. What have I done?
      ABEL. We have all sinned, and all will die.
          But God's not respecting your offerings
          Is a sign that you will be the first.
55   **CAIN.** You sound rather pleased about it.
      ABEL. Do you suppose I want to be the first?
          No, I am essentially a conservative person.
          And I can see, looking at my lambs,
          That dying's a grim business. I'm in no hurry.
60   It's only fit that you go first—you were born
              first.
          Vegetarian!
      CAIN. I don't understand. What have I done
          That was wrong, or you that was right?
          Father and Mother began the fault,
65   I know the story as well as you do.
      ABEL. You don't accept life as it is, that's
              your trouble.
          Things are the way they are, that's all.
          They've been that way from the beginning.
      CAIN. Which isn't so very long ago.
70   **ABEL.** And they will always be as they are.
          Accept it, Cain. Face up to reality.
      CAIN. That's easy for a winner to say.

(*Enter* ADAM *and* EVE.)
CAIN and **ABEL.** Father! Mother!
(*They bow their heads.*)
ADAM. That's right, respect. It's a proper respect
75   As from the children to the parents
    That keeps the world going round. It's a fine
       day,
    And life is what you make it, isn't that so?
    And both boys working hard, yes, that's right.
    "In the sweat of thy face shalt thou eat
       thy bread"
80   Is what He said to me, but it's not so bad
    When the children sweat for the father's bread.
(*He picks a tomato from* CAIN's *altar and eats it.*)
CAIN. Father, that is my offering to the Lord.
ADAM. Don't worry, I won't eat it all. Anyhow,
    The Lord seems to prefer the flesh and fat
85   That Abel provides. I must say
    That I agree. I'm eating this
    Only to stave off hunger till mealtime.
    Abel, I smell roast lamb. Good!
ABEL. Yes, the Lord God has received the essence,
90   And we may eat whatever is left over.
CAIN. It seems to me that everything is left except
    the smoke.
ABEL. Don't talk of what you don't understand.
ADAM. It is obvious, Cain, that you don't know
    The first principle of sacrifice. It is
95   The divine effluvium of the beast that rises
    To God in heaven, and does Him honor.
    A spiritual essence Himself, He feeds on spirit.
    The grosser parts are the leftovers of His meal,
    Which we may eat, if we do so with humble
      hearts.
100 **EVE.** Why doesn't He eat the divine effluvium
    Of Cain's vegetables?
ABEL.   Whoever heard
    Of burning vegetables? Our God
    Is an eater of meat, meat, meat.
ADAM. Mother, don't mix in the relations of man
    with God.
105   Remember what happened last time.
(*There is a silence.*)
EVE. It wasn't my fault. It was only a mistake.
ADAM. A mistake to end all mistakes.
EVE. You listened to me, wise as you are.

effluvium: vapor or odor.

spiritual essence: a being
without a body.

ADAM. It proves the wisdom of my not doing so
    again.

₁₁₀ He for God alone, and she for God in him;
    Remember that, and there won't be any trouble.

CAIN. Sir, what really did happen last time,
    I mean in the Garden?

ABEL. What's past is past. Cain still believes

₁₁₅ There's something that he doesn't understand,
    Or that you haven't told us, which would make
    Some difference to his situation.

EVE *(to Cain).* My poor boy, my poor, dear boy,
    I too
    Go over it and over it in my mind, I too,

₁₂₀ Though what I did is said to be so dreadful,
    Feel that the Lord's way with me
    Was very arbitrary, to say the least.

> **arbitrary:** based not on a rule but on chance or one's own wishes.

ADAM. Woman, enough. You'll make us more
    trouble.

ABEL. And as for Cain, he should have the tact

₁₂₅ Not to pursue a subject which so evidently
    Causes his mother pain.
    (to CAIN*)*
                      Also, our food is ready.
    You may do as you please about that slop of
        yours,
    But *this family* is going to eat.
    *(*CAIN *sits to one side, the rest to the other.* CAIN *starts*
           eating a tomato.)

ADAM. Not, however, before properly rendering
    thanks

₁₃₀ To the Most High. Cain, have the decency
    To control your appetite until Abel
    Has sanctified our meal with prayer. Abel.

ABEL. Permit us, O Lord, this tender beast
    Slain in Thy Holy Name, Amen.

₁₃₅ **ADAM.** Mm, good.

CAIN. Won't you let me have some? It smells good,
    And I would give you all this fruit.

ADAM. Dear boy, don't let us go all over this
    again.
    It's not that we don't care for you personally,

₁₄₀ But we simply cannot afford to offend the Lord.
    If He does not respect your offering, Cain,

> **presumptuous:** too bold.

    It would be presumptuous in us to do so,
    If He means to separate you by this sign,

We must not disobey.

145   **ABEL.** To each according to his labor, you know.

  CAIN. But I haven't done anything wrong—
As far as I'm aware, that is.

  ADAM. As far as you're aware, or we. Who knows
The hidden meaning of God's mysteries?

150   By the sign you are set off, and that's enough.

  ABEL. I'd set him further off. Suppose that God
In His displeasure should strike Cain
With fire from Heaven? I know that God
Can do whatever He will, but still

155   If we sit this close there might just be
an accident.

  CAIN (*moving a bit further away*).
I don't want to be a danger to you, you all
Seem to understand things so much better
than I do.
But what have I done wrong? Answer me that.

  ADAM. Ah, as to that, you would have to ask Him.
(*He points upward.*)

160   **CAIN.** Did He really speak to you, Himself—then?

  ADAM. He did indeed, yes. Your father has
spoken with God.

  CAIN. What does He look like?

  ADAM. Oh, you don't really see Him, you know,
He doesn't have a form. There was a Voice.

165   **EVE** (*covering her ears*). Don't. Don't remind me.
That voice!

  ADAM. Mother, have more respect. We are
talking
Of divine things. Besides, who was responsible
For His talking to us in that voice,
And saying what He said? Remember that,

170   Consider your sin, be quiet.

  ABEL. Cain thinks, because he is a gardener,
That he would have been at home in a Garden.
It's illogical, Cain, to suppose
The Garden of the Lord would be anything like
yours,

175   **CAIN.** Illogical, yes. Yet if I reason it out,
It does appear that God did once favor gardens,
Since, after all, He put our parents there.
And if I ask myself why He has turned against
Garden and gardener, I will have to answer

180   That what our parents did while they were there

blasphemy: disrespect
for God.

Was the thing that changed His mind.

ADAM. I will not have blasphemy, Cain,
And particularly not while we are at meat.
As for disrespect for your father,
185 I will not have that at any time. After all,
Your mother went through much suffering
To bring you into the world, while I
Labored to give you food and all good things.
For you to reward us with ingratitude
190 Proves, to my mind, a hidden fault in you,
And sufficiently explains why the All-Wise
Does not respect your offerings as Abel's;
Some wickedness, my boy, which is bringing
you to sin.

EVE. But truly, father, it was our fault.
195 It was my fault first, then it was yours.

ADAM. We may have made an error of judgment.
Does Cain suppose he could have done better?
We tried our best to give you boys
A decent life and bring you up to be honest,
200 Industrious, pleasing in the sight of the Lord.
As a matter of fact, I am convinced
It was a piece of luck to have got out of
that garden.
It was no place to bring up children in.
You would have had everything provided for
you.
205 No need to learn the manly virtues,
The dignity of toil, the courage of independence.
No, Cain, hard work never hurt anybody.
What happened to us was the will of God,
Which shows He did not mean us to sit around
210 On our behinds in a garden all our lives,
But to get out in the world and become
The masters of it.

ABEL.   Inventors of the knife,
The wheel, the bow.

ADAM. Sometimes I could bless that serpent!
215 **EVE.** Stop! What dreadful things you are saying.
Shame, labor, and the pains of birth
The woman knows. Those are the fruits
That grew on the forbidden tree, and I,
The first to sin, was the first to know them.
220 I shall be the first to know death also.

ADAM. Mother, don't excite yourself. What's
done is done.

As for death, no need to talk of that, I hope,
For many years.
ABEL. The little lambs are peaceful after death,
225   Mother. There's only a moment of fright,
And then it's over.
CAIN. But there's that moment, that small
moment.
A man might do anything, if he thought enough
How there's no way out but through that
moment.
230   He might become wild, and run away,
Knowing there was nowhere to run, he
might ...
ABEL. Might what?
CAIN. Kill.
ABEL. He might leave off babbling in that manner,
235   And remember he is a man, if not a very good
one.
CAIN. But if a man, even if not a very good one,
Is turned away by his God, what does he do?
Where does he go? What could he do
Worse than what is already done to him?
240   For there is God on the one hand,
And all the world on the other, and this man
Between them. Why should he care,
Seeing he cannot save himself?
ADAM. These are dangerous thoughts, Cain.
245   That man might better think
Wherein he has offended.
(The sky darkens. Thunder is heard, and lightning seen.)
ABEL. Aha! he's done it now, with his talk.
Did you think He would not have heard?
Did you consider the rest of us?
250 **CAIN.** I only meant to ask.
ABEL. You are being answered.
(He points to the sky.)
ADAM. I am afraid, Cain, that Abel is right.
I have faced up to God one time in my life,
It was enough. The coming storm
255   You brought down on yourself, and you must
face
The consequences. I am sorry for you.
Eve, come. Come, Abel. We shall seek shelter
elsewhere.
(They leave, and CAIN *stands alone. Lightning flashes,
sounds of thunder, then a stillness.)*

CAIN. Ah, they are right. I am going to die,
And I deserve to die. As Abel said,
260   There is no argument, the uneasy fear
I feel in my stomach tells me I am wrong,
Am guilty of everything, everything,
Though I cannot say what it is. Lord!
Lord God! Master! I am a wicked man,
265   The thoughts of my heart are wicked
And I don't know why. Punish me, Lord,
Punish me, but do not let me die.
(CAIN *kneels.*)
THE VOICE OF GOD (*in the silence*).
    Cain.
        Cain.
            Cain.
CAIN. Here I am.
270   **GOD.** What do you want?
CAIN. I want to know.
GOD. Ask.
CAIN. Why do you respect my brother's offerings
    and not mine?
GOD. That is not the question you want to ask.
275   **CAIN.** Why do You prefer Abel to me?
GOD. That again is not it. You must ask to the
    end.
(*A long silence.*)
CAIN. Why are things as they are?
GOD. I will debate it with you. Do you know
    That things are as they are?
280   **CAIN.** But—but they *are.* Besides,
    My father says they are.
GOD. Cain, I am your father.
CAIN. Sir, as you say.
GOD. Do you want things to be other than as
    they are?
285   **CAIN.** I want my offering to be acceptable, Sir.
    I want my offering to be preferred over Abel's.
    I want to be respected, even as he is now.
GOD. Why do you trouble yourself about it, then?
    The thing is easy. If you do well,
290   Will you not be accepted? And if you do not
        do well,
    Look, sin lies at the door.
CAIN. Sir, I do not understand.
GOD. Cain, Cain, I am trying to tell you.
    All things can be done, you must only

295 Do what you will. Things are as they are
Until you decide to change them,
But do not be surprised if afterward
Things are as they are again. What is to stop
     you
From ruling over Abel?
(Again after a silence.)
300 **CAIN.** I do not know.
(Thunder)
I do not know. I said I do not know.
He is not there and I am alone.
(The sky clears, the light grows stronger.)
And this is Abel's knife, which he left here
In his hurry to escape the storm he hoped
     would slay me.
305 And that storm was God.
And this is the knife which cuts the throats
Of acceptable sacrifices.
(Enter ABEL.)
ABEL. You're still alive. Surely the ways of the
     Lord
Are past understanding. Have you seen my knife?
310 **CAIN** *(still kneeling).* I have it here.
ABEL. Throw it to me then. I'm still uneasy
About coming close to you.
CAIN. I have spoken with God, Abel. If you want
     your knife,
Come over here and have it. God said things,
315 Abel, such as I never heard from you. He told
     me
About the will. Do what you will, He said.
And more than that. He said: You must
Do what you will. Abel, do you understand
That saying?
320 **ABEL** *(approaching).* The knife, I want the knife.
CAIN. Here, then.
(He rises, stabbing ABEL, who falls.)
My sacrifices shall be acceptable.
ABEL. My God, what have you done?
(He dies.)
CAIN *(standing over him).* I have done what I
     willed. I have changed
325 The way things are, and the first man's death
     is done.
It was not much, I have seen some of his lambs
Die harder.

GOD (*speaking casually, conversationally, without
thunder*).
Do you find it good, what you've done? Or bad?
CAIN (*as though talking to himself*).
Good? Bad? It was just my will that I did.
330   I do not know anything of good or bad.
GOD. Do you find that you have changed
Things as they are?
CAIN (*staring at* ABEL). There is this difference,
certainly.
And I have changed inside myself. I see now
335   That a man may be the master here.
GOD. Like that man on the ground?
CAIN. A man. Myself.
GOD. How peaceful he is, lying there.
CAIN. That's true, I feel uneasy, myself.
340   Abel, what have you to say to me now?
Well, speak up.
GOD. He will not speak.
CAIN. He is very quiet now, considering
How much he used to talk. How lonely
345   Everything has become! Mother! Father!
(*He shouts.*)
GOD. They will do to you as you have done to
him.
CAIN. Then I must run away.
GOD. Where will you run?
CAIN. Anywhere, to be alone.
350   There are no other people.
GOD. You're wrong about that. Everywhere
Men are beginning, and everywhere they
believe
Themselves to be alone, and everywhere
They are making the discovery of the conditions
355   Under which they are as they are. One of these
Discoveries has just been made, by you.
You will be alone, but alone among many,
Alone in every crowd.
CAIN. Seeing me set apart, they will kill me.
360   **GOD.** They would. But I have set my sign
Upon your forehead, that recognizing you,
Men will be afeared. Shunning you, scorning
you,
Blaming you, they may not kill you.
CAIN (*kneeling*). Lord God! You spoke, and I did
not know.

365 **GOD.** I send you away, Cain. You are one
Of my holy ones, discoverer of limits,
Your name is the name of one of the ways,
And you must bear it. You must bear
The everlasting fear no one can stop,
370 The everlasting life you do not want,
The smell of blood forever on your hand.
You are the discoverer of power, and you
Shall be honored among men that curse you.
And honored even in the moment of the curse.
375 From your discovery shall proceed
Great cities of men, and well defended,
And these men, your descendants, shall make
Weapons of war, and instruments of music,
Being drawn thereto by the nature of power;
380 But they will not be happy, and they will
    not know
Peace or any release from fear.
CAIN. May I not die?
GOD. Because of My sign, only you
May destroy yourself. And because of your fear,
385 You won't. For you have found
An idea of Me somewhat dangerous to consider,
And mankind will, I believe, honor your name
As one who has faced things as they are,
And changed them, and found them still the
    same.
390 **CAIN.** If I were sorry, would you raise Abel up?
GOD. No.
CAIN. Then I am not sorry. Because You have
    saved me
From everything but the necessity of being me,
I say it is Your fault. None of this need have
    happened.
395 And even my mother's temptation by the
    serpent in the Garden
Would not have happened but for You; I see
    now,
Having chosen myself, what her choice must
    have been.
GOD. Cain, I will tell you a secret.
CAIN. I am listening.
400 **GOD.** I was the serpent in the Garden.
CAIN. I can believe that, but nobody else will.
I see it so well, that You are the master of the
    will

That works two ways at once, whose action
Is its own punishment, the cause
405 That is its own result. It will be pain to me
To reject You, but I do it, in Your own world,
Where everything that is will speak of You.
And I will be deaf.
GOD. You do not reject Me. You cannot.
410 **CAIN.** I do not expect it to be easy.
(After a silence)
I said: I do not expect it to be easy.
But He is gone, I feel His absence.
As, after the storm's black accent,
The light grows wide and distant again,
415 So He is gone. Of all He said to me,
Only one thing remains. I send you away,
He said: Cain, I send you away.
But where is *Away?* Is it where Abel is,
My brother, as lonely and still as that?
(Enter ADAM *and* EVE; CAIN *turns away his face.)*
420 **ADAM** *(at a distance).* Was it the thunder, Abel,
the lightning?
(Coming closer, he sees that ABEL *is on the ground.)*
It can't be. There has been a mistake.
EVE. Abel, my son, my lamb.
(She runs to the corpse and throws herself down.)
ADAM. Monster! Unnatural child! Did you do
this?
Lord God, let it not go unpunished,

swiftly visited: i.e.,
let the punishment be
carried out quickly.

425 Let it be swiftly visited.
CAIN *(still turned away).* Suppose it was God that
struck Abel down?
Cannot the Lord do as He will do?
ADAM. Liar! I will never believe it, never.
CAIN. Well, then, it was a lie. I did it.
430 But had it been the other way, and I
The brother lying there, would you not have
said,
As I have heard you say so many times,
What the Lord does is well done?
ADAM. Vicious boy! Have you not done enough?
435 Would you go on to stand against your father?
EVE. Leave off, leave off. One son and the other
son,
All that I had, all that I cared to have,

One son and the other son, and from the
    beginning
This was the end I carried, the end we lay
    together
440   Taking our pleasure for, is now accomplished.
    CAIN. I stand, it seems, alone. Neither against
        Nor for father or mother or anything.
    ADAM. If the Lord God will not punish, I must.
    EVE. Leave off, leave off. All that we had
445   Is halved, and you would destroy the other half?
        Abel my son and Cain my son. Old man,
        It is your seed that from the beginning
        Was set at odds. You ate the fruit
        Of the tree of knowledge as well as I,
450   And sickened of it as well as I, and excited
        with lust
        As I swelled with the fruit of lust,
        And have you yet no knowledge?
    ADAM. Woman, be quiet. This is not woman's work.
    EVE. Oh, fool, what else if not woman's work?
455   The fruit of the curse has ripened till it fell,
        Can you refuse to swallow it? But you will
        swallow it,
        I tell you, stone and all, one son and the other
        son.
    ADAM. Cain, I am an old man, but it comes to me
        That I must do to you as you did to your brother.
460   **EVE.** Fooled in the Garden, and fooled out of it!
    CAIN (*turning his face to* ADAM, *who falls back*).
        Sir, you will do nothing. I am young and strong,
        And I have the knife—but no, that's not it,
        I do not want to stand against you, but I must.
    ADAM. There is a sign, a wound, there on your
        brow
465   Between the eyes. Cain, I am afraid of you.
        There is a terror written on your face.
    CAIN. And I am afraid of you. That is my fear
        You see written upon me, that your fear
        answers to.
        I am forbidden to be sorry for what I did.
470   Forbidden to pity you, forbidden to kiss
        My mother's tears, and everywhere
        In everything forbidden. I feel myself filled
        With this enormous power that I do not want.

This force that tells me I am to go,
475 To go on, always to go on, to go away
And see you both, and this place, never again.
EVE. My son, my only one, you won't go away?
I'll face the fear I see upon your face.
And you'll comfort me for what you did to me.
480 **ADAM.** And stay with me in my age? Cain, I accept it,
Though I shall never understand it, this
That you have done, this final thing
In a world where nothing seemed to end,
Is somehow the Lord God's doing. I fear you,
485 My son, but I will learn to still my fear,
If you will stay.
CAIN. No. I would change things if I could.
I tried to change things once, and the change
Is as you see; we cannot change things back,
490 Which may be the only change worth having,
So the future must be full of fear, which I
Would spare you. If this is riddling talk,
Let it go by; or, to speak plainly,
I am afraid my fear would make me kill you
495 If I stayed here.
EVE. This is the end
That we began with. Why should we not
Curse God and die?
ADAM. Woman, be careful.
EVE. I have been careful, full of care.
500 My son, my darling, why not kill us both?
It would be only what we did to you;
And that was only what was done to us.
CAIN. Mother, Mother, I must not hear you.
You and I, we understand things alike,
505 And that is curse enough, maybe. But he
May have his own curse, which we
Don't understand, that is, to go on.
Into the darkness, into the light,
510 That what I do to him is what he does to me,
And both of us compelled, or maybe
It is a blessing, the blindness of too much light
That comes from staring at the sun.
Father,
I'd bless you if I could, but I suspect
515 That God believes in you.
And now farewell,
If that is possible; try not to remember me.

(CAIN *goes. The scene begins to darken.*)
ADAM. Old woman, we are alone again, and the
    night
    Beginning to come down. Do you remember
520   The first night outside the Garden?
EVE. We slept in the cold sparkle of the
    angel's sword,
    Having cried ourselves asleep.
ADAM. If we went back, do you think, and stood
    At the gate, and said plainly, kill us
525   Or take us back, do you think . . . ?
EVE. No.
ADAM. You're right, we couldn't any more go
    back
    Than you could be my rib again, in my first
    sleep.
    The water in the rivers running out of Eden,
530   Where must that water be now, do you think?
EVE. It must be elsewhere, somewhere in the
    world;
    And yet I know those rivers glitter with water
    still.
    Abel my son and my son Cain, all that we had
    is gone.
    Old as we are, we come to the beginning again.
535 ADAM. Doing as we would, and doing as we
    must. . . .
    The darkness is so lonely, lonelier now
    Than on the first night, even, out of Eden.
    Having what we've had, and knowing what
    we know. . . .
EVE. What have we had, and what do we know?
540   The years are flickering as a dream, in which
    Our sons are grown and gone away. Husband,
    Take courage, come to my arms, husband and
    lord.
    It is the beginning of everything.
ADAM. Must we take the terrible night into our-
    selves
545   And make the morning of It? Again?
    Old woman, girl, bride of the first sleep,
    In pleasure and in bitterness all ways
    I love you till it comes death or daylight.

FOR CLOSE READING

1. How does Cain feel about killing at the beginning of the play?

2. According to Adam, who or what was responsible for his and Eve's ejection from the Garden? What are Eve's thoughts about this?

3. Why does Cain kill Abel?

FOR THOUGHT AND DISCUSSION

4. With which character or characters did you sympathize most? Why?

5. Why do you think that God speaks only to Cain?

6. Cain is often thought to be completely evil, yet in this play God calls him "one of my holy ones." How might you explain God's words?

7. Cain wanted to change "the way things are." How successful was he? Support your answer.

8. How has Cain changed by the end of the play? Adam? Eve? Explain.

9. Complete the following sentence: "Howard Nemerov's play *Cain* is about . . . " Write down as many answers as you can think of. Check the two or three that seem the most important to you.

The Great Flood

When the Lord saw how great was the wickedness of human beings on earth, and how their every thought and inclination were always wicked, he bitterly regretted that he had made mankind on earth. He said, "I shall wipe off the face of the earth this human race which I have created— yes, man and beast, creeping things and birds. I regret that I ever made them." Noah, however, had won the Lord's favor.

This is the story of Noah. Noah was a righteous man, the one blameless man of his time, and he walked with God. He had three sons: Shem, Ham, and Japheth. God saw that the world was corrupt and full of violence; and seeing this corruption, for the life of everyone on earth was corrupt, God said to Noah, "I am going to bring the whole human race to an end, for because of them the earth is full of violence. I am about to destroy them, and the earth along with them. Make yourself an ark with ribs of cypress; cover it with reeds and coat it inside and out with pitch. This **pitch:** tar. is to be its design: the length of the ark is to be three hundred cubits, its breadth fifty cubits, and its height **cubit:** about eighteen thirty cubits. You are to make a roof for the ark, inches. giving it a fall of one cubit when complete; put a door in the side of the ark, and build three decks, lower, middle, and upper. I am about to bring the waters of the flood over the earth to destroy from under heaven every human being that has the spirit of life; everything on earth shall perish. But with you I shall make my covenant, and you will go into the ark, you **covenant:** agreement. with your sons, your wife, and your sons' wives. You are to bring living creatures of every kind into the ark to keep them alive with you, two of each kind, a male and a female; two of every kind of bird, beast, and

Genesis 6:5–22; 7: 11–24; 8:6–12; 9:1–19 (Revised English Bible).

creeping thing are to come to you to be kept alive. See that you take and store by you every kind of food that can be eaten; this will be food for you and for them." Noah carried out exactly all God had commanded him. . . .

In the year when Noah was six hundred years old, on the seventeenth day of the second month, that very day all the springs of the great deep burst out, the windows of the heavens were opened, and rain fell on the earth for forty days and forty nights. That was the day Noah went into the ark with his sons, Shem, Ham, and Japheth, his own wife, and his three sons' wives. Wild animals of every kind, cattle of every kind, every kind of thing that creeps on the ground, and winged birds of every kind—all living creatures came two by two to Noah in the ark. Those which came were one male and one female of all living things; they came in as God had commanded Noah, and the Lord closed the door on him.

The flood continued on the earth for forty days, and the swelling waters lifted up the ark so that it rose high above the ground. The ark floated on the surface of the swollen waters as they increased over the earth. They increased more and more until they covered all the high mountains everywhere under heaven. The water increased until the mountains were covered to a depth of fifteen cubits. Every living thing that moved on earth perished: birds, cattle, wild animals, all creatures that swarm on the ground, and all human beings. Everything on dry land died, everything that had the breath of life in its nostrils. God wiped out every living creature that existed on earth, man and beast, creeping thing and bird; they were all wiped out over the whole earth, and only Noah and those who were with him in the ark survived. . . .

At the end of the forty days Noah opened the hatch that he had made in the ark, and sent out a raven; it continued flying to and fro until the water on the earth had dried up. Then Noah sent out a dove to see whether the water on the earth had subsided. But the dove found no place where she could settle because all the earth was under water, and so she came back to him in the ark. Noah reached out and

until . . . dried up: that is, it didn't return to the ark.

caught her, and brought her into the ark. He waited seven days more and again sent out the dove from the ark. She came back to him towards evening with a freshly plucked olive leaf in her beak. Noah knew then that the water had subsided from the earth's surface. He waited yet another seven days and, when he sent out the dove, she did not come back to him. . . .

Noah built an altar to the Lord and, taking beasts and birds of every kind that were ritually clean, he offered them as whole-offerings on it. When the Lord smelt the soothing odor, he said within himself, "Never again shall I put the earth under a curse because of mankind, however evil their inclination may be from their youth upwards, nor shall I ever again kill all living creatures, as I have just done.

"As long as the earth lasts,
seedtime and harvest, cold and heat,
summer and winter, day and night,
they will never cease."

God blessed Noah and his sons; he said to them, "Be fruitful and increase in numbers, and fill the earth. Fear and dread of you will come on all the animals on earth, on all the birds of the air, on everything that moves on the ground, and on all fish in the sea; they are made subject to you. Every creature that lives and moves will be food for you; I give them all to you, as I have given you every green plant. But you must never eat flesh with its life still in it, that is the blood. And further, for your life-blood I shall demand satisfaction; from every animal I shall require it, and from human beings also I shall require satisfaction for the death of their fellows.

"Anyone who sheds human blood,
for that human being his blood will be shed;
because in the image of God
has God made human beings.

"Be fruitful, then, and increase in number; people the earth and rule over it."

God said to Noah and his sons: "I am now establishing my covenant with you and with your descendants after you, and with every living creature that is with you, all birds and cattle, all the animals with you on earth, all that have come out of the ark. I shall sustain my covenant with you: never again will all living creatures be destroyed by the waters of a flood, never again will there be a flood to lay waste the earth."

God said, "For all generations to come, this is the sign which I am giving of the covenant between myself and you and all living creatures with you:

bow: rainbow.

> my bow I set in the clouds
> to be a sign of the covenant
> between myself and the earth.
> When I bring clouds over the earth,
> the rainbow will appear in the clouds.

"Then I shall remember the covenant which I have made with you and with all living creatures, and never again will the waters become a flood to destroy all creation. Whenever the bow appears in the cloud, I shall see it and remember the everlasting covenant between God and living creatures of every kind on earth." So God said to Noah, "This is the sign of the covenant which I have established with all that lives on earth."

The sons of Noah who came out of the ark were Shem, Ham, and Japheth; Ham was the father of Canaan. These three were sons of Noah, and their descendants spread over the whole earth.

FOR CLOSE READING

1. What seem to be the reasons for God's selection of Noah to build the ark?

2. Two birds are sent forth from the ark to test the earth. Which of the two brought the good news that the Flood had subsided?

3. List the two sets of promises that God makes to Noah, before and after the Flood.

FOR THOUGHT AND DISCUSSION

4. Which do you think is stronger in the story of Noah, its warning to the human race, or its reassurance? Explain.

Cain and Abel by Titian, sixteenth century. Sta. Maria della Salute, Venice, Italy. Erich Lessing/Art Resource.

Noah Releasing the Dove from the Ark, mosaic from St. Mark's Cathedral, Venice, before 1220. Erich Lessing/Art Resource.

ABOVE: *Dove with Olive Leaf* from Noah's Ark panel, Verdun Altar, the Abbey Klosterneuberg, Austria, by Nicholas of Verdun, 1180. Enamel and copper gilt. Erich Lessing/Art Resource.

BELOW: *Noah's Ark and the Return of the Dove,* twelfth-century altar. Sammlungen des Stiftes, Klosterneuburg, Austria. Erich Lessing/Art Resource.

PAGE 64: *The Tower of Babel,* detail from an oil on wood painting by Pieter Bruegel the Elder, 1563. The Kunsthistorisches Museum, Vienna.

5. The Great Flood may be one of the two or three Bible stories most memorable to young children. What elements do you think make the story so memorable? Why?

6. Three things in this story have become symbols: the dove, the olive branch, and the rainbow. What does each one mean for us today?

7. Compare and contrast the promises God makes to Noah before and after the Flood. What differences do you find? How might you account for the differences?

8. The Flood gives the human race a new beginning. How do the instructions God gives to Noah after the Flood compare with the instructions he gave to Adam and Eve? What details are repeated? What are people now permitted to eat? What is to be their relation to other creatures?

RESPONDING

1. **Writing** Write a description of life aboard the ark, or write a monologue expressing Noah's thoughts at various points in the story. (You may wish to conclude this project by listening to Bill Cosby's Noah monologues from his comedy recording *Bill Cosby Is a Very Funny Fellow, Right!)*

2. **Activity** By yourself or with classmates, construct a model ark.

3. **Activity** Noah's ark is a favorite topic of cartoonists. With a group of classmates, create an album of Noah cartoons. Be prepared to discuss in class any patterns or overall themes you find in the cartoons.

4. **Multicultural Connection** The dove, olive branch, and rainbow have certain meanings to cultures influenced by the Bible story of Noah. With a group of classmates, research other symbols used throughout the world to convey some of the same meanings.

Noah's Prayer

Translated by Rumer Godden

Lord,
What a menagerie!
Between Your downpour and these animal cries
one cannot hear oneself think!
5   The days are long,
Lord.
All this water makes my heart sink.
When will the ground cease to rock under my
    feet?
The days are long.
10   Master Raven has not come back.
Here is Your dove
Will she find us a twig of hope?
The days are long,
Lord.
15   Guide Your Ark to safety,
some zenith of rest,
where we can escape at last
from this brute slavery.
The days are long,
20   Lord.
Lead me until I reach the shore of Your covenant.

Amen

zenith: highest point.

Noah

He must wade out to a high point
and build an ark of the trees,
take two of each kind of happiness,
And send out
5 a pigeon that shall not return,
after the bubbling shriek of the drowned;
it shall land upon a rock.
God of his crying shall have made the flood
    subside.
10 He shall emerge
upon the earth, brown for grief
of its dead, and know no better
than before, save there is a promise
to cling to when the floods rise.

FOR THOUGHT AND DISCUSSION

1. In David Ignatow's "Noah," what would you say is
the speaker's strongest feeling about the Flood?
What details in the poem suggest this feeling?

2. According to the speaker, what knowledge does
Noah have when he emerges from the Ark? Would
you say that the outcome was worth it? Support
your opinion.

3. In the poem "Noah's Prayer," what aspect of life on
the ark seems to bother Noah most?

4. The Bible story of the Flood does not mention
Noah's thoughts and feelings. Do the portrayals of
Noah in Ignatow's "Noah" and "Noah's Prayer"
seem reasonable to you? Why or why not?

Babel: The City and the Tower

Shinar (shi'när): in what was later Babylonia; today southern Iraq.

bitumen (bə tü'mən): asphalt, used to cement bricks together.

dispersed: scattered.

Babel (bā'bəl): "gate of God" in Babylonian. It is also similar to the Hebrew word meaning "to confuse."

There was a time when all the world spoke a single language and used the same words. As people journeyed in the east, they came upon a plain in the land of Shinar and settled there. They said to one another, "Come, let us make bricks and bake them hard"; they used bricks for stone and bitumen for mortar. Then they said, "Let us build ourselves a city and a tower with its top in the heavens and make a name for ourselves, or we shall be dispersed over the face of the earth." The Lord came down to see the city and tower which they had built, and he said, "Here they are, one people with a single language, and now they have started to do this; from now on nothing they have a mind to do will be beyond their reach. Come, let us go down there and confuse their language, so that they will not understand what they say to one another." So the Lord dispersed them from there all over the earth, and they left off building the city. That is why it is called Babel, because there the Lord made a babble of the language of the whole world. It was from that place the Lord scattered people over the face of the earth.

FOR CLOSE READING

1. Under the following headings indicate the parts of the story *(a)* that are speeches by the people; *(b)* that are speeches by the Lord; *(c)* that describe the situation before construction of the tower; *(d)* that

Genesis 11:1–9 (Revised English Bible).

describe the situation after the Lord's actions; and *(e)* the sentence that links the two halves of the story.

2. What reason did the people give for building the tower?

FOR THOUGHT AND DISCUSSION

3. Why do you think the people wanted to "make a name for themselves"? In your opinion, are people different today?

4. In what ways is this story similar to the episode of the forbidden fruit in the Garden of Eden? In what ways is it different?

5. Examine the chart you made for Question One. What patterns do you find? What might these patterns of structure and language contribute to the story?

6. Which do you think is the uppermost concern of this story: the warning against too much ambition, the explanation of why people speak different languages, or something else? Explain.

RESPONDING

1. **Writing** Imagine this story happening one hundred years from now. What great human project would be like a tower of Babel? Try to use only ten sentences in your futuristic retelling.

2. **Activity** With a few classmates, and using whatever materials you wish, build a model of the tower of Babel.

3. **Humanities Connection** People throughout history have built enormous structures, from pyramids to cathedrals to skyscrapers. Make a collection of pictures of such structures, researching details of when and for what purpose they were constructed.

2

Ancestors of Israel

Abraham:
A Promise, a Test

God's Covenant with Abram

The Lord said to Abram, "Go forth from your native land and from your father's house to the land that I will show you.

I will make of you a great nation,
And I will bless you;
I will make your name great,
And you shall be a blessing.
I will bless those who bless you
And curse him that curses you;
And all the families of the earth
Shall bless themselves by you."

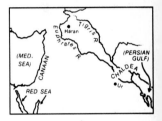

Abram went forth as the Lord had commanded him, and Lot went with him. Abram was seventy-five years old when he left Haran. Abram took his wife Sarai and his brother's son Lot, and all the wealth that they had amassed, and the persons that they had acquired in Haran; and they set out for the land of Canaan. . . .

Some time later, the word of the Lord came to Abram in a vision. He said,

"Fear not, Abram,
I am a shield to you;
Your reward shall be very great."

Canaan (kā′nən): the region between the Jordan River and the Mediterranean.

Genesis 12:1–5; 15:1–12, 17–21; 16:1–15; 18:1–15; 21:1–21; 22:1–14 (*Tanakh:* The New Jewish Publication Society Translation).
LEFT: *Sacrifice of Abraham* (Oshogbo), lino-cut by Jacob Afolabi, 1964. Courtesy of Ulli Beier.

But Abram said, "O Lord God, what can you give me, seeing that I shall die childless, and the one in charge of my household is Dammesek Eliezer!" Abram said further, "Since you have granted me no offspring, my steward will be my heir." He took him outside and said, "Look toward heaven and count the stars, if you are able to count them." And he added, "So shall your offspring be." And because he put his trust in the Lord, he reckoned it to his merit.

Then he said to him, "I am the Lord who brought you out from Ur of the Chaldeans to assign this land to you as a possession." And he said, "O Lord God, how shall I know that I am to possess it?" He answered, "Bring me a three-year-old heifer, a three-year-old she-goat, a three-year-old ram, a turtledove, and a young bird." He brought him all these and cut them in two, placing each half opposite the other; but he did not cut up the bird. Birds of prey came down upon the carcasses, and Abram drove them away. As the sun was about to set, a deep sleep fell upon Abram, and a great dark dread descended upon him. . . .

When the sun set and it was very dark, there appeared a smoking oven, and a flaming torch which passed between those pieces. On that day the Lord made a covenant with Abram, saying, "To your offspring I assign this land, from the river of Egypt to the great river, the river Euphrates: the Kenites, the Kenizzites, the Kadmonites, the Hittites, the Perizzites, the Rephaim, the Amorites, the Canaanites, the Girgashites, and the Jebusites."

The Birth of Ishmael

Sarai, Abram's wife, had borne him no children. She had an Egyptian maidservant whose name was Hagar. And Sarai said to Abram, "Look, the Lord has kept me from bearing. Consort with my maid; perhaps I shall have a son through her." And Abram heeded Sarai's request. So Sarai, Abram's wife, took her maid, Hagar the Egyptian—after Abram had dwelt in the land of Canaan ten years—and gave her to her husband Abram as concubine. He cohabited with Hagar and she conceived; and when she saw that she had conceived, her mistress was lowered in her esteem. And Sarai said to Abram, "The wrong done me is your fault! I myself put my maid in your

one . . . Eliezer: probably Abram's designated heir.

Ur . . . Chaldeans (ėr, kȯl dē′ənz): city on the Euphrates River.

heifer: a young cow.

pieces: carcasses referred to earlier.

lowered . . . esteem: Hagar lost respect for Sarai.

bosom; now that she sees that she is pregnant, I am lowered in her esteem. The Lord decide between you and me!" Abram said to Sarai, "Your maid is in your hands. Deal with her as you think right." Then Sarai treated her harshly, and she ran away from her.

An angel of the Lord found her by a spring of water in the wilderness, the spring on the road to Shur, and said, "Hagar, slave of Sarai, where have you come from, and where are you going?" And she said, "I am running away from my mistress Sarai."

And the angel of the Lord said to her, "Go back to your mistress, and submit to her harsh treatment." And the angel of the Lord said to her,

> "I will greatly increase your offspring,
> And they shall be too many to count."

The angel of the Lord said to her further,

> "Behold, you are with child
> And you shall bear a son;
> You shall call him Ishmael,
> For the Lord has paid heed to your suffering.
> He shall be a wild ass of a man.
> His hand against everyone,
> And everyone's hand against him;
> He shall dwell alongside of all his kinsmen."

Ishmael: In Hebrew, "God hears."

And she called the Lord who spoke to her, "You are El-ro-i," by which she meant, "Have I not gone on seeing after he saw me!" Therefore the well was called Beer-lahai-roi; it is between Kadesh and Bered. Hagar bore a son to Abram, and Abram gave the son that Hagar bore him the name Ishmael. . . .

El-ro-i: In Hebrew, "the God who sees."

The Birth of Isaac

The Lord appeared to him by the terebinths of Mamre; he was sitting at the entrance of the tent as the day grew hot. Looking up, he saw three men standing near him. As soon as he saw them, he ran from the entrance of the tent to greet them and, bowing to the ground, he said, "My lords, if it please you, do not go on past your servant. Let a little water be brought; bathe your feet and recline under the tree. And let me fetch a morsel of bread that you may refresh yourselves; then go on—seeing that you have

terebinths: great trees.
Mamre: near modern Hebron, twenty miles southwest of Jerusalem.

come your servant's way." They replied, "Do as you have said."

Abraham hastened into the tent to Sarah, and said, "Quick, three *seahs* of choice flour! Knead and make cakes!" Then Abraham ran to the herd, took a calf, tender and choice, and gave it to a servant-boy, who hastened to prepare it. He took curds and milk and the calf that had been prepared and set these before them; and he waited on them under the tree as they ate.

They said to him, "Where is your wife Sarah?" And he replied, "There, in the tent." Then one said, "I will return to you next year, and your wife Sarah shall have a son!" Sarah was listening at the entrance of the tent, which was behind him. Now Abraham and Sarah were old, advanced in years; Sarah had stopped having the periods of women. And Sarah laughed to herself, saying, "Now that I am withered, am I to have enjoyment—with my husband so old?" Then the Lord said to Abraham, "Why did Sarah laugh, saying 'Shall I in truth bear a child, old as I am?' Is anything too wondrous for the Lord? I will return to you at the same season next year, and Sarah shall have a son." Sarah lied, saying, "I did not laugh," for she was frightened. But he replied, "You did laugh.". . .

The Lord took note of Sarah as he had promised, and the Lord did for Sarah as he had spoken. Sarah conceived and bore a son to Abraham in his old age, at the set time of which God had spoken. Abraham gave his newborn, whom Sarah had borne him, the name Isaac. And when his son Isaac was eight days old, Abraham circumcised him, as God had commanded him. Now Abraham was a hundred years old when his son Isaac was born to him. Sarah said, "God has brought me laughter; everyone who hears will laugh with me." And she added,

> "Who would have said to Abraham
> That Sarah would suckle children!
> Yet I have borne a son in his old age."

The child grew up and was weaned, and Abraham held a great feast on the day that Isaac was weaned.

Abraham: God had changed the names of Abram and Sarai to **Abraham** ("father of very many") and **Sarah** ("princess") as a symbol of the covenant.

seahs: i.e., measures.

Isaac: Hebrew word meaning "he laughs."

suckle: nurse; breast-feed.

weaned: i.e., stopped nursing.

The Expulsion of Ishmael

Sarah saw the son whom Hagar the Egyptian had borne to Abraham playing. She said to Abraham, "Cast out that slave-woman and her son, for the son of that slave shall not share in the inheritance with my son Isaac." The matter distressed Abraham greatly, for it concerned a son of his. But God said to Abraham, "Do not be distressed over the boy or your slave; whatever Sarah tells you, do as she says, for it is through Isaac that offspring shall be continued for you. As for the son of the slave-woman, I will make a nation of him, too, for he is your seed."

Early next morning Abraham took some bread and a skin of water, and gave them to Hagar. He placed them over her shoulder, together with the child, and sent her away. And she wandered about in the wilderness of Beer-sheba. When the water was gone from the skin, she left the child under one of the bushes, and went and sat down at a distance, a bowshot away; for she thought, "Let me not look on as the child dies." And sitting thus afar, she burst into tears.

skin: leather container.

Beer-sheba: in the Negeb desert south of Canaan.

God heard the cry of the boy, and an angel of God called to Hagar from heaven and said to her, "What troubles you, Hagar? Fear not, for God has heeded the cry of the boy where he is. Come, lift up the boy and hold him by the hand, for I will make a great nation of him." Then God opened her eyes and she saw a well of water. She went and filled the skin with water, and let the boy drink. God was with the boy and he grew up; he dwelt in the wilderness and became a bowman. He lived in the wilderness of Paran; and his mother got a wife for him from the land of Egypt. . . .

The Test

Some time afterward, God put Abraham to the test. He said to him, "Abraham," and he answered, "Here I am." And he said, "Take your son, your favored one, Isaac, whom you love, and go to the land of Moriah, and offer him there as a burnt offering on one of the heights that I will point out to you." So early the next morning, Abraham saddled his ass and took with him two of his servants and his son Isaac.

Moriah (mō ri′ə): according to tradition, Jerusalem.

He split the wood for the burnt offering, and he set out for the place of which God had told him. On the third day Abraham looked up and saw the place from afar. Then Abraham said to his servants, "You stay here with the ass. The boy and I will go up there; we will worship and we will return to you."

Abraham took the wood for the burnt offering and put it on his son Isaac. He himself took the firestone and the knife; and the two walked off together. Then Isaac said to his father Abraham, "Father!" And he answered, "Yes, my son." And he said, "Here are the firestone and the wood; but where is the sheep for the burnt offering?" And Abraham said, "God will see to the sheep for His burnt offering, my son." And the two of them walked on together.

They arrived at the place of which God had told him. Abraham built an altar there; he laid out the wood; he bound his son Isaac; he laid him on the altar, on top of the wood. And Abraham picked up the knife to slay his son. Then an angel of the Lord called to him from heaven: "Abraham! Abraham!" And he answered, "Here I am." And he said, "Do not raise your hand against the boy, or do anything to him. For now I know that you fear God, since you have not withheld your son, your favored one, from me." When Abraham looked up, his eye fell upon a ram, caught in the thicket by its horns. So Abraham went and took the ram and offered it up as a burnt offering in place of his son. And Abraham named that site Adonai-yireh, whence the present saying, "On the mount of the Lord there is vision."

firestone: in Hebrew, "fire"; here, perhaps flint, to strike sparks for a fire.

fear: respect, obey, have confidence in.

Adonai-yireh: in Hebrew, "the Lord will see to," i.e., provide.

FOR CLOSE READING

1. What does God promise Abram when he tells him to leave his native land?

2. Twice Sarah takes action against her servant Hagar. What is her reason in each case?

3. What unusual details surround the birth of Isaac? How does Sarah react when she is told she will have a son?

4. What does God tell Abraham about the future of his son Ishmael?

FOR THOUGHT AND DISCUSSION

5. What might have been Abraham's arguments against the sacrifice of his son? If Abraham had protested, how might your opinion of him have been affected?

6. The proposed sacrifice of Isaac is described as a test of Abraham. In your opinion, at what other times has Abraham been tested? What do you learn about Abraham from each of these tests?

7. No mention is made of Abraham and Isaac's emotions during the episode on the mountain. In your opinion, would the story be more, or less, effective if you were told what the characters were feeling?

8. Compare the story of the expulsion of Hagar and Ishmael with the story of the sacrifice of Isaac. What similarities and what differences do you find in these two events involving Abraham's sons?

RESPONDING

1. Writing Have you ever felt seriously tested by a life experience? Briefly describe the circumstances and how the experience affected you.

2. Writing Retell the sacrifice story from Isaac's point of view, as if he were describing the events to a friend a few days after he and his father returned home.

3. Multicultural Connection God promised Abraham that he would make nations from both his sons. Many Arabs trace their descent from Abraham through Ishmael. Write a report on the Islamic traditions involving Ibrahim, Hajar, and Ismail.

Sarah

The angel said to me: "Why are you laughing?"
"Laughing! Not me! Who was laughing? I did not
  laugh. It was
A cough. I was coughing. Only hyenas laugh.
It was the cold I caught nine minutes after
5 Abraham married me: when I saw
How I was slender and beautiful, more and more
Slender and beautiful.
                              I was also
Clearing my throat; something inside of me
Is continually telling me something
10 I do not wish to hear: A joke: a big joke:
But the joke is always just on me.
He said: you will have more children than the
  sky's stars
And the seashore's sands, if you just wait patiently.
Wait: patiently: ninety years? You see
15 The joke's on me!"

FOR THOUGHT AND DISCUSSION

1. Laughter often expresses amusement and
happiness. In what other situations do people
laugh?

2. What does laughter express in the Bible story of
Isaac's birth? What does laughter express in this
poem?

The Parable of the Old Men and the Young

So Abram rose, and clave the wood, and went,   clave: split.
And took the fire with him, and a knife.
And as they sojourned both of them together,   sojourned: stayed.
Isaac the first-born spake and said, "My Father,
5   Behold the preparations, fire and iron,
But where the lamb for this burnt-offering?"
Then Abram bound the youth with belts and straps,
And builded parapets and trenches there,   parapets: walls,
And stretched for the knife to slay his son.   fortifications.
10 When lo! an angel called him out of heaven,
Saying, "Lay not thy hand upon the lad,
Neither do anything to him. Behold,
A ram, caught in a thicket by its horns;
Offer the Ram of Pride instead of him."
15 But the old man would not so, but slew his son,—
And half the seed of Europe, one by one.   seed: children,
                                                  descendants.

FOR THOUGHT AND DISCUSSION

1. What was your first reaction when you read the last two lines of this poem? Why do you think you had that reaction?

2. A parable is a story that illustrates a truth or lesson in a symbolic way. In this parable about war, whom or what does Abram represent? Isaac? What do you think is the truth or lesson?

3. In this poem, what does the angel tell Abram to sacrifice? Is such a sacrifice likely to prevent bloodshed? Explain.

The Father

Translated by Rasmus B. Anderson

The man whose story is here to be told was the wealthiest and most influential person in his parish; his name was Thord Överaas. He appeared in the priest's study one day, tall and earnest.

"I have gotten a son," said he, "and I wish to present him for baptism."

"What shall his name be?"

"Finn,—after my father."

"And the sponsors?"

They were mentioned, and proved to be the best men and women of Thord's relations in the parish.

"Is there anything else?" inquired the priest, and looked up.

The peasant hesitated a little.

"I should like very much to have him baptized by himself," said he, finally.

"That is to say, on a weekday?"

"Next Saturday, at twelve o'clock noon."

"Is there anything else?" inquired the priest.

"There is nothing else"; and the peasant twirled his cap, as though he were about to go.

Then the priest rose. "There is yet this, however," said he, and walking toward Thord, he took him by the hand and looked gravely into his eyes: "God grant that the child may become a blessing to you!"

One day sixteen years later, Thord stood once more in the priest's study.

"Really, you carry your age astonishingly well, Thord," said the priest; for he saw no change whatever in the man.

"That is because I have no troubles," replied Thord.

To this the priest said nothing, but after a while he asked: "What is your pleasure this evening?"

"I have come this evening about that son of mine who is to be confirmed tomorrow."

"He will stand number one."

"So I have heard; and here are ten dollars for the priest."

"Is there anything else I can do for you?" inquired the priest, fixing his eyes on Thord.

"There is nothing else."

Thord went out.

Eight years more rolled by, and then one day a noise was heard outside of the priest's study, for many men were approaching, and at their head was Thord, who entered first.

The priest looked up and recognized him.

"You come well attended this evening, Thord," said he.

"I am here to request that the banns may be published for my son; he is about to marry Karen Storliden, daughter of Gudmund, who stands here beside me."

"Why, that is the richest girl in the parish."

"So they say," replied the peasant, stroking back his hair with one hand.

The priest sat a while as if in deep thought, then entered the names in his book, without making any comments, and the men wrote their signatures underneath. Thord laid three dollars on the table.

"One is all I am to have," said the priest.

"I know that very well; but he is my only child; I want to do it handsomely."

The priest took the money.

"This is now the third time, Thord, that you have come here on your son's account."

"But now I am through with him," said Thord, and folding up his pocketbook he said farewell and walked away.

The men slowly followed him.

A fortnight later, the father and son were rowing across the lake, one calm, still day, to Storliden to make arrangements for the wedding.

"This thwart is not secure," said the son, and stood up to straighten the seat on which he was sitting.

At the same moment the board he was standing on slipped from under him; he threw out his arms, uttered a shriek, and fell overboard.

"Take hold of the oar!" shouted the father, springing to his feet and holding out the oar.

But when the son had made a couple of efforts he grew stiff.

"Wait a moment!" cried the father, and began to row toward his son.

Then the son rolled over on his back, gave his father one long look, and sank.

Thord could scarcely believe it; he held the boat still, and stared at the spot where his son had gone down, as though he must surely come to the surface again. There rose some bubbles, then some more, and finally one large one that burst; and the lake lay there as smooth and bright as a mirror again.

For three days and three nights people saw the father rowing round and round the spot, without taking either food or sleep; he was dragging the lake for the body of his son. And toward morning of the third day he found it, and carried it in his arms up over the hills to his gard.

It might have been about a year from that day, when the priest, late one autumn evening, heard some one in the passage outside of the door, carefully trying to find the latch. The priest opened the door, and in walked a tall, thin man, with bowed form and white hair. The priest looked long at him before he recognized him. It was Thord.

"Are you out walking so late?" said the priest, and stood still in front of him.

"Ah, yes! it is late," said Thord, and took a seat.

The priest sat down also, as though waiting. A long, long silence followed. At last Thord said,—

"I have something with me that I should like to give to the poor; I want it to be invested as a legacy in my son's name."

He rose, laid some money on the table, and sat down again. The priest counted it.

"It is a great deal of money," said he.

"It is half the price of my gard. I sold it today."

The priest sat long in silence. At last he asked, but gently,—

"What do you propose to do now, Thord?"

gard: fenced property; farm.

legacy: bequest; money or property left to a person by someone who has died.

"Something better."

They sat there for a while, Thord with downcast eyes, the priest with his eyes fixed on Thord. Presently the priest said, slowly and softly,—

"I think your son has at last brought you a true blessing."

"Yes, I think so myself," said Thord, looking up, while two big tears coursed slowly down his cheeks.

FOR CLOSE READING

1. What question does the priest repeat on Thord's first two visits?

2. What details show the father's great pride in his son?

3. How has Thord's appearance changed by the end of the story?

FOR THOUGHT AND DISCUSSION

4. Did you expect that something would happen to Thord's son? Why or why not?

5. Compare Thord's experiences with Abraham's. What did each man's son mean to him? What "sacrifice" does Thord make at the end of the story?

6. Both "The Father" and "The Parable of the Old Men and the Young" emphasize a father's pride. How might pride be a similar element of the biblical story of Abraham and Isaac? Explain.

Jacob: In Pursuit of Blessing

Like his grandfather, Abraham, and his father, Isaac, Jacob was said to be favored by God. Also called Israel, Jacob had an eventful life, some of which is told below.

Birth

This is the story of Isaac, son of Abraham. Abraham begot Isaac. Isaac was forty years old when he took to wife Rebekah, daughter of Bethuel the Aramean of Paddan-aram, sister of Laban the Aramean. Isaac pleaded with the Lord on behalf of his wife, because she was barren; and the Lord responded to his plea, and his wife Rebekah conceived. But the children struggled in her womb, and she said, "If so, why do I exist?" She went to inquire of the Lord, and the Lord answered her,

"Two nations are in your womb,
Two separate peoples shall issue from your
    body;
One people shall be mightier than the other,
And the older shall serve the younger."

When her time to give birth was at hand, there were twins in her womb. The first one emerged red, like a hairy mantle all over; so they named him Esau. Then his brother emerged, holding on to the heel of Esau; so they named him Jacob. Isaac was sixty years old when they were born.

Jacob: in Hebrew, "he follows at the heel."

Genesis 25:19–34; 27:1–29, 41–43; 28:10–17; 29:16–30; 32:22–32; 33 1–11 (*Tanakh:* The New Jewish Publication Society Translation).

Birthright and Blessing

When the boys grew up, Esau became a skillful hunter, a man of the outdoors; but Jacob was a mild man who stayed in camp. Isaac favored Esau because he had a fine taste for game; but Rebekah favored Jacob. Once when Jacob was cooking a stew, Esau came in from the open, famished. And Esau said to Jacob, "Give me some of that red stuff to gulp down, for I am famished"—which is why he was named Edom. Jacob said, "First sell me your birthright." And Esau said, "I am at the point of death, so of what use is my birthright to me?" But Jacob said, "Swear to me first." So he swore to him, and sold his birthright to Jacob. Jacob then gave Esau bread and lentil stew; he ate and drank, and he rose and went away. Thus did Esau spurn the birthright. . . .

birthright: the privilege of the first-born son to become the principal heir and head of the family.

When Isaac was old and his eyes were too dim to see, he called his older son Esau and said to him, "My son." He answered, "Here I am." And he said, "I am old now, and I do not know how soon I may die. Take your gear, your quiver and bow, and go out into the open and hunt me some game. Then prepare a dish for me such as I like, and bring it to me to eat, so that I may give you my innermost blessing before I die."

Rebekah had been listening as Isaac spoke to his son Esau. When Esau had gone out into the open to hunt game to bring home, Rebekah said to her son Jacob, "I overheard your father speaking to your brother Esau, saying, 'Bring me some game and prepare a dish for me to eat, that I may bless you, with the Lord's approval, before I die.' Now, my son, listen carefully as I instruct you. Go to the flock and fetch me two choice kids, and I will make of them a dish for your father, such as he likes. Then take it to your father to eat, in order that he may bless you before he dies." Jacob answered his mother Rebekah, "But my brother Esau is a hairy man and I am smooth-skinned. If my father touches me, I shall appear to him as a trickster and bring upon myself a curse, not a blessing." But his mother said to him, "Your curse, my son, be upon me! Just do as I say and go fetch them for me."

kids: young goats.

He got them and brought them to his mother, and his mother prepared a dish such as his father liked. Rebekah then took the best clothes of her older son Esau, which were there in the house, and had her younger son Jacob put them on; and she covered his hands and the hairless part of his neck with the skins of the kids. Then she put in the hands of her son Jacob the dish and the bread that she had prepared.

He went to his father and said, "Father." And he said, "Yes, which of my sons are you?" Jacob said to his father, "I am Esau, your firstborn; I have done as you told me. Pray sit up and eat of my game, that you may give me your innermost blessing." Isaac said to his son, "How did you succeed so quickly, my son?" And he said, "Because the Lord your God granted me good fortune." Isaac said to Jacob, "Come closer that I may feel you, my son—whether you are really my son Esau or not." So Jacob drew close to his father Isaac, who felt him and wondered. "The voice is the voice of Jacob, yet the hands are the hands of Esau." He did not recognize him, because his hands were hairy like those of his brother Esau; and so he blessed him.

He asked, "Are you really my son Esau?" And when he said, "I am," he said, "Serve me and let me eat of my son's game that I may give you my innermost blessing." So he served him and he ate, and he brought him wine and he drank. Then when his father Isaac said to him, "Come close and kiss me, my son'" and he went up and kissed him. And he smelled his clothes and he blessed him, saying "Ah, the smell of my son is like the smell of the fields that the Lord has blessed.

"May God give you
Of the dew of heaven and the fat of the earth,
Abundance of new grain and wine.
Let peoples serve you,
And nations bow to you;
Be master over your brothers,
And let your mother's sons bow to you.
Cursed be they who curse you,
Blessed they who bless you.". . .

Now Esau harbored a grudge against Jacob because of the blessing which his father had given him, and Esau said to himself, "Let but the mourning period of my father come, and I will kill my brother Jacob." When the words of her older son Esau were reported to Rebekah, she sent for her younger son Jacob and said to him, "Your brother Esau is

mourning . . . come: i.e., after my father dies.

consoling himself by planning to kill you. Now, my son, listen to me. Flee at once to Haran, to my brother Laban.". . .

Jacob's Dream

Jacob left Beer-sheba, and set out for Haran. He came upon a certain place and stopped there for the night, for the sun had set. Taking one of the stones of that place, he put it under his head and lay down in that place. He had a dream; a stairway was set on the ground and its top reached to the sky, and the angels of God were going up and down on it. And the Lord was standing beside him, and he said, "I am the Lord, the God of your father Abraham and the God of Isaac: the ground on which you are lying I will assign to you and to your offspring. Your descendants shall be as the dust of the earth; you shall spread out to the west and to the east, to the north and to the south. All the families of the earth shall bless themselves by you and your descendants. Remember, I am with you: I will protect you wherever you go and will bring you back to this land. I will not leave you until I have done what I have promised you."

stairway: in some versions, "ladder."

Jacob awoke from his sleep and said, "Surely the Lord is present in this place, and I did not know it!" Shaken, he said, "How awesome is this place! This is none other than the abode of God, and that is the gateway to heaven.". . .

abode of God: the Hebrew expression is *Beth-el.*

[Jacob was welcomed by Laban and began to work for him.]

Laboring for Love

When he had stayed with him a month's time, Laban said to Jacob, "Just because you are a kinsman, should you serve me for nothing? Tell me, what shall your wages be?" Now Laban had two daughters; the name of the older one was Leah, and the name of the younger was Rachel. Leah had weak eyes; Rachel was shapely and beautiful. Jacob loved Rachel; so he answered, "I will serve you seven years for your younger daughter Rachel." Laban said, "Better that I give her to you than that I should give her to an outsider. Stay with me." So Jacob served seven years for Rachel and they seemed to him but a few days because of his love for her.

Then Jacob said to Laban, "Give me my wife, for my time is fulfilled, that I may cohabit with her." And Laban gathered all the people of the place and made a feast. When evening came, he took his daughter Leah and brought her to him; and he cohabited with her. Laban had given his maidservant Zilpah to his daughter Leah as her maid. When morning came, there was Leah! So he said to Laban, "What is this you have done to me? I was in your service for Rachel! Why did you deceive me?" Laban said, "It is not the practice in our place to marry off the younger before the older. Wait until the bridal week of this one is over and we will give you that one too, provided you serve me another seven years." Jacob did so; he waited out the bridal week of the one, and then he gave him his daughter Rachel as wife. Laban had given his maidservant Bilhah to his daughter Rachel as her maid. And Jacob cohabited with Rachel also; indeed, he loved Rachel more than Leah. And he served him another seven years. . . .

brought her: brides wore heavy veils.

[After enjoying great success in his years with Laban, Jacob finally journeyed home. As he neared Canaan, he learned that Esau, with four hundred men, was coming out to meet him. Jacob sent gifts ahead, but prepared for the worst.]

Wrestling at Peniel

That same night he arose, and taking his two wives, his two maidservants, and his eleven children, he crossed the ford of the Jabbok. After taking them across the stream, he sent across all his possessions. Jacob was left alone. And a man wrestled with him until the break of dawn. When he saw that he had not prevailed against him, he wrenched Jacob's hip at its socket, so that the socket of his hip was strained as he wrestled with him. Then he said, "Let me go, for dawn is breaking." But he answered, "I will not let you go, unless you bless me." Said the other, "What is your name?" He replied, "Jacob." Said he, "Your name shall no longer be Jacob, but Israel, for you have striven with beings divine and human, and have prevailed." Jacob asked, "Pray tell me your name." But he said, "You must not ask my name!" And he took leave of him there. So Jacob named the place

ford: shallow place.

Israel: in Hebrew, "one who struggles with or for God."

Peniel, meaning, "I have seen a divine being face to face, yet my life has been preserved." The sun rose upon him as he passed Penuel, limping on his hip. That is why the children of Israel to this day do not eat the thigh muscle that is on the socket of the hip, since Jacob's hip socket was wrenched at the thigh muscle.

Peniel: in Hebrew, "the face of God."

Reconciliation

Looking up, Jacob saw Esau coming, accompanied by four hundred men. He divided the children among Leah, Rachel, and the two maids, putting the maids and their children first, Leah and her children next, and Rachel and Joseph last. He himself went on ahead and bowed low to the ground seven times until he was near his brother. Esau ran to greet him. He embraced him and, falling on his neck, he kissed him; and they wept. Looking about, he saw the women and the children. "Who," he asked, "are these with you?" He answered, "The children with whom God has favored your servant." Then the maids, with their children, came forward and bowed low; next Leah, with her children, came forward and bowed low; and last, Joseph and Rachel came forward and bowed low. And he asked, "What do you mean by all this company which I have met?" He answered, "To gain my lord's favor." Esau said, "I have enough, my brother; let what you have remain yours." But Jacob said, "No, I pray you, if you would do me this favor, accept from me this gift; for to see your face is like seeing the face of God, and you have received me favorably. Please accept my present which has been brought to you, for God has favored me and I have plenty." And when he urged him, he accepted.

Joseph: Rachel's only child at the time and Jacob's favorite.

this company: i.e., the herds of animals that Jacob had sent ahead to Esau as gifts.

FOR CLOSE READING

1. What does the Lord tell Rebekah before her children are born?

2. Briefly describe Esau and Jacob.

3. How does Jacob obtain the special blessing of his father?

4. Why does Jacob agree to work for Laban for seven years?

5. How does Jacob receive the name Israel?

FOR THOUGHT AND DISCUSSION

6. In your opinion, does Jacob get what he deserves? Explain.

7. What did you learn about Jacob's character from the birthright episode? What did you learn about Esau? What is your opinion of the behavior of each brother in this episode?

8. The Lord described Jacob's destiny before he was born. Do you think Rebekah's and Jacob's actions were necessary to fulfill that destiny? Explain.

9. What similarities do you find between the story of Jacob's blessing by Isaac and the story of Jacob's first wedding? How might these two events be connected?

10. How would you explain Esau's reaction to Jacob's homecoming?

11. How does Jacob change over the course of his life? Support your answer with details from the Bible passages.

12. Of all Jacob's experiences, which do you think had the greatest effect on his life? Explain.

RESPONDING

1. Writing In a monologue, express Jacob's thoughts at his reunion as he nervously walks toward his brother, then sees Esau break into a run.

2. Activity Using whatever materials you wish, create a model of the stairway/ladder of Jacob's dream.

3. Multicultural Connection While no one enjoys being tricked, people seem to enjoy tricky characters. Tricksters abound in the myths, folktales, fables, and legends of many cultures. Read stories about three such tricky characters from myth and folklore to learn what overall attitudes about cleverness are suggested. You might consider the Jack stories of American folklore; Coyote and Raven stories of Native American tribes; Loki stories from Scandinavian mythology; Anansi stories of West Africa; and Maui stories of Hawaii.

The Jacob's Ladder

The stairway is not
a thing of gleaming strands
a radiant evanescence
for angel's feet that only glance in their tread,
5   and need not
touch the stone

It is of stone.
A rosy stone that takes
a glowing tone of softness
10 only because behind it the sky is a doubtful,
a doubting
night gray.

A stairway of sharp
angles, solidly built.
15 One sees that the angels must spring
down from one step to the next, giving a little
lift of the wings:

and a man climbing
must scrape his knees, and bring
20 the grip of his hands into play. The cut stone
consoles his groping feet. Wings brush past him.
The poem ascends.

evanescence: a fading away; vanishing.

glance: i.e., touch lightly in passing.

FOR THOUGHT AND DISCUSSION

1. How does the poem's stairway compare with the stairway you imagined after reading the Bible story of Jacob's ladder?

2. Compare the ways angels and people travel on the stairway. Do you think this stairway was designed for angels or for people? Explain.

3. How did the last line affect your understanding of the poem?

Joseph: Favored and Cast Down

Jealous Brothers

sojourned: stayed.
line: family.

ornamented tunic: in some versions, "coat of many colors," a royal garment.

sheaves: bundles of cut grain.

Now Jacob was settled in the land where his father had sojourned, the land of Canaan. This, then is the line of Jacob: At seventeen years of age, Joseph tended the flocks with his brothers, as a helper to the sons of his father's wives Bilhah and Zilpah. And Joseph brought bad reports of them to their father. Now Israel loved Joseph best of all his sons, for he was the child of his old age; and he had made him an ornamented tunic. And when his brothers saw that their father loved him more than any of his brothers, they hated him so that they could not speak a friendly word to him.

Once Joseph had a dream which he told to his brothers; and they hated him even more. He said to them, "Hear this dream which I have dreamed: There we were binding sheaves in the field, when suddenly my sheaf stood up and remained upright; then your sheaves gathered around and bowed low to my sheaf." His brothers answered, "Do you mean to reign over us? Do you mean to rule over us?" and they hated him even more for his talk about his dreams.

He dreamed another dream and told it to his brothers, saying, "Look, I have had another dream: And this time, the sun, the moon, and eleven stars were bowing down to me." And when he told it to his father and brothers, his father berated him. "What," he said to him, "is this dream you have dreamed? Are we to come, I and your mother and your brothers, and bow low to you to the ground?" So his brothers were wrought up at him, and his father kept the matter in mind.

One time, when his brothers had gone to pasture their father's flock at Shechem, Israel said to Joseph,

Genesis 37:1–14a, 17b–35; 39:1–23 (*Tanakh*: The New Jewish Publication Society Translation).

"Your brothers are pasturing at Shechem. Come, I will send you to them." He answered, "I am ready." And he said to him, "Go and see how your brothers are and how the flocks are faring, and bring me back word.". . . So Joseph followed his brothers and found them at Dothan.

They saw him from afar, and before he came close to them they conspired to kill him. They said to one another, "Here comes that dreamer! Come now, let us kill him and throw him into one of the pits; and we can say, 'A savage beast devoured him.' We shall see what comes of his dreams!" But when Reuben heard it, he tried to save him from them. He said, "Let us not take his life." And Reuben went on, "Shed no blood! Cast him into that pit out in the wilderness, but do not touch him yourselves"—intending to save him from them and restore him to his father. When Joseph came up to his brothers, they stripped Joseph of his tunic, the ornamented tunic that he was wearing, and took him and cast him into the pit. The pit was empty; there was no water in it.

Reuben: the oldest brother.

Then they sat down to a meal. Looking up, they saw a caravan of Ishmaelites coming from Gilead, their camels bearing gum, balm, and ladanum to be taken to Egypt. Then Judah said to his brothers, "What do we gain by killing our brother and covering up his blood? Come, let us sell him to the Ishmaelites, but let us not do away with him ourselves. After all, he is our brother, our own flesh." His brothers agreed. When Midianite traders passed by, they pulled Joseph up out of the pit. They sold Joseph for twenty pieces of silver to the Ishmaelites, who brought Joseph to Egypt.

caravan: a group of travelers.

gum, balm, ladanum: valuable products derived from plants.

Judah: another of the older brothers.

When Reuben returned to the pit and saw that Joseph was not in the pit, he rent his clothes. Returning to his brothers, he said, "The boy is gone! Now, what am I to do?" Then they took Joseph's tunic, slaughtered a kid, and dipped the tunic in the blood. They had the ornamented tunic taken to their father, and they said, "We found this. Please examine it; is it your son's tunic or not?" He recognized it, and said, "My son's tunic! A savage beast devoured him! Joseph was torn by a beast!" Jacob rent his clothes, put sackcloth on his loins, and observed mourning for his son many days. All his sons and daughters sought

rent: tore.

kid: a young goat.

sackcloth: rough cloth worn as a sign of mourning.

loins: the middle portions of the body.

to comfort him; but he refused to be comforted,
saying, "No, I will go down mourning to my son in
Sheol." Thus his father bewailed him. . . .

In Potiphar's Service

courtier of Pharaoh: i.e.,
an officer of the Egyptian
king.

When Joseph was taken down to Egypt, a certain
Egyptian, Potiphar, a courtier of Pharaoh and
his chief steward, bought him from the Ishmaelites
who had brought him there. The Lord was with
Joseph, and he was a successful man; and he stayed in
the house of his Egyptian master. And when his
master saw that the Lord was with him and that the
Lord lent success to everything he undertook, he took
a liking to Joseph. He made him his personal
attendant and put him in charge of his household,
placing in his hands all that he owned. And from the
time that the Egyptian put him in charge of his
household and of all that he owned, the Lord blessed
his house for Joseph's sake, so that the blessing of the
Lord was upon everything that he owned, in the
house and outside. He left all that he had in Joseph's
hands and, with him there, he paid attention to
nothing save the food that he ate. Now Joseph was
well built and handsome.

After a time, his master's wife cast her eyes upon
Joseph and said, "Lie with me." But he refused. He
said to his master's wife, "Look, with me here, my
master gives no thought to anything in this house,
and all that he owns he has placed in my hands. He
wields no more authority in this house than I, and he
has withheld nothing from me except yourself, since
you are his wife. How then could I do this most
wicked thing, and sin before God?" And much as she
coaxed Joseph day after day, he did not yield to her
request to lie beside her, to be with her.

One such day, he came into the house to do his
work. None of the household being there inside, she
caught hold of him by his garment and said, "Lie with
me!" But he left his garment in her hand and got
away and fled outside. When she saw that he had left
it in her hand and had fled outside, she called out to
her servants and said to them, "Look, he had to bring
us a Hebrew to dally with us! This one came to lie
with me; but I screamed loud. And when he heard me
screaming at the top of my voice, he left his garment

with me and got away and fled outside." She kept his garment beside her, until his master came home. Then she told him the same story, saying, "The Hebrew slave whom you brought into our house came to me to dally with me; but when I screamed at the top of my voice, he left his garment with me and fled outside."

When his master heard the story that his wife told him, namely, "Thus and so your slave did to me," he was furious. So Joseph's master had him put in prison, where the king's prisoners were confined. But even while he was there in prison, the Lord was with Joseph: he extended kindness to him and disposed the chief jailer favorably toward him. The chief jailer put in Joseph's charge all the prisoners who were in that prison, and he was the one to carry out everything that was done there. The chief jailer did not supervise anything that was in Joseph's charge, because the Lord was with him, and whatever he did the Lord made successful.

FOR CLOSE READING

1. Why do Joseph's brothers dislike him?

2. In this passage, which of the brothers cares most about Joseph? What sentence shows this most clearly?

3. On three occasions Joseph is put into a low position. List those times and describe the situations.

FOR THOUGHT AND DISCUSSION

4. What is your impression of Joseph as a young man? Support your opinion from the text.

5. When the brothers are plotting to kill Joseph, they say, "Here comes that dreamer." Why do you suppose they use that word to show their hatred? People generally seem to be a little uneasy with those who claim to have unusual mental powers. Why do you think this is so?

6. What part does Joseph's clothing play in his success and misfortune?

7. To what extent is Joseph to blame for his difficulties? To what extent is he personally responsible for his successes?

8. A goat is killed in place of Joseph. Where has something like this happened before in the Bible? Compare and contrast the two episodes. What does it mean today to be made "the goat"?

RESPONDING

1. Activity "Ornamented tunic" or "coat of many colors," Joseph's garment symbolized that he was special to his father. With another classmate, design or describe an article of clothing that you think would express Joseph's special status if he lived in today's world.

2. Activity Depict in some medium (painting, collage, sculpture, needlepoint, etc.) one of Joseph's dreams.

3. Writing What kinds of clothing or uniform make you feel respect for the wearer? What kinds of clothing make you feel dislike or disapproval? amusement? Explain your reactions in an essay.

Joseph: His Brothers' Keeper

Pharaoh's Dreams

After two years' time, Pharaoh dreamed that he was standing by the Nile, when out of the Nile there came up seven cows, handsome and sturdy, and they grazed in the reed grass. But presently, seven other cows came up from the Nile close behind them, ugly and gaunt, and stood beside the cows on the bank of the Nile; and the ugly gaunt cows ate up the seven handsome sturdy cows. And Pharaoh awoke.

He fell asleep and dreamed a second time: Seven ears of grain, solid and healthy, grew on a single stalk. But close behind them sprouted seven ears, thin and scorched by the east wind. And the thin ears swallowed up the seven solid and full ears. Then Pharaoh awoke: it was a dream!

Next morning, his spirit was agitated, and he sent for all the magicians of Egypt, and all its wise men; and Pharaoh told them his dreams, but none could interpret them for Pharaoh.

The chief cupbearer then spoke up and said to Pharaoh, "I must make mention today of my offenses. Once Pharaoh was angry with his servants, and placed me in custody in the house of the chief steward, together with the chief baker. We had dreams the same night, he and I, each of us a dream with a meaning of its own. A Hebrew youth was there with us, a servant of the chief steward; and when we told him our dreams, he interpreted them for us, telling each of the meaning of his dream. And as he interpreted for us, so it came to pass: I was restored to my post, and the other was impaled."

offenses: faults, mistakes.

impaled: i.e., put to death on a stake. The Hebrew word can mean "to impale" or "to hang."

Genesis 41:1–16, 25–43; 42:1–28, 35–38; 43:1–44:18a; 44: 30b–45:28 (*Tanakh: The New Jewish Publication Society Translation*).

Thereupon Pharaoh sent for Joseph, and he was rushed from the dungeon. He had his hair cut and changed his clothes, and he appeared before Pharaoh. And Pharaoh said to Joseph, "I have had a dream, but no one can interpret it. Now I have heard it said of you that for you to hear a dream is to tell its meaning." Joseph answered Pharaoh, saying, "Not I! God will see to Pharaoh's welfare.". . .

And Joseph said to Pharaoh, "Pharaoh's dreams are one and the same: God has told Pharaoh what he is about to do. The seven healthy cows are seven years, and the seven healthy ears are seven years; it is the same dream. The seven lean and ugly cows that followed are seven years, as are also the seven empty ears scorched by the east wind; they are seven years of famine. It is just as I have told Pharaoh: God has revealed to Pharaoh what he is about to do. Immediately ahead are seven years of great abundance in all the land of Egypt. After them will come seven years of famine, and all the abundance in the land of Egypt will be forgotten. As the land is ravaged by famine, no trace of the abundance will be left in the land because of the famine thereafter, for it will be very severe. As for Pharaoh having had the same dream twice, it means that the matter has been determined by God, and that God will soon carry it out.

"Accordingly, let Pharaoh find a man of discernment and wisdom, and set him over the land of Egypt. And let Pharaoh take steps to appoint overseers over the land, and organize the land of Egypt in the seven years of plenty. Let all the food of these good years that are coming be gathered, and let the grain be collected under Pharaoh's authority as food to be stored in the cities. Let that food be a reserve for the land for the seven years of famine which will come upon the land of Egypt, so that the land may not perish in the famine."

The plan pleased Pharaoh and all his courtiers. And Pharaoh said to his courtiers, "Could we find another like him, a man in whom is the spirit of God?" So Pharaoh said to Joseph, "Since God has made all this known to you, there is none so discerning and wise as you. You shall be in charge of my court, and by your command shall all my people

famine: food shortage due to crop failure.

discernment: good judgment.

be directed; only with respect to the throne shall I be superior to you." Pharaoh further said to Joseph, "See, I put you in charge of all the land of Egypt." And removing his signet ring from his hand, Pharaoh put it on Joseph's hand; and he had him dressed in robes of fine linen, and put a gold chain about his neck. He had him ride in the chariot of his second-in-command, and they cried before him, "Abrek!" Thus he placed him over all the land of Egypt. . . .

signet ring: ring bearing official seal, symbol of authority.

Abrek: in other versions, "Bow down."

The Brothers' First Trip to Egypt

The seven years of abundance that the land of Egypt enjoyed came to an end, and the seven years of famine set in, just as Joseph had foretold. There was famine in all lands, but throughout the land of Egypt there was bread. And when all the land of Egypt felt the hunger, the people cried out to Pharaoh for bread; and Pharaoh said to all the Egyptians, "Go to Joseph; whatever he tells you, you shall do." Accordingly, when the famine became severe in the land of Egypt, Joseph laid open all that was within, and rationed out grain to the Egyptians. The famine, however, spread over the whole world. So all the world came to Joseph in Egypt to procure rations, for the famine had become severe throughout the world.

rationed out: gave in fixed amounts.

When Jacob saw that there were food rations to be had in Egypt, he said to his sons, "Why do you keep looking at one another? Now I hear," he went on, "that there are rations to be had in Egypt. Go and procure rations for us there, that we may live and not die." So ten of Joseph's brothers went down to get grain rations in Egypt; for Jacob did not send Joseph's brother Benjamin with his brothers, since he feared that he might meet with disaster. Thus the sons of Israel were among those who came to procure rations, for the famine extended to the land of Canaan.

Benjamin: of the twelve brothers, only Joseph and Benjamin, the youngest, were sons of Rachel, Jacob's favorite wife.

Now Joseph was the vizier of the land; it was he who dispensed rations to all the people of the land. And Joseph's brothers came and bowed low to him, with their faces to the ground. When Joseph saw his brothers, he recognized them; but he acted like a stranger toward them and spoke harshly to them. He asked them, "Where do you come from?" And they said, "From the land of Canaan, to procure food." For

vizier (vi zir′): governor.

procure: obtain; get.

though Joseph recognized his brothers, they did not recognize him. Recalling the dreams that he had dreamed about them, Joseph said to them, "You are spies, you have come to see the land in its nakedness." But they said to him, "No, my lord! Truly, your servants have come to procure food. We are all of us sons of the same man; we are honest men; your servants have never been spies!" And he said to them, "No, you have come to see the land in its nakedness!" And they replied, "We your servants were twelve brothers, sons of a certain man in the land of Canaan; the youngest, however, is now with our father, and one is no more." But Joseph said to them, "It is just as I have told you: You are spies! By this you shall be put to the test: unless your youngest brother comes here, by Pharaoh, you shall not depart from this place! Let one of you go and bring your brother, while the rest of you remain confined, that your words may be put to the test whether there is truth in you. Else, by Pharaoh, you are nothing but spies!" And he confined them in the guardhouse for three days.

On the third day Joseph said to them, "Do this and you shall live, for I am a God-fearing man. If you are honest men, let one of you brothers be held in your place of detention, while the rest of you go and take home rations for your starving households; but you must bring me your youngest brother, that your words may be verified and that you may not die." And they did accordingly. They said to one another, "Alas, we are being punished on account of our brother, because we looked on at his anguish, yet paid no heed as he pleaded with us. That is why this distress has come upon us." Then Reuben spoke up and said to them, "Did I not tell you, 'Do no wrong to the boy'? But you paid no heed. Now comes the reckoning for his blood." They did not know that Joseph understood, for there was an interpreter between him and them. He turned away from them and wept. But he came back to them and spoke to them; and he took Simeon from among them and had him bound before their eyes. Then Joseph gave orders to fill their bags with grain, return each one's money to his sack, and give them provisions for the journey; and this was done for them. So they loaded their asses with the rations and departed from there.

As one of them was opening his sack to give feed to his ass at the night encampment, he saw his money right there at the mouth of his bag. And he said to his brothers, "My money has been returned! It is here in my bag!" Their hearts sank; and, trembling, they turned to one another, saying, "What is this that God has done to us?". . .

As they were emptying their sacks, there, in each one's sack, was his money-bag! When they and their father saw their money-bags, they were dismayed. Their father Jacob said to them, "It is always me that you bereave: Joseph is no more and Simeon is no more, and now you would take away Benjamin. These things always happen to me!" Then Reuben said to his father, "You may kill my two sons if I do not bring him back to you. Put him in my care, and I will return him to you." But he said, "My son must not go down with you, for his brother is dead and he alone is left. If he meets with disaster on the journey you are taking, you will send my white head down to Sheol in grief."

dismayed: worried; upset.

bereave: leave desolate and alone.

white head: a reference to Jacob's white hair.

The Second Trip to Egypt

But the famine in the land was severe. And when they had eaten up the rations which they had brought from Egypt, their father said to them, "Go again and procure some food for us." But Judah said to him, "The man warned us, 'Do not let me see your faces unless your brother is with you.' If you will let our brother go with us, we will go down and procure food for you; but if you will not let him go, we will not go down, for the man said to us, 'Do not let me see your faces unless your brother is with you.'" And Israel said, "Why did you serve me so ill as to tell the man that you had another brother?" They replied, "But the man kept asking about us and our family, saying, 'Is your father still living? Have you another brother?' And we answered him accordingly. How were we to know that he would say, 'Bring your brother here'?"

Then Judah said to his father Israel, "Send the boy in my care, and let us be on our way, that we may live and not die—you and we and our children. I myself will be surety for him; you may hold me responsible: if I do not bring him back to you and set him before you, I shall stand guilty before you forever. For we

be surety: take responsibility.

could have been there and back twice if we had not dawdled."

Then their father Israel said to them, "If it must be so, do this: take some of the choice products of the land in your baggage; and carry them down as a gift for the man—some balm and some honey, gum, ladunum, pistachio nuts, and almonds. And take with you double the money, carrying back with you the money that was replaced in the mouths of your bags; perhaps it was a mistake. Take your brother too; and go back at once to the man. And may El Shaddai dispose the man to mercy toward you, that he may release to you your other brother, as well as Benjamin. As for me, if I am to be bereaved, I shall be bereaved."

So the men took that gift, and they took with them double the money, as well as Benjamin. They made their way down to Egypt, where they presented themselves to Joseph. When Joseph saw Benjamin with them, he said to his house steward, "Take the men into the house; slaughter and prepare an animal, for the men will dine with me at noon." The man did as Joseph said, and he brought the men into Joseph's house. But the men were frightened at being brought into Joseph's house. "It must be," they thought, "because of the money replaced in our bags the first time that we have been brought inside, as a pretext to attack us and seize us as slaves, with our pack animals." So they went up to Joseph's house steward and spoke to him at the entrance of the house. "If you please, my lord," they said, "we came down once before to procure food. But when we arrived at the night encampment and opened our bags, there was each one's money in the mouth of his bag, our money in full. So we have brought it back with us. And we have brought down with us other money to procure food. We do not know who put the money in our bags." He replied, "All is well with you; do not be afraid. Your God, the God of your father, must have put treasure in your bags for you. I got your payment." And he brought out Simeon to them.

Then the man brought the men into Joseph's house; he gave them water to bathe their feet, and he provided feed for their asses. They laid out their gifts to await Joseph's arrival at noon, for they had heard that they were to dine there.

El Shaddai: God Almighty.

pretext: excuse.

When Joseph came home, they presented to him the gifts that they had brought with them into the house, bowing low before him to the ground. He greeted them, and he said, "How is your aged father of whom you spoke? Is he still in good health?" They replied, "It is well with your servant our father; he is still in good health." And they bowed and made obeisance.

Looking about, he saw his brother Benjamin, his mother's son, and asked, "Is this your youngest brother of whom you spoke to me?" And he went on, "May God be gracious to you, my boy." With that, Joseph hurried out, for he was overcome with feeling toward his brother and was on the verge of tears; he went into a room and wept there. Then he washed his face, reappeared, and—now in control of himself—gave the order, "Serve the meal." They served him by himself, and them by themselves, and the Egyptians who ate with him by themselves; for the Egyptians could not dine with Hebrews, since that would be abhorrent to the Egyptians. As they were seated by his direction, from the oldest in order of his seniority to the youngest in the order of his youth, the men looked at one another in astonishment. Portions were served them from his table; but Benjamin's portion was several times that of anyone else. And they drank their fill with him.

Then he instructed his house steward as follows, "Fill the men's bags with food, as much as they can carry, and put each one's money in the mouth of his bag. Put my silver goblet in the mouth of the bag of the youngest one, together with his money for the rations." And he did as Joseph told him.

With the first light of morning, the men were sent off with their pack animals. They had just left the city and had not gone far, when Joseph said to his steward, "Up, go after the men! And when you overtake them, say to them, 'Why did you repay good with evil? It is the very one from which my master drinks and which he uses for divination. It was a wicked thing for you to do!'"

He overtook them and spoke those words to them. And they said to him, "Why does my lord say such things? Far be it from your servants to do anything of the kind! Here we brought back to you from the land of Canaan the money that we found in the mouths of our bags. How then could we have stolen any silver or gold from your master's house! Whichever of your servants it is found with shall die; the rest of us, moreover, shall become slaves to my lord." He replied, "Although what you are proposing is right, only the one with whom it is found shall be my slave; but the rest of you shall go free."

So each one hastened to lower his bag to the ground, and each one opened his bag. He searched, beginning with the oldest and ending with the youngest; and the goblet turned up in Benjamin's bag. At this they rent their clothes. Each reloaded his pack animal, and they returned to the city.

When Judah and his brothers reentered the house of Joseph, who was still there, they threw themselves on the ground before him. Joseph said to them, "What is this deed that you have done? Do you not know that a man like me practices divination?" Judah replied, "What can we say to my lord? How can we plead, how can we prove our innocence? God has uncovered the crime of your servants. Here we are, then, slaves of my lord, the rest of us as much as he in whose possession the goblet was found." But he replied, "Far be it from me to act thus! Only he in whose possession the goblet was found shall be my slave; the rest of you go back in peace to your father."

Then Judah went up to him and said, "Please, my lord, let your servant appeal to my lord, and do not be impatient with your servant. . . . Now, if I come to your servant my father and the boy is not with us—since his own life is so bound up with his—when he sees that the boy is not with us, he will die, and your servants will send the white head of your servant our father down to Sheol in grief. Now your servant has pledged himself for the boy to my father, saying 'If I do not bring him back to you, I shall stand guilty before my father forever.' Therefore, please let your servant remain as a slave to my lord instead of the boy, and let the boy go back with his brothers. For how can I go back to my father unless the boy is with me? Let me not be witness to the woe that would overtake my father!"

"I Am Joseph"

Joseph could no longer control himself before all his attendants, and he cried out, "Have everyone withdraw from me!" So there was no one else about when Joseph made himself known to his brothers. His sobs were so loud that the Egyptians could hear, and so the news reached Pharaoh's palace.

Joseph said to his brothers, "I am Joseph. Is my father still well?" But his brothers could not answer him, so dumfounded were they on account of him.

Then Joseph said to his brothers, "Come forward to me." And when they came forward, he said, "I am your brother Joseph, he whom you sold into Egypt. Now, do not be distressed or reproach yourselves because you sold me hither; it was to save life that God sent me ahead of you. It is now two years that there has been famine in the land, and there are still five years to come in which there shall be no yield from tilling. God has sent me ahead of you to ensure your survival on earth, and to save your lives in an extraordinary deliverance. So, it was not you who sent me here, but God; and he has made me a father to Pharaoh, lord of all his household, and ruler over the whole land of Egypt.

hither: to this place.

father to: chief under.

"Now, hurry back to my father and say to him: Thus says your son Joseph, 'God has made me lord of all Egypt; come down to me without delay. You will dwell in the region of Goshen, where you will be near me—you and your children and your grandchildren, your flocks and herds, and all that is yours. There I will provide for you—for there are yet five years of famine to come—that you and your household and all that is yours may not suffer want.' You can see for yourselves, and my brother Benjamin for himself, that it is indeed I who am speaking to you. And you must tell my father everything about my high station in Egypt and all that you have seen; and bring my father here with all speed."

Goshen (gō′shən): a very fertile area in Egypt.

With that he embraced his brother Benjamin around the neck and wept, and Benjamin wept on his neck. He kissed all his brothers and wept upon them; only then were his brothers able to talk to him.

The news reached Pharaoh's palace: "Joseph's brothers have come." Pharaoh and his courtiers were pleased. And Pharaoh said to Joseph, "Say to your brothers, 'Do as follows: load up your beasts and go at once to the land of Canaan. Take your father and your households and come to me; I will give you the best of the land of Egypt and you shall live off the fat of the land.' And you are bidden [to add], 'Do as follows; take from the land of Egypt wagons for your children and your wives, and bring your father here. And never mind your belongings, for the best of all the land of Egypt shall be yours.'"

The sons of Israel did so; Joseph gave them wagons as Pharaoh had commanded, and he supplied them with provisions for the journey. To each of them, moreover, he gave a change of clothing; but to Benjamin he gave three hundred pieces of silver and several changes of clothing. And to his father he sent the following: ten he-asses laden with the best things of Egypt, and ten she-asses laden with grain, bread, and provisions for his father on the journey. As he sent his brothers off on their way, he told them, "Do not be quarrelsome on the way."

They went up from Egypt and came to their father Jacob in the land of Canaan. And they told him, "Joseph is still alive; yes, he is ruler over the whole land of Egypt." His heart went numb, for he did not believe them. But when they recounted all that Joseph had sent to transport him, the spirit of their father Jacob revived. "Enough!" said Israel. "My son Joseph is still alive! I must go and see him before I die."

FOR CLOSE READING

1. How does Pharaoh learn of Joseph's special talents?

2. On several occasions in both parts of the story, Joseph becomes the favorite of an authority. Cite the occasions, the names of the people who promote Joseph, and the people who are ranked lower than Joseph.

3. Six dreams occur in the whole story of Joseph. List the people who have the dreams and what the dreams foretell.

FOR THOUGHT AND DISCUSSION

4. Which scene would you choose as the most important turning point in Joseph's life? Which scene is the point of strongest emotional tension?

5. What effect does each of the three pairs of dreams have on Joseph's life?

6. Explain the importance to the story of the following events: *(a)* Joseph imprisons his brothers; *(b)* Joseph has Simeon bound before his brothers' eyes; *(c)* Joseph threatens Benjamin with slavery. In your opinion, is Joseph tormenting his brothers or giving them a second chance? Explain.

7. Think of revenge stories you have read. In what ways are they similar to Joseph's story? In what ways are they different?

8. Certain images and situations occur several times throughout the story of Joseph; for example, "clothing," and being "cast down." What others do you find? What is the effect of these repeated situations on the reader?

9. In what ways have the brothers changed over the course of this story? Joseph? Support your opinions with examples.

RESPONDING

1. Writing Write an obituary notice that might have been published in an Egyptian newspaper after Joseph's death.

2. Activity Draw a plot line of the action in the story of Joseph, showing the high points and the low. Place on the drawing a small sketch of any object that seems significant to each turning point (bloody coat, a cup, etc.)

3

From Slavery to Freedom

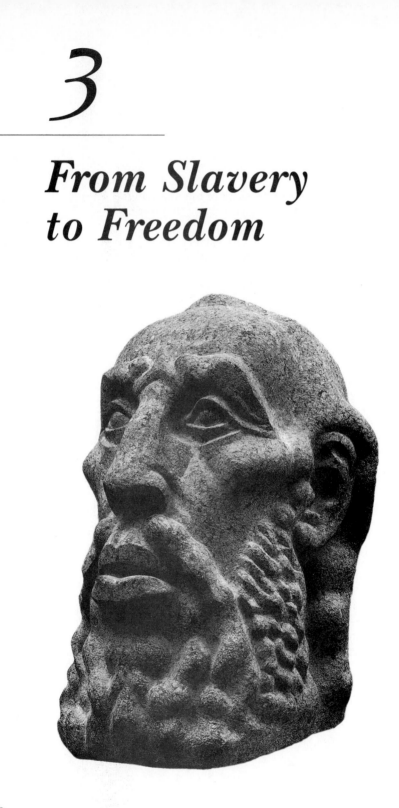

Moses: The Calling of a Leader

The Birth of Moses

Now there arose a new king over Egypt, who did not know Joseph. And he said to his people, "Behold, the people of Israel are too many and too mighty for us. Come, let us deal shrewdly with them, lest they multiply, and, if war befall us, they join our enemies and fight against us and escape from the land." Therefore they set taskmasters over them to afflict them with heavy burdens; and they built for Pharaoh store-cities, Pithom and Raamses. But the more they were oppressed, the more they multiplied and the more they spread abroad. And the Egyptians were in dread of the people of Israel. So they made the people of Israel serve with rigor, and made their lives bitter with hard service, in mortar and brick, and in all kinds of work in the field; in all their work they made them serve with rigor.

The king of Egypt said to the Hebrew midwives, one of whom was named Shiphrah and the other Puah, "When you serve as midwife to the Hebrew women, and see them upon the birthstool, if it is a son, you shall kill him; but if it is a daughter, she shall live." But the midwives feared God, and did not do as the king of Egypt commanded them, but let the male children live. So the king of Egypt called the midwives, and said to them, "Why have you done this, and let the male children live?" The midwives said to Pharaoh, "Because the Hebrew women are not like the Egyptian women; for they are vigorous and are delivered before the midwife comes to them." So

shrewdly: cleverly.

taskmasters: bosses for forced labor.

store-cities: supply depots (pi′thəm; rā am′sēz).

with rigor: harshly.

midwives: women who assist in childbirth.

upon the birthstool: giving birth.

feared: respected, obeyed, had confidence in.

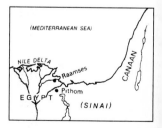

Exodus 1:8–3:14; 4:10–15, 18–20 (Revised Standard Version).

LEFT: *Moses*, granite sculpture by William Zorach, 1956. Collection of Columbia University, New York, Gift of Armand G. Erpf. Geoffrey Clements, photography.

God **dealt** well with the midwives; and the people **multiplied** and grew very strong. And because the midwives feared God he gave them families. Then Pharaoh commanded all his people, "Every son that is born to the Hebrews you shall cast into the Nile, but you shall let every daughter live."

house: tribe.

Now a man from the **house** of Levi went and took to wife a daughter of Levi. The woman conceived and bore a son; and when she saw that he was a goodly child, she hid him three months. And when she could hide him no longer she took for him a **basket** made of bulrushes, and daubed it with **bitumen** and **pitch**; and she put the child in it and placed it among the reeds at the river's brink. And his sister stood at a distance, to know what would be done to him. Now the daughter of Pharaoh came down to bathe at the river, and her maidens walked beside the river; she saw the basket among the reeds and sent her maid to fetch it. When she opened it she saw the child; and lo, the babe was crying. She took pity on him and said, "This is one of the Hebrews' children." Then his sister said to Pharaoh's daughter, "Shall I go and call you a nurse from the Hebrew women to nurse the child for you?" And Pharaoh's daughter said to her, "Go." So the girl went and called the child's mother. And Pharaoh's daughter said to her, "Take this child away, and nurse him for me, and I will give you your wages." So the woman took the child and nursed him. And the child grew, and she brought him to Pharaoh's daughter, and he became her son; and she named him **Moses**, for she said, "Because I drew him out of the water."

basket: the Hebrew word is the same one used for Noah's ark.

bitumen: asphalt used as cement.

pitch: tar.

Moses: the Hebrew word, *Mosheh*, means "he draws out," but Pharaoh's daughter seems to think it means "he is drawn out."

his people: the Hebrews.

A Stranger in a Strange Land

One day, when Moses had grown up, he went out to **his people** and looked on their burdens; and he saw an Egyptian beating a Hebrew, one of his people. He looked this way and that, and seeing no one he killed the Egyptian and hid him in the sand. When he went out the next day, behold, two Hebrews were struggling together; and he said to the man that did the wrong, "Why do you strike your fellow?" He answered, "Who made you a prince and a judge over us? Do you mean to kill me as you killed the

Egyptian?" Then Moses was afraid, and thought, "Surely the thing is known." When Pharaoh heard of it, he sought to kill Moses.

But Moses fled from Pharaoh, and stayed in the land of Midian; and he sat down by a well. Now the priest of Midian had seven daughters; and they came and drew water, and filled the troughs to water their father's flock. The shepherds came and drove them away; but Moses stood up and helped them, and watered their flock. When they came to their father Reuel, he said, "How is it that you have come so soon today?" They said, "An Egyptian delivered us out of the hand of the shepherds, and even drew water for us and watered the flock." He said to his daughters, "And where is he? Call him, that he may eat bread." And Moses was content to dwell with the man, and he gave Moses his daughter Zipporah. She bore a son, and he called his name Gershom; for he said, "I have been a sojourner in a foreign land."

In the course of those many days the king of Egypt died. And the people of Israel groaned under their bondage, and cried out for help, and their cry under bondage came up to God. And God heard their groaning, and God remembered his covenant with Abraham, with Isaac, and with Jacob. And God saw the people of Israel, and God knew their condition.

Midian: the Midianites and Hebrews had common ancestors.

Reuel (rü′əl): also called Jethro.

Gershom (gĕr′shəm): from the Hebrew words *ger* (stranger, alien) and *sham* (there).

The Burning Bush

Now Moses was keeping the flock of his father-in-law, Jethro, the priest of Midian; and he led his flock to the west side of the wilderness, and came to Horeb, the mountain of god. And the angel of the Lord appeared to him in a flame of fire out of the midst of a bush; and he looked, and lo, the bush was burning, yet it was not consumed. And Moses said, "I will turn aside and see this great sight, why the bush is not burnt." When the Lord saw that he turned aside to see, God called to him out of the bush, "Moses, Moses!" And he said, "Here am I." Then he said, "Do not come near; put off your shoes from your feet, for the place on which you are standing is holy ground." And he said, "I am the God of your father, the God of Abraham, the God of Isaac, and the God of Jacob." And Moses hid his face, for he was afraid to look at God.

Horeb (hôr′ eb): also called Sinai (si′nĭ).

affliction: suffering.

Then the Lord said, "I have seen the affliction of my people who are in Egypt, and have heard their cry because of their taskmasters; I know their sufferings, and I have come down to deliver them out of the hand of the Egyptians, and to bring them up out of that land to a good and broad land, a land flowing with milk and honey, to the place of the Canaanites, the Hittites, the Amorites, the Perizzites, the Hivites, and the Jebusites. And now, behold, the cry of the people of Israel has come to me, and I have seen the oppression with which the Egyptians oppress them. Come, I will send you to Pharaoh that you may bring

sons: descendants.

forth my people, the sons of Israel, out of Egypt." But Moses said to God, "Who am I that I should go to Pharaoh, and bring the sons of Israel out of Egypt?" He said, "But I will be with you; and this shall be the

sign: proof.

sign for you, that I have sent you: when you have brought forth the people out of Egypt, you shall serve God upon this mountain."

Then Moses said to God, "If I come to the people of Israel and say to them, 'The God of your fathers has sent me to you,' and they ask me, 'What is his name?' what shall I say to them?" God said to Moses,

I AM: the Hebrew word is close to the word that is translated "The Lord" in this translation (RSV).

"I AM WHO I AM." And he said, "Say this to the people of Israel, 'I AM has sent me to you.'" . . .

But Moses said to the Lord, "Oh, my Lord, I am not eloquent, either heretofore or since thou hast spoken to thy servant; but I am slow of speech and of

heretofore: before this time.

dumb: unable to talk.

tongue." The Lord said to him, "Who has made man's mouth? Who makes him dumb, or deaf, or seeing, or blind? Is it not I, the Lord? Now therefore go, and I will be with your mouth and teach you what you shall speak." But he said, "Oh, my Lord, send, I pray, some other person." Then the anger of the Lord was kindled against Moses and he said, "Is there not Aaron, your brother, the Levite? I know that he can speak well; and behold, he is coming out to meet you, and when he sees you he will be glad in his heart. And you shall speak to him and put the words in his mouth; and I will be with your mouth and with his mouth, and will teach you what you shall do. . . ."

Moses went back to Jethro his father-in-law and said to him, "Let me go back, I pray, to my kinsmen in Egypt and see whether they are still alive." And

Jethro said to Moses, "Go in peace." And the Lord said to Moses in Midian, "Go back to Egypt; for all the men who were seeking your life are dead." So Moses took his wife and his sons and set them on an ass, and went back to the land of Egypt; and in his hand Moses took the rod of God.

FOR CLOSE READING

1. What are the results of the Egyptian policy of oppressing the Hebrews?

2. How are the Pharaoh's two orders to kill male Hebrew babies obeyed?

3. What opposite roles do women play in the stories of Moses' birth and his stay in Midian?

4. For what reasons is Moses reluctant to accept God's call to leadership?

FOR THOUGHT AND DISCUSSION

5. Why do you think the Egyptians did not simply expel the Hebrews from the country? Can you think of other occasions when nations have reacted to "aliens" as the Egyptians do? How do the circumstances differ from those in the Bible story?

6. Pharaoh says that he will deal "shrewdly" with the Hebrews. How wise or clever are the measures he takes? In what ways do the Hebrew women deal "shrewdly" with Pharaoh?

7. Nowhere else in the Bible is the Hebrew word that is translated as "ark" or "basket" used except in the Noah and Moses stories. Assuming the word was chosen carefully, what do you suppose is the reason for connecting these two events?

8. In what ways is Moses an outsider? How is this indicated in the story? In your opinion, is there any connection between being an outsider and being a leader? Explain.

9. How do the following episodes relate to the assignment God later gives to Moses? *(a)* Moses rescues a Hebrew by killing an Egyptian; *(b)* he intervenes between two quarreling Hebrews; *(c)* he helps Reuel's daughters at the well.

10. Moses raises various objections at the burning bush, and God answers them in turn. From this interchange, what do you infer about the character of Moses? about God?

RESPONDING

1. **Writing** What is Pharaoh's reaction when he learns that his daughter has adopted a Hebrew baby? Write a dialogue between father and daughter.

2. **Activity** Create in some art medium (painting, sculpture, stained glass, etc.) an image of the burning bush.

3. **Multicultural Connection** There are many stories in various cultures about oppressed people resisting and outsmarting their oppressors. Find other examples of people cleverly overcoming oppression, then compare them with the story of the Hebrews in Egypt.

Go Down, Moses

When Israel was in Egypt's land,
　Let my people go!
Oppressed so hard they could not stand,
　Let my people go!

5　Go down, Moses,
　'Way down in Egypt's land,
　Tell old Pharaoh
　To let my people go!

10　"Thus spake the Lord," bold Moses said,
　"Let my people go!
If not, I'll smite your firstborn dead,
　Let my people go!"

　Go down, Moses,
　'Way down in Egypt's land.
15　Tell old Pharaoh
　To let my people go!

　"No more shall they in bondage toil,
　Let my people go!
Let them come out with Egypt's spoil,
20　Let my people go!"

　Go down, Moses,
　'Way down in Egypt's land.
　Tell old Pharaoh
　To let my people go!

FOR THOUGHT AND DISCUSSION

"Go Down, Moses" was originally sung by people in
slavery in America. What special meaning do you
think the Moses-Exodus story had to the first singers
of this song?

Challenging Pharaoh

"Let My People Go"

The Lord said to Aaron, "Go into the wilderness to meet Moses." So he went, and met him at the mountain of God and kissed him. And Moses told Aaron all the words of the Lord with which he had sent him, and all the signs which he had charged him to do. Then Moses and Aaron went and gathered together all the elders of the people of Israel. And Aaron spoke all the words which the Lord had spoken to Moses, and did the signs in the sight of the people. And the people believed; and when they heard that the Lord had visited the people of Israel and that he had seen their affliction, they bowed their heads and worshiped.

Afterward Moses and Aaron went to Pharaoh and said, "Thus says the Lord, the God of Israel, 'Let my people go, that they may hold a feast to me in the wilderness.'" But Pharaoh said, "Who is the Lord, that I should heed his voice and let Israel go? I do not know the Lord, and moreover I will not let Israel go." Then they said, "The God of the Hebrews has met with us; let us go, we pray, a three days' journey into the wilderness, and sacrifice to the Lord our God, lest

he fall upon us with pestilence or with the sword." But the king of Egypt said to them, "Moses and Aaron, why do you take the people away from their work? Get to your burdens.". . .The same day Pharaoh commanded the taskmasters of the people and their foremen, "You shall no longer give the people straw to make bricks, as heretofore; let them go and gather straw for themselves. But the number of bricks which they made heretofore you shall lay upon them, you shall by no means lessen it; for they are idle; therefore they cry, 'Let us go and offer sacrifice to our god.' Let

Exodus 4:27–5:4; 5:6–9, 15–23; 7:14–24; 11:1–9; 12: 1–13, 29–36; 14: 5–14, 19–29, 31 (Revised Standard Version).

heavier work be laid upon the men that they may labor at it and pay no regard to lying words.". . .

Then the foremen of the people of Israel came and cried to Pharaoh, "Why do you deal thus with your servants? No straw is given to your servants, yet they say to us, 'Make bricks!' And behold, your servants are beaten; but the fault is in your own people." But he said, "You are idle, you are idle; therefore you say, 'Let us go and sacrifice to the Lord.' Go now, and work; for no straw shall be given you, but you shall deliver the same number of bricks." The foremen of the people of Israel saw that they were in evil plight, when they said, "You shall by no means lessen your daily number of bricks." They met Moses and Aaron, who were waiting for them, as they came forth from Pharaoh; and they said to them, "The Lord look upon you and judge, because you have made us offensive in the sight of Pharaoh and his servants, and have put a sword in their hand to kill us."

evil plight: great trouble.

Then Moses turned again to the Lord and said, "O Lord, why hast thou done evil to this people? Why didst thou ever send me? For since I came to Pharaoh to speak in thy name, he has done evil to this people, and thou hast not delivered thy people at all.". . .

evil: harm.

delivered: rescued.

The Plagues

Then the Lord said to Moses, "Pharaoh's heart is hardened, he refuses to let the people go. Go to Pharaoh in the morning, as he is going out to the water; wait for him by the river's brink, and take in your hand the rod which was turned into a serpent. And you shall say to him, 'The Lord, the God of the Hebrews, sent me to you, saying, "Let my people go, that they may serve me in the wilderness; and behold, you have not yet obeyed." Thus says the Lord, "By this you shall know that I am the Lord: behold, I will strike the water that is in the Nile with the rod that is in my hand, and it shall be turned to blood, and the fish in the Nile shall die, and the Nile shall become foul, and the Egyptians will loathe to drink water from the Nile." ' " And the Lord said to Moses, "Say to Aaron, 'Take your rod and stretch out your hand over the waters of Egypt, over their rivers, their canals, and their ponds, and all their pools of water, that they may become blood; and there shall be blood

rod . . . serpent: a miraculous sign given to Moses at the burning bush and repeated before Pharaoh.

loathe: hate.

throughout all the land of Egypt, both in vessels of wood and in vessels of stone.'"

Moses and Aaron did as the Lord commanded; in the sight of Pharaoh and in the sight of his servants, he lifted up the rod and struck the water that was in the Nile, and all the water that was in the Nile turned to blood. And the fish in the Nile died; and the Nile became foul, so that the Egyptians could not drink water from the Nile; and there was blood throughout all the land of Egypt. But the magicians of Egypt did the same by their secret arts; so Pharaoh's heart remained hardened, and he would not listen to them; as the Lord had said. Pharaoh turned and went into

his house, and he did not lay even this to heart. And all the Egyptians dug round about the Nile for water to drink, for they could not drink the water of the Nile. . . .

[*Pharaoh resisted eight more plagues, including swarms of frogs, gnats, flies, and locusts; boils and cattle disease; hail; and daylong darkness.*]

The Lord said to Moses, "Yet one plague more I will bring upon Pharaoh and upon Egypt; afterwards

he will let you go hence; when he lets you go, he will drive you away completely. Speak now in the hearing of the people, that they ask, every man of his

neighbor and every woman of her neighbor, jewelry of silver and gold." And the Lord gave the people

favor in the sight of the Egyptians. Moreover, the man Moses was very great in the land of Egypt, in the sight of Pharaoh's servants and in the sight of the people.

And Moses said, "Thus says the Lord: About midnight I will go forth in the midst of Egypt; and all the first-born in the land of Egypt shall die, from the first-born of Pharaoh who sits upon his throne, even

to the first-born of the maidservant who is behind the mill; and all the first-born of the cattle. And there shall be a great cry throughout all the land of Egypt, such as there has never been, nor ever shall be again. But against any of the people of Israel, either man or beast, not a dog shall growl; that you may know that the Lord makes a distinction between the Egyptians and Israel. And all these your servants shall come down to me, and bow down to me, saying, 'Get you out, and all the people who follow you.' And after that I will go out." And he went out from Pharaoh in hot anger. Then the Lord said to Moses, "Pharaoh will not listen to you; that my wonders may be multiplied in the land of Egypt.". . .

The Passover

The Lord said to Moses and Aaron in the land of Egypt, "This month shall be for you the beginning of months; it shall be the first month of the year for you. Tell all the congregation of Israel that on the tenth day of this month they shall take every man a lamb according to their fathers' houses, a lamb for a household; and if the household is too small for a lamb, then a man and his neighbor next to his house shall take according to the number of persons; according to what each can eat you shall make your count for the lamb. Your lamb shall be without blemish, a male a year old; you shall take it from the sheep or from the goats; and you shall keep it until the fourteenth day of this month, when the whole assembly of the congregation of Israel shall kill their lambs in the evening. Then they shall take some of the blood, and put it on the two doorposts and the lintel of the houses in which they eat them. They shall eat the flesh that night, roasted; with unleavened bread and bitter herbs they shall eat it. Do not eat any of it raw or boiled with water, but roasted, its head with its legs and its inner parts. And you shall let none of it remain until the morning, anything that remains until the morning you shall burn. In this manner you shall eat it: your loins girded, your sandals on your feet, and your staff in your hand; and you shall eat it in haste. It is the Lord's passover. For I will pass through the land of Egypt that night, and I will smite all the first-born in the land of Egypt, both man and beast; and on all the gods of Egypt I will execute judgments: I am the Lord. The blood shall be a sign for you, upon the houses where you are; and when I see the blood, I will pass over you, and no plague shall fall upon you to destroy you, when I smite the land of Egypt.". . .

At midnight the Lord smote all the first-born in the land of Egypt, from the first-born of Pharaoh who

goats: i.e., a kid could take the place of a lamb.

lintel: top of the door frame.

unleavened: without yeast, which takes time to rise.

loins girded: belt fastened, for travel.

passover: movement of the Lord over Egypt.

smite: strike.

sat on his throne to the first-born of the captive who was in the dungeon, and all the first-born of the cattle. And Pharaoh rose up in the night, he, and all his servants, and all the Egyptians; and there was a great cry in Egypt, for there was not a house where one was not dead. And he summoned Moses and Aaron by night, and said, "Rise up, go forth from among my people, both you and the people of Israel; and go, serve the Lord, as you have said. Take your flocks and your herds, as you have said, and be gone; and bless me also!"

The Exodus

And the Egyptians were urgent with the people, to send them out of the land in haste; for they said, "We are all dead men." So the people took their dough before it was leavened, their kneading bowls being bound up in their mantles on their shoulders. The people of Israel had also done as Moses told them, for they had asked of the Egyptians jewelry of silver and of gold, and clothing; and the Lord had given the people favor in the sight of the Egyptians, so that they let them have what they asked. Thus they despoiled the Egyptians. . . .

When the king of Egypt was told that the people had fled, the mind of Pharaoh and his servants was changed toward the people, and they said, "What is this we have done, that we have let Israel go from serving us?" So he made ready his chariot and took his army with him, and took six hundred picked chariots and all the other chariots of Egypt with officers over all of them. And the Lord hardened the heart of Pharaoh king of Egypt and he pursued the people of Israel as they went forth defiantly. The Egyptians pursued them, all Pharaoh's horses and chariots and his horsemen and his army, and overtook them encamped at the sea, by Pi-hahiroth, in front of Baal-zephon.

When Pharaoh drew near, the people of Israel lifted up their eyes, and behold, the Egyptians were marching after them; and they were in great fear. And the people of Israel cried out to the Lord; and they said to Moses, "Is it because there are no graves in Egypt that you have taken us away to die in the

mantles: cloaks, capes.

despoiled: took the possessions of.

sea: according to tradition, the Red Sea.

wilderness? What have you done to us, in bringing us out of Egypt? Is not this what we said to you in Egypt, 'Let us alone and let us serve the Egyptians'? For it would have been better for us to serve the Egyptians than to die in the wilderness." And Moses said to the people, "Fear not, stand firm and see the salvation of the Lord, which he will work for you today; for the Egyptians whom you see today, you shall never see again. The Lord will fight for you, and you have only to be still.". . .

salvation: deliverance.

Parting the Sea

Then the angel of God who went before the host of Israel moved and went behind them; and the pillar of cloud moved from before them and stood behind them, coming between the host of Egypt and the host of Israel. And there was the cloud and the darkness; and the night passed without one coming near the other all night.

host: army.

pillar: column.

Then Moses stretched out his hand over the sea; and the Lord drove the sea back by a strong east wind all night, and made the sea dry land, and the waters were divided. And the people of Israel went into the midst of the sea on dry ground, the waters being a wall to them on their right hand and on their left. The Egyptians pursued, and went in after them into the midst of the sea, all Pharaoh's horses, his chariots, and his horsemen. And in the morning watch the Lord in the pillar of fire and of cloud looked down upon the host of the Egyptians, and discomfited the host of the Egyptians, clogging their chariot wheels so that they drove heavily; and the Egyptians said, "Let us flee from before Israel; for the Lord fights for them against the Egyptians."

watch: hours.

discomfited: threw into panic.

Then the Lord said to Moses, "Stretch out your hand over the sea, that the water may come back upon the Egyptians, upon their chariots, and upon their horsemen." So Moses stretched forth his hand over the sea, and the sea returned to its wonted flow when the morning appeared; and the Egyptians fled into it, and the Lord routed the Egyptians in the midst of the sea. The waters returned and covered the chariots and the horsemen and all the host of Pharaoh that had followed them into the sea; not so much as

wonted: normal, usual.
fled into it: i.e., tried to return.
routed: put to flight.

one of them remained. But the people of Israel walked on dry ground through the sea, the waters being a wall to them on their right hand and on their left.

... And Israel saw the great work which the Lord did against the Egyptians, and the people feared the Lord; and they believed in the Lord and in his servant Moses.

FOR CLOSE READING

1. What do Moses and Aaron first ask of Pharaoh and what reasons do they give? How does Pharaoh respond?

2. By what means are the people of Israel protected when the Lord passes over Egypt?

3. When Pharaoh tells Moses and Aaron to "be gone," he adds a personal request. What is that request?

4. What specific actions does the Lord perform during the escape from Egypt?

FOR THOUGHT AND DISCUSSION

5. What was for you the most intense moment in this part of the Exodus story? Why?

6. Why is Pharaoh unconvinced when the water of the Nile is "turned to blood"? What would you say is the difference between magic and miracles?

7. The Lord gives detailed instructions regarding the Hebrew feast. For what reasons do you think they are to dress for travel and to eat "in haste"?

8. Do you think it was right for the Hebrews to ask for the Egyptians' jewelry? Explain.

9. At one point Moses asks, "O Lord, why hast thou done evil to this people?" People often question God's actions. Why do you think they do so?

RESPONDING

1. Writing In a monologue, express Pharaoh's thoughts at his moment of greatest despair.

2. Multicultural Connection The Passover remains to this day a vital holiday for Jews. If you have never seen a Passover family meal, or seder, find out about the holiday customs and write a report.

3. Multicultural Connection In what ways do people attach religious meaning to food and eating today? Examine customs regarding food in some culture other than your own. You might focus on prayers before meals, the eating of specific types of food at special meals, fasting, and prohibitions about certain foods.

Moses

i walk on bones
snakes twisting
in my hand
locusts breaking my mouth
5   an old man
leaving slavery.
home is burning in me
like a bush
God got his eye on.

FOR THOUGHT AND DISCUSSION

1. Who do you think is speaking in this poem?

2. The speaker says that home is like a burning bush.
In what way may that be true? Considering what
took place at the original burning bush, how
appropriate is this figure of speech?

Runagate Runagate

I.

Runs falls rises stumbles on from darkness into darkness
and the darkness thicketed with shapes of terror
and the hunters pursuing and the hounds pursuing
and the night cold and the night long and the river
to cross and the jack-muh-lanterns beckoning beckoning
and blackness ahead and when shall I reach that somewhere
morning and keep on going and never turn back and keep on going

> Runagate
> Runagate
> Runagate

Runagate: a runaway;
here a runaway slave.

Many thousands rise and go
many thousands crossing over

> O mythic North
> O star-shaped yonder Bible city.

Some go weeping and some rejoicing
some in coffins and some in carriages
some in silks and some in shackles

> Rise and go or fare you well

No more auction block for me
no more driver's lash for me

> If you see my Pompey, 30 yrs of age,
> new breeches, plain stockings, negro shoes;
> if you see my Anna, likely young mulatto
> branded E on the right cheek, R on the left,
> catch them if you can and notify subscriber.
> Catch them if you can, but it won't be easy.

Pompey: name of a
slave.

They'll dart underground when you try to catch
    them,
plunge into quicksand, whirlpools, mazes,
turn into scorpions when you try to catch them.

30   And before I'll be a slave
I'll be buried in my grave

North star and bonanza gold
I'm bound for the freedom, freedom-bound
and oh Susyanna don't you cry for me

35   Runagate

                    Runagate

    II.

Rises from their anguish and their power,

Harriet Tubman:
fugitive slave who led
other slaves to freedom
by means of the "under-
ground railroad"—a
secret arrangement by
anti-slavery people for
helping fugitive slaves to
escape to Canada and
other places of safety.

patterolers: reference to
patrollers who searched
for runaways.

                    Harriet Tubman,

                woman of earth, whipscarred,
40   a summoning, a shining

                    Mean to be free

And this was the way of it, brethren brethren,
way we journeyed from Can't to Can.
Moon so bright and no place to hide,
45   the cry up and the patterollers riding,
hound dogs belling in bladed air.
And fear starts a-murbling, Never make it,
we'll never make it. *Hush that now,*
and she's turned upon us, levelled pistol
50   glinting in the moonlight:
Dead folks can't jaybird-talk, she says;
you keep on going now or die, she says.

Wanted   Harriet Tubman   alias the General
alias Moses   Stealer of Slaves

Garrison . . . Brown: 55   In league with Garrison   Alcott   Emerson
anti-slavery leaders.   Garrett   Douglass   Thoreau   John Brown
                              Armed and known to be Dangerous
                              Wanted   Reward   Dead or Alive

Tell me, Ezekiel, oh tell me do you see
60   mailed Jehovah coming to deliver me?

Hoot-owl calling in the ghosted air,
five times calling to the hants in the air.
Shadow of a face in the scary leaves,
shadow of a voice in the talking leaves:

65   Come ride-a my train

Oh that train, ghost-story train
through swamp and savanna movering movering,
over trestles of dew, through caves of the wish,
Midnight Special on a sabre track movering movering,
70   *first stop Mercy and the last Hallelujah.*

Come ride-a my train

Mean mean mean to be free.

mailed: wearing armor.

hants: ghosts.

savanna: grassland.

FOR THOUGHT AND DISCUSSION

1. Reread the first seven lines of the poem. What
would you say is the strongest impression or
feeling created by these lines?

2. Who is speaking in lines 21–29? Why do you think
this section is included in the poem?

3. Who says "Hush that now" in line 48? How is this
person like Moses?

RESPONDING

1. Activity How many specific sounds do you "hear"
in this poem? Tape-record as many of these sounds
as you can and assemble them into a soundtrack for
this poem.

2. Activity With several classmates, prepare a choral
reading of this poem. You may want to experiment
with dramatic lighting, music, and sound effects.

In the Wilderness

Manna from Heaven

Then they came to Elim, where there were twelve springs of water and seventy palm trees; and they encamped there by the water.

They set out from Elim, and all the congregation of the people of Israel came to the wilderness of Sin, which is between Elim and Sinai, on the fifteenth day of the second month after they had departed from the land of Egypt. And the whole congregation of the people of Israel murmured against Moses and Aaron in the wilderness, and said to them, "Would that we had died by the hand of the Lord in the land of Egypt, when we sat by the fleshpots and ate bread to the full; for you have brought us out into this wilderness to kill this whole assembly with hunger.". . .

And Moses said to Aaron, "Say to the whole congregation of the people of Israel, 'Come near before the Lord, for he has heard your murmurings.'" And as Aaron spoke to the whole congregation of the people of Israel, they looked toward the wilderness, and behold, the glory of the Lord appeared in the cloud. And the Lord said to Moses, "I have heard the murmurings of the people of Israel; say to them, 'At twilight you shall eat flesh, and in the morning you shall be filled with bread; then you shall know that I am the Lord your God.'"

In the evening quails came up and covered the camp; and in the morning dew lay round about the camp. And when the dew had gone up, there was on the face of the wilderness a fine, flakelike thing, fine as hoarfrost on the ground. When the people of Israel saw it, they said to one another, "What is it?" For they did not know what it was. And Moses said

Sin: Hebrew place name; not related to the word "sin."

murmured: complained.

fleshpots: jars of meat.

flesh: meat.

hoarfrost: light frost.
what is it: the Hebrew expression is *man hu*.

Exodus 15:27; 16:1–3, 9–15, 31, 35; 19:1–6a, 16–19; 20:1–21; 31:18; 32: 1–7, 15–20, 30–34; 33:7–11a, 12–13, 17–20; 34:4–5, 27–35. Deuteronomy 31:14–18; 34:1–12. Joshua 1:1–3; 6:1–7, 15–16, 20 (Revised Standard Version).

Moses Crossing the Red Sea, detail from a mininature in an illuminated Haggadah. The British Library Board.

ABOVE: *Moses and the Tables of the Law* by Shalom of Safed. After 1957. The Israel Museum, Jerusalem.

RIGHT: *Deborah Riding into Battle with Barak*, detail from a French illuminated miniature in the Psalter of St. Louis, 1252-1270. The Bibliothèque Nationale, Paris.

BELOW: *Moses and the Law* by Rembrandt van Rijn. Staaliche Museen zu Berlin, photo by Jörg P. Anders.

Samson and the Lion, bronze engraved aquamanile (ewer), Lorraine or Upper Rhine, thirteenth century. Courtesy of the Museum of Fine Arts, Boston, Benjamin Shelton Fund.

to them, "It is the bread which the Lord has given you to eat. . . . "

Now the house of Israel called its name manna; it was like coriander seed, white, and the taste of it was like wafers made with honey. . . . And the people of Israel ate the manna forty years, till they came to a habitable land; they ate the manna, till they came to the border of the land of Canaan. . . .

coriander seed: a flavorful fruit.

The Ten Commandments

On the third new moon after the people of Israel had gone forth out of the land of Egypt, on that day they came into the wilderness of Sinai. And when they set out from Rephidim and came into the wilderness of Sinai, they encamped in the wilderness; and there Israel encamped before the mountain. And Moses went up to God, and the Lord called to him out of the mountain, saying, "Thus you shall say to the house of Jacob, and tell the people of Israel: You have seen what I did to the Egyptians, and how I bore you on eagles' wings and brought you to myself. Now therefore, if you will obey my voice and keep my covenant, you shall be my own possession among all peoples; for all the earth is mine, and you shall be to me a kingdom of priests and a holy nation. . . . "

On the morning of the third day there were thunders and lightnings, and a thick cloud upon the mountain, and a very loud trumpet blast, so that all the people who were in the camp trembled. Then Moses brought the people out of the camp to meet God; and they took their stand at the foot of the mountain. And Mount Sinai was wrapped in smoke, because the Lord descended upon it in fire; and the smoke of it went up like the smoke of a kiln, and the whole mountain quaked greatly. And as the sound of the trumpet grew louder and louder, Moses spoke, and God answered him in thunder. . . .

kiln: furnace for baking pottery.

And God spoke all these words, saying,

"I am the Lord your God, who brought you out of the land of Egypt, out of the house of bondage.

"You shall have no other gods before me.

"You shall not make for yourself a graven image, or any likeness of anything that is in heaven above, or that is in the earth beneath, or that is in the water under the earth; you shall not bow down to them or

The commandments are divided and numbered in different ways by various religious groups.

graven: carved.

serve them; for I the Lord your God am a jealous God, visiting the iniquity of the fathers upon the children to the third and the fourth generation of those who hate me, but showing steadfast love to thousands of those who love me and keep my commandments.

"You shall not take the name of the Lord your God in vain; for the Lord will not hold him guiltless who takes his name in vain.

"Remember the sabbath day, to keep it holy. Six days you shall labor, and do all your work; but the seventh day is a sabbath to the Lord your God; in it you shall not do any work, you, or your son, or your daughter, or your manservant, or your maidservant, or your cattle, or the sojourner who is within your gates; for in six days the Lord made heaven and earth, the sea, and all that is in them, and rested the seventh day; therefore the Lord blessed the sabbath day and hallowed it.

"Honor your father and your mother, that your days may be long in the land which the Lord your God gives you."

"You shall not kill.

"You shall not commit adultery.

"You shall not steal.

"You shall not bear false witness against your neighbor.

"You shall not covet your neighbor's house; you shall not covet your neighbor's wife, or his manservant, or his maidservant, or his ox, or his ass, or anything that is your neighbor's."

Now when all the people perceived the thunderings and the lightnings and the sound of the trumpet and the mountain smoking, the people were afraid and trembled; and they stood afar off, and said to Moses, "You speak to us, and we will hear; but let not God speak to us, lest we die." And Moses said to the people, "Do not fear; for God has come to prove you, and that the fear of him may be before your eyes, that you may not sin."

And the people stood afar off, while Moses drew near to the thick darkness where God was. . . . "

And he gave to Moses, when he had made an end of speaking with him upon Mount Sinai, the two tables of the testimony, tables of stone, written with the finger of God.

tables: tablets.

testimony: commandments.

The Golden Calf

When the people saw that Moses delayed to come down from the mountain, the people gathered themselves together to Aaron, and said to him, "Up, make us gods, who shall go before us; as for this Moses, the man who brought us up out of the land of Egypt, we do not know what has become of him." And Aaron said to them, "Take off the rings of gold which are in the ears of your wives, your sons, and your daughters, and bring them to me." So all the people took off the rings of gold which were in their ears, and brought them to Aaron. And he received the gold at their hand, and fashioned it with a graving tool, and made a molten calf; and they said, "These are your gods, O Israel, who brought you up out of the land of Egypt!" When Aaron saw this, he built an altar before it; and Aaron made proclamation and said, "Tomorrow shall be a feast to the Lord." And they rose up early on the morrow, and offered burnt offerings and brought peace offerings; and the people sat down to eat and drink, and rose up to play.

molten: produced by melting and pouring into a mold.

And the Lord said to Moses, "Go down; for our people, whom you brought up out of the land of Egypt, have corrupted themselves. . . . "

And Moses turned, and went down from the mountain with the two tables of the testimony in his hands, tables that were written on both sides; on the one side and on the other were they written. And the tables were the work of God, and the writing was the writing of God, graven upon the tables. When Joshua heard the noise of the people as they shouted, he said to Moses, "There is a noise of war in the camp." But he said, "It is not the sound of shouting for victory, or the sound of the cry of defeat, but the sound of singing that I hear." And as soon as he came near the camp and saw the calf and the dancing, Moses' anger burned hot, and he threw the tables out of his hands and broke them at the foot of the mountain. And he took the calf which they had made, and burnt it with fire, and ground it to powder, and scattered it upon

Joshua: Moses' assistant, who had gone partway up the mountain with him.

the water, and made the people of Israel drink of it. . . .

Talking with God

On the morrow Moses said to the people, "You have sinned a great sin. And now I will go up to the Lord; perhaps I can make atonement for your sin." So Moses returned to the Lord and said, "Alas, this people have sinned a great sin; they have made for themselves gods of gold. But now, if thou wilt forgive their sin—and if not, blot me, I pray thee, out of thy book which thou hast written." But the Lord said to Moses, "Whoever has sinned against me, him will I blot out of my book. But now go, lead the people to the place of which I have spoken to you; behold, my angel shall go before you. Nevertheless, in the day when I visit, I will visit their sin upon them.". . .

Now Moses used to take the tent and pitch it outside the camp, far off from the camp; and he called it the tent of meeting. And every one who sought the Lord would go out to the tent of meeting, which was outside the camp. Whenever Moses went out to the tent, all the people rose up, and every man stood at his tent door, and looked after Moses, until he had gone into the tent. When Moses entered the tent, the pillar of cloud would descend and stand at the door of the tent, all the people would rise up and worship, every man at his tent door. Thus the Lord used to speak to Moses face to face, as a man speaks to his friend. . . .

Moses said to the Lord, "See, thou sayest to me, 'Bring up this people'; but thou hast not let me know whom thou wilt send with me. Yet thou hast said, 'I know you by name, and you have also found favor in my sight.' Now therefore, I pray thee, if I have found favor in thy sight, show me now thy ways, that I may know thee and find favor in thy sight. Consider too that this nation is thy people.". . .

And the Lord said to Moses, "This very thing that you have spoken I will do; for you have found favor in my sight, and I know you by name." Moses said, "I pray thee, show me thy glory." And he said, "I will make all my goodness pass before you, and will

make atonement: get forgiveness.

book: i.e., list of righteous people.

I will visit . . . upon them: at the appropriate time I will punish them for their sin.

meeting: i.e., meeting God.

proclaim before you my name 'The LORD'; and I will be gracious to whom I will be gracious, and will show mercy on whom I will show mercy. But," he said, "you cannot see my face; for man shall not see me and live."

. . . So Moses cut two tables of stone like the first; and he rose early in the morning and went up on Mount Sinai, as the Lord had commanded him, and took in his hand the two tables of stone. And the Lord descended in the cloud and stood with him there, and proclaimed the name of the Lord. . . .

And the Lord said to Moses, "Write these words; in accordance with these words I have made a covenant with you and with Israel." And he was there with the Lord forty days and forty nights; he neither ate bread nor drank water. And he wrote upon the tables the words of the covenant, the ten commandments.

When Moses came down from Mount Sinai, with the two tables of the testimony in his hand as he came down from the mountain, Moses did not know that the skin of his face shone because he had been talking with God. And when Aaron and all the people of Israel saw Moses, behold, the skin of his face shone, and they were afraid to come near him. But Moses called to them; and Aaron and all the leaders of the congregation returned to him, and Moses talked with them. And afterward all the people of Israel came near, and he gave them in commandment all that the Lord had spoken with him in Mount Sinai. And when Moses had finished speaking with them, he put a veil on his face; but whenever Moses went in before the Lord to speak with him, he took the veil off, until he came out; and when he came out, and told the people of Israel what he was commanded, the people of Israel saw the face of Moses, that the skin of Moses' face shone; and Moses would put the veil upon his face again, until he went in to speak with him. . . .

[The people of Israel remained in the wilderness for forty years—more than an entire generation.]

"The LORD": God's personal name. The original Hebrew is Yahweh, meaning "he creates" or "he causes to be." Eventually, out of respect for God's holiness, the word Adonai ("my Lord") was substituted for Yahweh whenever the Bible was read aloud

be gracious: show favor.

shone: often pictured as rays of light from his face. Sometimes Moses is portrayed with horns on his head because early translators did not know that the same Hebrew word can mean both "horns" or "rays of light."

The Death of Moses

Deut. 31:14.

commission him: tell him his duties.

And the Lord said to Moses, "Behold, the days approach when you must die; call Joshua, and present yourselves in the tent of meeting, that I may commission him." And Moses and Joshua went and presented themselves in the tent of meeting. And the Lord appeared in the tent in a pillar of cloud; and the pillar of cloud stood by the door of the tent.

And the Lord said to Moses, "Behold, you are about to sleep with your fathers; then this people will rise and play the harlot after the strange gods of the land, where they go to be among them, and they will forsake me and break my covenant which I have made with them. Then my anger will be kindled against them in that day, and I will forsake them and hide my face from them, and they will be devoured; and many evils and troubles will come upon them, so that they will say in that day, 'Have not these evils come upon us because our God is not among us?' And I will surely hide my face in that day on account of all the evil which they have done, because they have turned to other gods. . . ."

And Moses went up from the plains of Moab to Mount Nebo, to the top of Pisgah, which is opposite Jericho. And the Lord showed him all the land, Gilead as far as Dan, all Naphtali, the land of Ephraim and Manesseh, all the land of Judah as far as the western sea, the Negeb, and the Plain, that is, the valley of Jericho the city of palm trees, as far as Zoar. And the Lord said to him, "This is the land of which I swore to Abraham, to Isaac, and to Jacob, 'I will give it to your descendants.' I have let you see it with your eyes, but

you shall not go: earlier Moses had somehow sinned against God by striking a rock to provide water; for this he was not permitted to enter Canaan.

abated: weakened.

you shall not go over there." So Moses the servant of the Lord died there in the land of Moab, according to the word of the Lord, and he buried him in the valley in the land of Moab opposite Beth-peor; but no man knows the place of his burial to this day. Moses was a hundred and twenty years old when he died; his eye was not dim, nor his natural force abated. And the people of Israel wept for Moses in the plains of Moab thirty days; then the days of weeping and mourning for Moses were ended.

And Joshua the son of Nun was full of the spirit of wisdom, for Moses had laid his hands upon him; so the people of Israel obeyed him, and did as the Lord had commanded Moses. And there has not arisen a prophet since in Israel like Moses, whom the Lord knew face to face, none like him for all the signs and the wonders which the Lord sent him to do in the land of Egypt, to Pharaoh and to all his servants and to all his land, and for all the mighty power and all the great and terrible deeds which Moses wrought in the sight of all Israel.

terrible: awesome.
wrought: did.

The Fall of Jericho

After the death of Moses the servant of the Lord, the Lord said to Joshua the son of Nun, Moses' minister, "Moses my servant is dead; now therefore arise, go over this Jordan, you and all this people, into the land which I am giving to them, to the people of Israel. Every place that the sole of your foot will tread upon I have given to you, as I promised to Moses. . . .

Joshua 1:1

Now Jericho was shut up from within and from without because of the people of Israel; none went out, and none came in. And the Lord said to Joshua, "See, I have given into your hand Jericho, with its king and mighty men of valor. You shall march around the city, all the men of war going around the city once. Thus shall you do for six days. And seven priests shall bear seven trumpets of rams' horns before the ark; and on the seventh day you shall march around the city seven times, the priests blowing the trumpets. And when they make a long blast with the ram's horn, as soon as you hear the sound of the trumpet, then all the people shall shout with a great shout; and the wall of the city will fall down flat, and the people shall go up every man straight before him." So Joshua the son of Nun called the priests and said to them, "Take up the ark of the covenant, and let seven priests bear seven trumpets of rams' horns before the ark of the Lord." And he said to the people, "Go forward; march around the city, and let the armed men pass on before the ark of the Lord.". . .

On the seventh day they rose early at the dawn of day, and marched around the city in the same manner seven times: it was only on that day they marched around the city seven times. And at the seventh time, when the priests had blown the trumpets, Joshua said

Joshua 6:1
Jericho: a major city at the southern end of the Jordan Valley.

ark: a large chest thought to contain the tablets from Sinai; regarded by the Israelites as the place where God sat invisibly enthroned.

to the people, "Shout; for the Lord has given you the city. . . ."

So the people shouted, and the trumpets were blown. As soon as the people heard the sound of the trumpet, the people raised a great shout, and the wall fell down flat, so that the people went up into the city, every man straight before him, and they took the city.

FOR CLOSE READING

1. How long were the Hebrews in the wilderness?

2. How did the Lord first answer the "murmurings" of the people against Moses?

3. What did the Hebrews do while Moses was on Mount Sinai?

4. Briefly describe how Jericho was captured.

FOR THOUGHT AND DISCUSSION

5. Considering their circumstances as the Hebrews emerge from Egypt, in what ways might they benefit from an extended period in the wilderness?

6. Beginning with Moses' early youth, how does the story prepare the reader for the people's lack of trust in Moses and the Lord at the foot of Mount Sinai?

7. If the Lord will not forgive the people for their sin, Moses asks that he himself be blotted out. What does this response tell you about Moses? his relation to God? to his people?

8. In your opinion, what heroic qualities does Moses possess? What is his greatest achievement as a leader? Consider some other hero in history. What circumstances and what personal characteristics does that person have in common with Moses?

RESPONDING

1. **Writing** Imagine that you are Moses near the end of life. Write a last entry in your journal. What do you regard as the key events of your life? What are you proudest of? What do you regret?

2. **Activity** Create the front page of a newspaper reporting the arrival of the people of Israel in the land of Canaan. Work in teams to produce articles on the crossing of the Jordan River, an eyewitness account of the battle of Jericho, a review of the wilderness years, an editorial tribute to Moses; others might create a map of the wanderings and a "photograph" of the falling walls of Jericho.

3. **Activity** Using photographs cut from old magazines, create a collage that illustrates how the modern world seems to be responding to one or more of the Ten Commandments.

4. **Humanities Connection** Moses has been a favorite subject of painters and sculptors. Find and compare several images of Moses in art books or other sources. Choose the one image that you think best expresses the character of Moses and explain why you chose it.

The Latest Decalogue

Decalogue: the ten commandments.

Thou shalt have one God only; Who
Would be at the expense of two?
No graven images may be
Worshiped, except the currency.
5 Swear not at all; for, for thy curse
Thine enemy is none the worse.
At church on Sunday to attend
Will serve to keep the world thy friend.
Honor thy parents; that is, all
10 From whom advancement may befall.
Thou shalt not kill; but need'st not strive

officiously: i.e., too aggressively or eagerly.

Officiously to keep alive.
Do not adultery commit;
Advantage rarely comes of it.
15 Thou shalt not steal; an empty feat,

lucrative: profitable

When it's so lucrative to cheat.
Bear not false witness; let the lie
Have time on its own wings to fly.
Thou shalt not covet, but tradition
20 Approves all forms of competition.

FOR THOUGHT AND DISCUSSION

1. The speaker offers several reasons for obeying the commandments. Summarize those reasons in one or two sentences.

2. What seems to be the speaker's feeling about society's response to the Ten Commandments?

3. This poem was first published in 1862. How do you think the poet might change it if he were writing today?

The Murder of Moses

By reason of despair we set forth behind you
And followed the pillar of fire like a doubt,
To hold to belief wanted a sign,
Called the miracle of the staff and the plagues
5 Natural phenomena.

wanted: needed.

We questioned the expediency of the march,
Gossiped about you. What was escape
To the fear of going forward and Pharaoh's wheels?
When the chariots mired and the army flooded
10 Our cry of horror was one with theirs.

expediency: usefulness, desirability.

You always went alone, a little ahead,
Prophecy disturbed you, you were not a fanatic.
The women said you were meek, the men
Regarded you as a typical leader.
15 You and your black wife might have been
  foreigners.

black wife: during the years in the wilderness Moses married a Cushite (Ethiopian) woman.

We even discussed your parentage; were you
  really a Jew?
We remembered how Joseph had made himself a
  prince,
All of us shared in the recognition
Of his skill of management, sense of propriety,
20 Devotion to his brothers and Israel.

We hated you daily. Our children died. The water
  spilled.
It was as if you were trying to lose us one by one.
Our wandering seemed the wandering of your
  mind,
The cloud believed we were tireless,
25 We expressed our contempt and our boredom
  openly.

At last you ascended the rock; at last returned.
Your anger that day was probably His.
When we saw you come down from the mountain,
    your skin alight
And the stones of our law flashing,
30 We fled like animals and the dancers scattered.

We watched where you overturned the calf on the
    fire,
We hid when you broke the tablets on the rock,
We wept when we drank the mixture of gold and
    water.
We had hoped you were lost or had left us.

defilement: dishonor.   35 This was the day of our greatest defilement.

You were simple of heart; you were sorry for
    Miriam,

Miriam: Moses' sister,
who was afflicted with
leprosy by God.

You reasoned with Aaron, who was your enemy.
However often you cheered us with songs and
    prayers
We cursed you again. The serpent bit us,
40 And mouth to mouth you entreated the Lord for
    our sake.

At the end of it all we gave you the gift of death.
Invasion and generalship were spared you.
The hand of our direction, resignedly you fell,
And while officers prepared for the river-crossing
45 The One God blessed you and covered you with
    earth.

Though you were mortal and once committed
    murder
You assumed the burden of the covenant,
Spoke for the world and for our understanding.

converse: conversation.   Converse with God made you a thinker,
50 Taught us all early justice, made us a race.

FOR THOUGHT AND DISCUSSION

1. The title says "murder." Why do you suppose the poet chose that word?

2. The speaker says "the men/Regarded you as a typical leader." What does this mean to you?

3. Choose one of the following lines from the poem and explain what you think it means: line 23, line 40, or line 50.

4. What does this poem say about the difficulties of being a leader? about the difficulties of being a follower?

from The Tables of the Law

Translated by H. T. Lowe-Porter

This excerpt from a novella describes
Moses' experiences on Mount Sinai.

Accordingly Moses crossed the wilderness on his
staff, his wide-set eyes bent on the mount of God,
which was smoking like a chimney and often spewing
out fire. It had an odd shape, the mountain: cracks
and ridges ran round it, seeming to divide it into
several stories. They looked like paths running round
it, but they were not: only terracelike gradations with
yellow rear walls. By the third day the pilgrim had
crossed the foothills to the rugged base; now he began
to climb, his fist closed round his staff, which he set
before him as he mounted the pathless, trackless,
blackened, scalded waste. Hours and hours he
mounted, pace by pace, higher and higher into the
nearness of God; as far as ever a human being could.
For after a while the sulphurous vapors, smelling like
hot metal, so filled the air that he gasped for breath
and began to cough. Yet he got up to the topmost
ridge just below the peak, where there was an
extended view on both sides over the bare desert
range and beyond the wilderness toward Kadesh. He
could even see the little tribal encampment, closer in
and far down in the depths.

Here Moses, coughing, found a cavity in the
mountain wall, with a roof formed by a ledge of rock
that should protect him from flying stones and
molten streams. Here he set up his rest and took time
to get his breath. And now he prepared to embark
upon the task which God had laid upon him. Under
all the difficulties (the metallic vapors oppressed his
chest and even made the water taste of sulphur), the
work was to take him forty days and forty nights.

But why so long? The question is an idle one. God's whole moral law, in permanently compact and compendious form, binding to all time, had to be composed and graven on the stone of His own mountain, in order that Moses might carry it down to his father's crude, confused, bewildered folk, down to the enclosure where they were waiting. It should be among them, from generation to generation, inviolably graven as well in their minds and hearts and their flesh and blood, the quintessence of human good behavior. God commanded him loudly from out of his own breast to hew two tables from the living rock and write the decrees on them, five on one and five on the other—in all, ten decrees. To make the tablets, to smooth them and shape them to be adequate bearers of the eternal law—that in itself was no small thing. One man alone, even though he had broad wrists and had drunk the milk of a stone-mason's daughter, might not for many days accomplish it. Actually the making of the tables took a quarter of the forty days. But the writing itself, when he came to it, was a problem that might well bring Moses' stay on the hilltop to more than forty days. For how was he to write? In his Theban boarding school he had learned the decorative picture writing of the Egyptians and its cursive adaptation; also the cramped cuneiform of the formal script practiced in the region of the Euphrates and employed by the kings of the earth to exchange ideas on earthen shards. And among the Midianites he had got acquainted with a third kind of semantic magic expressed in symbols, such as eyes, crosses, beetles, rings, and various kinds of wavy lines. This kind of writing was used in the land of Sinai; it was a clumsy attempt to imitate Egyptian picture writing, but it did not manage to symbolize whole words and things— only syllables to be read together. Moses saw that no one of these three methods of putting down ideas would serve in the present case, for the simple reason that all of them depended on the language they expressed by signs. Not in Babylonian or Egyptian or the jargon of the Bedouins of Sinai—not in any one of these could he possibly write down the ten decrees. No, they must and could only be written in the

compendious: concise.

inviolably graven: permanently carved, never to be changed.

quintessence: most perfect example.

cursive: written with letters joined together.

cuneiform: (kyü nē′ə form): an early type of writing using a pointed stick to press wedge-shaped marks into clay.

earthen shards: broken pieces of pottery.

semantic: having to do with the meaning of words.

Bedouins: (bed′ü ənz) desert wanderers; nomads.

tongue of the fathers' seed—the idiom it spoke, the dialect he himself used in his formative task; and that no matter whether they could read it or not. Indeed, how should they read it, when it could scarcely be written and there did not yet exist any semantic magic whatever for the tongue they talked in?

Fervently, with all his heart, Moses wished for it: for a kind of simple writing that they would be able to read quite quickly; one that they, children as they were, could learn in a few days—and it followed that such a one, God's help being nigh, could also be thought out and invented in no longer time. For thought out and invented a kind of writing had got to be, since it did not exist.

What a pressing, oppressive task! He had not measured it beforehand. He had thought only of "writing"—not at all of the fact that one could not just "write." His head glowed and steamed like a furnace; it was like the top of the peak itself, on fire with the fervor of his hopes for his people. He felt as though rays streamed from his head; as though horns came out on his brow for very strain of desire and pure inspiration. He could not invent signs for all the words his people used, nor for the syllables which composed them. The vocabulary of the people down there in the camp was small enough. But even so it would need so many symbols that they could not be invented in the limited number of days at his command; much less could the people learn to read them. So Moses contrived something else—and horns stood forth from his head out of sheer pride of his god-invention. He classified the sounds of the language: those made with the lips, with the tongue and palate, and with the throat; and he divided off from them the smaller group of open sounds which became words only when they were included in combinations with the others. Of those others there were not so very many—a bare twenty; and if you gave them signs which regularly obliged anyone pronouncing them to buzz or hiss, to huff or puff, or mumble or rumble, then you might adapt your sounds and combine them into words and pictures of things, paying no heed to those in the other group, which came in automatically anyhow. You could make as many combinations as you liked, and that

horns: There was a tradition in art of depicting Moses with horns on his head, because early translators did not know that the same Hebrew word can mean both "horns" and "rays of light."

not only in the language spoken by his father's people but in any language whatever. You could even write Egyptian and Babylonian with them.

A god-inspiration! An inspiration with horns to it! It was like to its source, to the Invisible and Spiritual whence it came, who possessed all the world, and who, though He had especially elected the stock down below for His own, yet He was Lord everywhere and all over on earth. But it was also an inspiration peculiarly apt for Moses' immediate and urgent purpose and for the necessity out of which it was born—for the brief and binding text of the law. Of course, this was first to be impressed upon the seed which Moses had led out of Egypt, because God and he had a common love to it. But just as the handful of arbitrary signs might be used to write down all the words of all the tongues of all the people on earth, and just as Jahwe was omnipotent over all these, so also the text which Moses intended to set down by means of those signs should likewise be universal. It should be a compendium of such a kind as to serve everywhere on earth and to all the peoples on it as a foundation stone of morality and good conduct.

So, then, Moses—his head on fire—began by scratching his signs on the rocky wall in loose imitation of the sounds the Sinai people made, conjuring them up in his mind as he went. With his graving tool he scratched on the rock the signs he had made to represent the burrs and purrs and whirrs, the hisses and buzzes, the humming and gurgling of his father's native tongue. He set them down in an order that pleased his ear—and lo, with them one could set down the whole world in writing: the signs that took up space and those that took none, the derived and the contrived—in short, everything on earth.

And he wrote; I mean, he drilled and chiseled and scooped at the splintery stone of the tables; for these he had prepared beforehand with great pains, during the time he had spent cogitating his script. The whole took him rather more than forty days—and no wonder!

Young Joshua came up to him a few times, to fetch water and bread. The people did not need to know this: they believed that Moses sojourned up

stock: people.

arbitrary: determined by chance.

Jahwe: (yä′ wā): also Yahweh; a way of pronouncing the Hebrew YHWH, usually translated "the Lord." A variant is Jehovah.

conjuring them: making them appear.

cogitating: thinking over.

there sustained solely by God's presence and His words, and Joshua for strategic reasons preferred them to remain in this belief.

Moses rose with the dawn and labored till the sun set back in the desert. We must picture him there, sitting bare to the waist, his breast hairy, with the strong arms bequeathed him by his father the slain water-bearer; with wide-set eyes, flattened nose, and parted grizzling beard; chewing a pancake, coughing now and then from the metallic vapors, and in the sweat of his brow hewing at the tables, filing and planing. Squatting before them as he leaned against the rocky wall, he toiled away with great attention to detail; first drawing his pothooks, his magic runes, with the graver and then drilling them into the stone.

He wrote on the first table:

I, Jahwe, am thy God; thou shalt have no other gods before me.

Thou shalt not make unto thyself any graven image.

Thou shalt not take my name in vain.

Be mindful of my day to keep it holy.

Honor thy father and thy mother.

And on the other table he wrote:

Thou shalt not kill.

Thou shalt not commit adultery.

Thou shalt not steal.

Thou shalt not affront thy neighbor by bearing false witness.

Thou shalt not cast a covetous eye upon thy neighbor's goods.

This was what he wrote, leaving out the vowels, which were taken for granted. And while he worked it seemed to him as though rays like a pair of horns stood out from the hair of his brow.

When Joshua came up for the last time he stayed a little longer than before, in fact, two whole days, for Moses was not done with his work, and they wanted to go down together. The youth admired and warmly praised what his master had done, consoling him in the matter of a few letters which, despite all Moses' loving care and greatly to his distress, had got splintered and were illegible. Joshua assured him that the general effect was unharmed.

As a finishing touch in Joshua's presence Moses colored the letters he had engraved. He did with his own blood, that they might stand out better. No other coloring matter was at hand; so he pricked his strong arm with the tool and carefully let the drops of blood run into the outlines of the letters, so that they showed red against the stone. When the script was dry, Moses took a table under each arm, handed to the young man the staff which had supported him on his climb; and so they went down together from the mountain of God to the tribal encampment opposite in the desert.

FOR CLOSE READING

1. According to this account, what must Moses invent before he begins to write on the tablets?

2. What part does Joshua play in this story?

3. How is the mountain described?

4. Make a list of details that Mann adds to the Bible story.

FOR THOUGHT AND DISCUSSION

5. What do you think is the most significant change Mann makes in this retelling of the story of the Ten Commandments? Why?

6. According to this story, how is Moses' system of writing different from the three methods already being used by the Egyptians and others? What are the advantages of the new system of writing?

7. Which do you think has had the greater impact on the human race: a system of laws or a system of writing? Explain.

Joshua Fit the Battle of Jericho

Joshua fit the battle of Jericho,
Jericho, Jericho,
Joshua fit the battle of Jericho,
And the walls came tumbling down.

5   You may talk about your king of Gideon
Talk about your man of Saul,
There's none like good old Joshua
At the battle of Jericho.

Up to the walls of Jericho
10   He marched with spear in hand;
"Go blow them ram horns," Joshua cried,
"'Cause the battle is in my hand."

Then the lamb ram sheep horns began to blow,
Trumpets began to sound,
15   Joshua commanded the children to shout,
And the walls came tumbling down.

That morning,
Joshua fit the battle of Jericho,
Jericho, Jericho,
20   Joshua fit the battle of Jericho,
And the walls came tumbling down.

FOR THOUGHT AND DISCUSSION

1. Why do you think the song says that "there's none like good old Joshua"?

2. Like "Go Down, Moses" (page 115), this song was originally sung by people in slavery. What special meaning might Joshua's victory have for people in such circumstances? How might it apply to groups of people in the world today?

4
Israel's Youthful Days

Deborah and Jael: Victory for Israel

The Book of Judges *is a series of stories that follow a pattern. In each story the Israelites stray from righteousness; God sends a foreign power to oppress them; they cry to God for help; a God-appointed leader—a "judge"—arises in Israel to deliver them; and they return to God and his law. The most prominent of these successive leaders are Ehud, Deborah, Gideon, Jephthah, and Samson. This chapter includes the stories of Deborah and Samson.*

After Ehud died, the Israelites once again did evil in the eyes of the Lord. So the Lord sold them into the hands of Jabin, a king of Canaan, who reigned in Hazor. The commander of his army was Sisera, who lived in Harosheth Haggoyim. Because he had nine hundred iron chariots and had cruelly oppressed the Israelites for twenty years, they cried to the Lord for help.

iron: the Israelites had only the softer bronze metal.

Deborah, a prophetess, the wife of Lappidoth, was leading Israel at that time. She held court under the Palm of Deborah between Ramah and Bethel in the hill country of Ephraim, and the Israelites came to her to have their disputes decided. She sent for Barak son of Abinoam from Kedesh in Naphtali and said to him, "The Lord, the God of Israel, commands you: 'Go, take with you ten thousand men of Naphtali and Zebulun and lead the way to Mount Tabor. I will lure Sisera, the commander of Jabin's army, with his chariots and his troops to the Kishon River and give him into your hands.'"

prophetess: among the judges, Deborah is the only prophet (one who speaks for God) and only woman.

Judges 4:1–9, 12–22; 5:1, 3–5, 11d, 19–31 (New International Version).
LEFT: *Ruth Brings Gleanings to Naomi*, detail from a full-page illuminated miniature in an Old Testament, French, about 1250. The Pierpont Morgan Library.

Barak said to her, "If you go with me, I will go; but if you don't go with me, I won't go."

"Very well," Deborah said, "I will go with you. But because of the way you are going about this, the honor will not be yours, for the Lord will hand Sisera over to a woman." So Deborah went with Barak to Kedesh . . . .

When they told Sisera that Barak son of Abinoam had gone up to Mount Tabor, Sisera gathered together his nine hundred iron chariots and all the men with him, from Harosheth Haggoyim to the Kishon River.

Then Deborah said to Barak, "Go! This is the day the Lord has given Sisera into your hands. Has not the Lord gone ahead of you?" So Barak went down Mount Tabor, followed by ten thousand men. At Barak's advance, the Lord routed Sisera and all his chariots and army by the sword, and Sisera abandoned his chariot and fled on foot. But Barak pursued the chariots and army as far as Harosheth Haggoyim. All the troops of Sisera fell by the sword; not a man was left.

Kenites: sheep-herding people distantly related to the Israelites.

Sisera, however, fled on foot to the tent of Jael, the wife of Heber the Kenite, because there were friendly relations between Jabin king of Hazor and the clan of Heber the Kenite.

Jael went out to meet Sisera and said to him, "Come, my lord, come right in. Don't be afraid." So he entered her tent, and she put a covering over him.

"I'm thirsty," he said. "Please give me some water." She opened a skin of milk, gave him a drink, and covered him up.

"Stand in the doorway of the tent," he told her. "If someone comes by and asks you, 'Is anyone here?' say 'No.'"

But Jael, Heber's wife, picked up a tent peg and a hammer and went quietly to him while he lay fast asleep, exhausted. She drove the peg through his temple into the ground, and he died.

Barak came by in pursuit of Sisera, and Jael went out to meet him. "Come," she said, "I will show you the man you're looking for." So he went in with her, and there lay Sisera with the tent peg through his temple—dead. On that day Deborah and Barak son of Abinoam sang this song: . . .

The song of Deborah and Barak retells the story in poetic and slightly different form.

"Hear this, you kings! Listen, you rulers!
I will sing to the Lord, I will sing;
I will make music to the Lord, the God of Israel.

O Lord, when you went out from Seir,
    when you marched from the land of Edom,
the earth shook, the heavens poured,
    the clouds poured down water.
The mountains quaked before the Lord,
        the One of Sinai,
    before the Lord, the God of Israel. . . .

Then the people of the Lord
    went down to the city gates. . . .

"Kings came, they fought;
    the kings of Canaan fought
at Taanach by the waters of Megiddo,
    but they carried off no silver, no plunder.
From the heavens the stars fought,
    from their courses they fought against Sisera.
The river Kishon swept them away,
    the age-old river, the river Kishon.
    March on, my soul; be strong!
Then thundered the horses' hoofs—
    galloping, galloping go his mighty steeds.
'Curse Meroz,' said the angel of the Lord.
    'Curse its people bitterly,
because they did not come to help the Lord,
    to help the Lord against the mighty.'

"Most blessed of women be Jael,
    the wife of Heber the Kenite,
    most blessed of tent-dwelling women.
He asked for water, and she gave him milk;
    in a bowl fit for nobles she brought him
        curdled milk.
Her hand reached for the tent peg,
    her right hand for the workman's hammer.
She struck Sisera, she crushed his head,
    she shattered and pierced his temple.
At her feet he sank,
    he fell; there he lay.
At her feet he sank, he fell;
    where he sank, there he fell—dead.

Seir, Edom: regions
south of Israel.

courses: paths across the
sky.

Meroz: probably a
nearby Israelite village.

Through the window peered Sisera's mother;
   behind the lattice she cried out,
'Why is his chariot so long in coming?
   Why is the clatter of his chariots delayed?'
The wisest of her ladies answer her;
   indeed, she keeps saying to herself,

spoils: loot.

'Are they not finding and dividing the spoils:
   a girl or two for each man,
   colorful garments as plunder for Sisera,
   colorful garments embroidered,
   highly embroidered garments for my neck—
all this as plunder?'

"So may all your enemies perish, O Lord!
   But may they who love you be like the sun
   when it rises in its strength."

FOR CLOSE READING

1. What military advantage did Sisera have over the Israelites?

2. What part does Barak play in this story?

3. In the song of Deborah and Barak, how is nature shown to be on the side of the Israelites?

FOR THOUGHT AND DISCUSSION

4. Consider the parts played by men and by women in this story. What effect do these unusual roles have on the story and why?

5. The death of Sisera is described in prose and in poetry. Which description had the stronger impact on you? Why?

6. What would you say are the main differences between the prose and the poetic accounts of events? What are the advantages of each way of telling the story? of including both versions?

7. Near its end, the victory song concentrates on Sisera's mother and the other Canaanite women. What do you feel is the effect of this scene?

RESPONDING

1. Writing The fables of Aesop and others often end with a "moral." For example, "The Fox and the Crow" has as its moral, "Don't be greedy." Create a moral for the story of Deborah and Jael.

2. Activity With several classmates, prepare a choral reading of the song of Deborah and Barak. If possible, prepare a musical soundtrack to accompany your reading.

3. Multicultural Connection Many songs commemorate events in the history of a people; "The Star-Spangled Banner" is one example. Examine one or more national anthems or folk songs of heroes and great events and report on characteristics they seem to have in common.

Sisera

fared: can mean "ate" or "experienced good or bad treatment."

kite: a hawk.

viscera (vis′ər ə): guts.

Sisera, dead by hammer and nail, fared worst
Where he fared well; the woman had fed him first.
After the kill Deborah came,
A holy kite to claim the heathen viscera.
5 Is not her song impressive? All the same,
I am for Sisera

rhetoric: i.e., style, effectiveness.

supplanted: forced out, replaced.

polemic: argument.

descanted: sang.

Whose ruin had rhetoric enough and fitness
For Deborah's prophecy, so are God's enemies
    supplanted.
She needed no polemic, as God was her witness
10 Gloriously to publish the story condensed:
'The stars in their courses fought against
Sisera,' she descanted.

The hostess it was, who pinned the villain mute;
But Deborah whittled her fine art, the keener to
    spike him
15 On a final point: 'His women wait for the loot.'
So, from God's poets may God perfectly defend
Sisera and all the rest of us like him,
With whom the stars contend.

FOR THOUGHT AND DISCUSSION

1. It was Jael who killed Sisera. Why do you suppose the speaker says that Deborah "spiked" him?

2. In the last lines of the poem, the speaker suggests a link or bond with Sisera. Why do you think the speaker feels this bond?

3. What are your feelings about Sisera and his death? Why?

The Story of Samson

The Birth of Samson

A certain man of Zorah, named Manoah, from the clan of the Danites, had a wife who was sterile and remained childless. The angel of the Lord appeared to her and said, "You are sterile and childless, but you are going to conceive and have a son. Now see to it that you drink no wine or other fermented drink and that you do not eat anything unclean, because you will conceive and give birth to a son. No razor may be used on his head, because the boy is to be a Nazirite, set apart to God from birth, and he will begin the deliverance of Israel from the hands of the Philistines.". . .

The woman gave birth to a boy and named him Samson. He grew and the Lord blessed him, and the spirit of the Lord began to stir him while he was in Mahaneh Dan, between Zorah and Eshtaol.

The Riddle Betrayed

Samson went down to Timnah and saw there a young Philistine woman. When he returned, he said to his father and mother, "I have seen a Philistine woman in Timnah; now get her for me as my wife."

His father and mother replied, "Isn't there an acceptable woman among your relatives or among all our people? Must you go to the uncircumcised Philistines to get a wife?"

But Samson said to his father, "Get her for me. She's the right one for me." (His parents did not know that this was from the Lord, who was seeking an occasion to confront the Philistines; for at that time they were ruling over Israel.) Samson went down to Timnah together with his father and mother. As they approached the vineyards of Timnah, suddenly a

unclean: meat of animals forbidden as food by the Lord.

Nazirite: holy person. One of the vows of a Nazirite was not to cut his hair. (Not to be confused with Nazarene, a person from Nazareth.)

Philistines: traditional enemies of the Israelites. They arrived in Canaan by sea. (The name Palestine is derived from Philistine.)

uncircumcised: i.e., not Jewish.

occasion: excuse.

Judges 13: 2–5, 24–25; 14:1–15:16; 16:1–23, 25–31 (New International Version).

young lion came roaring toward him. The spirit of the Lord came upon him in power, so that he tore the lion apart with his bare hands as he might have torn a young goat. But he told neither his father nor his mother what he had done. Then he went down and talked with the woman, and he liked her.

carcass: dead body.

Some time later, when he went back to marry her, he turned aside to look at the lion's carcass. In it was a swarm of bees and some honey, which he scooped out with his hands and ate as he went along. When he rejoined his parents, he gave them some, and they too ate it. But he did not tell them that he had taken the honey from the lion's carcass.

Now his father went down to see the woman. And Samson made a feast there, as was customary for bridegrooms. When he appeared, he was given thirty companions.

"Let me tell you a riddle," Samson said to them. "If you can give me the answer within the seven days of the feast, I will give you thirty linen garments and thirty sets of clothes."

"Tell us your riddle," they said. "Let's hear it."

He replied,

"Out of the eater, something to eat;
  out of the strong, something sweet."

For three days they could not give the answer.

On the fourth day, they said to Samson's wife, "Coax your husband into explaining the riddle for us, or we will burn you and your father's household to death. Did you invite us here to rob us?"

Then Samson's wife threw herself on him, sobbing, "You hate me! You don't really love me. You've given my people a riddle, but you haven't told me the answer."

"I haven't even explained it to my father or mother," he replied, "so why should I explain it to you?" She cried the whole seven days of the feast. So on the seventh day he finally told her, because she continued to press him. She in turn explained the riddle to her people.

Before sunset on the seventh day the men of the town said to him,

"What is sweeter than honey?
    What is stronger than a lion?"

Samson said to them,

"If you had not plowed with my heifer,
    you would not have solved my riddle."

Then the spirit of the Lord came upon him in power. He went down to Ashkelon, struck down thirty of their men, stripped them of their belongings and gave their clothes to those who had explained the riddle. Burning with anger, he went up to his father's house. And Samson's wife was given to the friend who had attended him at his wedding.

was given to: married.

Samson's Revenge

Later on, at the time of wheat harvest, Samson took a young goat and went to visit his wife. He said, "I'm going to my wife's room." But her father would not let him go in.

"I was so sure you thoroughly hated her," he said, "that I gave her to your friend. Isn't her younger sister more attractive? Take her instead."

Samson said to them, "This time I have a right to get even with the Philistines; I will really harm them." So he went out and caught three hundred foxes and tied them tail to tail in pairs. He then fastened a torch to every pair of tails, lit the torches and let the foxes loose in the standing grain of the Philistines. He burned up the shocks and standing grain, together with the vineyards and olive groves.

shocks: piles of cut grain stalks.

When the Philistines asked, "Who did this?" they were told, "Samson, the Timnite's son-in-law, because his wife was given to his friend."

So the Philistines went up and burned her and her father to death. Samson said to them, "Since you've acted like this, I won't stop until I get my revenge on you." He attacked them viciously and slaughtered many of them. Then he went down and stayed in a cave in the rock of Etam.

The Philistines went up and camped in Judah, spreading out near Lehi. The men of Judah asked, "Why have you come to fight us?"

"We have come to take Samson prisoner," they answered, "to do to him as he did to us."

Then three thousand men from Judah went down to the cave in the rock of Etam and said to Samson, "Don't you realize that the Philistines are rulers over us? What have you done to us?"

He answered, "I merely did to them what they did to me."

They said to him, "We've come to tie you up and hand you over to the Philistines."

Samson said, "Swear to me that you won't kill me yourselves."

"Agreed," they answered. "We will only tie you up and hand you over to them. We will not kill you." So they bound him with two new ropes and led him up from the rock. As he approached Lehi, the Philistines came toward him shouting. The spirit of the Lord came upon him in power. The ropes on his arms became like charred flax, and the bindings dropped from his hands. Finding a fresh jawbone of a donkey, he grabbed it and struck down a thousand men.

Then Samson said,

> "With a donkey's jawbone
> I have made donkeys of them.
> With a donkey's jawbone
> I have killed a thousand men." . . .

The Gates of Gaza

One day Samson went to Gaza, where he saw a prostitute. He went in to spend the night with her. The people of Gaza were told, "Samson is here!" So they surrounded the place and lay in wait for him all night at the city gate. They made no move during the night, saying, "At dawn we'll kill him."

But Samson lay there only until the middle of the night. Then he got up and took hold of the doors of the city gate, together with the two posts, and tore them loose, bar and all. He lifted them to his shoulders and carried them to the top of the hill that faces Hebron.

like . . . flax: i.e., like burned threads. Flax is a plant fiber that is spun into thread and woven into linen.

Samson and Delilah

Some time later, he fell in love with a woman in the Valley of Sorek whose name was Delilah. The rulers of the Philistines went to her and said, "See if you can lure him into showing you the secret of his great strength and how we can overpower him so we may tie him up and subdue him. Each one of us will give you eleven hundred shekels of silver."

So Delilah said to Samson, "Tell me the secret of your great strength and how you can be tied up and subdued."

Samson answered her, "If anyone ties me with seven fresh thongs that have not been dried, I'll become as weak as any other man."

Then the rulers of the Philistines brought her seven fresh thongs that had not been dried, and she tied him with them. With men hidden in the room, she called to him, "Samson, the Philistines are upon you!" But he snapped the thongs as easily as a piece of string snaps when it comes close to a flame. So the secret of his strength was not discovered.

Then Delilah said to Samson, "You have made a fool of me; you lied to me. Come now, tell me how you can be tied."

He said, "If anyone ties me securely with new ropes that have never been used, I'll become as weak as any other man."

So Delilah took new ropes and tied him with them. Then, with men hidden in the room, she called to him, "Samson, the Philistines are upon you!" But he snapped the ropes off his arms as if they were threads.

Delilah then said to Samson, "Until now, you have been making a fool of me and lying to me. Tell me how you can be tied."

He replied, "If you weave the seven braids of my head into the fabric on the loom and tighten it with the pin, I'll become as weak as any other man." So while he was sleeping, Delilah took the seven braids of his head, wove them into the fabric and tightened it with the pin.

shekels: here, coins or pieces.

thongs: narrow strips of leather.

loom: weaving machine.

Again she called to him, "Samson, the Philistines are upon you!" He awoke from his sleep and pulled up the pin and the loom, with the fabric.

Then she said to him, "How can you say, 'I love you,' when you won't confide in me? This is the third time you have made a fool of me and haven't told me the secret of your great strength." With such nagging she prodded him day after day until he was tired to death.

So he told her everything. "No razor has ever been used on my head," he said, "because I have been a Nazirite set apart to God since birth. If my head were shaved, my strength would leave me, and I would become as weak as any other man."

When Delilah saw that he had told her everything, she sent word to the rulers of the Philistines, "Come back once more; he has told me everything." So the rulers of the Philistines returned with the silver in their hands. Having put him to sleep on her lap, she called a man to shave off the seven braids of his hair, and so began to subdue him. And his strength left him.

Then she called, "Samson, the Philistines are upon you!"

He awoke from his sleep and thought, "I'll go out as before and shake myself free." But he did not know that the Lord had left him.

Samson in Chains

Then the Philistines seized him, gouged out his eyes and took him down to Gaza. Binding him with bronze shackles, they set him to grinding in the prison. But the hair on his head began to grow again after it had been shaved.

grinding: crushing grain by turning a heavy stone wheel on it.

Now the rulers of the Philistines assembled to offer a great sacrifice to Dagon their god and to celebrate, saying, "Our god has delivered Samson, our enemy, into our hands."

While they were in high spirits, they shouted, "Bring out Samson to entertain us." So they called Samson out of the prison, and he performed for them.

When they stood him among the pillars, Samson said to the servant who held his hand, "Put me where I can feel the pillars that support the temple, so that I may lean against them." Now the temple was crowded with men and women; all the rulers of the Philistines were there, and on the roof were about three thousand men and women watching Samson perform.

Then Samson prayed to the Lord, "O Sovereign Lord, remember me. O God, please strengthen me just once more, and let me with one blow get revenge on the Philistines for my two eyes." Then Samson reached toward the two central pillars on which the temple stood. Bracing himself against them, his right hand on the one and his left hand on the other, Samson said, "Let me die with the Philistines!" Then he pushed with all his might, and down came the temple on the rulers and all the people in it. Thus he killed many more when he died than while he lived.

Then his brothers and his father's whole family went down to get him. They brought him back and buried him between Zorah and Eshtaol in the tomb of Manoah his father. He had led Israel twenty years.

FOR CLOSE READING

1. List the occasions and the reasons Samson does harm to the Philistines. Which of his feats are clever tricks? Which are acts of sheer strength?

2. Describe the methods Delilah and the daughter of Timnah use to get what they want from Samson.

3. Write down as many of Samson's characteristics as you can, and give at least one example of each.

4. After he is blinded by the Philistines, what is the first task Samson is given to do?

FOR THOUGHT AND DISCUSSION

5. Samson's characteristics seem both good and bad. Why do you suppose such a person is chosen to save Israel from the Philistines?

6. What kind of person is Delilah? Support your opinion with details of the story.

7. What pattern do you notice in Samson's life? Describe that pattern in one or two sentences.

8. Some people never change their character or behavior. What would you say of Samson in this respect? Support your answer with examples.

9. Samson is one of the few persons in the Bible with a special birth story foretelling a special destiny. In what ways do you think Samson lived up to expectations or failed to do so?

RESPONDING

1. Writing Describe an episode from this story from the viewpoint of one of the women in Samson's life.

2. Activity With a group of classmates, create a cartoon strip that illustrates episodes of Samson's life.

3. Activity Imagine that you are producing a movie on the life of Samson. What present-day actors and actresses would you cast in the key roles? Who would direct your movie? Create a poster to promote your movie.

4. Multicultural Connection Heroes of great physical strength appear in folk tales and myths of many cultures, for example, Hercules in Greek mythology and Paul Bunyan and John Henry in American folklore. Look up stories of one or more of these mighty heroes and compare them to Samson in terms of their deeds, their deaths, and their wisdom.

VACHEL LINDSAY

How Samson Bore Away the Gates of Gaza

Once, in a night as black as ink,
She drove him out when he would not drink.
Round the house there were men in wait
Asleep in rows by the Gaza gate.
5 But the Holy Spirit was in this man.
Like a gentle wind he crept and ran.
("It is midnight," said the big town clock.)

He lifted the gates up, post and lock.
The hole in the wall was high and wide
10 When he bore away old Gaza's pride
Into the deep of the night:—
The bold Jack Johnson Israelite,—
Samson—
The Judge,
15 The Nazirite.

Jack Johnson: first African American to be heavyweight boxing champion.

The air was black, like the smoke of a dragon.
Samson's heart was as big as a wagon.
He sang like a shining golden fountain.
He sweated up to the top of the mountain.
20 He threw down the gates with a noise like
     judgment.
And the quails all ran with the big arousement.

But he wept—"I must not love tough queens,
And spend on them my hard earned means.
I told that girl I would drink no more.
25 Therefore she drove me from her door.
Oh sorrow!
Sorrow!
I cannot hide.
Oh Lord look down from your chariot side.

30 You made me Judge, and I am not wise.
I am weak as a sheep for all my size."

Let Samson
Be coming
Into your mind.

35 The moon shone out, the stars were gay.
He saw the foxes run and play.

rent: tore.

He rent his garments, he rolled around
In deep repentance on the ground.
Then he felt a honey in his soul.

grace abounding: great
mercy (from God).

40 Grace abounding made him whole.
Then he saw the Lord in a chariot blue.
The gorgeous stallions whinnied and flew.
The iron wheels hummed an old hymn-tune
And crunched in thunder over the moon.

45 And Samson shouted to the sky:
"My Lord, my Lord is riding high."

Like a steed, he pawed the gates with his hoof.
He rattled the gates like rocks on the roof,
And danced in the night

50 On the mountain-top,
Danced in the deep of the night:
The Judge, the holy Nazirite,
Whom ropes and chains could never bind.

Let Samson
55 *Be coming*
Into your mind.

Whirling his arms, like a top he sped.
His long black hair flew round his head
Like an outstretched net of silky cord,

60 Like a wheel of the chariot of the Lord.

Let Samson
Be coming
Into your mind.

Samson saw the sun anew.
65 He left the gates in the grass and dew.

a-nigh: nearby.

He went to a county-seat a-nigh
Found a harlot proud and high:

Philistine that no man could tame—
Delilah was her lady-name.
70   Oh sorrow,
Sorrow,
She was too wise.
She cut off his hair,
She put out his eyes.

75   *Let Samson*
Be coming
Into your mind.

FOR THOUGHT AND DISCUSSION

1. Though the poem concentrates on the "gates of Gaza" episode, several words and phrases hint at other events in Samson's life. How many of these hints can you find?

2. What emotions does Samson express in this poem? How?

3. What do you think the speaker means by "Let Samson/Be coming/Into your mind"?

The Story of Ruth

Moab (mō´ab): a country east of the Dead Sea. The Moabites and Israelites were traditional enemies.

A Time of Bitterness

In the days when the judges ruled, there was a famine in the land, and a man from Bethlehem in Judah, together with his wife and two sons, went to live for a while in the country of Moab. The man's name was Elimelech, his wife's name was Naomi, and the names of his two sons were Mahlon and Kilion. They were Ephrathites from Bethlehem, Judah. And they went to Moab and lived there.

Now Elimelech, Naomi's husband, died, and she was left with her two sons. They married Moabite women, one named Orpah and the other Ruth. After they had lived there about ten years, both Mahlon and Kilion also died, and Naomi was left without her two sons and her husband.

When she heard in Moab that the Lord had come to the aid of his people by providing food for them, Naomi and her daughters-in-law prepared to return home from there. With her two daughters-in-law she left the place where she had been living and set out on the road that would take them back to the land of Judah.

Then Naomi said to her two daughters-in-law, "Go back, each of you, to your mother's home. May the Lord show kindness to you, as you have shown to your dead and to me. May the Lord grant that each of you will find rest in the home of another husband."

Then she kissed them and they wept aloud and said to her, "We will go back with you to your people."

sons . . . your husbands: according to Israelite law, an unmarried man must wed his dead brother's widow if she is childless, to preserve his line of descent.

But Naomi said, "Return home, my daughters. Why would you come with me? Am I going to have any more sons, who could become your husbands? Return home, my daughters; I am too old to have

Ruth 1:1–4:17 (New International Version).

another husband. Even if I thought there was still hope for me—even if I had a husband tonight and then gave birth to sons—would you wait until they grew up? Would you remain unmarried for them? No, my daughters. It is more bitter for me than for you, because the Lord's hand has gone out against me!"

At this they wept again. Then Orpah kissed her mother-in-law good-by, but Ruth clung to her.

"Look," said Naomi, "your sister-in-law is going back to her people and her gods. Go back with her."

But Ruth replied, "Don't urge me to leave you or to turn back from you. Where you go I will go, and where you stay I will stay. Your people will be my people and your God my God. Where you die I will die, and there I will be buried. May the Lord deal with me, be it ever so severely, if anything but death separates you and me." When Naomi realized that Ruth was determined to go with her, she stopped urging her.

So the two women went on until they came to Bethlehem. When they arrived in Bethlehem, the whole town was stirred because of them, and the women exclaimed, "Can this be Naomi?"

"Don't call me Naomi," she told them. "Call me Mara, because the Almighty has made my life very bitter. I went away full, but the Lord has brought me back empty. Why call me Naomi? The Lord has afflicted me; the Almighty has brought misfortune upon me."

So Naomi returned from Moab accompanied by Ruth the Moabitess, her daughter-in-law, arriving in Bethlehem as the barley harvest was beginning.

Ruth Gleans

Now Naomi had a relative on her husband's side, from the clan of Elimelech, a man of standing, whose name was Boaz.

And Ruth the Moabitess said to Naomi, "Let me go to the fields and pick up the leftover grain behind anyone in whose eyes I find favor."

Naomi said to her, "Go ahead, my daughter." So she went out and began to glean in the fields behind the harvesters. As it turned out, she found herself

Naomi: in Hebrew, "pleasant."

Mara: in Hebrew, "bitter"

Boaz (bō′az).

glean: gather fallen grains that, according to Israelite law, were left by the reapers for the poor.

working in a field belonging to Boaz, who was from the clan of Elimelech.

Just then Boaz arrived from Bethlehem and greeted the harvesters, "The Lord be with you!"

"The Lord bless you!" they called back.

Boaz asked the foreman of his harvesters, "Whose young woman is that?"

The foreman replied, "She is the Moabitess who came back from Moab with Naomi. She said, 'Please let me glean and gather among the sheaves behind the harvesters.' She went into the field and has worked steadily from morning till now, except for a short rest in the shelter."

So Boaz said to Ruth, "My daughter, listen to me. Don't go and glean in another field and don't go away from here. Stay here with my servant girls. Watch the field where the men are harvesting, and follow along after the girls. I have told the men not to touch you. And whenever you are thirsty, go and get a drink from the water jars the men have filled."

At this, she bowed down with her face to the ground. She exclaimed, "Why have I found such favor in your eyes that you notice me—a foreigner?"

Boaz replied, "I've been told all about what you have done for your mother-in-law since the death of your husband—how you left your father and mother and your homeland and came to live with a people you did not know before. May the Lord repay you for what you have done. May you be richly rewarded by the Lord, the God of Israel, under whose wings you have come to take refuge."

"May I continue to find favor in your eyes, my lord," she said. "You have given me comfort and have spoken kindly to your servant—though I do not have the standing of one of your servant girls."

At mealtime Boaz said to her, "Come over here. Have some bread and dip it in the wine vinegar."

When she sat down with the harvesters, he offered her some roasted grain. She ate all she wanted and had some left over. As she got up to glean, Boaz gave orders to his men, "Even if she gathers among the sheaves, don't embarrass her. Rather, pull out some stalks for her from the bundles and leave them for her to pick up, and don't rebuke her."

sheaves: bundles of cut grain stalks.

So Ruth gleaned in the field until evening. Then she threshed the barley she had gathered, and it amounted to about an ephah. She carried it back to town, and her mother-in-law saw how much she had gathered. Ruth also brought out and gave her what she had left over after she had eaten enough.

ephah (e′fə): about a bushel.

Naomi Advises Ruth

Her mother-in-law asked her, "Where did you glean today? Where did you work? Blessed be the man who took notice of you!"

Then Ruth told her mother-in-law about the one at whose place she had been working. "The name of the man I worked with today is Boaz," she said.

"The Lord bless him!" Naomi said to her daughter-in-law. "He has not stopped showing his kindness to the living and the dead." She added, "That man is our close relative; he is one of our kinsman-redeemers."

he . . . kinsman-redeemers: i.e., he might perform the duty of a kinsman to marry the widow.

Then Ruth the Moabitess said, "He even said to me, 'Stay with my workers until they finish harvesting all my grain.'"

Naomi said to Ruth her daughter-in-law, "It will be good for you, my daughter, to go with his girls, because in someone else's field you might be harmed."

So Ruth stayed close to the servant girls of Boaz to glean until the barley and wheat harvests were finished. And she lived with her mother-in-law.

One day Naomi her mother-in-law said to her, "My daughter, should I not try to find a home for you, where you will be well provided for? Is not Boaz, with whose servant girls you have been, a kinsman of ours? Tonight he will be winnowing barley on the threshing floor. Wash and perfume yourself, and put on your best clothes. Then go down to the threshing floor, but don't let him know you are there until he has finished eating and drinking. When he lies down, note the place where he is lying. Then go and uncover his feet and lie down. He will tell you what to do."

winnowing: sifting the chaff from grain.

"I will do whatever you say," Ruth answered. So she went down to the threshing floor and did everything her mother-in-law told her to do.

When Boaz had finished eating and drinking and

Since Ruth's husband left no brother to marry her, the law required his near-est unmarried relative to wed her. Naomi is advising Ruth to make her claim to Boaz in this unusual and symbolic way.

was in good spirits, he went over to lie down at the far end of the grain pile. Ruth approached quietly, uncovered his feet and lay down. In the middle of the night something startled the man, and he turned and discovered a woman lying at his feet.

"Who are you?" he asked.

"I am your servant Ruth," she said. "Spread the corner of your garment over me, since you are a kinsman-redeemer."

"The Lord bless you, my daughter," he replied. "This kindness is greater than that which you showed earlier: You have not run after the younger men, whether rich or poor. And now, my daughter, don't be afraid. I will do for you all you ask. All my fellow townsmen know that you are a woman of noble character. Although it is true that I am near of kin, there is a kinsman-redeemer nearer than I. Stay here for the night, and in the morning if he wants to redeem, good; let him redeem. But if he is not willing, as surely as the Lord lives I will do it. Lie here until morning."

So she lay at his feet until morning, but got up before anyone could be recognized; and he said, "Don't let it be known that a woman came to the threshing floor."

He also said, "Bring me the shawl you are wearing and hold it out." When she did so, he poured into it six measures of barley and put it on her. Then he went back to town.

When Ruth came to her mother-in-law, Naomi asked, "How did it go, my daughter?"

Then she told her everything Boaz had done for her and added, "He gave me these six measures of barley, saying, 'Don't go back to your mother-in-law empty-handed.'"

Then Naomi said, "Wait, my daughter, until you find out what happens. For the man will not rest until the matter is settled today."

Boaz Takes Action

Meanwhile Boaz went up to the town gate and sat there. When the kinsman-redeemer he had mentioned came along, Boaz said, "Come over here, my friend, and sit down." So he went over and sat down.

kindness: i.e., act of family loyalty.

gate: where legal agreements were made before witnesses.

Boaz took ten of the elders of the town and said, "Sit here," and they did so. Then he said to the kinsman-redeemer, "Naomi, who has come back from Moab, is selling the piece of land that belonged to our brother Elimelech. I thought I should bring the matter to your attention and suggest that you buy it in the presence of these seated here and in the presence of the elders of my people. If you will redeem it, do so. But if you will not, tell me, so I will know. For no one has the right to do it except you, and I am next in line."

"I will redeem it," he said.

Then Boaz said, "On the day you buy the land from Naomi and from Ruth the Moabitess, you acquire the dead man's widow, in order to maintain the name of the dead with his property."

At this, the kinsman-redeemer said, "Then I cannot redeem it because I might endanger my own estate. You redeem it yourself. I cannot do it."

endanger ... estate: i.e., by taking responsibility for Ruth and her future children, he might reduce the inheritance of his other children.

(Now in earlier times in Israel, for the redemption and transfer of property to become final, one party took off his sandal and gave it to the other. This was the method of legalizing transactions in Israel.)

So the kinsman-redeemer said to Boaz, "Buy it yourself." And he removed his sandal.

Then Boaz announced to the elders and all the people, "Today you are witnesses that I have bought from Naomi all the property of Elimelech, Kilion and Mahlon. I have also acquired Ruth the Moabitess, Mahlon's widow, as my wife, in order to maintain the name of the dead with his property, so that his name will not disappear from among his family or from the town records. Today you are witnesses!"

Then the elders and all those at the gate said, "We are witnesses. May the Lord make the woman who is coming into your home like Rachel and Leah, who together built up the house of Israel. May you have standing in Ephrathah and be famous in Bethlehem. Through the offspring the Lord gives you by this young woman, may your family be like that of Perez, whom Tamar bore to Judah."

Rachel and Leah: wives of Jacob, "mothers of Israel."

Perez: Judah's son Perez was an ancestor of Boaz, born to a widow who, like Ruth, claimed the right of kinship.

So Boaz took Ruth and she became his wife. Then he went to her, and the Lord enabled her to conceive, and she gave birth to a son. The women said to Naomi: "Praise be to the Lord, who this day has not left you without a kinsman-redeemer. May he become famous throughout Israel! He will renew your life and sustain you in your old age. For your daughter-in-law, who loves you and who is better to you than seven sons, has given him birth."

Then Naomi took the child, laid him in her lap and cared for him. The women living there said, "Naomi has a son." And they named him Obed. He was the father of Jesse, the father of David.

FOR CLOSE READING

1. What are the conditions in Bethlehem when Naomi leaves for Moab? when she returns with Ruth?

2. Naomi says, "I went away full, but the Lord has brought me back empty." List the occasions in the story that Ruth brings something to Naomi to overcome her emptiness.

3. What references to widowhood, childlessness, and famine can you find in this story? What references to abundant harvest and fruitful marriage?

FOR THOUGHT AND DISCUSSION

4. What do you think is the moment of greatest suspense in this story? What techniques are used to increase the tension of this moment?

5. What obligations and responsibilities do relatives have for one another today? In what ways are such obligations similar to and different from those in this story?

6. What is your opinion of the law concerning gleaning as a way of providing for those in need? Can you think of any modern equivalents to this system? Explain.

7. What does Ruth "glean" besides grain? What does Naomi glean—personally and through Ruth? In what sense does Boaz glean?

8. This is a story of various kinds of emptiness and fullness. Give examples of each and explain how they contribute to the overall effect of the story.

Women

Women have no wilderness in them,
They are provident instead,
Content in the tight hot cell of their hearts
To eat dusty bread.

provident: careful and economical.

5 They do not see cattle cropping red winter grass,
They do not hear
Snow water going down under culverts
Shallow and clear.

They wait, when they should turn to journeys,
10 They stiffen, when they should bend.
They use against themselves that benevolence
To which no man is friend.

benevolence: good will; kindly feeling.

They cannot think of so many crops to a field
Or of clean wood cleft by an ax.
15 Their love is an eager meaninglessness
Too tense, or too lax.

They hear in every whisper that speaks to them
A shout and a cry.
As like as not, when they take life over their door-
sills
20 They should let it go by.

FOR THOUGHT AND DISCUSSION

1. According to the speaker, what are some
characteristics of women?

2. Which of the women in Bible passages you have
read seem to fit the speaker's description? Explain.

3. Do you agree or disagree with the speaker's
description? Support your opinion with examples
from your own experience and reading.

5

Anointed Kings

Saul:
The Mighty Are Fallen

Saul Is Anointed

There was a man of Benjamin whose name was Kish, the son of Abiel, son of Zeror, son of Becorath, son of Aphiah, a Benjaminite, a man of wealth; and he had a son whose name was Saul, a handsome young man. There was not a man among the people of Israel more handsome than he; from his shoulders upward he was taller than any of the people.

from ... taller: he was a head taller.

Now the asses of Kish, Saul's father, were lost. So Kish said to Saul his son, "Take one of the servants with you, and arise, go and look for the asses." And they passed through the hill country of Ephraim and passed through the land of Shalishah, but they did not find them. . . .

When they came to the land of Zuph, Saul said to his servant who was with him, "Come, let us go back, lest my father cease to care about the asses and become anxious about us." But he said to him, "Behold, there is a man of God in this city, and he is a man that is held in honor; all that he says comes true. Let us go there; perhaps he can tell us about the journey on which we have set out." . . .

As they went up the hill to the city, they met young maidens coming out to draw water, and said to them, "Is the seer here?" They answered, "He is; behold, he is just ahead of you. . . ."

seer: prophet, one who spoke for God.

Now the day before Saul came, the Lord had revealed to Samuel: "Tomorrow about this time I will

1 Samuel 9:1–4a, 5–6, 11–12a, 15–19, 26–27; 10:1a, 9a; 11:1–11, 15a; 15:1–3, 5, 7–9a, 13–16, 22–28, 35a; 16:14; 18:6–8a, 9; 28:3–15a, 18–19b; 31:1–5. 2 Samuel 1:17, 19–20, 23–27 (Revised Standard Version).
LEFT: *David and Goliath*. The British Library, Oriental and India Office Collections.

send to you a man from the land of Benjamin, and you shall anoint him to be prince over my people Israel. He shall save my people from the hand of the Philistines; for I have seen the affliction of my people, because their cry has come to me." When Samuel saw Saul, the Lord told him, "Here is the man of whom I spoke to you! He it is who shall rule over my people." Then Saul approached Samuel in the gate, and said, "Tell me where is the house of the seer?" Samuel answered Saul, "I am the seer; go up before me to the high place, for today you shall eat with me, and in the morning I will let you go and will tell you all that is on your mind. . . ."

Then at the break of dawn Samuel called to Saul upon the roof, "Up, that I may send you on your way." So Saul arose, and both he and Samuel went out into the street.

As they were going down to the outskirts of the city, Samuel said to Saul, "Tell the servant to pass on before us, and when he has passed on stop here yourself for a while, that I may make known to you the word of God."

Then Samuel took a vial of oil and poured it on his head, and kissed him and said, "Has not the Lord anointed you to be prince over his people Israel? And you shall reign over the people of the Lord and you will save them from the hand of their enemies round about. . . ."

When he turned his back to leave Samuel, God gave him another heart . . . .

The Defeat of the Ammonites

Then Nahash the Ammonite went up and besieged Jabesh-gilead; and all the men of Jabesh said to Nahash, "Make a treaty with us, and we will serve you." But Nahash the Ammonite said to them, "On this condition I will make a treaty with you, that I gouge out all your right eyes, and thus put disgrace upon all Israel." The elders of Jabesh said to him, "Give us seven days respite that we may send messengers through all the territory of Israel. Then, if there is no one to save us, we will give ourselves up to you." When the messengers came to Gibeah of Saul, they reported the matter in the ears of the people; and all the people wept aloud.

anoint: sprinkle his head with oil (as a sign that God appointed him king).

affliction: suffering.

high place: At that time there were shrines to God on certain hills in Israel.

vial: small bottle.

Ammonites: enemies to the east of Israel.

respite: delay.

of Saul: i.e., where he lived.

Now Saul was coming from the field behind the oxen; and Saul said, "What ails the people, that they are weeping?" So they told him the tidings of the men of Jabesh. And the spirit of God came mightily upon Saul when he heard these words, and his anger was greatly kindled. He took a yoke of oxen, and cut them in pieces and sent them throughout all the territory of Israel by the hand of messengers, saying, "Whoever does not come out after Saul and Samuel, so shall it be done to his oxen!" Then the dread of the Lord fell upon the people, and they came out as one man. When he mustered them at Bezek, the men of Israel were three hundred thousand, and the men of Judah thirty thousand. And they said to the messengers who had come, "Thus shall you say to the men of Jabesh-gilead: 'Tomorrow, by the time the sun is hot, you shall have deliverance.'" When the messengers came and told the men of Jabesh, they were glad. Therefore the men of Jabesh said, "Tomorrow we will give ourselves up to you, and you may do to us whatever seems good to you." And on the morrow Saul put the people in three companies; and they came into the midst of the camp in the morning watch, and cut down the Ammonites until the heat of the day; and those who survived were scattered, so that no two of them were left together.

. . . So all the people went to Gilgal, and there they made Saul king before the Lord in Gilgal.

tidings: news.

yoke: pair.

mustered: assembled.

Israel, Judah: names for the ten northern tribes and for the two southern tribes.

said: i.e., to Nahash, the enemy king.

Saul Is Rejected

And Samuel said to Saul, "The Lord sent me to anoint you king over his people Israel; now therefore hearken to the words of the Lord. Thus says the Lord of hosts, 'I will punish what Amalek did to Israel in opposing them on the way, when they came up out of Egypt. Now go and smite Amalek, and utterly destroy all that they have; do not spare them, but kill both man and woman, infant and suckling, ox and sheep, camel and ass.'"

. . . And Saul came to the city of Amalek, and lay in wait in the valley. . . . And Saul defeated the Amalekites, from Havilah as far as Shur, which is east of Egypt. And he took Agag the king of the Amalekites alive, and utterly destroyed all the people with the edge of the sword. But Saul and the people

hosts: armies.

Amalek: the Amalekites, southern enemies.

suckling: nursing infant.

spared Agag, and the best of the sheep and of the oxen and of the fatlings, and the lambs, and all that was good, and would not utterly destroy them . . . .

And Samuel came to Saul, and Saul said to him, "Blessed be you to the Lord; I have performed the commandment of the Lord." And Samuel said, "What then is this bleating of the sheep in my ears, and the lowing of the oxen which I hear?" Saul said, "They have brought them from the Amalekites; for the people spared the best of the sheep and of the oxen, to sacrifice to the Lord your God; and the rest we have utterly destroyed." Then Samuel said to Saul, "Stop! I will tell you what the Lord said to me this night." And he said to him, "Say on.". . . And Samuel said,

lowing (lō′ing): mooing.

"Has the Lord as great delight in burnt offerings
    and sacrifices,
as in obeying the voice of the Lord?
Behold, to obey is better than sacrifice,
and to hearken than the fat of rams.
For rebellion is as the sin of divination,
and stubbornness is as iniquity and idolatry.
Because you have rejected the word of the
    Lord,
he has also rejected you from being king."

hearken: listen.
divination: witchcraft.
iniquity: wickedness.
idolatry: worshiping
idols.

transgressed: disobeyed.

And Saul said to Samuel, "I have sinned; for I have transgressed the commandment of the Lord and your words, because I feared the people and obeyed their voice. Now therefore, I pray, pardon my sin, and return with me, that I may worship the Lord." And Samuel said to Saul, "I will not return with you; for you have rejected the word of the Lord, and the Lord has rejected you from being king over Israel." As Samuel turned to go away, Saul laid hold upon the skirt of his robe, and it tore. And Samuel said to him, "The Lord has torn the kingdom of Israel from you this day, and has given it to a neighbor of yours, who is better than you. . . ."

And Samuel did not see Saul again until the day of his death, but Samuel grieved over Saul. . . .

Now the spirit of the Lord departed from Saul, and an evil spirit from the Lord tormented him. . . .

[A stalemate between Saul's army and the Philistines is ended when a young shepherd, David, kills the enemy champion, Goliath, a story that will be told later. This victory brings Saul no peace of mind.]

Saul's Envy

As they were coming home, when David returned from slaying the Philistine, the women came out of all the cities of Israel, singing and dancing, to meet King Saul, with timbrels, with songs of joy, and with instruments of music. And the women sang to one another as they made merry,

> "Saul has slain his thousands,
> And David his ten thousands."

And Saul was very angry, and this saying displeased him; he said, "They have ascribed to David ten thousands, and to me they have ascribed thousands; and what more can he have but the kingdom?" And Saul eyed David from that day on.

[Saul's envy turns to hatred. Though David is now his son-in-law and best friend of his son Jonathan, Saul tries to kill him. While he is pursuing David, the Philistines again invade Israel.]

The "Witch" of Endor

Now Samuel had died, and all Israel had mourned for him and buried him in Ramah, his own city. And Saul had put the mediums and the wizards out of the land. The Philistines assembled, and came and encamped at Shunem; and Saul gathered all Israel, and they encamped at Gilboa. When Saul saw the army of the Philistines, he was afraid, and his heart trembled greatly. And when Saul inquired of the Lord, the Lord did not answer him, either by dreams, or by Urim, or by prophets. Then Saul said to his servants, "Seek out for me a woman who is a medium, that I may go to her and inquire of her." And his servants said to him, "Behold, there is a medium at Endor."

timbrels: tambourines, hand drums that jingle when shaken.

ascribed: given credit.

put . . . land: banned and driven out people who dealt with spirits.

Urim (ŭr′im): holy objects used to tell the will of God.

medium at Endor: traditionally called "the witch of Endor."

So Saul disguised himself and put on other garments, and went, he and two men with him; and they came to the woman by night. And he said, "Divine for me by a spirit, and bring up for me whomever I shall name to you." The woman said to him, "Surely you know what Saul has done, how he has cut off the mediums and the wizards from the land. Why then are you laying a snare for my life to bring about my death?" But Saul swore to her by the Lord, "As the Lord lives, no punishment shall come upon you for this thing." Then the woman said, "Whom shall I bring up for you?" He said, "Bring up Samuel for me." When the woman saw Samuel, she cried out with a loud voice; and the woman said to Saul, "Why have you deceived me? You are Saul." The king said to her, "Have no fear; what do you see?" And the woman said to Saul, "I see a god coming up out of the earth." He said to her, "What is his appearance?" And she said, "An old man is coming up; and he is wrapped in a robe." And Saul knew that it was Samuel, and he bowed with his face to the ground, and did obeisance.

Then Samuel said to Saul, "Why have you disturbed me by bringing me up?" ... "Because you did not obey the voice of the Lord, and did not carry out his fierce wrath against Amalek, therefore the Lord has done this thing to you this day. Moreover the Lord will give Israel also with you into the hand of the Philistines; and tomorrow you and your sons shall be with me . . . ."

Saul's Death

Now the Philistines fought against Israel; and the men of Israel fled before the Philistines, and fell slain on Mount Gilboa. And the Philistines overtook Saul and his sons; and the Philistines slew Jonathan and Abinadab and Malchishua, the sons of Saul. The battle pressed hard upon Saul, and the archers found him; and he was badly wounded by the archers. Then Saul said to his armor-bearer, "Draw your sword, and thrust me through with it, lest these uncircumcised come and thrust me through, and make sport of me." But his armor-bearer would not; for he feared greatly. Therefore Saul took his own sword, and fell upon it. And when his armor-bearer saw that Saul was dead, he also fell upon his sword, and died with him. . . .

divine for me: tell my fortune.

snare: trap.

god: i.e., a spirit, a supernatural being.

did obeisance: lay flat on the ground in submission.

armor-bearer: an assistant who carries combat gear.

uncircumcised: i.e., not Jewish.

And David lamented with this lamentation over
Saul and Jonathan his son . . .

> "Thy glory, O Israel, is slain upon thy high
>   places!
> How are the mighty fallen!
> Tell it not in Gath,
> publish it not in the streets of Ashkelon;
> lest the daughters of the Philistines rejoice,
> lest the daughters of the uncircumcised
>   exult. . . .
>
> Saul and Jonathan, beloved and lovely!
> In life and in death they were not divided;
> they were swifter than eagles,
> they were stronger than lions.
>
> Ye daughters of Israel, weep over Saul,
> who clothed you daintily in scarlet,
> who put ornaments of gold upon your apparel.
>
> How are the mighty fallen
> in the midst of the battle!
>
> Jonathan lies slain upon the high places.
> I am distressed for you, my brother Jonathan;
> very pleasant have you been to me;
> your love to me was wonderful,
> passing the love of women.
>
> How are the mighty fallen,
> and the weapons of war perished!"

2 Sam. 1:17.

**lamented with this
lamentation:** (created
and) sang this song of
sorrow.

Gath, Ashkelon: two of
the main Philistine cities.

exult: rejoice.

lovely: pleasant.

daintily: beautifully.

FOR CLOSE READING

1. Saul is named ruler twice. Describe the two
occasions; tell who is present and what reason is
given for his being named king.

2. After the Amalekite battle, how does Samuel know
immediately that Saul has disobeyed the Lord?

3. Why is Saul angry at what the women sang about
David and himself?

4. What does the spirit of Samuel at Endor foretell to
Saul?

FOR THOUGHT AND DISCUSSION

5. Saul could have been anointed by Samuel *after* the battle of Jabesh-gilead. What difference would that shift have made in the story?

6. Saul is named leader by God; later, the people "made Saul king." This double approval suggests two responsibilities: to God and to his people's needs. In what ways might Saul have felt a conflict between these two responsibilities?

7. Why do you think Saul disguises himself for his visit to the medium at Endor?

8. In your opinion, to what extent is Saul responsible for what happens to him? Support your answer from the text.

RESPONDING

1. Writing Saul is in his tent on the evening before his final battle with the Philistines. Express his thoughts in his letter home to his wife.

2. Writing What is a tragedy? a tragic hero? In what way might the story of Saul fit your definitions? In a short essay, compare and contrast the story of Saul with that of a tragic hero you have studied.

3. Writing Write an account of Saul's death as it might be reported in a modern newspaper. Include a brief history of his accomplishments and importance.

4. Humanities Connection Select passages from classical or contemporary music that might be used as background to David's lament for Saul and Jonathan. You may wish to prepare a reading of David's lament with your chosen music.

WILLIAM SHAKESPEARE

The Death of Kings

Let's talk of graves, of worms and epitaphs;
Make dust our paper and with rainy eyes
Write sorrow on the bosom of the earth . . .

For God's sake, let us sit upon the ground
5 And tell sad stories of the death of kings:
How some have been depos'd; some slain in war;
Some haunted by the ghosts they have depos'd;
Some poisoned by their wives; some sleeping
    kill'd;
All murdered: for within the hollow crown
10 That rounds the mortal temples of a king
Keeps Death his court and there the antic sits,
Scoffing his state and grinning at his pomp,
Allowing him a breath, a little scene,
To monarchize, be fear'd and kill with looks,
15 Infusing him with self and vain conceit,
As if this flesh which walls about our life
Were brass impregnable, and humour'd thus
Comes at the last and with a little pin
Bores through his castle wall, and farewell king!

Richard II, Act 3, Scene 2

epitaphs: short statements in memory of people who have died, usually put on grave stones.

depos'd: removed from power.

antic: clown, jester.

infusing: i.e., filling.

impregnable: able to resist attack.

humour'd thus: having been amused (referring to Death).

FOR THOUGHT AND DISCUSSION

1. According to the passage, what are the various ways in which kings are "removed"? To what extent might this passage apply to modern heads of state?

2. What seems to be the speaker's attitude about "the death of kings"? How do his feelings differ from David's feelings after the deaths of Saul and Jonathan?

David: Young Champion of Israel

*This unit includes three episodes
from David's long and eventful life.
The first occurs while Saul is still king.*

David Is Anointed

The Lord said to Samuel, "How long will you grieve over Saul, seeing I have rejected him from being king over Israel? Fill your horn with oil, and go; I will send you to Jesse the Bethlehemite, for I have provided for myself a king among his sons." . . . Samuel did what the Lord commanded, and came to Bethlehem. . . . And he consecrated Jesse and his sons, and invited them to the sacrifice.

When they came, he looked on Eliab and thought, "Surely the Lord's anointed is before him." But the Lord said to Samuel, "Do not look on his appearance or on the height of his stature, because I have rejected him; for the Lord sees not as man sees; man looks on the outward appearance, but the Lord looks on the heart." Then Jesse called Abinadab, and made him pass before Samuel. And he said, "Neither has the Lord chosen this one." Then Jesse made Shammah pass by. And he said, "Neither has the Lord chosen this one." And Jesse made seven of his sons pass before Samuel. And Samuel said to Jesse, "The Lord has not chosen these." And Samuel said to Jesse, "Are all your sons here?" And he said, "There remains yet the youngest, but behold, he is keeping the sheep." And Samuel said to Jesse, "Send and fetch him; for we will not sit down till he comes here." And he sent, and brought him in. Now he was ruddy, and had beautiful eyes, and was handsome. And the Lord

horn: container made of an animal's horn.

consecrated: purified.

before him: i.e., this one.

ruddy: healthy in color; pink-cheeked.

I Samuel 16:1, 4, 5d–13; 17:1–9, 11a, 13a, 15–16a, 17–51 (Revised Standard Version).

said, "Arise, anoint him; for this is he." Then Samuel took the horn of oil, and anointed him in the midst of his brothers; and the spirit of the Lord came mightily upon David from that day forward. And Samuel rose up, and went to Ramah. . . .

David and Goliath

Now the Philistines gathered their armies for battle; and they were gathered at Socoh, which belongs to Judah, and encamped between Socoh and Azekah, in Ephes-dammim. And Saul and the men of Israel were gathered, and encamped in the valley of Elah, and drew up in line of battle against the Philistines. And the Philistines stood on the mountain on the one side, and Israel stood on the mountain on the other side, with a valley between them. And there came out from the camp of the Philistines a champion named Goliath, of Gath, whose height was six cubits and a span. He had a helmet of bronze on his head, and he was armed with a coat of mail, and the weight of the coat was five thousand shekels of bronze. And he had greaves of bronze upon his legs, and a javelin of bronze slung between his shoulders. And the shaft of his spear was like a weaver's beam, and his spear's head weighed six hundred shekels of iron; and his shield-bearer went before him. He stood and shouted to the ranks of Israel, "Why have you come out to draw up for battle? Am I not a Philistine, and are you not servants of Saul? Choose a man for yourselves, and let him come down to me. If he is able to fight with me and kill me, then we will be your servants; but if I prevail against him and kill him, then you shall be our servants and serve us." . . . When Saul and all Israel heard these words of the Philistine, they were dismayed and greatly afraid.

. . . The three eldest sons of Jesse had followed Saul to the battle . . . but David went back and forth from Saul to feed his father's sheep at Bethlehem. For forty days the Philistine came forward and took his stand, morning and evening.

And Jesse said to David his son, "Take for your brothers an ephah of this parched grain, and these ten loaves, and carry them quickly to the camp to your brothers; also take these ten cheeses to the commander of their thousand. See how your brothers fare, and bring some token from them."

Philistines: traditional enemies of the Israelites.

six cubits...span: Goliath is between nine and ten feet tall.

five thousand shekels: about one hundred sixty pounds.

greaves: leg guards.

weaver's beam: i.e., about three inches thick.

six hundred shekels: about twenty pounds.

prevail against: defeat.

ephah (ē′fə): about a bushel.

Now Saul, and they, and all the men of Israel, were in the valley of Elah, fighting with the Philistines. And David rose early in the morning, and left the sheep with a keeper, and took the provisions, and went, as Jesse had commanded him; and he came to the encampment as the host was going forth to the battle line, shouting the war cry. And Israel and the Philistines drew up for battle, army against army. And David left the things in charge of the keeper of the baggage, and ran to the ranks, and went and greeted his brothers. As he talked with them, behold, the champion, the Philistine of Gath, Goliath by name, came up out of the ranks of the Philistines, and spoke the same words as before. And David heard him.

All the men of Israel, when they saw the man, fled from him, and were much afraid. And the men of Israel said, "Have you seen this man who has come up? Surely he has come up to defy Israel; and the man who kills him, the king will enrich with great riches, and will give him his daughter, and make his father's

house free in Israel." And David said to the men who stood by him, "What shall be done for the man who kills this Philistine, and takes away the reproach from Israel? For who is this uncircumcised Philistine, that he should defy the armies of the living God?" And the people answered him in the same way, "So shall it be done to the man who kills him."

Now Eliab his eldest brother heard when he spoke to the men; and Eliab's anger was kindled against David, and he said, "Why have you come down? And with whom have you left those few sheep

in the wilderness? I know your presumption, and the evil of your heart; for you have come down to see the battle." And David said, "What have I done now? Was it not but a word?" And he turned away from him toward another, and spoke in the same way; and the people answered him again as before.

When the words which David spoke were heard, they repeated them before Saul; and he sent for him. And David said to Saul, "Let no man's heart fail

because of him; your servant will go and fight with this Philistine." And Saul said to David, "You are not able to go against this Philistine to fight with him; for you are but a youth, and he has been a man of war from his youth." But David said to Saul, "Your servant used to keep sheep for his father; and when there came a lion, or a bear, and took a lamb from the flock, I went after him and smote him and delivered it out of his mouth; and if he arose against me, I caught him by his beard, and smote him and killed him. Your servant has killed both lions and bears; and this uncircumcised Philistine shall be one of them, seeing he has defied the armies of the living God." And David said, "The Lord who delivered me from the paw of the lion and from the paw of the bear, will deliver me from the hand of this Philistine." And Saul said to David, "Go, and the Lord be with you!" Then Saul clothed David with his armor; he put a helmet of bronze on his head, and clothed him with a coat of mail. And David girded his sword over his armor, and he tried in vain to go, for he was not used to them. Then David said to Saul, "I cannot go with these; for I am not used to them." And David put them off. Then he took his staff in his hand, and chose five smooth stones from the brook, and put them in his shepherd's bag, in his wallet; his sling was in his hand, and he drew near to the Philistine.

smote: struck.

And the Philistine came on and drew near to David, with his shield-bearer in front of him. And when the Philistine looked, and saw David, he disdained him; for he was but a youth, ruddy and comely in appearance. And the Philistine said to David, "Am I a dog, that you come to me with sticks?" And the Philistine cursed David by his gods. The Philistine said to David, "Come to me, and I will give your flesh to the birds of the air and to the beasts of the field." Then David said to the Philistine, "You come to me with a sword and with a spear and with a javelin; but I come to you in the name of the Lord of hosts, the God of the armies of Israel, whom you have defied. This day the Lord will deliver you into my hand, and I will strike you down, and cut off your head; and I will give the dead bodies of the host of the Philistines this day to the birds of the air and to the wild beasts of the earth; that all the earth may know that there is a God in Israel, and that all this assembly may know that the Lord saves not with sword and spear; for the battle is the Lord's and he will give you into our hand."

sling: a weapon consisting of a pouch with two cords. It is whirled over the head to throw a stone with great force when one of the cords is released.

disdained: scorned.

comely: handsome.

When the Philistine arose and came and drew near to meet David, David ran quickly toward the battle line to meet the Philistine. And David put his hand in his bag and took out a stone, and slung it, and struck the Philistine on his forehead; the stone sank into his forehead, and he fell on his face to the ground.

So David prevailed over the Philistine with a sling and with a stone, and struck the Philistine, and killed him; there was no sword in the hand of David. Then David ran and stood over the Philistine, and took his sword and drew it out of its sheath, and killed him, and cut off his head with it. When the Philistines saw that their champion was dead, they fled.

FOR CLOSE READING

1. How many sons of Jesse does Samuel inspect before he discovers David?

2. Samuel is told that "the Lord sees not as man sees." How is this explained?

3. Why is David confident he can defeat Goliath?

4. Why does David decide not to wear Saul's armor?

5. What is Goliath's "outward appearance" before the combat? David's? List as many differences as you can between the two.

FOR THOUGHT AND DISCUSSION

6. In what ways do "outward appearances" reveal a person's character? In what ways do they mislead? Do you think it is ever possible for a person to "look on the heart" of another person, almost as the Lord does? Support your opinions with examples.

7. Descriptions of important characters in the Bible usually have few details. Goliath, by contrast, is described in specific detail. What dramatic effects result from this description?

8. What is your impression of David as a young man? Try to describe him in a single sentence.

9. The story of David and Goliath is one of the best-known Bible stories. What aspects of the story make it so appealing?

RESPONDING

1. Writing Describe the duel between David and Goliath from one of the following viewpoints: (*a*) one of David's brothers; (*b*) a Philistine soldier; (*c*) an Israelite soldier.

2. Writing David is one of several younger children in the Bible who is favored over older siblings. Based on your experiences and observations of family life, describe the advantages and disadvantages of being one of the following: (*a*) oldest; (*b*) youngest; (*c*) middle; (*d*) only child.

3. Activity Describe the "match" between David and Goliath as if you were a radio sports reporter. You may wish to record your broadcast, complete with crowd noise and other sound effects.

4. Humanities Connection David has been a favorite subject of artists and sculptors throughout history. Find as many portrayals of the young David as you can, select the one that most closely fits your impression of him, and say why you chose it.

After Goliath

The first shot out of that sling
Was enough to finish the thing:
The champion laid out cold
Before half the programs were sold.
5 And then, what howls of dismay
From his fans in their dense array:
From aldermen, adjutants, aunts,
Administrators of grants,
Assurance-men, auctioneers,
10 Advisers about careers,
And advertisers, of course,
Plus the obvious b——s in force—
The whole reprehensible throng
Ten times an alphabet strong.
15 But such an auspicious debut
Was a little too good to be true,
Our victor sensed; the applause
From those who supported his cause
Sounded shrill and excessive now,
20 And who were they, anyhow?
Academics, actors who lecture,
Apostles of architecture,
Ancient-gods-of-the-abdomen men,
Angst-pushers, adherents of Zen,
25 Alastors, austenites, A-test
Abolishers—even the straightest
Of issues looks pretty oblique
When a movement turns into a clique,
The conqueror mused, as he stopped
30 By the sword his opponent had dropped:
Trophy, or means of attack
On the rapturous crowd at his back?
He shrugged and left it, resigned
To a new battle, fought in the mind,
35 For faith that his quarrel was just,
That the right man lay in the dust.

array: formation.

adjutants: military administrative officers.

assurance: insurance.

reprehensible: deserving blame.

auspicious: favorable.

angst: anxiety.

alastors: avengers.

austenites: admirers of the novelist Jane Austen.

oblique (ə blēkʹ): not straightforward; unclear.

clique (klēk): a small, exclusive group.

ABOVE: *The Sorrows of the King*, cut-out gouache by Henri Matisse, 1952. Courtesy of the Musée National d'Art Moderne, Paris © SPADEM, Paris 1975.

BELOW: *David*, detail from marble statue by Michelangelo, 1501-1504. Scala Art Resource.

ABOVE: *Elijah and the Angel* by Giovanni Andrea Carlone, Assissi, Italy. Alinari/Regione Umbria/Art Resource.
RIGHT: *Jonah Cast Up*, marble, eastern Mediterranean, mid-third century. The Cleveland Museum of Art, John L. Severance Fund.
PAGE 200: *A Prophet* by Jan Provost. Museo del Prado, Madrid.

See "After Goliath" on page 196.

FOR THOUGHT AND DISCUSSION

1. Have you ever accomplished something or won a victory "too good to be true"? If so, how were you affected by that experience?

2. Amis has said that this poem "is something I had been trying to get said for a long time: that there is a disappointing lack of contrast between the enemies of progress . . . and those theoretically on the side of progress." How does the poem suggest "disappointment"? How does it suggest the "lack of contrast" between the two opposing groups?

3. What does David consider doing with Goliath's sword? Why do you think he does not do it?

David and Bathsheba

David has now been king for many years, has led his armies to many victories, and has greatly expanded his empire. He has established Jerusalem as his capital and built a palace there.

Joab (jō′ab): the commander of David's army.

In the spring of the year, the time when kings go forth to battle, David sent Joab, and his servants with him, and all Israel; and they ravaged the Ammonites, and besieged Rabbah. But David remained at Jerusalem.

It happened late one afternoon, when David arose from his couch and was walking upon the roof of the king's house, that he saw from the roof a woman bathing; and the woman was very beautiful. And David sent and inquired about the woman. And one said, "Is not this Bathsheba, the daughter of Eliam, the wife of Uriah the Hittite?" So David sent messengers, and took her; and she came to him, and he lay with her.... Then she returned to her house. And the woman conceived; and she sent and told David, "I am with child."

So David sent word to Joab, "Send me Uriah the Hittite." And Joab sent Uriah to David. When Uriah came to him, David asked how Joab was doing, and how the people fared, and how the war prospered. Then David said to Uriah, "Go down to your house, and wash your feet." And Uriah went out of the king's house, and there followed him a present from the king. But Uriah slept at the door of the king's house, with all the servants of his lord, and did not go down to his house. When they told David, "Uriah did not go down to his house," David said to Uriah, "Have you not come from a journey? Why did you

wash your feet: i.e., clean up after the trip.

2 Samuel 11:1–4b, 4d–11, 14–18, 23–27; 12:1–10, 13–15a (Revised Standard Version).

not go down to your house?" Uriah said to David, "The ark and Israel and Judah dwell in booths; and my lord Joab and the servants of my lord are camping in the open field; shall I then go to my house, to eat and to drink, and to lie with my wife? As you live, and as your soul lives, I will not do this thing.". . .

In the morning David wrote a letter to Joab, and sent it by the hand of Uriah. In the letter he wrote, "Set Uriah in the forefront of the hardest fighting, and then draw back from him, that he may be struck down, and die." And as Joab was besieging the city, he assigned Uriah to the place where he knew there were valiant men. And the men of the city came out and fought with Joab; and some of the servants of David among the people fell. Uriah the Hittite was slain also. Then Joab sent and told David all the news about the fighting . . . .

The messenger said to David, "The men gained an advantage over us, and came out against us in the field; but we drove them back to the entrance of the gate. Then the archers shot at your servants from the wall; some of the king's servants are dead; and your servant Uriah the Hittite is dead also." David said to the messenger, "Thus shall you say to Joab, 'Do not let this matter trouble you, for the sword devours now one and now another; strengthen your attack upon the city, and overthrow it.' And encourage him."

When the wife of Uriah heard that Uriah her husband was dead, she made lamentation for her husband. And when the mourning was over, David sent and brought her to his house, and she became his wife, and bore him a son. But the thing that David had done displeased the Lord.

And the Lord sent Nathan to David. He came to him, and said to him, "There were two men in a certain city, the one rich and the other poor. The rich man had very many flocks and herds; but the poor man had nothing but one little ewe lamb, which he had bought. And he brought it up, and it grew up with him and with his children; it used to eat of his morsel, and drink from his cup, and lie in his bosom, and it was like a daughter to him. Now there came a traveler to the rich man, and he was unwilling to take one of his own flock or herd to prepare for the

ark: the Ark of the Covenant, the sacred chest probably containing the tablets of the law given to Moses. The ark was regarded as the seat on which God sat invisibly enthroned.

booths: temporary shelters on the battlefield.

valiant: brave.

devours: i.e., kills.

Nathan: a prophet.

ewe: female.

morsel: bit of food.

wayfarer who had come to him, but he took the poor man's lamb, and prepared it for the man who had come to him." Then David's anger was greatly kindled against the man; and he said to Nathan, "As the Lord lives, the man who has done this deserves to die; and he shall restore the lamb fourfold, because he did this thing, and because he had no pity."

Nathan said to David, "You are the man. Thus says the Lord, the God of Israel, 'I anointed you king over Israel, and I delivered you out of the hand of Saul; and I gave you your master's house, and your master's wives into your bosom, and gave you the house of Israel and of Judah; and if this were too little, I would add to you as much more. Why have you despised the word of the Lord, to do what is evil in his sight?

You have smitten Uriah the Hittite with the sword, and have taken his wife to be your wife, and have slain him with the sword of the Ammonites.

Now therefore the sword shall never depart from your house, because you have despised me, and have taken the wife of Uriah the Hittite to be your wife.'. . . 'Behold, I will raise up evil against you out of your own house. . . .'" David said to Nathan, "I have sinned against the Lord." And Nathan said to David, "The Lord also has put away your sin; you shall not die. Nevertheless, because by this deed you have utterly scorned the Lord, the child that is born to you shall die." Then Nathan went to his house.

FOR CLOSE READING

1. How many occasions can you find where David "sent" some person or some message?

2. What reason does Uriah give for not returning to his home?

3. How does David respond when he learns of Uriah's death?

FOR THOUGHT AND DISCUSSION

4. How does the David portrayed in this story compare with the David who fought Goliath? In what ways has he changed? How would you account for the changes?

5. What differences in character and actions do you see between David and Uriah? What hints are there in the story that prepare us for the statement that the Lord is displeased?

6. Why do you suppose Nathan begins with a story rather than a direct accusation of David?

7. Given David's early career, why is it significant that Nathan speaks of a cherished lamb? What other details of Nathan's parable apply to David's actions?

8. Compare the sins of Saul and David. Compare their punishments. Why do you think David's life and throne are spared and Saul's are not?

RESPONDING

1. Writing You are Bathsheba. What are your thoughts after learning of Uriah's death? Do you suspect that anyone is responsible?

2. Writing From history or current events, choose a person that you feel has been guilty of some wrong. Using Nathan's parable as a model, write a brief story that will indirectly accuse that person of the wrong.

The Rebellion of Absalom

Now an old man, David is challenged by his ambitious son.

Now in all Israel there was no one so much to be praised for his beauty as Absalom; from the sole of his foot to the crown of his head there was no blemish in him. And when he cut the hair of his head (for at the end of every year he used to cut it; when it was heavy on him, he cut it), he weighed the hair of his head, two hundred shekels by the king's weight. . . .

two hundred shekels: about five pounds.

After this Absalom got himself a chariot and horses, and fifty men to run before him. And Absalom used to rise early and stand beside the way of the gate; and when any man had a suit to come before the king for judgment, Absalom would call to him, and say, "From what city are you?" And when he said, "Your servant is of such and such a tribe in Israel," Absalom would say to him, "See, your claims are good and right; but there is no man deputed by the king to hear you." Absalom said moreover, "Oh that I were judge in the land! Then every man with a suit or cause might come to me, and I would give him justice." And whenever a man came near to do obeisance, to him, he would put out his hand, and take hold of him, and kiss him. Thus Absalom did to all of Israel who came to the king for judgment; so Absalom stole the hearts of the men of Israel.

a suit to come: a case to bring.

deputed: appointed.

And at the end of four years Absalom said to the king, "Pray let me go and pay my vow, which I have vowed to the Lord, in Hebron. For your servant vowed a vow while I dwelt at Geshur in Aram,

Hebron (hē′brən): David's capital city before he moved to Jerusalem. Absalom was born there.

2 Samuel 14:25–27; 15:1–16a, 23; 18:1–5, 9–15, 31–33 (Revised Standard Version).

saying, 'If the Lord will indeed bring me back to Jerusalem, then I will offer worship to the Lord.'" The king said to him, "Go in peace." So he arose, and went to Hebron. But Absalom sent secret messengers throughout all the tribes of Israel saying, "As soon as you hear the sound of the trumpet, then say, 'Absalom is king at Hebron!'" With Absalom went two hundred men from Jerusalem who were invited guests, and they went in their simplicity, and knew nothing. And while Absalom was offering the sacrifices, he sent for Ahithophel the Gilonite, David's counselor, from his city Giloh. And the conspiracy grew strong, and the people with Absalom kept increasing.

And a messenger came to David, saying, "The hearts of the men of Israel have gone after Absalom." Then David said to all his servants who were with him at Jerusalem, "Arise, and let us flee; or else there will be no escape for us from Absalom; go in haste, lest he overtake us quickly, and bring down evil upon us, and smite the city with the edge of the sword." And the king's servants said to the king, "Behold, your servants are ready to do whatever my lord the king decides." So the king went forth, and all his household after him. . . .

And all the country wept aloud as all the people passed by, and the king crossed the brook Kidron, and all the people passed on toward the wilderness. . . .

brook Kidron (kē′drən): the city boundary.

Then David mustered the men who were with him, and set over them commanders of thousands and commanders of hundreds. And David sent forth the army, one third under the command of Joab, one third under the command of Abishai the son of Zeruiah, Joab's brother, and one third under the command of Ittai the Gittite. And the king said to the men, "I myself will also go out with you." But the men said, "You shall not go out. For if we flee, they will not care about us. If half of us die, they will not care about us. But you are worth ten thousand of us; therefore it is better that you send us help from the city." The king said to them, "Whatever seems best to you I will do." So the king stood at the side of the gate, while all the army marched out by hundreds and by thousands. And the king ordered Joab and

mustered: assembled.

the city: David's headquarters, located east of the Jordan River.

Abishai and Ittai, "Deal gently for my sake with the young man Absalom." And all the people heard when the king gave orders to all the commanders about Absalom. . . .

And Absalom chanced to meet the servants of David. Absalom was riding upon his mule, and the mule went under the thick branches of a great oak, and his **head** caught fast in the oak, and he was left hanging between heaven and earth, while the mule that was under him went on. And a certain man saw it, and told Joab, "Behold, I saw Absalom hanging in an oak." Joab said to the man who told him, "What, you saw him! Why then did you not strike him there to the ground? I would have been glad to give you ten pieces of silver and a **girdle**." But the man said to Joab, "Even if I felt in my hand the weight of a thousand pieces of silver, I would not put forth my hand against the king's son; for in our hearing the king commanded you and Abishai and Ittai, 'For my sake protect the young man Absalom.' On the other hand, if I had dealt treacherously against his life (and there is nothing hidden from the king), then you yourself would have **stood aloof**." Joab said, "I will not waste time like this with you." And he took three darts in his hand, and thrust them into the heart of Absalom, while he was still alive in the oak. And ten young men, Joab's armor-bearers, surrounded Absalom and struck him, and killed him. . . .

And behold, the **Cushite** came; and the Cushite said, "Good tidings for my lord the king! For the Lord has delivered you this day from the power of all who rose up against you." The king said to the Cushite, "Is it well with the young man Absalom?" And the Cushite answered, "May the enemies of my lord the king, and all who rise up against you for evil, be like that young man." And the king was deeply moved, and went up to the **chamber** over the gate, and wept; and as he went, he said, "O my son Absalom, my son, my son Absalom! Would I had died instead of you, O Absalom, my son, my son!"

head: some translations say "hair."

girdle: belt.

stood aloof: kept out of it.

Cushite: Ethiopian servant.

chamber: room.

FOR CLOSE READING

1. How does Absalom go about gaining power for himself?

2. What instructions does David give his generals before the battle against the rebels?

3. How is Absalom caught and killed?

FOR THOUGHT AND DISCUSSION

4. Whose story is being told in this passage: David's or Absalom's? How does Absalom compare with the young David portrayed earlier—in appearance? in character?

5. Why do you think Joab insists on killing Absalom? What does the conversation between Joab and his soldier reveal about the relation between officers and common soldiers?

6. The three David stories in this unit give radically different pictures of the man at crucial moments of his life. Which story did you find most appealing? most moving? Why?

7. Compare David's public life as soldier and king with his personal life. What differences do you find? How does the Absalom episode fit into both areas of David's life?

RESPONDING

1. Writing You are David near the end of your long life. An interviewer asks what you think was the turning point of your life. What is your answer and explanation?

2. Activity Sketch or paint a portrait of Absalom.

6

God's Prophets

Elijah:
The Only One Left

Approximately forty years after the death of David, the nation of Israel was divided. The Northern Kingdom retained the name Israel; the Southern Kingdom, ruled by descendants of David, was called Judah. The rulers of the two kingdoms often "did evil in the sight of the Lord," which led to greater activity by a series of prophets—people who spoke for God.

Elijah was a prophet in the Northern Kingdom during the reign of Ahab, a king who was strongly influenced by his foreign wife, Jezebel. Ahab angered the Lord by introducing the worship of Baal (bā'əl), a Canaanite god of storm and rain.

Fed by Ravens

Now Elijah the Tishbite, of Tishbe in Gilead, said to Ahab, "As the Lord the God of Israel lives, before whom I stand, there shall be neither dew nor rain these years, except by my word." The word of the Lord came to him, saying, "Go from here and turn eastward, and hide yourself by the Wadi Cherith, which is east of the Jordan. You shall drink from the wadi, and I have commanded the ravens to feed you there." So he went and did according to the word of the Lord; he went and lived by the Wadi Cherith, which is east of the Jordan. The ravens brought him bread and meat in the morning, and bread and meat in the evening; and he drank from the wadi. But after a while the wadi dried up, because there was no rain in the land.

Gilead (gil'ē əd): region east of the Jordan River.

him: Elijah.
wadi (wä'dē): a stream bed that has flowing water only during the rainy season.

---

1 Kings 17:1–24; 18:1–2, 17–46; 19:1–18; 21:1–11, 15–24 (New Revised Standard Version).
LEFT: Marble bust of a prophet by Giovanni Pisano. Museo Civico, Pisa.

The Widow and Her Son

Then the word of the Lord came to him, saying, "Go now to Zarephath, which belongs to Sidon, and live there; for I have commanded a widow there to feed you." So he set out and went to Zarephath. When he came to the gate of the town, a widow was there gathering sticks; he called to her and said, "Bring me a little water in a vessel, so that I may drink." As she was going to bring it, he called to her and said, "Bring me a morsel of bread in your hand." But she said, "As the Lord your God lives, I have nothing baked, only a handful of meal in a jar, and a little oil in a jug; I am now gathering a couple of sticks, so that I may go home and prepare it for myself and my son, that we may eat it, and die." Elijah said to her, "Do not be afraid; go and do as you have said; but first make me a little cake of it and bring it to me, and afterwards make something for yourself and your son. For thus says the Lord the God of Israel: The jar of meal will not be emptied and the jug of oil will not fail until the day that the Lord sends rain on the earth." She went and did as Elijah said, so that she as well as he and her household ate for many days. The jar of meal was not emptied, neither did the jug of oil fail, according to the word of the Lord that he spoke by Elijah.

meal: coarsely ground grain.

After this the son of the woman, the mistress of the house, became ill; his illness was so severe that there was no breath left in him. She then said to Elijah, "What have you against me, O man of God? You have come to me to bring my sin to remembrance, and to cause the death of my son!" But he said to her, "Give me your son." He took him from her bosom, carried him up into the upper chamber where he was lodging, and laid him on his own bed. He cried out to the Lord, "O Lord my God, have you brought calamity even upon the widow with whom I am staying, by killing her son?" Then he stretched himself upon the child three times, and cried out to the Lord, "O Lord my God, let this child's life come into him again." The Lord listened to the voice of Elijah; the life of the child came into him again, and he revived. Elijah took the child, brought him down from the upper chamber into the house, and gave him to his mother; then Elijah said, "See, your son is alive." So the woman said to Elijah, "Now I know that you are a man of God, and that the word of the Lord in your mouth is truth." . . .

The Contest on Mount Carmel

After many days the word of the Lord came to Elijah, in the third year of the drought, saying, "Go, present yourself to Ahab; I will send rain on the earth." So Elijah went to present himself to Ahab. The famine was severe in Samaria. . . .

When Ahab saw Elijah, Ahab said to him, "Is it you, the troubler of Israel?" He answered, "I have not troubled Israel; but you have, and your father's house, because you have forsaken the commandments of the Lord and followed the Baals. Now therefore have all Israel assemble for me at Mount Carmel, with the four hundred fifty prophets of Baal and the four hundred prophets of Asherah, who eat at Jezebel's table."

So Ahab sent to all the Israelites, and assembled the prophets at Mount Carmel. Elijah then came near to all the people, and said, "How long will you go limping with two different opinions? If the Lord is God, follow him; but if Baal, then follow him." The people did not answer him a word. Then Elijah said to the people, "I, even I only, am left a prophet of the Lord; but Baal's prophets number four hundred fifty. Let two bulls be given to us; let them choose one bull for themselves, cut it in pieces, and lay it on the wood, but put no fire to it; I will prepare the other bull and lay it on the wood, but put no fire to it. Then you call on the name of your god and I will call on the name of the Lord; the god who answers by fire is indeed God." All the people answered, "Well spoken!" Then Elijah said to the prophets of Baal, "Choose for yourselves one bull and prepare it first, for you are many; then call on the name of your god, but put no fire to it." So they took the bull that was given them, prepared it, and called on the name of Baal from morning until noon, crying, "O Baal, answer us!" But there was no voice, and no answer. They limped about the altar that they had made. At noon Elijah mocked them, saying, "Cry aloud! Surely he is a god; either he is meditating, or he has wandered away, or he is on a journey, or perhaps he is asleep and must

Samaria: the capital city of the Northern Kingdom.

Baals: Baal (bā′əl) was a Canaanite god of storm and rain.

Asherah (ə shir′ə): a goddess associated with the worship of Baal.

be awakened." Then they cried aloud and, as was their custom, they cut themselves with swords and lances until the blood gushed out over them. As midday passed, they raved on until the time of the offering of the oblation, but there was no voice, no answer, and no response.

Then Elijah said to all the people, "Come closer to me"; and all the people came closer to him. First he repaired the altar of the Lord that had been thrown down; Elijah took twelve stones, according to the number of the tribes of the sons of Jacob, to whom the word of the Lord came, saying, "Israel shall be your name"; with the stones he built an altar in the name of the Lord. Then he made a trench around the altar, large enough to contain two measures of seed. Next he put the wood in order, cut the bull in pieces, and laid it on the wood. He said, "Fill four jars with water and pour it on the burnt offering and on the wood." Then he said, "Do it a second time"; and they did it a second time. Again he said, "Do it a third time"; and they did it a third time, so that the water ran all around the altar, and filled the trench also with water.

At the time of the offering of the oblation, the prophet Elijah came near and said, "O Lord, God of Abraham, Isaac, and Israel, let it be known this day that you are God in Israel, that I am your servant, and that I have done all these things at your bidding. Answer me, O Lord, answer me, so that this people may know that you, O Lord, are God, and that you have turned their hearts back." Then the fire of the Lord fell and consumed the burnt offering, the wood, the stones, and the dust, and even licked up the water that was in the trench. When all the people saw it, they fell on their faces and said, "The Lord indeed is God; the Lord indeed is God." Elijah said to them, "Seize the prophets of Baal; do not let one of them escape." Then they seized them; and Elijah brought them down to the Wadi Kishon, and killed them there.

Elijah said to Ahab, "Go up, eat and drink; for there is a sound of rushing rain." So Ahab went up to eat and to drink. Elijah went up to the top of Carmel; there he bowed himself down upon the earth and put his face between his knees. He said to his servant, "Go up now, look toward the sea." He went up and

---

raved: shouted wildly.

offering . . . oblation: i.e., the midafternoon sacrifice.

looked, and said, "There is nothing." Then he said, "Go again seven times." At the seventh time he said, "Look, a little cloud no bigger than a person's hand is rising out of the sea." Then he said, "Go say to Ahab, 'Harness your chariot and go down before the rain stops you.'" In a little while the heavens grew black with clouds and wind; there was a heavy rain. Ahab rode off and went to Jezreel. But the hand of the Lord was on Elijah; he girded up his loins and ran in front of Ahab to the entrance of Jezreel.

Jezreel: Ahab's summer home.

girded up his loins: fastened his belt; got ready for action.

"I Alone Am Left"

Ahab told Jezebel all that Elijah had done, and how he had killed all the prophets with the sword. Then Jezebel sent a messenger to Elijah, saying, "So may the gods do to me, and more also, if I do not make your life like the life of one of them by this time tomorrow." Then he was afraid; he got up and fled for his life, and came to Beer-sheba, which belongs to Judah; he left his servant there.

But he himself went a day's journey into the wilderness, and came and sat down under a solitary broom tree. He asked that he might die: "It is enough; now, O Lord, take away my life, for I am no better than my ancestors." Then he lay down under the broom tree and fell asleep. Suddenly an angel touched him and said to him, "Get up and eat." He looked, and there at his head was a cake baked on hot stones, and a jar of water. He ate and drank, and lay down again. The angel of the Lord came a second time, touched him and said, "Get up and eat, otherwise the journey will be too much for you." He got up, and ate and drank; then he went in the strength of that food forty days and forty nights to Horeb the mount of God. At that place he came to a cave, and spent the night there.

Horeb: also, Mount Sinai, on which Moses received the commandments.

Then the word of the Lord came to him, saying, "What are you doing here, Elijah?" He answered, "I have been very zealous for the Lord, the God of hosts; for the Israelites have forsaken your covenant, thrown down your altars, and killed your prophets with the sword. I alone am left, and they are seeking my life, to take it away."

covenant: agreement.

He said, "Go out and stand on the mountain before the Lord, for the Lord is about to pass by."

Now there was a great wind, so strong that it was splitting mountains and breaking rocks in pieces before the Lord, but the Lord was not in the wind; and after the wind an earthquake, but the Lord was not in the earthquake; and after the earthquake a fire, but the Lord was not in the fire; and after the fire a sound of sheer silence. When Elijah heard it, he wrapped his face in his mantle and went out and stood at the entrance of the cave. Then there came a voice to him that said, "What are you doing here, Elijah?" He answered, "I have been very zealous for the Lord, the God of hosts; for the Israelites have forsaken your covenant, thrown down your altars, and killed your prophets with the sword. I alone am left, and they are seeking my life, to take it away." Then the Lord said to him, "Go, return on your way to the wilderness of Damascus; when you arrive, you shall anoint Hazael as king over Aram. Also you shall anoint Jehu son of Nimshi as king over Israel; and you shall anoint Elisha son of Shaphat of Abel-meholah as prophet in your place. Whoever escapes from the sword of Hazael, Jehu shall kill; and whoever escapes from the sword of Jehu, Elisha shall kill. Yet I will leave seven thousand in Israel, all the knees that have not bowed to Baal, and every mouth that has not kissed him.". . .

Naboth's Vineyard

Later the following events took place: Naboth the Jezreelite had a vineyard in Jezreel, beside the palace of King Ahab of Samaria. And Ahab said to Naboth, "Give me your vineyard, so that I may have it for a vegetable garden, because it is near my house; I will give you a better vineyard for it; or, if it seems good to you, I will give you its value in money." But Naboth said to Ahab, "The Lord forbid that I should give you my ancestral inheritance." Ahab went home resentful and sullen because of what Naboth the Jezreelite had said to him; for he had said, "I will not give you my ancestral inheritance." He lay down on his bed, turned away his face, and would not eat.

His wife Jezebel came to him and said, "Why are you so depressed that you will not eat?" He said to her, "Because I spoke to Naboth the Jezreelite and said to him, 'Give me your vineyard for money; or else, if you prefer, I will give you another vineyard for it'; but he answered, 'I will not give you my vineyard.'" His wife Jezebel said to him, "Do you now govern Israel? Get up, eat some food, and be cheerful; I will give you the vineyard of Naboth the Jezreelite."

So she wrote letters in Ahab's name and sealed them with his seal; she sent the letters to the elders and the nobles who lived with Naboth in his city. She wrote in the letters, "Proclaim a fast, and seat Naboth at the head of the assembly; seat two scoundrels opposite him, and have them bring a charge against him, saying, 'You have cursed God and the king.' Then take him out, and stone him to death." The men of his city, the elders and the nobles who lived in his city, did as Jezebel had sent word to them. . . .

two scoundrels: by law, two witnesses were needed to prove an accusation.

As soon as Jezebel heard that Naboth had been stoned and was dead, Jezebel said to Ahab, "Go, take possession of the vineyard of Naboth the Jezreelite, which he refused to give you for money; for Naboth is not alive, but dead." As soon as Ahab heard that Naboth was dead, Ahab set out to go down to the vineyard of Naboth the Jezreelite, to take possession of it.

Then the word of the Lord came to Elijah the Tishbite, saying: Go down to meet King Ahab of Israel, who rules in Samaria; he is now in the vineyard of Naboth, where he has gone to take possession. You shall say to him, "Thus says the Lord: Have you killed, and also taken possession?" You shall say to him, "Thus says the Lord: In the place where dogs licked up the blood of Naboth, dogs will also lick up your blood."

Ahab said to Elijah, "Have you found me, O my enemy?" He answered, "I have found you. Because you have sold yourself to do what is evil in the sight of the Lord, I will bring disaster on you; I will consume you, and will cut off from Ahab every male, bond or free, in Israel; and I will make your house like the house of Jeroboam son of Nebat, and like the house of Baasha son of Ahijah, because you have provoked me to anger and have caused Israel to sin. Also concerning Jezebel the Lord said, 'The dogs shall eat Jezebel within the bounds of Jezreel.' Anyone belonging to Ahab who dies in the city the dogs shall eat; and anyone of his who dies in the open country the birds of the air shall eat."

Jeroboam . . . Baasha: former kings of Israel whose families had been destroyed by prophet-led revolutions.

FOR CLOSE READING

1. How many journeys does Elijah make? from where to where?

2. In their contest with Elijah, how do the prophets of Baal appeal to their god? How does Elijah make the Lord's demonstration of power more dramatic?

3. List the miracles that Elijah performs through the power of the Lord. How do the people who witness or benefit from these miracles respond to them?

4. How does Ahab get the vineyard of Naboth?

FOR THOUGHT AND DISCUSSION

5. Consider Elijah's experiences on Mount Carmel (the contest with the prophets of Baal) and his experiences on Mount Horeb (in the cave). On both occasions Elijah states that he is the only one left. Compare and contrast his feelings in the two situations.

6. The Lord responds to Elijah both on Mount Carmel and on Mount Horeb. How does the story in each case "build up" to this moment? In your opinion, which response is more dramatic? Why?

7. Would you say that Elijah's low spirits on Mount Horeb are caused mainly by: (*a*) Fear for his life? (*b*) A sense of personal failure? (*c*) Disappointment that Israel has forsaken the Lord? (*d*) Another reason? Support your choice with details from the story.

8. What does the episode of Naboth's vineyard reveal about Ahab's character? about Jezebel's?

9. The hero of Henrik Ibsen's play *The Enemy of the People* states: "The strongest man in the world is he who stands most alone." Think of people who have stood alone. How do their actions support or contradict this statement?

RESPONDING

1. **Writing** You are Jezebel. Write an entry in your diary that expresses your feelings about Elijah and your husband after the episode of Naboth's vineyard.

2. **Activity** Depict the contest between Elijah and the prophets of Baal in some form of art.

Amos: Let Justice Roll Down

A migrant worker, harvesting or herding from place to place, Amos spoke out in the Northern Kingdom approximately a century after Elijah. For the rich in Israel, this was a time of peace and prosperity; for the poor, it was a time of hardship.

In the passage below, Amos begins by telling his audience in Israel how their enemies have sinned—the Syrians (whose capital is Damascus) to the northeast, the Ammonites and the Moabites to the south and east. As a climax Amos shocks the people of Israel with their own injustices to the poor.

Tekoa (tǝko′ǝ): city in Judah. Amos was born in the Southern Kingdom.

The words of Amos, who was among the shepherds of Tekoa, which he saw concerning Israel in the days of King Uzziah of Judah and in the days of King Jeroboam son of Joash of Israel, two years before the earthquake.

And he said:

Zion: hill in Jerusalem on which the temple of the Lord stood.

The Lord roars from Zion,
    and utters his voice from Jerusalem;
the pastures of the shepherds wither,
    and the top of Carmel dries up.

Thus says the Lord:

transgressions: sins.
revoke: cancel, take back.
threshed . . . iron: this may refer to a means of executing prisoners by running horse-drawn sledges over them.

For three transgressions of Damascus,
    and for four, I will not revoke the punishment."
because they have threshed Gilead
    with threshing sledges of iron.
So I will send a fire on the house of Hazael,
    and it shall devour the strongholds of Ben-hadad.

Amos 1:1–5, 13–15; 2:1–3, 6–7, 13, 15–16; 5:18–24; 7:10–15; 3:3–8 (New Revised Standard Version).

I will break the gate bars of Damascus,
  and cut off the inhabitants from the Valley of Aven,
and the one who holds the scepter from Beth-eden;
  and the people of Aram shall go into exile to Kir,
                    says the Lord. . . .

bars: the great beams that hold shut the city gate.

holds the scepter: rules.

Thus says the Lord:
For three transgressions of the Ammonites,
  and for four, I will not revoke the punishment;
because they have ripped open pregnant women in
    Gilead
  in order to enlarge their territory.
So I will kindle a fire against the wall of Rabbah,
  fire that shall devour its strongholds,
with shouting on the day of the battle,
  with a storm on the day of the whirlwind;
then their king shall go into exile,
  he and his officials together,
                    says the Lord. . . .

Thus says the Lord:
For three transgressions of Moab,
  and for four, I will not revoke the punishment;
because he burned to lime
  the bones of the king of Edom.
So I will send a fire on Moab,
  and it shall devour the strongholds of Kerioth,
and Moab shall die amid uproar,
  amid shouting and the sound of the trumpet;
I will cut off the ruler from its midst,
  and will kill all its officials with him,
                    says the Lord. . . .

he: i.e., the kingdom of Moab.

burned . . . bones: it was a great sin not to give a body proper burial.

Thus says the Lord:
For three transgressions of Israel,
  and for four, I will not revoke the punishment;
because they sell the righteous for silver,
  and the needy for a pair of sandals—
they who trample the head of the poor into the
    dust of the earth,
  and push the afflicted out of the way; . . .
So, I will press you down in your place,
  just as a cart presses down when it is full of
    sheaves. . . .

those who handle the bow shall not stand,
and those who are swift of foot shall not save
themselves,
nor shall those who ride horses save their lives;
and those who are stout of heart among the mighty
shall flee away naked in that day,
says the Lord. . . .

day of the Lord: the annual festival in which the people of Israel anticipate the time when God would establish his world-wide rule by defeating their enemies. The Israelites believed it would be a time of rejoicing for them; Amos disagrees.

Alas for you who desire the day of the Lord!
Why do you want the day of the Lord?
It is darkness, not light;
as if someone had fled from a lion,
and was met by a bear;
or went into the house and rested a hand against
the wall,
and was bitten by a snake.
Is not the day of the Lord darkness, not light,
and gloom with no brightness in it?

I hate, I despise your festivals,
and I take no delight in your solemn assemblies.
Even though you offer me your burnt offerings and
grain offerings,
I will not accept them;

fatted: fattened.

and the offerings of well-being of your fatted
animals
I will not look upon.
Take away from me the noise of your songs;
I will not listen to the melody of your harps.

justice: social justice.

But let justice roll down like waters,
and righteousness like an everflowing stream. . . .

Then Amaziah, the priest of Bethel, sent to King Jeroboam of Israel, saying, "Amos has conspired against you in the very center of the house of Israel; the land is not able to bear all his words. For thus Amos has said,

'Jeroboam shall die by the sword,
and Israel must go into exile
away from this land.'"

seer: prophet.

And Amaziah said to Amos, "O seer, go, flee away to the land of Judah, earn your bread there, and prophesy there; but never again prophesy at Bethel, for it is the king's sanctuary, and it is a temple of the kingdom."

Then Amos answered Amaziah, "I am no prophet, nor a prophet's son; but I am a herdsman, and a dresser of sycamore trees, and the Lord took me from following the flock, and the Lord said to me, 'Go, prophesy to my people Israel.'". . .

> Do two walk together
> unless they have made an appointment?
> Does a lion roar in the forest,
> when it has no prey?
> Does a young lion cry out from its den,
> if it has caught nothing?
> Does a bird fall into a snare on the earth,
> when there is no trap for it?
> Does a snare spring up from the ground,
> when it has taken nothing?
> Is a trumpet blown in a city,
> and the people are not afraid?
> Does disaster befall a city,
> unless the Lord has done it?
> Surely the Lord God does nothing,
> without revealing his secret
> to his servants the prophets.
> The lion has roared;
> who will not fear?
> The Lord God has spoken;
> who can but prophesy?

dresser . . . trees: in the Middle East the sycamore is a type of fig tree. Amos tended the blossoms so that the figs could ripen properly.

taken: caught.

FOR CLOSE READING

1. What four countries are condemned in this passage? What differences do you find between the offenses of Israel and the offenses of the first three countries?

2. What country is Amos from? What country does he mainly speak against? What is his occupation?

3. How do the people in power respond to Amos's message? Where is this shown?

FOR THOUGHT AND DISCUSSION

4. In his "transgressions" prophecies, how does Amos emphasize and dramatize his message? Why do you think he begins by accusing Israel's enemies?

5. For what reasons might people in Israel be likely to object to Amos as a prophet?

6. In what ways might Amos's way of making a living have influenced his prophetic message?

7. What do you think Amos means when he says he is "no prophet"?

RESPONDING

1. Writing Using Amos's pattern ("For three transgressions of . . .") write a statement against some injustice you see in today's world.

2. Writing Choose a recent or current public figure whom you regard as a modern Amos. In a brief essay, compare this person with Amos.

3. Activity Collect photographs from newspapers and magazines to create a collage, a scrapbook, or a poster that will illustrate your views on a modern injustice.

4. Multicultural Connection A Turkish proverb says "He who tells the truth should have one foot in the stirrup." Make a collection of proverbs and sayings from other countries about truth telling and truth tellers. Which of them seem to apply to Amos's experiences? Prepare a brief report for your classmates.

5. Humanities Connection Prepare a brief report (illustrated with photographs from newspapers or magazines) showing how Amos's words "let justice roll down like waters" are used in Maya Lin's Civil Rights Memorial in Montgomery, Alabama.

Prophets for a New Day

1.

As the Word came to prophets of old,
As the burning bush spoke to Moses,
And the fiery coals cleansed the lips of Isaiah;
As the wheeling cloud in the sky
5   Clothed the message of Ezekiel;
So the Word of fire burns today
On the lips of our prophets in an evil age——
Our sooth-sayers and doom-tellers and doers
   of the Word.
So the Word of the Lord stirs again
10   These passionate people toward deliverance.
As Amos, Shepherd of Tekoa, spoke
To the captive children of Judah,
Preaching to the dispossessed and the poor,
So today in the pulpits and the jails,
15   On the highways and in the byways,
A fearless shepherd speaks at last
To his suffering weary sheep.

soothsayers: people who foretell the future.

dispossessed: people who have lost their home or land.

2.

So, kneeling by the river bank
Comes the vision to a valley of believers
20   So in flaming flags of stars in the sky
And in the breaking dawn of a blinding sun
The lamp of truth is lighted in the Temple
And the oil of devotion is burning at midnight
So the glittering censer in the Temple
25   Trembles in the presence of the priests
And the pillars of the doorposts move
And the incense rises in smoke

censer: container in which incense is burned.

And the dark faces of the sufferers
Gleam in the new morning
30   The complaining faces glow
And the winds of freedom begin to blow
While the Word descends on the waiting
    World below.

3.

A beast is among us.
His mark is on the land.
35   His horns and his hands and his lips are gory
    with our blood.

pestilence: disease.   He is War and Famine and Pestilence
He is Death and Destruction and Trouble
And he walks in our houses at noonday
And devours our defenders at midnight.
40   He is the demon who drives us with whips of fear
And in his cowardice
He cries out against liberty
He cries out against humanity
Against all dignity of green valleys and high hills
45   Against clean winds blowing through our living;
Against the broken bodies of our brothers.
He has crushed them with a stone.
He drinks our tears for water
And he drinks our blood for wine;

ravenous: intensely 50   He eats our flesh like a ravenous lion
hungry.   And he drives us out of the city
to be stabbed on a lonely hill.

FOR THOUGHT AND DISCUSSION

1. In a poem filled with biblical references and images, what lines suggest modern times?

2. In the Bible prophets frequently brought bad news to their people. What kind of news is being prophesied here?

3. The "beast among us" is given many names. Sum up the meaning of the beast in a single sentence and explain your choice of words.

4. According to the poem, what kind of people are the "prophets for a new day"?

5. Whom would you classify as a prophet in today's world? Why?

6. Sum up the three parts of the poem in one sentence each. How does the tone or feeling of the last section differ from the rest of the poem?

Jonah:
A Reluctant Prophet

Nineveh (nin′ə və): the capital of one of Israel's most hated enemies, this city was a symbol of cruelty and violence.

Joppa: modern Jaffa, on the eastern edge of the Mediterranean.

Tarshish: perhaps located on the southern coast of Spain, on the outer edge of the then-known world.

cast lots: i.e., choose by chance (probably using marked stones).

Now the word of the Lord came to Jonah son of Amittai, saying, "Go at once to Nineveh, that great city, and cry out against it; for their wickedness has come up before me." But Jonah set out to flee to Tarshish from the presence of the Lord. He went down to Joppa and found a ship going to Tarshish; so he paid his fare and went on board, to go with them to Tarshish, away from the presence of the Lord.

But the Lord hurled a great wind upon the sea, and such a mighty storm came upon the sea that the ship threatened to break up. Then the mariners were afraid, and each cried to his god. They threw the cargo that was in the ship into the sea, to lighten it for them. Jonah, meanwhile, had gone down into the hold of the ship and had lain down and was fast asleep. The captain came and said to him, "What are you doing sound asleep? Get up, call on your god! Perhaps the god will spare us a thought so that we do not perish."

The sailors said to one another, "Come, let us cast lots, so that we may know on whose account this calamity has come upon us." So they cast lots, and the lot fell on Jonah. Then they said to him, "Tell us why this calamity has come upon us. What is your occupation? Where do you come from? What is your country? And of what people are you?" "I am a Hebrew," he replied. "I worship the Lord, the God of heaven, who made the sea and the dry land." Then the men were even more afraid, and said to him, "What is this that you have done!" For the men knew that he was fleeing from the presence of the Lord, because he had told them so.

Jonah 1:1–2:6, 10; 3:1–4:11 (New Revised Standard Version).

Then they said to him, "What shall we do to you, that the sea may quiet down for us?" For the sea was growing more and more tempestuous. He said to them, "Pick me up and throw me into the sea; then the sea will quiet down for you; for I know it is because of me that this great storm has come upon you." Nevertheless the men rowed hard to bring the ship back to land, but they could not, for the sea grew more and more stormy against them. Then they cried out to the Lord, "Please, O Lord, we pray, do not let us perish on account of this man's life. Do not make us guilty of innocent blood; for you, O Lord, have done as it pleased you." So they picked Jonah up and threw him into the sea; and the sea ceased from its raging. Then the men feared the Lord even more, and they offered a sacrifice to the Lord and made vows.

But the Lord provided a large fish to swallow up Jonah; and Jonah was in the belly of the fish three days and three nights.

Then Jonah prayed to the Lord his God from the belly of the fish, saying,

"I called to the Lord out of my distress,
    and he answered me;
out of the belly of Sheol I cried,
    and you heard my voice.
You cast me into the deep,
    into the heart of the seas,
    and the flood surrounded me;
all your waves and your billows passed over me.
Then I said, 'I am driven away from your sight;
how shall I look again
    upon your holy temple?'
The waters closed in over me;
    the deep surrounded me;
weeds were wrapped around my head
    at the roots of the mountains." . . .

Sheol: place of the dead, here depicted as a city with gates located under the waters.

Then the Lord spoke to the fish, and it spewed Jonah out upon the dry land.

spewed: in other versions, "vomited."

The word of the Lord came to Jonah a second time, saying. "Get up, go to Nineveh, that great city, and proclaim to it the message that I tell you." So Jonah set out and went to Nineveh, according to the word of the Lord. Now Nineveh was an exceedingly large city, a three days' walk across. Jonah began to go into the city, going a day's walk. And he cried out, "Forty days more, and Nineveh shall be overthrown!" And the people of Nineveh believed God; they proclaimed a fast, and everyone, great and small, put on sackcloth.

When the news reached the king of Nineveh, he rose from his throne, removed his robe, covered himself with sackcloth, and sat in ashes. Then he had a proclamation made in Nineveh: "By the decree of the king and his nobles: No human being or animal, no herd or flock shall taste anything. They shall not feed, nor shall they drink water. Human beings and animals shall be covered with sackcloth, and they shall cry mightily to God. All shall turn from their evil ways and from the violence that is in their hands. Who knows? God may relent and change his mind; he may turn from his fierce anger, so that we do not perish."

When God saw what they did, how they turned from their evil ways, God changed his mind about the calamity that he had said he would bring upon them; and he did not do it.

But this was very displeasing to Jonah, and he became angry. He prayed to the Lord and said, "O Lord! Is not this what I said while I was still in my own country? That is why I fled to Tarshish at the beginning; for I knew that you are a gracious God and merciful, slow to anger, and abounding in steadfast love, and ready to relent from punishing. And now, O Lord, please take my life from me, for it is better for me to die than to live." And the Lord said, "Is it right for you to be angry?" Then Jonah went out of the city and sat down east of the city, and made a booth for himself there. He sat under it in the shade, waiting to see what would become of the city.

The Lord God appointed a bush, and made it come up over Jonah, to give shade over his head, to save him from his discomfort; so Jonah was very happy about the bush. But when dawn came up the next day, God appointed a worm that attacked the bush, so that it withered. When the sun rose, God prepared a sultry east wind, and the sun beat down on the head of Jonah so that he was faint and asked that he might die. He said, "It is better for me to die than to live."

sackcloth: rough cloth worn as a sign of mourning or penitence for a sin.

sat in ashes: another sign of mourning or penitence.

booth: shelter.

appointed: ordered up; created.

sultry: very hot.

But God said to Jonah, "Is it right for you to be angry about the bush?" And he said, "Yes, angry enough to die." Then the Lord said, "You are concerned about the bush, for which you did not labor and which you did not grow; it came into being in a night and perished in a night. And should I not be concerned about Nineveh, that great city, in which there are more than a hundred and twenty thousand persons who do not know their right hand from their left, and also many animals?"

FOR CLOSE READING

1. What suggestion does Jonah make to the sailors to end the storm?

2. At what two times does the Lord show sympathy and mercy to Jonah? How does Jonah react in each case?

3. How do the sailors react when they find that God has spared them? How do the Ninevites react when they hear Jonah's message?

4. What is Jonah's message to the Ninevites?

FOR THOUGHT AND DISCUSSION

5. Compare Jonah's reactions to the Lord with the reactions of the sailors and the Ninevites. Why do you suppose this contrast is made so clearly?

6. Some have called the story of Jonah a satire that makes fun of Jonah. What moments of satire and humor can you find in the story? What do you think is the effect of the satire?

7. What "lesson" do you think the Lord is teaching Jonah? How does each episode in the story relate to that lesson?

8. Why do you think Jonah is angry when he hears that the Lord has spared Nineveh?

9. The story ends with the Lord's question. Do you think the story would have been more, or less, effective if it had been a statement? if Jonah's answer were given? Why? How might Jonah have answered?

10. Consider Elijah, Amos, and Jonah as prophets. Which man, in your opinion, had the most difficult job? Who was the most successful? Which prophet made the strongest impression on you? Why?

RESPONDING

1. **Writing** You are Jonah. Describe your experiences in a letter home to your family.

2. **Activity** Tell the story of Jonah as a cartoon strip.

3. **Activity** Using whatever art medium you wish, show Jonah in the belly of the fish.

4. **Activity** Look up *Jonah* in a dictionary. What does it mean to say that someone is a "Jonah"? What other expressions can you think of that use biblical names in a similar way?

Jonah

Translated by Miller Williams

I could damn all things equally. Don't ask me
in the name of what.
In the name of Isaiah, the prophet,
but with the gesture
5 grotesque and incomplete
of his cohort Jonah
who was never able to finish his petty commission
given to the lows and highs of good and evil,
the shifting circumstances of history,
10 that left him lost in the uncertainty
of a whale's belly.
Like Jonah, the clown of heaven,
obstinate always
in finishing his minor assignments,
15 the incendiary briefcase under the sweaty armpit,
the umbrella worn down to a lightning rod.
Above him, the uncertainty of Jehovah,
swaying between forgiveness and fury,
between taking him up and flinging him down
20 an old tool of uncertain usefulness
fallen at last into perfect disuse.

I will end also under a tree
but like those old drunken bums
who despise all things equally,
25 don't ask me anything,
all I know is we will be destroyed.
I see as a blind man
the hand of the lord whose name I don't
remember,

grotesque: odd or
unnatural.

cohort: (kō´hôrt):
associate or follower.

commission: assignment.

incendiary: causing fires,
violence, or rebellion.

the delicate fingers twisted and clumsy.
30 And something else, that has nothing to do
with this. I remember something
like that—
no, no it was more. A thing,
it doesn't matter.
35 I don't know again where I'm going

Lord, in thy abandonment, attend me.

FOR THOUGHT AND DISCUSSION

1. What words and phrases reveal the speaker's opinion of Jonah? To what extent do you think that opinion is justified?

2. How does the speaker link his own life to Jonah's?

3. In line 7, the speaker says Jonah "was never able to finish his petty commission." What do you think the speaker means?

4. How would you describe the speaker's mood up to the last line of the poem? What are the speaker's feelings in the last line?

It Should Happen to a Dog

Author's Note

It Should Happen to a Dog is a serio-comic strip, which, those who know the story of Jonah will see, is faithful to the original. If the characters speak as people we know personally, it is because there is no other way for us to know characters. If Jonah is somewhat familiar in his manner of address to the Almighty—it is because one may assume that a greater intimacy exists between Prophets and their source of instruction than does for the rest of us.

In the staging of *It Should Happen to a Dog*, a coatstand is required from which the rope of the ship is hung, and upon which any practical props may also hang. The coatstand becomes the tree in the last scene, and should be placed behind Jonah's back in full view of the audience by the Angel or by a property man who may be written in at the director's discretion. A thunder-sheet will be found useful. The characters should be dressed in an anachronistic selection of garments suggestive of our own time and of biblical times, and the piece should be played at a fast tempo.

As to the message of the story—"Why should I not spare Nineveh?" This is, one hopes, how God feels about Man—unlike Man, who is less tolerant of himself.

Characters

JONAH
A MAN

SCENE I

traveler: traveling
salesman (one of many
British words and
expressions in the play).

braces: suspenders
(British).

pitch: sidewalk sales
stand.

JONAH. Please, please, what do you want from my life? He won't leave me alone. All these years I've been running—a traveler—Jonah, the traveler, representing Top Hat; Braces For The Trousers; Fair Lady Fancy Buttons; Hold Tight Hair Grips—only good brands in the suitcase. Ask them in Tarshish, ask them in Aleppo, in Carthage even; they all know Jonah ben Amittai, regular call once a month for more than thirty years. I don't complain only I'm tired of running, that's all. Now at last I'm tired. I get this good pitch here—at last—so I shouldn't have to run with a suitcase any more. And still he nags me. All right. I heard. I'm going. What happens to me shouldn't happen to a dog.

(A man stands in his way.)

MAN. It's a nice pitch you got here.

JONAH. It's nice.

MAN. So what are you looking so down in the mouth for?

JONAH. What's the use of talking? It has to happen to me.

MAN. What happens?

JONAH. This dream.

MAN. Dream?

JONAH. I tell you, this is a most terrible dream. The voice comes like the voice of a bird. In the middle hours of the night it comes chirping, chirping, "The end of the world is at hand. The end of the world is at hand."

MAN. Could be right. It wouldn't be the first time.

JONAH. So all right then, let it be the end of the world. Is it my business? Am I to blame?

MAN. And this is all the voice says?

JONAH *(lying).* Certainly that's all. Isn't it enough? What else should it say?

MAN. Nothing. Only if that is all the voice says you got nothing to worry about. Look—if it *is* the end of the world, what can you do? On the other

hand—if it isn't—you got nothing to worry about.
I'll take a quarter ounce Archangel Gabriel tobacco.
JONAH *(handing him a small packet of tobacco).* That's a
good brand. I opened up the Tarshish territory for
Archangel Gabriel.
MAN. I never smoke nothing else. *(Starts to go out)*
JONAH. Ay, ay.
MAN. Oh. *(Giving coin)* Chirp, chirp? Chirp, chirp,
heh, heh. *(As he goes)*
JONAH. I hate birds. You know what it says? "Arise,
Jonah, arise. Go to Nineveh, that great city, and cry
against it." I ask you. Why pick on me? Why sort
me out? Chirp, chirp, It's in my head the whole
time. Once I could sleep fifteen hours—like a short
course of death. No more. I don't sleep that good
no more. I hate birds. *(To God)* All right, I'm
going—to the docks—for a ship—I'm going. *(He
walks into the next area and set-up.)*

SCENE II

*(The same man as before, as a sailor, is untying a rope from
a capstan as* JONAH *enters.)*
JONAH *(to God).* Certainly I'm on my way. By ship.
You expect me to fly? If you are so clever and in
such a hurry, make me sprout a couple of wings so
I'll take off. It's quicker by air. But so far is only
invented the ship. *(To the* SAILOR*)* Which way
you going, shipmate?
SAILOR. Tarshish.
JONAH. You don't say. I got a lot of friends there. It's
a beautiful place. In Tarshish they got more people
over a hundred years old than anywhere else.
SAILOR. Who wants to live so long?
JONAH. In some circumstances, chirp, chirp, who
gets a chance to live so long? Tarshish, eh? *(Aside)*
It seems silly, if I'm going all this way to Nineveh
(where I am certainly eventually going) why don't
I break my journey and look up a few old friends
in Tarshish. Why not? It's a crime? *(To the* SAILOR*)*
You can take passengers?
SAILOR. First class or tourist?
JONAH. In the old days when I was traveling for
myself, nothing but first class for J. B. Amittai. But
in these circumstances, one tourist.
SAILOR. Single or return?

JONAH. What's the matter with you? Return, of course. I got a wonderful little business waiting for me when I come back.

SAILOR *(shouts).* One more tourist coming up. Tarshish return.

JONAH *(aside, as he begins to board ship).* I'll spend a couple of days there to build my strength up and then I'll give such a shout against Nineveh. After all, it's a tough territory, and what difference can a couple of days make? Thank you. *(Sits)* Oh, it's a beautiful day for sailing.

SAILOR. Any more for the *Skylark?*

(Black out)

SCENE III

(JONAH sleeps on some bales of goods. The SAILOR wakes him.)

JONAH. Chirp, chirp. The end of the world is at hand. *(He wakes up.)*

SAILOR. If it isn't troubling you.

JONAH. The weather's come over black all of a sudden.

SAILOR. In all my years I never knew a storm this time of year.

JONAH. Are we far from Tarshish?

SAILOR. Are you barmy? We been stuck out here the past five hours, and all the wind does is try to blow us back. In all my years I never see anything like it.

JONAH. Very interesting phenomena. Like St. Ermin's fire; caused by electricity in the atmosphere, you understand? And take the sea serpent, for example.

SAILOR. I will.

JONAH. The sea serpent is really a very big eel. Science proves it.

SAILOR. I don't take any chances. After I tried every trick I know, I pray. *(He prays for a few moments. Then he looks at JONAH.)* You too, guv'ner.

JONAH. I already said my prayers today. To duplicate is just silly. When it comes to the evening I'll say my evening prayers.

barmy: crazy.

St. Ermin's fire: Jonah means St. Elmo's fire, a glowing light sometimes seen during storms at sea.

SAILOR. Don't take no chances. Pray now.

JONAH. It should happen to a dog what happens to me. Listen, God. Stop messing me about. Didn't I give you my word of honor I will go to Nineveh? Ask anybody anywhere in these big territories. Jonah's word is his bond. *(A gale begins to blow.)* Do me a favor just this once. I will catch the first boat from Tarshish to Nineveh. The very first boat. *(The gale blows stronger.)*

SAILOR. Did you make a sacrifice yet? We got all the passengers making sacrifices to all the different gods. That way we must hit the right god sooner or later and he'll stop the storm. Guv'ner, did you make a sacrifice yet?

JONAH. Here. I sacrifice this beautiful meat pie. I only ate a small portion of it.

SAILOR. Right. Throw it overboard with an appropriate prayer.

JONAH. Here, God. And remember I'm catching the first boat from Tarshish. All right? *(He throws the pie overboard. The pie is thrown straight back, and* JONAH *catches it. The* SAILOR *looks at him significantly, then calls out.)*

SAILOR. Aye, aye. This is it folks.

JONAH. It's a perfectly natural phenomena.

SAILOR. This man is the troublemaker.

JONAH. It's got a perfectly natural explanation.

SAILOR. His sacrifice was definitely refused. He's the one. Overboard with him—overboard. *(He advances on* JONAH.*)*

JONAH. You can't do this to me. I am on very important business. I can drown in there. What happens to me should happen to a dog. *(He backs away from the influence of the* SAILOR *till he falls overboard and the gale stops and the sun comes out.)*

SAILOR. I never did like the look of that fella. To me, he always looked a troublemaker. Uh? What? *(He follows the progress of* JONAH *in the water.)* You could live a thousand years, you wouldn't see a man swallowed by a whale. But who would believe such a story.

(Black out)

SCENE IV

(JONAH *gropes in the dark, then strikes a match.*)

JONAH. Faugh—it smells like Billingsgate in here. All right. Now what am I supposed to do. Now I can't go to Nineveh. All I wanted to do was to go to Nineveh and cry against it, and look at me. Maybe I'm dead. I must be dead. Who would have thought that being dead was a blackout in a fish shop? Maybe *this is* the end of the world. But if it isn't, if, for example, don't laugh, I happen to have been swallowed by a whale, tee-hee, I categorically put it on record that if I could go to Nineveh at this moment I would definitely and unconditionally go to Nineveh at this moment. (*A crash of thunder; lightning.* JONAH *executes a double somersault into the light. Looks round, amazed*) Honestly, God, sometimes I can't make you out. You've got such a mysterious way of carrying on. (*He stretches himself.*) So where's Tarshish? Tarshish. (*Disgusted*) If I'm not dead and if I'm not mistaken and if my memory serves me right that great city in the distance is—*Nineveh*. It should happen to a dog. (*Exit, towards Nineveh.*)

SCENE V

KING (*enters, sits, sorts papers, looks up*). Jonah B. Amittai.

JONAH. Yes, Your Majesty.

KING. You are up on a charge of vagrancy.

JONAH. Uh?

KING. Vagrancy.

JONAH. Oh.

KING. Also it seems you have been talking a lot of seditious nonsense about the end of the world is at hand. Also—what's this? Also you keep saying "chirp, chirp." This official work is beginning to get me down. All night long I get the most terrible dreams. Mmm—what have you got to say for yourself?

JONAH. Just a minute. (*He mounts the throne and sings.*) The Lord saith: Cry out against Nineveh, that great city, for their wickedness is come up before me. Stop. Yet forty days and Nineveh shall be overthrown. Stop. The end of the world is at

Billingsgate: formerly, a fish market in London.

vagrancy: wandering about without ability to earn a living.

seditious: stirring up discontent or rebellion.

stop: period. (Jonah is delivering his message in the style of a telegram.)

hand. Stop. Repent lest ye perish. End of message. And that, Your Majesty, in short is what I am instructed to tell you. *(Sits)* Personally it makes no difference to me. I should be just as pleased for Nineveh not to be destroyed. For my part it can go on being as wicked as you like, though, if you was to ask my opinion, as a businessman of some experience, I'll tell you straight out that honesty is always the best policy. A satisfied client is better than government consols. Especially as, I am instructed to tell you, the government is not going to last too long, anyway.

consols: bonds, securities (British).

KING. What's the source of your information?

JONAH. A little bird tells me every night.

KING *(alarmed).* A bird?

JONAH. A little bird. Chirp, chirp. It makes just like that.

KING. What color the feathers?

JONAH. The feathers! One wing is blue, the other wing white, the breast red, the tail purple, but the funny thing is, this bird has one brown eye and—

KING. —and the other a blue!

JONAH. You are familiar with it?

KING. I have been getting the same dream.

JONAH. Oh. So *your* little bird tells me one hundred times nightly to come to Nineveh and inform *you* that in forty days from now *you* are completely in liquidation. And that's what *I'm* telling *you?* It's a madhouse here!

you . . . liquidation: i.e., your business will be ended; you will be dead.

KING *(stands up and tears his robe).* Let neither man nor beast, herd nor flock, taste anything. Let them not eat food nor drink water; but let man and beast be covered with sackcloth and cry mightily unto God. Yea, let them turn every one from his evil way, and from the violence that is in their hands. Let them turn from the violence that is in their hands for the sake of the smallest bird, for the bird also is God. *(To* JONAH*)* Who can tell if God will turn and repent, and turn away from his fierce anger, that we perish not?

JONAH. Who can tell? But if you ask my opinion, I don't think so. Otherwise he doesn't go to all this trouble. No, king, this is the end. Still, you can always try. There's no charge for trying.

(Exeunt)

SCENE VI

Bank Holiday Monday:
an end-of-summer
British holiday.

(JONAH *is sitting on a rock in the scorching sun. In the background a celebratory fairground noise, like a Bank Holiday Monday.)*

JONAH. It should happen to a dog, what happens to me. Here after all this the King himself takes my personal word that in forty days it is the end of the world; and what happens? The forty-first day is proclaimed a national holiday. Government stock rises, and I am the biggest bloody fool in the Middle East. I am a laughingstock, that's all, a laughingstock. I don't move. I'm going to sit here until I get a sunstroke. You can do what you like with Nineveh, Miniver, Shminever. I'm finished. "Yet forty days and Nineveh shall be overthrown." *(Laughter off and voices singing: "Jonah, Jonah—He pulled a boner.")* Listen to 'em. Laugh your heads off! Three-four hours I won't hear you anymore. And I won't hear that damned bird either no more. I hate birds. *(A shadow is thrown over JONAH.)* What's this? By my life. A tree! *(A palm tree has sprung up from nowhere. He reaches down a coconut.)* What do you know? Coconuts as well with a patent zipper. You just pull it open and drink the milk. Ice cold. Delicious. And what's this. The *Tarshish Gazette.* Well, this is certainly a novelty. *(Reads)* Aha. I see that Mrs. Zinkin has been presented with her third daughter. That's bad. Young Fyvel is opening a café espresso bar on the High Street. That's a good position. He should do well. It's just like a summer holiday here now, and believe me, I earned a vacation. This is certainly a wonderful place you made here, Lord. I got to hand it to you. For land development you're the tops.

(Standing beside him is the MAN *dressed as an angel.* JONAH *sees him and looks away, back to his paper.)*

ANGEL. A beautiful day.

JONAH. Yes, it's certainly marvelous weather we're having.

ANGEL. That's a remarkable palm tree. *(He reaches out for a coconut.)* This I never saw before.

JONAH. It's got a zipper.

ANGEL. What will He think of next, eh? *(He offers the coconut to the irritable* JONAH.)

JONAH (*throwing down the newspaper*). All right. Cut out the performance. You are an angel, right?

ANGEL. I must give you credit, Jonah. You're certainly quick off the mark.

JONAH. But an angel?

ANGEL. Archangel.

JONAH. Oh—so now what do I have to do? Go back to Nineveh? Tell the King the Lord has changed his mind again? He is going to give him ten more days and then bring the world to an end? He made a laughingstock of me.

ANGEL. What can you do?

JONAH. Admitted. But at the same time this is a terrible way to treat someone who goes through all the trouble I go through. For what—only He knows. And He won't tell. (*Turns, bangs into tree.*) Feh! Fancy trees yet!

ANGEL (*wheedling*). That's certainly a *wonderful* tree. Help yourself.

JONAH. Perhaps just another coconut. These coconuts are delicious. (*As he turns the tree withers, collapsing into dust; that is, the coatstand is removed.*) What a terrible thing to happen. Such a wonderful tree. With such trees mankind could live in plenty for ever. A quick death from some palm tree disease, I suppose?

ANGEL. It's a small worm crawls through the arterial system of the tree, cuts off the life from the heart. And boom.

JONAH. A quick death to that worm.

ANGEL. Ah. You notice something. How annoyed you are with this worm which after all only killed a tree, which after all didn't cause you an hour's work. After all, you don't hear God complain; He made the tree to come up in a night. He can make it go down the night after.

JONAH. It cranks me such a beautiful tree should die like that, apart from now I am in the sun again and can catch a sunstroke any minute. Pity about the tree. Hey-hey. This is some kind of parable, ain't it? You are trying to teach me something, isn't it?

ANGEL. That's my boy. By this little experiment He is saying, if you feel sorry for the tree, which after all didn't cost you anything, why shouldn't He feel sorry for Nineveh, that great city, in which there are one hundred and twenty thousand human

cranks: upsets.

parable: short story with a moral.

beings on whom after all He has taken a great deal of trouble even if they still don't know what time it is, or their left hand from the right hand. Also much cattle.

JONAH. You got a point there, there was never any harm in those cattle. But if you don't mind a question——

ANGEL. Any help I can give you.

JONAH. If God knew right from the start exactly what He is going to do about everything—right?

ANGEL. That's right.

JONAH. Then He knows He isn't going to destroy Nineveh. Right?

ANGEL. Right!

JONAH. Then what does He want of my life? What's the point of all this expensive business with whales and palm trees and so on?

ANGEL. You mankind, you can't see no further than your nose.

JONAH. So what's the answer?

ANGEL. You see—*(long pause)* frankly, I don't know.

JONAH. It should happen to a dog.

ANGEL. Me too. After all, it's no joke following you or any other prophet I happen to get assigned to around the whole time. You think it's such a wonderful thing to be an angel and do a few conjuring tricks? It *should* happen to a dog.

JONAH. On the other hand, come to think of it, whose dogs are we?

ANGEL. We are the dogs of God.

JONAH. So——

ANGEL. Nu?

Nu?: well then?

JONAH. Whatever happens to a dog——

ANGEL. —must happen to us, eh? *(He chuckles with admiration.)*

JONAH. Can you give me a lift back home?

ANGEL. It's a pleasure. (JONAH *jumps on* ANGEL's *back.)*

JONAH. On the way we could call in at Tarshish. I got a lot of friends there.

ANGEL. That's a good idea. So have I. *(As they go out)* Did you hear that young Fyvel opened a café espresso bar on the High Street?

JONAH. I read it in the paper. He's a clever boy.

(Curtain)

FOR CLOSE READING

1. What happens to the sacrifice that Jonah throws overboard during the storm?

2. List at least three details or incidents in the play that are not in the Bible story of Jonah.

3. In this play, why is Jonah angry when Nineveh is spared?

FOR THOUGHT AND DISCUSSION

4. In this account, Jonah is a salesman as well as a prophet. What might these two roles have in common?

5. Suppose this play were staged as "realistically" as possible, with detailed scenery and special effects instead of a coatstand and a rope. How do you think the play would be affected?

6. Why do you think the author added the detail about the king's dream? Why do you suppose he used an angel, rather than God's voice, in Scene VI?

7. The Bible story ends with God's question. What important question does Jonah ask in the final scene of the play? Compare and contrast the two questions.

8. In his introduction the author says his play is "faithful to the original." To what extent is he correct? He also calls the play a "serio-comic strip." Which moments of the play seem most comic to you? most serious?

7
Varieties of
Biblical Poetry

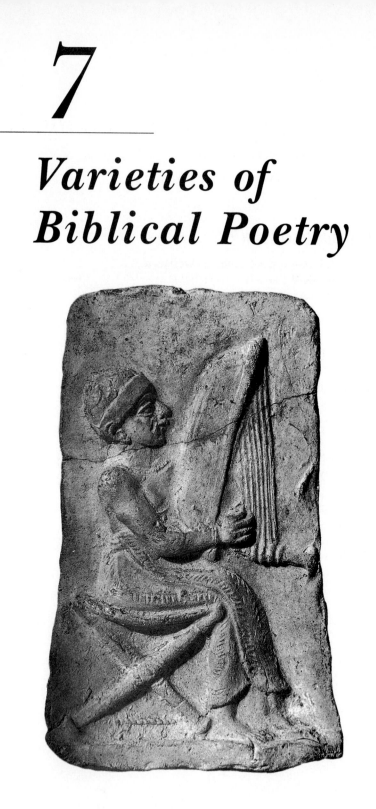

A Song of Trust

The Lord is my shepherd, I shall not want.
   He makes me lie down in green pastures;
he leads me beside still waters;
   he restores my soul.   restores: renews.
He leads me in right paths
   for his name's sake.

Even though I walk through the darkest valley,
   I fear no evil;
for you are with me;
   your rod and your staff—
   they comfort me.
You prepare a table before me
   in the presence of my enemies;
you anoint my head with oil;   anoint ... oil: a
   my cup overflows.   sign of God's blessing.

Surely goodness and mercy shall follow me
   all the days of my life,
and I shall dwell in the house of the Lord
   my whole life long.

                              Psalm 23

FOR THOUGHT AND DISCUSSION

1. Why do you think the speaker calls the Lord "you"
only in the second stanza?

2. Sum up each of the stanzas in a sentence. What
different emphasis does each stanza have?

All Bible passages in Unit 7 are from the New Revised Standard Version.
LEFT: Terra cotta plaque of seated harpist from Ischali, Iraq. Old Babylonian
Period. Courtesy of the Oriental Institute, University of Chicago.

A Song of Zion

Zion is the hill in Jerusalem on which the
temple was built; it is often used poetically to
refer to all Jerusalem, "the city of God."

refuge: i.e., protector.

Gₒd is our refuge and strength,
    a very present help in trouble.
Therefore we will not fear, though the earth
        should change,
    though the mountains shake in the heart of the sea;
though its waters roar and foam,
    though the mountains tremble with its tumult.

There is a river whose streams make glad the
        city of God,
    the holy habitation of the Most High.
God is in the midst of the city; it shall not be moved;
    God will help it when the morning dawns.

totter: shake, as if about
to fall.

The nations are in an uproar, the kingdoms totter;
    he utters his voice, the earth melts.

hosts: armies.

The Lord of hosts is with us;
    the God of Jacob is our refuge.

desolations: ruins.

Come, behold the works of the Lord;
    see what desolations he has brought on the earth.
He makes wars cease to the end of the earth;
    he breaks the bow, and shatters the spear;
    he burns the shields with fire.
"Be still, and know that I am God!
    I am exalted among the nations,
    I am exalted in the earth."
The Lord of hosts is with us;
    the God of Jacob is our refuge.

Psalm 46

FOR THOUGHT AND DISCUSSION

1. God is described as a refuge from threat or danger in each stanza. How would you describe the threat represented in each stanza?

2. Some scholars see a thematic relationship between the river of Zion and the rivers that flow out of the garden of Eden. What "refuge" is provided by each place?

3. Compare and contrast the description of God in Psalm 46 with the description in Psalm 23.

4. Read the two psalms aloud. What similarities and differences do you notice?

5. Often in Hebrew poetry, one line will be followed by another that is very similar in rhythm and meaning. For example: "The Lord of hosts is with us;/the God of Jacob is our refuge." What other examples can you find in Psalms 23 and 46? What are some of the effects of this technique?

i thank You God

i thank You God for most this amazing
day:for the leaping greenly spirits of trees
and a blue true dream of sky;and for everything
which is natural which is infinite which is yes

₅ (i who have died am alive again today,
and this is the sun's birthday;this is the birth
day of life and love and wings:and of the gay
great happening illimitably earth)

illimitably: infinitely.

how should tasting touching hearing seeing
₁₀ breathing any—lifted from the no
of all nothing—human merely being
doubt unimaginable You?

(now the ears of my ears awake and
now the eyes of my eyes are opened)

FOR THOUGHT AND DISCUSSION

1. Why is the speaker grateful to God? What do you
think is meant by "i who have died"?

2. What special meanings does the speaker seem to
give to the words "yes" and "no"?

3. Cummings is known for the unusual punctuation
and phrasing of his poems. How does the style of
this poem help express the speaker's emotions?

Songs of Lament

These poems refer to a time of exile. Jerusalem has been conquered by the Babylonians, and many people of Judah have been taken away as captives. This period of exile will be explored further in Unit 9.

How lonely sits the city
    that once was full of people!
How like a widow she has become,
    she that was great among the nations!
She that was a princess among the provinces
    has become a vassal.

vassal: servant.

She weeps bitterly in the night,
    with tears on her cheeks;
among all her lovers
    she has no one to comfort her;
all her friends have dealt treacherously with her,
    they have become her enemies.

treacherously: disloyally.

Judah has gone into exile with suffering
    and hard servitude;
she lives now among the nations,
    and finds no resting place;
her pursuers have all overtaken her
    in the midst of her distress.

servitude: slavery.

The roads to Zion mourn,
    for no one comes to the festivals;
all her gates are desolate,
    her priests groan;
her young girls grieve,
    and her lot is bitter. . . .

Zion: Jerusalem.

Lamentations 1:1–4

How the Lord in his anger
    has humiliated daughter Zion!
He has thrown down from heaven to earth
    the splendor of Israel;
he has not remembered his footstool
    in the day of his anger.

The Lord has destroyed without mercy
    all the dwellings of Jacob;
in his wrath he has broken down
    the strongholds of daughter Judah;
he has brought down to the ground in dishonor
    the kingdoms and its rulers.

He has cut down in fierce anger
    all the might of Israel;
he has withdrawn his right hand from them
    in the face of the enemy;
he has burned like a flaming fire in Jacob,
    consuming all around.

He has bent his bow like an enemy,
    with his right hand set like a foe;
he has killed all in whom we took pride
    in the tent of daughter Zion;
he has poured out his fury like fire. . . .

Lamentations 2: 1–4

But you, O Lord, reign forever;
    your throne endures to all generations.
Why have you forgotten us completely?
    Why have you forsaken us these many days?
Restore us to yourself, O Lord, that we may be
        restored;
    renew our days as of old—
unless you have utterly rejected us,
    and are angry with us beyond measure.

Lamentations 5: 19–22

footstool: a metaphor for Jerusalem as the earthly extension of God's throne.

Jacob: Israel.

By the rivers of Babylon—
 there we sat down and there we wept
 when we remembered Zion.
On the willows there
 we hung up our harps.
For there our captors
 asked us for songs,
and our tormentors asked for mirth, saying,   **mirth:** laughter.
 "Sing us one of the songs of Zion!"

How could we sing the Lord's song
 in a foreign land?
If I forget you, O Jerusalem,
 let my right hand wither!
Let my tongue cling to the roof of my mouth,
 if I do not remember you,
if I do not set Jerusalem
 above my highest joy. . . .

Psalm 137: 1–6

FOR THOUGHT AND DISCUSSION

1. These songs of lament use many words that have
 sad meanings or connotations. For example, the
 first song has "lonely" and "widow" in the opening
 three lines. What other words and phrases have a
 similar effect? How do these effects differ from
 poem to poem?

2. How is God portrayed in Lam. 2:1–4? How is this
 description different from the descriptions of God
 given in Psalms 23 and 46?

3. Both Psalms 23 and 137 each refer to waters and
 "enemies" or "captors." What different impressions
 are created by these references in each poem?

4. What feelings are expressed about Zion/Jerusalem
 in these poems?

5. Which of these poems made the strongest
 impression on you? Why?

A Song of Comfort

Comfort, O comfort my people,
    says your God.
Speak tenderly to Jerusalem,
    and cry to her
that she has served her term,
    that her penalty is paid,
that she has received from the Lord's hand
    double for all her sins.

A voice cries out:
"In the wilderness prepare the way of the Lord.
    make straight in the desert a highway for our God.
Every valley shall be lifted up,
    and every mountain and hill be made low;
the uneven ground shall become level,
    and the rough places a plain.
Then the glory of the Lord shall be revealed,
    and all people shall see it together,
for the mouth of the Lord has spoken."

A voice says, "Cry out!"
    And I said, "What shall I cry?
All people are grass,
    their constancy is like the flower of the field.
The grass withers, the flower fades,
    when the breath of the Lord blows upon it;
    surely the people are grass."
The grass withers, the flower fades;
    but the word of our God will stand forever.

Get you up to a high mountain,
    O Zion, herald of good tidings;
lift up your voice with strength,
    O Jerusalem, herald of good tidings,
    lift it up, do not fear;

constancy: faithfulness.

herald . . . tidings:
announcer of good news.

say to the cities of Judah,
   "Here is your God!"
See, the Lord God comes with might,
   and his arm rules for him;
his reward is with him,
   and his recompense before him.

recompense: fair payment; justice.

He will feed his flock like a shepherd;
   he will gather the lambs in his arms,
and carry them in his bosom,
   and gently lead the mother sheep. . . .

Why do you say, O Jacob,
   and speak, O Israel,
"My way is hidden from the Lord,
   and my right is disregarded by my God"?
Have you not known? Have you not heard?
The Lord is the everlasting God,
   the Creator of the ends of the earth.
He does not faint or grow weary;
   his understanding is unsearchable.

unsearchable: cannot be discovered; mysterious.

He gives power to the faint,
   and strengthens the powerless.
Even youths will faint and be weary,
   and the young will fall exhausted;
but those who wait for the Lord shall renew their
     strength,
   they shall mount up with wings like eagles,
they shall run and not be weary,
   they shall walk and not faint.

Isaiah 40: 1–11, 27–31

FOR THOUGHT AND DISCUSSION

1. What are the "good tidings" of this song?

2. As in Psalm 23, God is described in this passage as a shepherd. How might this image create a feeling of comfort?

3. What does "grass" symbolize in this song?

4. This song states that humans are "grass," but can also be "like eagles." How do you explain these contrasting images?

5. As you have seen, one technique of Hebrew poetry is to use similar language and meaning in two or more lines; another technique is to *contrast* two or more lines. For example: "The grass withers, the flower fades;/but the word of our God will stand forever." What other examples of this use of contrast can you find in this poem and other biblical poetry you have read? What are some of the effects of this pattern?

RESPONDING

1. **Writing** Create your own title for each of the biblical poems.

2. **Activity** Make a poster or banner that illustrates a phrase from one of these poems.

3. **Activity** Prepare a choral reading of the Song of Comfort from Isaiah 40. How many different voices do you "hear" in this passage? Assign parts to individuals or to groups of voices.

4. **Activity** Set one or more of these poems to music (adapting an existing melody or composing your own).

5. **Humanities Connection** Psalms and other Hebrew poetry are the source of many religious songs and hymns—and secular popular music as well. Find and listen to music based on biblical poetry.

Sayings of the Wise

1

Three things are too wonderful for me;
  four I do not understand:
the way of an eagle in the sky,
  the way of a snake on a rock,
the way of a ship on the high seas,
  and the way of a man with a girl.

2

The words of a whisperer are like delicious morsels;
  they go down into the inner parts of the body.

morsels: small bits of food.

3

Like vinegar on a wound
  is one who sings songs to a heavy heart.
Like a moth in clothing or a worm in wood,
  sorrow gnaws at the human heart.

4

Better is a neighbor who is nearby
  than kindred who are far away.

kindred: relatives.

5

The sated appetite spurns honey,
  but to a ravenous appetite even the bitter is sweet.

sated: fully satisfied.
ravenous: starving.

Proverbs (1) 30:18–19; (2) 18:8; (3) 25:20; (4) 27:10; (5) 27:7; (6) 6:6–11; (7) 11:16; (8) 23: 4–5; (9) 22:2; (10) 30:33; (11) 26:27; (12) 10:9; (13) 21:13; (14) 23:29–35; (15) 14:13; (16) 14:10; (17) 27:19; (18) 21:2; (19) Ecclesiastes 9:11–12 (New Revised Standard Version).

6

Go to the ant, you lazybones;
    consider its ways, and be wise.
Without having any chief
    or officer or ruler,
it prepares its food in summer,
    and gathers its sustenance in harvest.
How long will you lie there, O lazybones?
    When will you rise from your sleep?
A little sleep, a little slumber,
    a little folding of the hands to rest,
and poverty will come upon you like a robber,
    and want, like an armed warrior.

sustenance: food, provisions.

want: neediness.

7

A gracious woman gets honor,
    but she who hates virtue is covered with shame.
The timid become destitute,
    but the aggressive gain riches.

destitute: extremely needy.

8

Do not wear yourself out to get rich;
    be wise enough to desist.
When your eyes light upon it, it is gone;
    for suddenly it takes wings to itself,
    flying like an eagle toward heaven.

desist: stop.

9

The rich and the poor have this in common:
    the Lord is the maker of them all.

10

For as pressing milk produces curds,
    and pressing the nose produces blood,
    so pressing anger produces strife.

curds: thickened part of sour milk, used to form cheese.

strife: fighting.

11

Whoever digs a pit will fall into it,
    and a stone will come back on the one who starts it
      rolling.

12

Whoever walks in integrity walks securely,
    but whoever follows perverse ways will be found
      out.

integrity: honesty, uprightness.
perverse: corrupt.

13

If you close your ear to the cry of the poor,
    you will cry out and not be heard.

14

Who has woe? Who has sorrow?
    Who has strife? Who has complaining?
Who has wounds without cause?
    Who has redness of eyes?
Those who linger late over wine,
    those who keep trying mixed wines.
Do not look at wine when it is red,
    when it sparkles in the cup
    and goes down smoothly.
At the last it bites like a serpent,
    and stings like an adder.
Your eyes will see strange things,
    and your mind utter perverse things.
You will be like one who lies down in the midst of the
      sea,
    like one who lies on the top of a mast.
"They struck me," you will say, "but I was not hurt;
    they beat me, but I did not feel it.
When shall I awake?
    I will seek another drink."

adder: a poisonous snake.

15

Even in laughter the heart is sad,
    and the end of joy is grief.

16

The heart knows its own bitterness,
   and no stranger shares its joy.

17

Just as water reflects the face,
   so one human heart reflects another.

18

All deeds are right in the sight of the doer,
   but the Lord weighs the heart.

19

chance: luck.

   Again I saw that under the sun the race is not to
the swift, nor the battle to the strong, nor bread to the
wise, nor riches to the intelligent, nor favor to the
skillful; but time and chance happen to them all. For
no one can anticipate the time of disaster. Like fish
taken in a cruel net, and like birds caught in a snare,
so mortals are snared at a time of calamity, when it
suddenly falls upon them.

FOR THOUGHT AND DISCUSSION

1. Which of these sayings seem most closely related to
your own experiences of life? Which one appealed
to you most? Why?

2. What seem to be the main topics or concerns of
these sayings? How would you describe the kind of
"wisdom" they express?

3. Some of these proverbs are based on the similarities
of two or more things (see number 3). Others are
based on the differences between two things (see
number 5). Find at least one more example of each
type.

A Time for Everything

For everything there is a season, and a time for
every matter under heaven:
    a time to be born, and a time to die;
    a time to plant, and a time to pluck up what is
       planted;
    a time to kill, and a time to heal;
    a time to break down, and a time to build up;
    a time to weep, and a time to laugh;
    a time to mourn, and a time to dance;
    a time to throw away stones, and a time to
       gather stones together;
    a time to embrace, and a time to refrain from
       embracing;
    a time to seek, and a time to lose;
    a time to keep, and a time to throw away;
    a time to tear, and a time to sew;
    a time to keep silence, and a time to speak;
    a time to love, and a time to hate;
    a time for war, and a time for peace.

refrain: keep back.

Ecclesiastes 3:1–8

FOR THOUGHT AND DISCUSSION

1. In one sentence, describe the first impression this
passage had on you.

2. In your opinion, are any aspects of human life not
covered in this passage? Explain.

3. In what ways might this passage apply to attitudes
people have toward life?

4. Suppose after reading this passage someone asked, "But how do you tell what 'time' it is?" How would you respond?

RESPONDING

1. Activity Greeting cards are now available for all occasions of life. Prepare a series of greeting cards using only phrases taken from this passage of Ecclesiastes. Try to cover as many occasions of life as you can.

2. Activity How do the words of Ecclesiastes connect with events in the world today? Work in small groups, with each group having that day's copy of a daily newspaper. Each group tries to find as many specific illustrations of "times" mentioned in Ecclesiastes as possible. (For example, the obituary page is an obvious link to "a time to die.") Share results with the whole class.

3. Humanities Connection Pete Seeger developed this passage from Ecclesiastes into the song "Turn! Turn! Turn!" that was made into a popular recording by the rock group The Byrds in the late 1960s. Listen to this recording and discuss any differences you notice in content and overall impressions between the Bible passage and the song.

A Song of Love

I am a rose of Sharon,
   a lily of the valleys.

As a lily among brambles,
   so is my love among maidens.

As an apple tree among the trees of the wood,
   so is my beloved among young men,
With great delight I sat in his shadow,
   and his fruit was sweet to my taste.
He brought me to the banqueting house,
   and his intention toward me was love.
Sustain me with raisins,
   refresh me with apples;
   for I am faint with love.
O that his left hand were under my head,
   and that his right hand embraced me!
I adjure you, O daughters of Jerusalem,
   by the gazelles or the wild does:
do not stir up or awaken love
   until it is ready!

The voice of my beloved!
   Look, he comes,
leaping upon the mountains,
   bounding over the hills.
My beloved is like a gazelle
   or a young stag.
Look, there he stands
   behind our wall,
gazing in at the windows,
   looking through the lattice.
My beloved speaks and says to me:
"Arise, my love, my fair one,
   and come away;

Sharon: fertile region of Israel near the shore of the Mediterranean Sea.

brambles: prickly shrubs.

faint: weak.

adjure: solemnly beg.
gazelles: small graceful antelopes.
does (dōz): female deer.

lattice: a network of thin wooden strips within a window frame.

for now the winter is past,
  the rain is over and gone.
The flowers appear on the earth;
  the time of singing has come,
and the voice of the turtledove
  is heard in our land.
The fig tree puts forth its figs,
  and the vines are in blossom;
  they give forth fragrance.
Arise, my love, my fair one,
  and come away.
O my dove, in the clefts of the rock,
  in the covert of the cliff,
let me see your face,
  let me hear your voice;
for your voice is sweet,
  and your face is lovely.
Catch us the foxes,
  the little foxes,
that ruin the vineyards—
  for our vineyards are in blossom."

My beloved is mine and I am his;
  he pastures his flock among the lilies.
Until the day breathes
  and the shadows flee,
turn, my beloved, be like a gazelle
  or a young stag on the cleft mountains.

Song of Solomon 2:1–17

turtledove: a small bird, like a pigeon.

covert: hiding place.

FOR THOUGHT AND DISCUSSION

1. Who seems to be speaking in this poem? to whom? What details suggest that two people are speaking back and forth?

2. In line 8 the speaker mentions "taste." What other physical senses are mentioned or implied in this poem? What is the effect of these sensory details?

3. How do the references to the creatures and fruits of nature help express the emotions of the two lovers?

A Hymn to Love

Among the writings of early Christians that form the New Testament are epistles, or letters, written by Paul the apostle to help newly formed churches. The passage that follows, celebrated for its poetic beauty, is from Paul's first letter to the church at Corinth. It is printed here in poetic form.

If I speak in the tongues of mortals and of angels,
    but do not have love,
I am a noisy gong or a clanging cymbal.
And if I have prophetic powers,
    and understand all mysteries and all knowledge,
    and if I have all faith, so as to remove mountains,
    but do not have love,
I am nothing.
If I give away all my possessions,
    and if I hand over my body so that I may boast
    but do not have love,
I gain nothing.

> tongues: languages.

> hand over . . . boast: i.e., seek glory by dying as a martyr.

Love is patient; love is kind;
    love is not envious or boastful or arrogant or rude.
It does not insist on its own way;
    it is not irritable or resentful;
it does not rejoice in wrongdoing,
    but rejoices in the truth.
It bears all things, believes all things,
    hopes all things, endures all things.

Love never ends.
    But as for prophecies, they will come to an end;
    as for tongues, they will cease;
    as for knowledge, it will come to an end.

For we know only in part, and we prophesy only in part;
  but when the complete comes, the partial will come to
  an end.
When I was a child, I spoke like a child,
  I thought like a child, I reasoned like a child;
when I became an adult, I put an end to childish ways.
For now we see in a mirror, dimly,
  but then we will see face to face.
Now I know only in part;
  then I will know fully, even as I have been fully known.

abide: remain

And now faith, hope, and love abide, these three;
  and the greatest of these is love.

1 Corinthians 13

FOR CLOSE READING

1. In the first stanza, what gifts or abilities are wasted in the absence of love?

2. In the second stanza, what words describe what love is? what love is not?

3. What does the third stanza suggest about human abilities in the present ("now")? When will this change?

FOR THOUGHT AND DISCUSSION

4. What would you say is the main idea of each of the three stanzas?

5. How does the main idea of the third stanza relate to those of the first two stanzas?

6. Consider the statements in the second stanza about what love is and is not. How do they compare with your own understandings about love? What, if anything, would you add to or subtract from the list in the second stanza?

7. Love has many forms, including romantic love, brotherly love, and selfless love. Which do you think is meant here? Support your answer from the text.

8. Consider this passage as a persuasive argument. How convincing is the speaker's conclusion that love is the greatest virtue?

RESPONDING

1. Writing Choose one of the gifts or abilities mentioned in the first stanza and defend its virtues—even though it is limited.

2. Activity In some artistic medium, express the theme of this poem.

3. Activity Set this poem to music.

8

Why Do the Righteous Suffer?

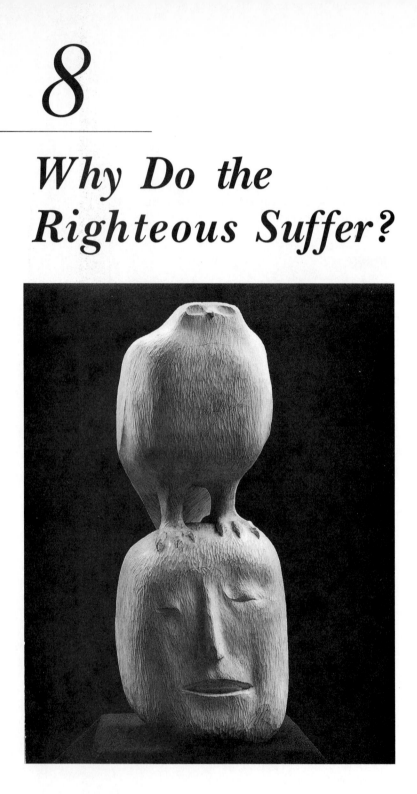

The Story of Job

Prologue

There lived in the land of Uz a man of blameless and upright life named Job, who feared God and set his face against wrongdoing. He had seven sons and three daughters; and he owned seven thousand sheep, three thousand camels, five hundred yoke of oxen, and five hundred she-donkeys, together with a large number of slaves. Thus Job was the greatest man in all the East.

His sons used to meet together and give, each in turn, a banquet in his own house, and they would send and invite their three sisters to eat and drink with them. Then, when a round of banquets was over, Job would send for his children and sanctify them, rising early in the morning and sacrificing a whole-offering for each of them; for he thought that they might somehow have sinned against God and committed blasphemy in their hearts. This Job did regularly.

The day came when the members of the court of heaven took their places in the presence of the Lord, and the Adversary, Satan, was there among them. The Lord asked him where he had been. "Ranging over the earth," said the Adversary, "from end to end." The Lord asked him, "Have you considered my servant Job? You will find no one like him on earth, a man of blameless and upright life, who fears God and sets his face against wrongdoing." "Has not Job good reason to be godfearing?" answered the Adversary. "Have you not hedged him round on every side with your protection, him and his family, and all his

feared: respected, obeyed, had confidence in.

sanctify: bless, make holy.

committed blasphemy: insulted God.

Adversary, Satan: the Hebrew word for Satan means "opponent." Here he acts like a prosecuting attorney.

hedged ... side: surrounded.

Job 1:1–3:4, 20–23; 4:1–9; 5:17–18; 6:1, 14–15, 21, 24; 7:9–12, 16–18, 20–21; 8:1–3, 8–10, 20–21; 9:1–2, 19–24, 30–33; 11:1–8; 12:1–3; 13: 4–9, 12; 14:1–2, 12b, 14–22; 19:23–27; 27:1–6; 29:2, 7–10, 15–16; 31:1–2, `5–6, 9, 13, 16–17, 19–20, 22, 29, 33, 35–37; 38:1–7, 34–38; 39:19–22, 25–28; 40:2–8, 10, 12–14; 41:1–5, 31–34; 42:1–17 (Revised English Bible).

LEFT: *Oppressed Man*, sculpture of pine painted white by Leonard Baskin, 1960. Whitney Museum of American Art, New York.

possessions? Whatever he does you bless, and everywhere his herds have increased beyond measure. But just stretch out your hand and touch all that he has, and see if he will not curse you to your face." "Very well," said the Lord. "All that he has is in your power; only the man himself you must not touch." With that the Adversary left the Lord's presence.

On the day when Job's sons and daughters were eating and drinking in the eldest brother's house, a messenger came to Job and said, "The oxen were plowing and the donkeys were grazing near them, when the Sabaeans swooped down and carried them off, after putting the herdsmen to the sword; only I have escaped to bring you the news." While he was still speaking, another messenger arrived and said, "God's fire flashed from heaven, striking the sheep and the shepherds and burning them up; only I have escaped to bring you the news." While he was still speaking, another arrived and said, "The Chaldaeans, three bands of them, have made a raid on the camels and carried them off, after putting those tending them to the sword; only I have escaped to bring you the news." While this man was speaking, yet another arrived and said, "Your sons and daughters were eating and drinking in their eldest brother's house, when suddenly a whirlwind swept across from the desert and struck the four corners of the house, which fell on the young people. They are dead, and only I have escaped to bring you the news. At this Job stood up, tore his cloak, shaved his head, and threw himself prostrate on the ground, saying:

> "Naked came I from the womb,
> naked I shall return whence I came.
> The Lord gives and the Lord takes away;
> blessed be the name of the Lord."

Throughout all this Job did not sin, or did he ascribe any fault to God.

Once again the day came when the members of the court of heaven took their places in the presence of the Lord, and the Adversary was there among them. The Lord enquired where he had been. "Ranging over the earth," said the Adversary, "from

whirlwind: wind storm.

ascribe any fault to: blame.

end to end." The Lord asked, "Have you considered my servant Job? You will find no one like him on the earth, a man of blameless and upright life, who fears God and sets his face against wrongdoing. You incited me to ruin him without cause, but he still holds fast to his integrity." The Adversary replied, "Skin for skin! To save himself there is nothing a man will withhold. But just reach out your hand and touch his bones and his flesh, and see if he will not curse you to your face." The Lord said to the Adversary, "So be it. He is in your power; only spare his life."

When the Adversary left the Lord's presence, he afflicted Job with running sores from the soles of his feet to the crown of his head, and Job took a piece of a broken pot to scratch himself as he sat among the ashes. His wife said to him, "Why do you still hold fast to your integrity? Curse God, and die!" He answered, "You talk as any impious woman might talk. If we accept good from God, shall we not accept evil?" Throughout all this, Job did not utter one sinful word.

When Job's three friends, Eliphaz of Teman, Bildad of Shuah, and Zophar of Naamah, heard of all these calamities which had overtaken him, they set out from their homes, arranging to go and condole with him and comfort him. But when they first saw him from a distance, they did not recognize him; they wept aloud, tore their cloaks, and tossed dust into the air over their heads. For seven days and seven nights they sat beside him on the ground, and none of them spoke a word to him, for they saw that his suffering was very great.

skin for skin: i.e., a fair exchange. The meaning of this ancient proverb is probably related to Satan's next statement.

running: oozing.

impious: disrespectful to God.

calamities: great troubles.
condole: sympathize.

Job Speaks

After this Job broke his silence and cursed the day of his birth:

> Perish the day when I was born,
> and the night which said, "A boy is conceived"!
> May that day turn to darkness;
> may God above not look for it,
> nor the light of dawn shine on it. . . .
> Why should the sufferer be born to see the light?
> Why is life given to those who find it so bitter?

They long for death but it does not come,
they seek it more eagerly than hidden treasure.
They are glad when they reach the grave;

exult: rejoice.

when they come to the tomb they exult.
Why should a man be born to wander blindly,
hedged about by God on every side?. . .

Eliphaz Speaks and Job Answers

Job 4:1.

Then Eliphaz the Temanite spoke up:

venture: risk.

If one should venture a word with you, would
you lose patience?
Yet who could curb his tongue any longer?
Think how you once encouraged many,
how you braced feeble arms,
how a word from you upheld those who
stumbled
and put strength into failing knees.

adversity: hardship,
suffering.

But now adversity comes on you, and you are
impatient;
it touches you, and you are dismayed.
Does your piety give you no assurance?
Does your blameless life afford you no hope?
For consider, has any innocent person ever
perished?
Where have the upright ever been destroyed?
This is what I have seen:

plow mischief: plant
seeds of sin.

those who plow mischief and sow trouble
reap no other harvest.
They perish at the blast of God;
they are shrivelled by the breath of his nostrils. . . .

rebukes: scolds.

Happy indeed are they whom God rebukes!
Therefore do not reject the Almighty's discipline.
For, though he wounds, he will bind up;
the hands that harm will heal. . . .

Job answered: . . .

Job 6:14.

Devotion is due from his friends
to one who despairs and loses faith in the
Almighty;

torrent: rushing stream
of water.

but my brothers have been deceptive as a torrent,
like the watercourses of torrents that run dry. . . .
Just so unreliable have you now been to me:

you felt dismay and took fright. . . .
Tell me plainly, and I shall listen in silence;
show me where I have been at fault. . . .
As a cloud breaks up and disperses,
so no one who goes down to Sheol ever comes back;   **Sheol:** place of the dead.
he never returns to his house,
and his abode knows him no more.
But I cannot hold my peace;
I shall speak out in my anguish of spirit
and complain in my bitterness of soul.
Am I the monster of the deep, am I the sea
    serpent,
that you set a watch over me?. . .   **you:** Job is now speaking
I am in despair, I have no desire to live;   to God.
let me alone, for my days are but a breath.
What is man, that you make much of him
and turn your thoughts towards him,
only to punish him morning after morning
or to test him every hour of the day?. . .
Will you not look away from me for an instant,
leave me long enough to swallow my spittle?   **spittle:** saliva.
If I have sinned, what harm can I do you,
you watcher of the human heart?
Why have you made me your target?
Why have I become a burden to you?
Why do you not pardon my offense
and take away my guilt?
For soon I shall lie in the dust of the grave;
you may seek me, but I shall be no more.

Bildad Speaks and Job Answers
Then Bildad the Shuhite spoke up: **Job 8:1.**

How long will you go on saying such things,
those long-winded ramblings of an old man?
Does God pervert justice?
Does the Almighty pervert what is right?. . .   **pervert:** overturn; go
Enquire now of older generations   against.
and consider the experience of their forefathers;
for we are but of yesterday and know nothing;
our days on earth are but a passing shadow.
Will they not teach you and tell you
and pour out the wisdom of their minds?. . .
Be sure, God will not spurn the blameless man,   **spurn:** reject.

nor will he clasp the hand of the wrongdoer.
He will yet fill your mouth with laughter,
and shouts of joy will be on your lips. . . .

Job 9:1. Job answered:

Indeed, this I know for the truth:
that no one can win his case against God. . . .
If the appeal is to force, see how mighty he is;
if to justice, who can compel him to give me a
    hearing?
Though I am in the right, he condemns me out
    of my own mouth;
though I am blameless, he makes me out to be
    crooked.

myself . . . nothing: I consider myself of no importance.

Blameless, I say; of myself
I reck nothing, I hold my life cheap.
But it is all one; therefore I declare,
"He destroys blameless and wicked alike."
When a sudden flood brings death,
he mocks the plight of the innocent.
When a country is delivered into the power of
    the wicked,
he blindfolds the eyes of its judges. . . .
Though I were to wash myself with soap
and cleanse my hands with lye,

miry: muddy.

you would thrust me into the miry pit
and my clothes would render me loathsome.
God is not as I am, not someone I can challenge,
and say, "Let us confront one another in court."

arbitrate: act as a judge.

If only there were one to arbitrate between us
and impose his authority on us both. . . .

Zophar Speaks and Job Answers
Job 11:1. Then Zophar the Naamathite spoke up:

spate: flood.
glib of tongue: i.e., smooth talker.

Is this spate of words to go unanswered?
Must the glib of tongue always be right?
Is your endless talk to reduce others to silence?
When you speak irreverently, is no one to take
    you to task?
You claim that your opinions are sound;
you say to God, "I am spotless in your sight."

But if only God would speak
and open his lips to reply,
to expound to you the secrets of wisdom,   **expound:** explain.
for wonderful are its achievements!
Know then that God exacts from you   **exacts:** demands.
less than your sin deserves.
Can you fathom the mystery of God,   **fathom:** find out.
or attain to the limits of the Almighty?
They are higher than the heavens. What can you
   do?
They are deeper than Sheol. What can you
   know?. . .

Job answered: **Job 12:1.**

No doubt you are intelligent people,
and when you die, wisdom will perish!
But I have sense, as well as you;
in no way do I fall short of you;
what gifts indeed have you that others have
   not?. . .
I am ready to argue with God,
while you go on smearing truth with your
   falsehoods,
one and all stitching a patchwork of lies.
If only you would be silent
and let silence be your wisdom!
Listen, now, to my arguments;
attend while I put my case.   **attend:** pay attention.
Is it on God's behalf that you speak so wickedly,
In his defense that you voice what is false?
Must you take God's part,
putting his case for him?
Will all go well when he examines you?
Can you deceive him as you could a human
   being?. . .
Your moralizing talk is so much dross,   **dross:** rubbish.
your arguments crumble like clay. . . .

Job States His Case to God
Every being born of woman is short-lived and   **Job 14:1.**
   full of trouble.
He blossoms like a flower and withers away;

fleeting as a shadow, he does not endure. . . .
If a man dies, can he live again?
I would not lose hope, however long my service,
waiting for my relief to come.
You would summon me, and I would answer;
you would long to see the creature you have
    made,
whereas now you count my every step,
watching all my errant course.
Every offense of mine is stored in your bag,

where you keep my iniquity under seal.
Yet as a falling mountainside is swept away,
and a rock is dislodged from its place,
as water wears away stone,

and a cloudburst scours the soil from the land,
so you have wiped out the hope of frail man;
finally you overpower him, and he is gone;
with changed appearance he is banished from
    your sight.
His sons may rise to honor, but he is unaware of it;
they may sink into obscurity, but he knows it not.
His kinsfolk are grieved for him
and his slaves mourn his loss. . . .

Job 19:23.

Would that my words might be written down,
that they might be engraved in an inscription,

incised: cut (into stone).

incised with an iron tool and filled with lead,
carved in rock as a witness!

vindicator: one who
justifies.

But I know that my vindicator lives
and that he will rise last to speak in court;

discern: see, recognize.

I shall discern my witness standing at my side
and see my defending counsel, even God
    himself,
whom I shall see with my own eyes,
I myself and no other. . . .

Job Speaks to His Comforters

Job 27:1.

Then Job resumed his discourse:

I swear by the living God, who has denied me
    justice,
by the Almighty, who has filled me with
    bitterness,

that so long as there is any life left in me
and the breath of God is in my nostrils,
no untrue word will pass my lips,
nor will my tongue utter any falsehood.
Far be it from me to concede that you are right!   concede: admit.
Till I cease to be, I shall not abandon my claim of
    innocence.
I maintain and shall never give up the rightness
    of my cause;
so long as I live, I shall not change.

If only I could go back to the old days,   Job 29:2.
to the time when God was watching over me . . . .
When I went out of my gate up to the town
to take my seat in the public square,
young men saw me and kept back out of sight,
old men rose to their feet,
men in authority broke off their talk
and put their hands to their lips;
the voices of the nobles died away,
and every man held his tongue. . . .
I was eyes to the blind
and feet to the lame;
I was a father to the needy,
and I took up the stranger's cause. . . .
I have taken an oath   Job 31:1.
never to let my eyes linger on a girl. . . .
I swear I have had no dealings with falsehood
and have not gone hotfoot after deceit.   gone hotfoot: chased.
Let God weigh me in the scales of justice,
and he will know that I am blameless! . . .
If my heart has been enticed by a woman   enticed: tempted.
or I have lurked by my neighbour's door . . .
If I ever rejected the plea of my slave or
    slave-girl
when they brought a complaint against me . . .
If I have withheld from the poor what they
    needed
or made the widow's eye grow dim with tears;
if I have eaten my portion of food by myself,
and the fatherless child has not shared it with
    me . . .
if I have seen anyone perish for lack of clothing
or a poor man with nothing to cover him;

if his body had no cause to bless me,
because he was not kept warm with a fleece
     from my flock . . .
then may my shoulder-blade be torn from my
     shoulder,
my arm be wrenched out of its socket!

Have I rejoiced at the ruin of anyone who hated me
or been filled with glee when misfortune
     overtook him? . . .
Have I ever concealed my misdeeds as others do,
keeping my guilt hidden within my breast? . . .
Let me but call a witness in my defense!
Let the Almighty state his case against me!

indictment: legal list of
accusations.

If my accuser had written out his indictment,
I should not keep silence and remain indoors.
No! I should flaunt it on my shoulder
and wear it like a crown on my head;
I should plead the whole record of my life
and present that in court as my defense. . . .

Job 38:1.

The Lord Answers

Then the Lord answered Job out of the tempest:

darkens counsel: hides
wisdom.
devoid: empty.

Who is this who darkens counsel
with words devoid of knowledge?
Brace yourself and stand up like a man;
I shall put questions to you, and you must
     answer.
Where were you when I laid the earth's
     foundations?
Tell me, if you know and understand.

fixed its dimensions: set
its boundaries.

Who fixed its dimensions? Surely you know!
Who stretched a measuring line over it?
On what do its supporting pillars rest?
Who set its corner-stone in place,
while the morning stars sang in chorus
and the sons of God all shouted for joy? . . .
Can you command the clouds
to envelop you in a deluge of rain?
If you bid lightning speed on its way,
will it say to you, "I am ready"?
Who put wisdom in depths of darkness
and veiled understanding in secrecy?

Who is wise enough to marshal the rain-clouds
and empty the cisterns of heaven,
when the dusty soil sets in a dense mass,
and the clods of earth stick fast together? . . .
Do you give the horse his strength?
Have you clothed his neck with a mane?
Do you make him quiver like a locust's wings,
when his shrill neighing strikes terror?
He shows his mettle as he paws and prances;
in his might he charges the armored line.
He scorns alarms and knows no dismay;
he does not shy away before the sword. . . .
Trembling with eagerness, he devours the
    ground
and when the trumpet sounds there is no
    holding him;
at the trumpet-call he cries "Aha!"
and from afar he scents the battle,
the shouting of the captains, and the war cries.
Does your skill teach the hawk to use its pinions
and spread its wings towards the south?
Do you instruct the eagle to soar aloft
and build its nest high up?
It dwells among the rocks and there it has its
    nest,
secure on a rocky crag. . . .
Is it for a man who disputes with the Almighty
    to be stubborn?
Should he who argues with God answer back?

Job answered the Lord:

What reply can I give you, I who carry no
    weight?
I put my finger to my lips.
I have spoken once; I shall not answer again;
twice have I spoken; I shall do so no more.

Then the Lord answered Job out of the tempest:

Brace yourself and stand up like a man;
I shall put questions to you, and you must
    answer.
Would you dare deny that I am just,
or put me in the wrong to prove yourself right? . . .

marshal: arrange, gather.
cisterns: reservoirs, storage tanks.

Job 39:19

mettle: spirit.

pinions: feathers.

Job 40:1

shroud: cover, hide.

Deck yourself out, if you can, in pride and dignity,
array yourself in pomp and splendor. . . .
look on all who are proud, and bring them low,
crush the wicked where they stand;
bury them in the earth together,
and shroud them in an unknown grave.
Then I in turn would acknowledge
that your own right hand could save you. . . .

Job 41:1.
whale: in other versions,
"Leviathan," a sea
monster representing
disorder and evil.

Can you lift out the whale with a gaff
or slip a noose round its tongue?
Can you pass a rope through its nose
or pierce its jaw with a hook?
Will it take to pleading with you for mercy
or beg for its life with soft words?
Will it enter into an agreement with you
to become your slave for life?
Will you toy with it as with a bird
or keep it on a leash for your girls? . . .

cauldron: kettle.

He makes the deep water boil like a cauldron,
he churns up the lake like ointment in a mixing
    bowl.
He leaves a shining trail behind him,
and in his wake the great river is like white hair.
He has no equal on earth,
a creature utterly fearless.
He looks down on all, even the highest;
over all proud beasts he is king.

Job Responds

Job answered the Lord:

I know that you can do all things
and that no purpose is beyond you.
You ask: Who is this obscuring counsel yet
    lacking knowledge?
But I have spoken of things
which I have not understood,
things too wonderful for me to know.
Listen, and let me speak. You said:
I shall put questions to you, and you must
    answer.

I knew of you then only by report,
but now I see you with my own eyes.
Therefore I yield,
repenting in dust and ashes.

Epilogue

When the Lord had finished speaking to Job, he said to Eliphaz the Temanite, "My anger is aroused against you and your two friends, because, unlike my servant Job, you have not spoken as you ought about me. Now take seven bulls and seven rams, go to my servant Job and offer a whole-offering for yourselves, and he will intercede for you. I shall surely show him favor by not being harsh with you because you have not spoken as you ought about me, as he has done." Then Eliphaz the Temanite and Bildad the Shuhite and Zophar the Naamathite went and carried out the Lord's command, and the Lord showed favor to Job when he had interceded for his friends.

intercede for you: ask favors on your behalf.

The Lord restored Job's fortunes, and gave him twice the possessions he had before. All Job's brothers and sisters and his acquaintance of former days came and feasted with him in his home. They consoled and comforted him for all the misfortunes which the Lord had inflicted on him, and each of them gave him a sheep and a gold ring. Thus the Lord blessed the end of Job's life more than the beginning: he had fourteen thousand sheep and six thousand camels, a thousand yoke of oxen, and as many she-donkeys. He also had seven sons and three daughters; he named his eldest daughter Jemimah, the second Keziah, and the third Keren-happuch. There were no women in all the world so beautiful as Job's daughters; and their father gave them an inheritance with their brothers.

Thereafter Job lived another hundred and forty years; he saw his sons and his grandsons to four generations, and he died at a very great age.

FOR CLOSE READING

1. What limits does God place upon Satan before each of the times Job is tested?

2. How do Eliphaz, Bildad, and Zophar respond when they first meet Job? How does their attitude change during their talks with him?

3. Give three points or arguments made by Job's "comforters."

4. How does Job's wealth at the end compare with his possessions at the beginning of the story?

FOR THOUGHT AND DISCUSSION

5. Why do you think God accepts Satan's challenge?

6. What impression do you get of Satan from his discussions with God? Whom do you consider responsible for Job's suffering, Satan, God, or Job himself? Explain.

7. In the Prologue, what is the effect of the repeated phrase, "While he was still speaking"?

8. Even after his last, physical affliction, Job refuses to curse God and seems to accept his fate: "If we accept good from God, shall we not accept evil?" How do you explain the seeming change in attitude expressed in Job's very next speech?

9. In what way does "dialogue" help explore a complex issue? In what ways does it get in the way? What would be gained or lost if Job had had only one comforter? no comforter?

10. What is your opinion of Eliphaz, Bildad, and Zophar as friends? as advisers? Why do you think God criticizes these men at the end of the story?

11. What would you say is Job's tone of voice when he tells his comforters "No doubt you are intelligent people / and when you die, wisdom will perish!"?

12. Beginning on page 276, Job defends his righteousness. What flaws, if any, do you find in this self-portrait? Why do you suppose God finally accepts Job's challenge after this speech?

13. What do you think is the purpose of God's questions to Job? In what tone of voice do you think God asks these questions?

14. Do you think Job repents: (*a*) because he has been overwhelmed by a full understanding of God's power; (*b*) because his questions have been answered; (*c*) because he has had a first-hand experience of God; (*d*) because he is convinced, after all, that he deserved the suffering he received? Why do you think so? Can you suggest any other possible reasons for Job's repentance?

15. Select a passage from the story of Job that you find particularly powerful or moving. What features of language—rhythm, imagery, and so on—make the passage effective? Do you respond more to the meaning of the words or to the style of language? Explain.

RESPONDING

1. **Writing** Create a conversation between Job and his wife about his troubles. If possible, perform this dialogue in class.

2. **Activity** Prepare a dramatic reading for the class of God's speech out of the tempest or some other passage of your choice.

3. **Humanities Connection** Collect and record passages of music that express the mood or feeling of various parts of the story of Job. For example, what kind of music would you use to suggest the peace and prosperity that Job enjoys in the Prologue? What music would you use to suggest the catastrophes? the dialogues with the comforters? God's speeches? Job's recovery? If possible, tape-record your sequence of music to make a "tone poem" of the story of Job.

from A Masque of Reason

*In this passage from a dramatic poem,
God is speaking to Job.*

Yes, by and by. But first a larger matter.
I've had you on my mind a thousand years
To thank you someday for the way you helped me
Establish once for all the principle
There's no connection man can reason out
Between his just deserts and what he gets.
Virtue may fail and wickedness succeed.
'Twas a great demonstration we put on.
I should have spoken sooner had I found
The word I wanted. You would have supposed
One who in the beginning *was* the Word
Would be in a position to command it.
I have to wait for words like anyone.
Too long I've owed you this apology
For the apparently unmeaning sorrow
You were afflicted with in those old days.
But it was of the essence of the trial
You shouldn't understand it at the time.
It had to seem unmeaning to have meaning.
And it came out all right. I have no doubt
You realize by now the part you played
To stultify the Deuteronomist
And change the tenor of religious thought.
My thanks are to you for releasing me
From moral bondage to the human race.
The only free will there at first was man's,
Who could do good or evil as he chose.
I had no choice but I must follow him
With forfeits and rewards he understood—

5

10

15

20

25

just deserts (di zėrts′):
deserved reward or
punishment.

stultify . . .
Deuteronomist: i.e.,
block the lawmaker.
The biblical book of
Deuteronomy stresses
that breaking the law will
bring God's judgment,
while obedience will
bring blessing.

30 Unless I liked to suffer loss of worship.
I had to prosper good and punish evil.
You changed all that. You set me free to reign.
You are the Emancipator of your God,
And as such I promote you to a saint.

Emancipator: one who frees.

FOR THOUGHT AND DISCUSSION

1. What impression do you get of God from this speech? Choose three words to describe him.

2. According to this speech, what "principle" was established by Job's ordeal (lines 4–7)? How would you say this came about?

3. How do you suppose Job would respond to this explanation of his suffering?

4. If the system of reward and punishment is as unfair as this speech suggests, what reasons would you say still exist for being good and virtuous?

H . G . W E L L S

The Prologue
in Heaven

In this passage from the novel
The Undying Fire, *God and Satan*
continue their discussion about Job.

Now, as in the ancient story, it is a reception of the sons of God.

The Master of the gathering, to whom one might reasonably attribute a sublime boredom, seeing that everything that can possibly happen is necessarily known to him, displays on the contrary as lively an interest in his interlocutor as ever. This interlocutor is of course Satan, the Unexpected. . . .

interlocutor (in'ter lok'ye ter): participant in a conversation.

"There was a certain man in the land of Uz whose name was Job."

"We remember him."

"We had a wager of sorts," said Satan. "It was some time ago."

"The wager was never distinct—and now that you remind me of it, there is no record of your paying."

"Did I lose or win? The issue was obscured by discussion. How those men did talk! You intervened. There was no decision."

intervened: i.e., stepped in, became involved.

"You lost, Satan," said a great Being of Light who bore a book. "The wager was whether Job would lose faith in God and curse him. He was afflicted in every way, and particularly by the conversation of his friends. But there remains an undying fire in man."

Satan rested his dark face on his hand, and looked down between his knees through the pellucid floor to

pellucid: transparent.

that little eddying in the ether which makes our world. "Job," he said, "lives still."

Then after an interval: "The whole earth is now—Job."

Satan delights equally in statistics and in quoting scripture. He leant back in his seat with an expression of quiet satisfaction. "Job," he said, in easy narrative tones, "lived to a great age. After his disagreeable experiences he lived one hundred and forty years. He had again seven sons and three daughters, and he saw his offspring for four generations. So much is classical. These ten children brought him seventy grandchildren, who again prospered generally and had large families. (It was a prolific strain.) And now if we allow three generations to a century, and the reality is rather more than that, and if we take the survival rate as roughly three to a family, and if we agree with your excellent Bishop Ussher that Job lived about thirty-five centuries ago, that gives us——How many? Three to the hundred and fifth power?... It is at any rate a sum vastly in excess of the present population of the earth.... You have globes and rolls and swords and stars here; has anyone a slide rule?"

But the computation was brushed aside.

"A thousand years in my sight are but as yesterday when it is past. I will grant what you seek to prove; that Job has become mankind."

The dark regard of Satan smote down through the quivering universe and left the toiling light waves behind. "See there," he said pointing. "My old friend on his little planet—Adam—Job—Man—like a roast on a spit. It is time we had another wager."

God condescended to look with Satan at mankind, circling between day and night. "Whether he will curse or bless?"

"Whether he will even remember God."

"I have given my promise that I will at last restore Adam."

The downcast face smiled faintly.

"These questions change from age to age," said Satan.

"The Whole remains the same."

"The story grows longer in either direction," said Satan, speaking as one who thinks aloud; "past and

eddying in the ether: i.e., a small whirling current in space.

prolific strain: productive race or breed.

Bishop Ussher: a 17th-century churchman and scholar known for his now-disputed dating of biblical events.

regard: gaze.

like . . . on a spit: i.e., like meat stuck on a rod, turning over a flame.

restore Adam: i.e., on Judgment Day.

future unfold together. . . . When the first atoms jarred I was there, and so conflict was there—and progress. The days of the old story have each expanded to hundreds of millions of years now, and still I am in them all. The sharks and crawling monsters of the early seas, the first things that crept out of the water into the jungle of fronds and stems, the early reptiles, the leaping and flying dragons of the great age of life, the mighty beasts of hoof and horn that came later; they all feared and suffered and were perplexed. At last came this Man of yours, out of the woods, hairy, beetle-browed and bloodstained, peering not too hopefully for that Eden-bower of the ancient story. It wasn't there. There never had been a garden. He had fallen before he arose, and the weeds and thorns are as ancient as the flowers. The Fall goes back in time now beyond man, beyond the world, beyond imagination. The very stars were born in sin. . . .

bower: sheltered garden.

"If we can still call it sin," mused Satan.

"On a little planet this Thing arises, this red earth, this Adam, this Edomite, this Job. He builds cities, he tills the earth, he catches the lightning and makes a slave of it, he changes the breed of beast and grain. Clever things to do, but still petty things. You say that in some manner he is to come up at last to *this*. . . . He is too foolish and too weak. His achievements only illuminate his limitations. Look at his little brain boxed up from growth in a skull of bone! Look at his bag of a body full of rags and rudiments, a haggis of diseases! His life is decay. . . . *Does* he grow? I do not see it. Has he made any perceptible step forward in quality in the last ten thousand years? He quarrels endlessly and aimlessly with himself. . . . In a little while his planet will cool and freeze."

rudiments: undeveloped parts.

haggis: a kind of stew or meat pudding.

"In the end he will rule over the stars," said the voice that was above Satan. "My spirit is in him."

Satan shaded his face with his hand from the effulgence about him. He said no more for a time, but sat watching mankind as a boy might sit on the bank of a stream and watch the fry of minnows in the clear water of a shallow.

effulgence (i ful´ jəns): brilliant light, radiance.

fry of minnows: school of tiny fish.

"Nay," he said at last, "but it is incredible. It is impossible. I have disturbed and afflicted him long enough. I have driven him as far as he can be driven. But now I am moved to pity. Let us end this dispute. It has been interesting, but now—— Is it not enough? It grows cruel. He has reached his limit. Let us give him a little peace now, Lord, a little season of sunshine and plenty, and then some painless universal pestilence and so let him die."

"He is immortal and he does but begin."

"He is mortal and near his end. At times no doubt he has a certain air that seems to promise understanding and mastery in his world; it is but an air; give me the power to afflict and subdue him but a little, and after a few squeaks of faith and hope he will whine and collapse like any other beast. He will behave like any kindred creature with a smaller brain and a larger jaw; he too is doomed to suffer to no purpose, to struggle by instinct merely to live, to endure for a season and then to pass. . . . Give me but the power and you shall see his courage snap like a rotten string."

"You may do all that you will to him, only you must not slay him. For my spirit is in him."

"That he will cast out of his own accord—when I have ruined his hopes, mocked his sacrifices, blackened his skies and filled his veins with torture. . . . But it is too easy to do. Let me just slay him now and end his story. Then let us begin another, a different one, and something more amusing. Let us, for example, put brains—and this Soul of yours—into the ants or the bees or the beavers! Or take up the octopus, already a very tactful and intelligent creature!"

"No; but do as you have said, Satan. For you also are my instrument. Try Man to the uttermost. See if he is indeed no more than a little stir amidst the slime, a fuss in the mud that signifies nothing. . . ."

The Satan, his face hidden in shadow, seemed not to hear this, but remained still and intent upon the world of men.

pestilence: deadly disease.

FOR CLOSE READING

1. Quote statements from this passage that express Satan's and God's views of human nature.

2. According to Satan, what should God do with the human race? Why?

FOR THOUGHT AND DISCUSSION

3. How is Satan portrayed in this passage? How does this Satan compare with the biblical Satan?

4. Why do you suppose Satan says "there was no decision" in the "wager" about Job?

5. What do you think God means by "Job has become mankind"?

6. This passage expresses both optimistic and pessimistic opinions about humanity. Give some arguments on both sides. Which do you tend to agree with? Why?

Job

They did not know his face
Where the chin rested on the sunken breastbone,
So changed it was, emptied, rinsed out and dried,
And for some future purpose put aside.
5 Expecting torment, they were much perplexed.

His world had gone
And he sat isolated, foul and flyblown,   **flyblown:** covered with
Without a world, with nothing but a mind   the eggs of flies.
Staggered to silence since it could not find
10 Language to utter its amazing text.

For where was Job?
In some strange state, unknown and yet well-known,
A mask that stared hollowly in God's breath,
Mind that perceived the irrelevance of death,   **percieved . . . irrelevance:**
15 And the astonished heart unmoved, unvexed.   saw the unimportance.

                                                           unvexed: not angered or
They did not see his soul   annoyed.
Perched like a bird upon the broken hearthstone,   **hearthstone:** the floor of
Piping incessantly above the ashes   a fireplace, often a
What next what next what next what next what next   symbol of home and
                                                           family.

FOR THOUGHT AND DISCUSSION

1. Who do you think are "they" in line 1? What do they see when they look at Job? What are they unable to see?

2. In your opinion, what words in the poem are most effective in suggesting Job's physical state? his mental state?

3. Why is Job silent?

4. To what is Job's soul compared? How does this comparison affect your feelings about Job?

from J. B.

[*J. B. is a modern Job, a millionaire who has lost his children and his fortune through war, accident, and murder. In this scene J. B. and his wife Sarah struggle to find some meaning to their tragedy.*

The setting of the entire play is a huge circus tent where a sort of sideshow has been set up, including a six-foot-high platform, a wooden ladder, a table, and several chairs. At the beginning of the play two old actors come onstage to put on masks and play the roles of God and Satan; they observe J. B.'s experiences from the "heavenly" platform. Satan is played by Nickles; throughout this scene he speaks to God, who remains silent and unseen on the platform. The other characters in this scene, on the ground, are Mrs. Adams, her young daughter Jolly, Mrs. Murphy, Mrs. Lesure, and Mrs. Botticelli.]

Scene 8

(*There is no light but the glow on the canvas sky, which holds the looming, leaning shadows. They fade as a match is struck. It flares in* SARAH's *hand, showing her face, and glimmers out against the wick of a dirty lantern. As the light of the lantern rises,* J. B. *is seen lying on the broken propped-up table, naked but for a few rags of clothing.* SARAH *looks at him in the new light, shudders, lets her head drop into her hands. There is a long silence and then a movement in the darkness of the open door where four* WOMEN *and a young* GIRL *stand, their arms filled with blankets and newspapers. They come forward slowly into the light.*)

NICKLES (*unseen, his cracked, cackling voice drifting down from the darkness of the platform overhead*).
Never fails! Never fails!
Count on you to make a mess of it!
Every blessed blundering time
You hit at one man you blast thousands.

5 Think of that Flood of yours—a massacre!
Now you've fumbled it again:
Tumbled a whole city down
To blister one man's skin with agony.
(NICKLES's *white coat appears at the foot of the ladder. The* WOMEN, *in the circle of the lantern, are walking slowly around* J. B. *and* SARAH, *staring at them as though they were figures in a show window.*)

NICKLES. Look at your works! Those shivering women

10 Sheltering under any crumbling
Heap to keep the sky out! Weeping!
MRS. ADAMS. That's him.
JOLLY ADAMS.   Who's him?
MRS. ADAMS.   Grammar, Jolly.

15 **MRS. LESURE.** Who did she say it was?
MRS. MURPHY.   Him she said it was.
        Poor soul!
MRS. LESURE. Look at them sores on him!
MRS. ADAMS. Don't look child. You'll remember them.

20 **JOLLY ADAMS** (*proudly*). Every sore I seen I remember.
MRS. BOTTICELLI. Who did she say it was?
MRS. MURPHY.   Him.
MRS. ADAMS. That's his wife.
MRS. LESURE.   She's pretty.

25 **MRS. BOTTICELLI.**   Ain't she.
        Looks like somebody we've seen.
MRS. ADAMS. (*snooting her*). I don't believe you would have seen her:
        Pictured possibly—her picture
        Posted in the penthouse.

30 **MRS. BOTTICELLI.**   Puce with pants?
MRS. ADAMS. No, the negligee.
MRS. BOTTICELLI.   The net?
MRS. ADAMS. The simple silk.
                        Oh la! With sequins?

puce (pyüs): a purplish brown.

MRS. MURPHY. Here's a place to park your
    poodle—
    Nice cool floor.
MRS. LESURE. Shove over, dearie.
(The WOMEN *settle themselves on their newspapers off at
the edge of the circle of light.* NICKLES *has perched
himself on a chair at the side. Silence.)*
J. B. *(a whisper).* God let me die!
(NICKLES *leers up into the dark toward the unseen
platform.)*
SARAH *(her voice dead).* You think He'd help you
    Even to that?
(Silence. SARAH *looks up, turning her face away from* J. B.
She speaks without passion, almost mechanically.)
SARAH.   God is our enemy.
J. B. No. . . . No. . . . No. . . . Don't
    Say that Sarah!
(SARAH's *head turns toward him slowly as though
dragged against her will. She stares and cannot look
away.)*
                 God had something
    Hidden from our hearts to show.
NICKLES. She knows! She's looking at it!
J. B.   Try to
    sleep.
SARAH *(bitterly).* He should have kept it hidden.
J. B. Sleep now.
SARAH.   You don't have to see it:
    I do.
J. B.   Yes, I know.
NICKLES *(a cackle).* He knows!
    He's back behind it and he knows!
    If he could see what she can see
    There's something else he might be knowing.
J. B. Once I knew a charm for sleeping—
    Not as forgetfulness but gift,
    Not as sleep but second sight,
    Come and from my eyelids lift
    The dead of night.
SARAH.   The dead . . .
                       of night . . .
(She drops her head to her knees, whispering.)
    Come and from my eyelids lift
    The dead of night.
(Silence.)

J. B.   Out of sleep
Something of our own comes back to us:
A drowned man's garment from the sea.
(SARAH *turns the lantern down. Silence. Then the voices
of the* WOMEN, *low.*)
MRS. BOTTICELLI. Poor thing!
70 **MRS. MURPHY.**   Poor thing!
Not a chick not a child between them.
MRS. ADAMS. First their daughters. Then their sons.
MRS. MURPHY. First son first. Blew him to pieces.

mischance: bad luck.

More mischance it was than war.
75 Asleep on their feet in the frost they walked
into it.

two . . . viaduct: two of
J. B.'s and Sarah's
children were killed in
an auto accident.

MRS. ADAMS. Two at the viaduct. That makes three.
JOLLY ADAMS (*a child's chant*). Jolly saw the picture!
The picture!
MRS. ADAMS. Jolly Adams, you keep quiet.
JOLLY ADAMS. Wanna know? The whole of the
viaduct. . . .
80 **MRS. ADAMS.** Never again will you look at them!
Never!
MRS. LESURE. Them magazines! They're awful!
Which?

the little one: J. B.'s
youngest daughter had
been murdered.

MRS. MURPHY. And after that the little one.
MRS. BOTTICELLI.   Who in the
World are they talking about, the little one?
85 What are they talking?
MRS. LESURE.   I don't know.
Somebody dogged by death it must be.
MRS. BOTTICELLI. Him it must be.
MRS. LESURE.   Who's him?
90 **MRS. ADAMS.** You know who.
MRS. MURPHY.   You remember. . . .
MRS. ADAMS.   Hush! The child!
MRS. MURPHY.   Back of the lumberyard.
MRS. LESURE. Oh! Him!
95 **MRS. MURPHY.**   Who did you think it was—
Penthouse and negligees, daughters and dying?
MRS. BOTTICELLI. Him? That's him? The
millionaire?
MRS. LESURE.   Millionaires he buys like cabbages.
MRS. MURPHY. He couldn't buy cabbages now by
the look of him:
100 The rags he's got on.

MRS. BOTTICELLI. Look at them sores!

MRS. MURPHY. All that's left him now is her.

MRS. BOTTICELLI. Still that's something—a good woman.

MRS. MURPHY. What good is a woman to him with that hide on him?—

105 Or he to her if you think of it.

MRS. ADAMS.   Don't!

MRS. LESURE. Can you blame her?

MRS. MURPHY.   I don't blame her. All I say is she's no comfort.

110 She won't cuddle.

MRS. ADAMS.   Really, Mrs. . . .

MRS. MURPHY. Murphy call me. What's got into you?. . .

.   .   .

MRS. ADAMS. None of that! We have a child here! *(Silence.)*

.   .   .

115 **MRS. MURPHY.** Roll a little nearer, dearie, Me backside's froze.

MRS. LESURE.   You smell of roses.

MRS. MURPHY. Neither do you but you're warm.

MRS. BOTTICELLI.   Well,

120 Good night, ladies. Good night, ladies. . . .

(Silence. Out of the silence, felt rather than heard at first, a sound of sobbing, a muffled, monotonous sound like the heavy beat of a heart.)

J. B. If you could only sleep a little Now they're quiet, now they're still.

SARAH *(her voice broken).* I try. But oh I close my eyes and . . .

Eyes are open there to meet me!

(Silence. Then SARAH's *voice in an agony of bitterness.)*

125 My poor babies! Oh, my babies!

(J. B. pulls himself up, sits huddled on his table in the feeble light of the lamp, his rags about him.)

J. B. *(gently).* Go to sleep.

SARAH.   Go! Go where?

If there were darkness I'd go there.

If there were night I'd lay me down in it.

130 God has shut the night against me.

God has set the dark alight

With horror blazing blind as day
When I go toward it . . .
                            close my eyes.
135 **J. B.** I know. I know those waking eyes.
His will is everywhere against us—
Even in our sleep, our dreams. . . .
NICKLES *(a snort of laughter up toward the dark of the platform). Your* will, *his* peace!
Doesn't seem to grasp that, does he?
140 Give him another needling twinge
Between the withers and the works—
He'll understand you better.
J. B.   If I
Knew. . . . If I knew why!
145 **NICKLES.**   If he knew
Why he wouldn't be there. He'd be
Strangling, drowning, suffocating,
Diving for a sidewalk somewhere. . . .
J. B. What I *can't* bear is the blindness—
150 Meaninglessness—the numb blow
Fallen in the stumbling night.
SARAH *(starting violently to her feet).* Has death no
meaning? Pain no meaning?
(She points at his body.)
Even these suppurating sores—
Have they no meaning for you?
155 **NICKLES.**   Ah!
J. B. *(from his heart's pain).* God will not punish
without cause.
(NICKLES *doubles up in spasms of soundless laughter.)*
J. B. God is just.
SARAH *(hysterically).* God is just!
If God is just our slaughtered children
160 Stank with sin, were rotten with it!
(She controls herself with difficulty, turns toward him, reaches her arms out, lets them fall.)
Oh, my dear! my dear! my dear!
Does God demand deception of us?
Purchase His innocence by ours?
Must we be guilty for Him?—bear
165 The burden of the world's malevolence
For Him who made the world?
J. B.   He
Knows the guilt is mine. He must know:
Has He not punished it? He knows its

withers: i.e., shoulder blades.

suppurating (sup′yə rāt ing): oozing.

malevolence (mə lev′ə ləns): ill will; spite.

170 Name, its time, its face, its circumstance,
The figure of its day, the door,
The opening of the door, the room, the moment. . . .
SARAH *(fiercely).* And you? Do you? You do not
know it.
Your punishment is all you know.
(She moves toward the door, stops, turns.)
175 I will not stay here if you lie—
Connive in your destruction, cringe to it:
Not if you betray my children...

I will not stay to listen. . . .

180   They are
Dead and they were innocent: I will not
Let you sacrifice their deaths
To make injustice justice and God good!
J. B. *(covering his face with his hands).* My heart beats.
I cannot answer it.
185 **SARAH.** If you buy quiet with their innocence—
Theirs or yours . . .
(Softly.)
                        I will not love you.
J. B. I have no choice but to be guilty.
SARAH *(her voice rising).* We have the choice to
live or die,
190 All of us . . .
                 curse God and die. . . .
(Silence.)
J. B. God is God or we are nothing—
Mayflies that leave their husks behind—
Our tiny lives ridiculous—a suffering
195 Not even sad that Someone Somewhere
Laughs at as we laugh at apes.
We have no choice but to be guilty.
God is unthinkable if we are innocent.
*(SARAH turns, runs soundlessly out of the circle of light,
out of the door. The* WOMEN *stir.* MRS. MURPHY
comes up on her elbow.)
MRS. MURPHY. What did I say? I said she'd walk
out on him.
200 **MRS. LESURE.** She did.
MRS. BOTTICELLI.   Did she?
MRS. MURPHY.   His hide was too
much for her.

connive: cooperate secretly.

mayflies: fragile, short-lived insects.

MRS. BOTTICELLI. His hide or his heart.

MRS. MURPHY. The hide
comes between.

205   **MRS. BOTTICELLI.** The heart is the stranger.

MRS. MURPHY. Oh,
stranger!
It's always strange, the heart is: only
It's the skin we ever know.

J. B. *(raising his head).* Sarah, why do you not speak
to me? Sarah?
(Silence.)

210   **MRS. ADAMS.** Now he knows.

MRS. MURPHY. And he's alone now.
*(J. B.'s head falls forward onto his knees. Silence. Out of the
silence his voice in an agony of prayer.)*

J. B. Show me my guilt, O God!

NICKLES. His
Guilt! His! You heard that didn't you?

215   He wants to feel the feel of guilt—
That putrid poultice of the soul
That draws the poison in, not out—
Inverted catheter! You going to show him?
(Silence. NICKLES rises, moves toward the ladder.)
Well? You going to show him . . . Jahveh?
(Silence. He crosses to the ladder's foot.)

220   Where are those cold comforters of yours
Who justify the ways of God to
Job by making Job responsible?—
Those three upholders of the world—
Defenders of the universe—where are they?
*(Silence. He starts up the ladder. Stops. The jeering tone is
gone. His voice is bitter.)*

225   Must be almost time for comfort!. . .
(NICKLES *vanishes into the darkness above. The light
fades.)*

---

poultice: a poultice is a mass of herbs applied to reduce swelling. Nickles's image suggests that the guilt poultice has an opposite effect.

catheter (kath′ə tər): a slender tube inserted into any cavity of the body to drain fluids.

Jahveh (yä′vā): a way of pronouncing the Hebrew YHWH, usually translated "the Lord." Other variants are Yahweh and Jehovah.

FOR CLOSE READING

1. Even before the first speech, a grim, depressing mood is created in this scene. How is this done?

2. How many directions for silence do you find in this scene?

3. What information about J. B. and Sarah is given in the women's conversation in lines 69–120?

FOR THOUGHT AND DISCUSSION

4. Why do you think this scene includes so many silences? In what way does silence play a role in the biblical story of Job?

5. How would you describe the conversations of the women in lines 69–120? Apart from the necessary information these conversations provide, what other effects do they have on the scene?

6. What feelings about J. B. and Sarah are expressed by Nickles? by the women? What would be gained or lost if Nickles and the women were omitted from the scene?

7. Job's wife is mentioned only once in the Bible story. How reasonable do you think the playwright's portrayal of Sarah seems?

8. Which character made the stronger impression on you, J. B. or Sarah? Why? In your opinion, who seems to be suffering more? Why do you think so?

9. Why do you think J. B. insists that he must be guilty? Why do you think Sarah disagrees so strongly?

New Hampshire, February

crevices: cracks.

Nature had made them hide in crevices,
Two wasps so cold they looked like bark.
Why I do not know, but I took them
And I put them
5 In a metal pan, both day and dark.

Like God . . .
Michaelangelo: a reference
to a well-known scene by
the artist Michaelangelo
on the ceiling of the
Sistine Chapel in Rome.

preened: i.e., prepared
themselves.

quite: completely.

Like God touching his finger to Adam
I felt, and thought of Michaelangelo,
For whenever I breathed on them,
The slightest breath,
10 They leaped, and preened as if to go.

My breath controlled them always quite.
More sensitive than electric sparks
They came into life
Or they withdrew to ice,
15 While I watched, suspending remarks.

career: rush; rapid
movement.

Then one in a blind career got out,
And fell to the kitchen floor. I
Crushed him with my cold ski boot,
By accident. The other
20 Had not the wit to try or die.

shirk: avoid.

And so the other is still my pet.
The moral of this is plain.
But I will shirk it.
You will not like it. And
25 God does not live to explain.

FOR THOUGHT AND DISCUSSION

1. Controlling the wasps makes the speaker feel "like God." Have you ever had such "godlike" feelings? What were the circumstances?

2. Although this poem makes no mention of Job, what connections do you find between it and the story of Job?

3. What do you think is the "moral" of this poem? The speaker claims "You will not like it." Is he right? Explain.

9

In the Midst of the Enemy

The Victory of Judith

Nebuchadnezzar (neb/ə kəd nez/ər), *here described as king of Assyria, has sent his commander-in-chief Holofernes* (hol/ə fėr/nēz) *with a huge army to attack the countries west of his kingdom. To protect Jerusalem and the temple, the Israelites decide to resist. The citizens of Bethulia, under the leadership of Uzziah, try to block Holofernes' army in the hill-country passes, but the situation seems hopeless until Judith comes forward with a plan.*

Roman Catholic Bibles include the Book of Judith in the Old Testament; other Christian Bibles do not, though in some Judith appears in a section called "The Apocrypha." Jewish Bibles do not include Judith.

The Assyrians Threaten Bethulia

The following day Holofernes issued orders to his whole army and to the whole host of auxiliaries who had joined him, to break camp and march on Bethulia, to occupy the mountain passes and so open the campaign against the Israelites. The troops broke camp that same day. The actual fighting force numbered one hundred and twenty thousand infantry and twelve thousand cavalry, not to mention the baggage train with the vast number of men on foot concerned with that. . . .

Judith 7:1–2, 19–20, 23–24, 26–27; 8:1a, 2–3a, 4–11, 32b–34; 10:1–6a, 9–17, 21–23; 12:10–12, 15–20; 13:1–17; 14:11–18; 15:1–3, 12–13 (New Jerusalem Bible).

LEFT: *Daniel in the Lion's Den*, Souvigny Bible, Ms. 1, fol. 185v, French, late 12th c. Giraudon/Art Resource.

The Israelites called on the Lord their God, dispirited because the enemy had surrounded them and cut all line of retreat. For thirty-four days the Assyrian army, infantry, chariots, cavalrymen, had them surrounded. Every water-jar the inhabitants of Bethulia had was empty. . . .

Young men, women, children, the whole people thronged clamoring round Uzziah and the chief men of the town, shouting in the presence of the assembled elders. "May God be judge between you and us! For you have done us great harm, by not suing for peace with the Assyrians. . . . Call them in at once; hand the whole town over to be sacked by Holofernes' men and all his army. After all, we should be much better off as their booty than we are now; no doubt we shall be enslaved, but at least we shall be alive and not see our little ones dying before our eyes or our wives and children perishing.". . .

Judith was informed at the time of what had happened. . . . Her husband Manasseh, of her own tribe and family, had died at the time of the barley harvest. He was supervising the men as they bound up the sheaves in the field when he caught sunstroke and had to take to his bed. He died in Bethulia, his home town. . . . As a widow, Judith stayed inside her home for three years and four months. She had had an upper room built for herself on the roof. She wore sackcloth next to the skin and dressed in widow's weeds. She fasted every day of her widowhood except for the Sabbath eve, the Sabbath itself, the eve of New Moon, the feast of New Moon and the joyful festivals of the house of Israel. Now she was very beautiful, charming to see. Her husband Manasseh had left her gold and silver, menservants and maidservants, herds and land; and she lived among all her possessions without anyone finding a word to say against her, so devoutly did she fear God.

Hearing how the water shortage had demoralized the people and how they had complained bitterly to the headman of the town, and being also told what Uzziah had said to them and how he had given them his oath to surrender the town to the Assyrians in five days' time, Judith immediately sent the serving-woman who ran her household to summon Chabris

dispirited: discouraged.

bound . . . sheaves: tied up bundles of grain stalks.

sackcloth: rough fabric worn as a sign of mourning.

fear: honor, respect.

and Charmis, two elders of the town. When these came in she said:

"Listen to me, leaders of the people of Bethulia. You were wrong to speak to the people as you did today and to bind yourself by oath, in defiance of God, to surrender the town to our enemies if the Lord did not come to your help within a set number of days. . . .

"I intend to do something, the memory of which will be handed down to the children of our race from age to age. Tonight you must be at the gate of the town. I shall make my way out with my attendant. Before the time fixed by you for surrendering the town to our enemies, the Lord will make use of me to rescue Israel. You must not ask what I intend to do; I shall not tell you until I have done it.". . .

Judith Sets Her Plan in Motion

When she had finished praying, she got up from the floor, summoned her maid and went down into the rooms which she used on Sabbath days and festivals. There she removed the sackcloth she was wearing and taking off her widow's dress, she washed all over, anointed herself plentifully with perfumes, dressed her hair, wrapped a turban round it and put on the robe of joy she used to wear when her husband Manasseh was alive. She put sandals on her feet, put on her necklaces, bracelets, rings, earrings and all her jewellery, and made herself beautiful enough to beguile the eye of any man who saw her. Then she handed her maid a skin of wine and a flask of oil, filled a bag with barley girdle-cakes, cakes of dried fruit and pure loaves, and wrapping all these provisions up gave them to her as well. They then went out, making for the town of Bethulia. . . .

dressed: arranged.

beguile: attract.

girdle-cakes: probably similar to pancakes.

Judith worshiped God, and then she said, "Have the town gate opened for me so that I can go out and fulfill all the wishes you expressed to me." They did as she asked and gave orders to the young men to open the gate for her. This done, Judith went out accompanied by her maid, while the men of the town watched her all the way down the mountain and across the valley, until they lost sight of her.

As the women were making straight through the valley, an advance unit of Assyrians intercepted them, and, seizing Judith, began to question her. "Which side are you on? Where do you come from? Where are you going?" "I am a daughter of the Hebrews," she replied, "and I am fleeing from them since they will soon be your prey. I am on my way to see Holofernes, the general of your army, to give him trustworthy information. I shall show him the road to take if he wants to capture all the hill-country without losing one man or one life." As the men listened to what she was saying, they stared in astonishment at the sight of such a beautiful woman. "It will prove the saving of you," they said to her, "coming down to see our master of your own accord. You had better go to his tent; some of our men will escort you and hand you over to him. Once you are in his presence do not be afraid. Tell him what you have just told us and you will be well treated." They then detailed a hundred of their men as escort for herself and her attendant, and these led them to the tent of Holofernes. . . .

prey: victims.

Holofernes was resting on his bed under a canopy of purple and gold studded with emeralds and precious stones. The men announced her and he came out to the entrance to the tent, with silver torches carried before him.

canopy: a rooflike covering hung from bedposts.

When Judith confronted the general and his adjutant, the beauty of her face astonished them all. She fell on her face and did homage to him, but his servants raised her from the ground. . . .

adjutant: assistant.
did homage: showed honor and respect.

On the fourth day Holofernes gave a banquet, inviting only his own staff and none of the other officers. He said to Bagoas, the eunuch in charge of his personal affairs, "Go and persuade that Hebrew woman you are looking after to come and join us and eat and drink in our company. We shall be disgraced if we let a woman like this go without seducing her. If we do not seduce her, everyone will laugh at us.". . .

So she got up and put on her dress and all her feminine adornments. Her maid preceded her, and on the floor in front of Holofernes spread the fleece which Bagoas had given Judith for her daily use to lie on as she ate.

Judith came in and took her place. The heart of

Holofernes was ravished at the sight; his very soul was stirred. He was seized with a violent desire to sleep with her; and indeed since the first day he saw her, he had been waiting for an opportunity to seduce her. "Drink then!" Holofernes said, "Enjoy yourself, with us!" "I am delighted to do so, my lord, for since my birth I have never felt my life more worthwhile than today." She took what her maid had prepared, and ate and drank facing him. Holofernes was so enchanted with her that he drank far more wine than he had drunk on any other day in his life.

It grew late and his staff hurried away. Bagoas closed the tent from the outside, having shown out those who still lingered in his lord's presence. They went to their beds wearied with too much drinking, and Judith was left alone in the tent with Holofernes who had collapsed wine-sodden on his bed. Judith then told her maid to stay just outside the bedroom and wait for her to come out, as she did every morning. She had let it be understood she would be going out to her prayers and had also spoken of her intention to Bagoas.

By now everyone had left Holofernes, and no one, either important or unimportant, was left in the bedroom. Standing beside the bed, Judith murmured to herself:

Lord God, to whom all strength belongs,
prosper what my hands are now to do
for the greater glory of Jerusalem;
now is the time to recover your heritage
and to further my plans
to crush the enemies arrayed against us.

With that she went up to the bedpost by Holofernes' head and took down his scimitar; coming closer to the bed she caught him by the hair and said, "Make me strong today, Lord God of Israel!" Twice she struck at his neck with all her might, and cut off his head. She then rolled his body off the bed and pulled down the canopy from the bedposts. After which, she went out and gave the head of Holofernes to her maid who put it in her food bag. The two then left the camp together, as they always did when they

scimitar (sim′ə tər): curved sword.

went to pray. Once they were out of the camp, they skirted the ravine, climbed the slope to Bethulia and made for the gates.

Judith's Triumph

From a distance, Judith shouted to the guards on the gates, "Open the gate! Open! For the Lord our God is with us still, displaying his strength in Israel and his might against our enemies, as he has done today!" Hearing her voice, the townsmen hurried down to the town gate and summoned the elders. Everyone, great and small, came running down, since her arrival was unexpected. They threw the gate open, welcomed the women, lit a fire to see by and crowded round them. Then Judith raised her voice and said, "Praise God! Praise him! Praise the God who has not withdrawn his mercy from the house of Israel, but has shattered our enemies by my hand tonight!" She pulled the head out of the bag and held it for them to see. "This is the head of Holofernes, general-in-chief of the Assyrian army; here is the canopy under which he lay drunk! The Lord has struck him down by the hand of a woman! Glory to the Lord who has protected me in the course I took! My face seduced him, only to his own undoing; he committed no sin with me to shame me or disgrace me."

prostrated themselves: lay flat on the ground.

Overcome with emotion, the people all prostrated themselves and worshipped God, exclaiming with one voice, "Blessings on you, our God, for confounding your people's enemies today!". . .

At daybreak they hung the head of Holofernes on the ramparts. Every man took his arms and they all went out in groups to the slopes of the mountain. Seeing this, the Assyrians sent word to their leaders, who in turn reported to the generals, the captains of thousands and all the other officers; and these in their turn reported to the tent of Holofernes. "Rouse our master," they said to his major-domo, "these slaves have dared to march down on us to attack—and to be wiped out to a man!" Bagoas went inside and struck the curtain dividing the tent, thinking that Holofernes

major-domo: chief servant.

was sleeping with Judith. But as no one seemed to hear, he drew the curtain and went into the bedroom, to find him thrown down dead on the threshold, with his head cut off. He gave a great shout, wept, sobbed, shrieked and rent his clothes. He then went into the tent which Judith had occupied and could not find her either. Then, rushing out to the men, he shouted, "The slaves have rebelled! A single Hebrew woman has brought shame on the house of Nebuchadnezzar. Holofernes is lying dead on the ground without his head!"

rent: tore.

When the men who were still in their tents heard the news they were appalled. Panic-stricken and trembling, no two of them could keep together, the rout was complete, with one accord they fled along every track across the plain or through the mountains. The men who had been bivouacking in the mountains round Bethulia were fleeing too. Then all the Israelite warriors charged down on them. . . .

bivouacking (biv′ wak ing): camping.

All the women of Israel, hurrying to see her, formed choirs of dancers in her honor. Judith took wands of vine-leaves in her hand and distributed them to the women who accompanied her; she and her companions put on wreaths of olive. Then she took her place at the head of the procession and led the women as they danced. All the men of Israel, armed and garlanded, followed them, singing hymns. . . .

wands: branches.

garlanded: wearing strings of flowers.

FOR CLOSE READING

1. What details of the story emphasize the power of the Assyrians? What details emphasize the troubles of the Israelites?

2. What do you learn about Judith from the description on page 306? Choose three words to describe her.

3. How does Judith meet the enemy commander? After she kills Holofernes, how is she able to escape?

4. At what points in the story are people surprised or amazed?

FOR THOUGHT AND DISCUSSION

5. Why do you suppose Judith does not reveal her plans before she leaves Bethulia? How is the story affected by this withholding of information?

6. Judith tells Holofernes, "I have never felt my life more worthwhile than today." How do you suppose Holofernes interprets her statement? What do you think Judith means?

7. Why do you think Judith brings Holofernes' head and canopy back to Bethulia?

8. What methods does the story use to create suspense and increase the tension at key moments?

9. It might be argued that Judith was able to succeed only because of her great beauty. What other qualities of Judith might be equally important or more important?

RESPONDING

1. Writing If a woman today took action against her nation's enemies as Judith did, what do you think would be the public's reaction? Discuss your opinion in a brief paper.

2. Activity Using whatever art medium you wish, create a portrait of Judith in all her finery.

3. Humanities Connection Study the portrait of Judith on page 329, then examine other paintings of Judith in art books. What similarities and what differences do you find?

DANIEL

The Rescue of Susanna

King Nebuchadnezzar defeated Judah and brought many Jewish captives back to Babylonia. The king chose certain promising young men from the Jews to serve at the royal court, where they were educated and given new names. One of these young men was Daniel, who was renamed Belteshazzar.

Roman Catholic Bibles include Susanna in the Book of Daniel; other Christian Bibles do not, though in some Susanna appears in a section called "The Apocrypha." Jewish Bibles do not include Susanna.

In Babylon there lived a man named Joakim. He was married to a woman called Susanna daughter of Hilkiah, a woman of great beauty; and she was God-fearing, for her parents were worthy people and had instructed their daughter in the law of Moses. Joakim was a very rich man and had a garden by his house; he used to be visited by a considerable number of the Jews, since he was held in greater respect than any other man. Two elderly men had been selected from the people, that year, to act as judges. . . . These men were often at Joakim's house, and all who were engaged in litigation used to come to them. At midday, when the people had gone away, Susanna would take a walk in her husband's garden. The two elders, who used to watch her every day as she came in to take her walk, gradually began to desire her. They threw reason aside, making no effort to turn their eyes to heaven, and forgetting the demands of virtue. Both were inflamed by passion for her, but

litigation: law suits.

Daniel 13:1–5a, 6–56, 58–64 (New Jerusalem Bible).

they hid their desire from each other, for they were ashamed to admit the longing to sleep with her, but they made sure of watching her every day. One day, having parted with the words, "Let us go home, then, it is time for the midday meal," they went off in different directions, only to retrace their steps and find themselves face to face again. Obliged then to explain, they admitted their desire and agreed to look for an opportunity of surprising her alone. So they waited for a favorable moment; and one day Susanna came as usual, accompanied only by two young maidservants. The day was hot and she wanted to bathe in the garden. There was no one about except the two elders, spying on her from their hiding place. She said to the servants, "Bring me some oil and balsam and shut the garden door while I bathe." They did as they were told, shutting the garden door and going back to the house by a side entrance to fetch what she had asked for; they knew nothing about the elders, for they had concealed themselves.

Hardly were the maids gone than the two elders sprang up and rushed upon her. "Look," they said, "the garden door is shut, no one can see us. We want to have you, so give in and let us! Refuse, and we shall both give evidence that a young man was with you and that this was why you sent your maids away." Susanna sighed. "I am trapped," she said, "whatever I do. If I agree, it means death for me; if I resist, I cannot get away from you. But I prefer to fall innocent into your power than to sin in the eyes of the Lord." She then cried out as loud as she could. The two elders began shouting too, putting the blame on her, and one of them ran to open the garden door. The household, hearing the shouting in the garden, rushed out by the side entrance to see what had happened to her. Once the elders had told their story, the servants were thoroughly taken aback, since nothing of this sort had ever been said of Susanna.

Next day a meeting was held at the house of her husband Joakim. The two elders arrived, full of their wicked plea against Susanna, to have her put to death. They addressed the company, "Summon Susanna daughter of Hilkiah and wife of Joakim." She was sent for, and came accompanied by her parents, her children and all her relations. Susanna was very

obliged: required.

Note that there are two doors to the garden: toward the house and to the outside.

death: i.e., the penalty for adultery in Jewish law.

taken aback: shocked.

graceful and beautiful to look at; she was veiled, so the wretches made her unveil in order to feast their eyes on her beauty. All her own people were weeping, and so were all the others who saw her. The two elders stood up, with all the people round them, and laid their hands on her head. Tearfully she turned her eyes to heaven, her heart confident in God. The elders then spoke, "While we were walking by ourselves in the garden, this woman arrived with two maids. She shut the garden door and then dismissed the servants. A young man, who had been hiding, went over to her and they lay together. From the end of the garden where we were, we saw this crime taking place and hurried towards them. Though we saw them together, we were unable to catch the man: he was too strong for us; he opened the door and took to his heels. We did, however, catch this woman and ask her who the young man was. She refused to tell us. That is our evidence."

Since they were elders of the people and judges, the assembly accepted their word: Susanna was condemned to death. She cried out as loud as she could, "Eternal God, you know all secrets and everything before it happens; you know that they have given false evidence against me. And now I must die, innocent as I am of everything their malice has invented against me!"

> malice: wickedness.

The Lord heard her cry and, as she was being led away to die, he roused the holy spirit residing in a young boy called Daniel who began to shout, "I am innocent of this woman's death!" At this all the people turned to him and asked, "What do you mean by that?" Standing in the middle of the crowd, he replied, "Are you so stupid, children of Israel, as to condemn a daughter of Israel unheard, and without troubling to find out the truth? Go back to the scene of the trial: these men have given false evidence against her."

All the people hurried back, and the elders said to Daniel, "Come and sit with us and tell us what you mean, since God has given you the gifts that elders have." Daniel said, "Keep the men well apart from each other, for I want to question them." When the men had been separated, Daniel had one of them brought to him. "You have grown old in wickedness,"

> elders: other men, not the two accusers.

he said, "and now the sins of your earlier days have overtaken you, you with your unjust judgments, your condemnation of the innocent, your acquittal of the guilty, although the Lord has said, 'You must not put the innocent and upright to death.' Now then, since you saw her so clearly, tell me what sort of tree you saw them lying under." He replied, "Under an acacia tree." Daniel said, "Indeed! Your lie recoils on your own head: the angel of God has already received from him your sentence and will cut you in half." He dismissed the man, ordered the other to be brought and said to him, "Son of Canaan, not of Judah, beauty has seduced you, lust has led your heart astray! . . . Now then, tell me what sort of tree you surprised them under." He replied, "Under an aspen tree." Daniel said, "Indeed! Your lie recoils on your own head: the angel of God is waiting with a sword to rend you in half, and destroy the pair of you."

Then the whole assembly shouted, blessing God, the savior of those who trust in him. And they turned on the two elders whom Daniel had convicted of false evidence out of their own mouths. As the law of Moses prescribes, they were given the same punishment as they had schemed to inflict on their neighbor. They were put to death. And thus, that day, an innocent life was saved. Hilkiah and his wife gave thanks to God for their daughter Susanna, and so did her husband Joakim and all his relations, because she had been acquitted of anything dishonorable.

From that day onwards, Daniel's reputation stood high with the people.

son of Canaan: i.e., Daniel is insulting the elder by calling him a non-Jew.

FOR CLOSE READING

1. Why are Daniel and the other Jews living in Babylon?

2. What is the reaction of the servants when they first hear the charge against Susanna?

3. What method does Daniel use to reveal the lies of the two elders?

FOR THOUGHT AND DISCUSSION

4. What kind of person is Susanna? What evidence in the story—from her own actions and words and those of others—support your opinion?

5. Review the actions and testimony of the two elders at the beginning of the trial. What details do you think should have made the people suspicious of their story?

6. Why do you suppose the people accepted the word of the two elders without question? Why do you suppose the other elders immediately agreed to listen to Daniel? Can you think of modern examples of such behavior?

7. Whose story is being told in this passage, Susanna's or Daniel's? Explain.

RESPONDING

1. Writing You are a reporter at the trial of Susanna. Write a newspaper story, complete with a headline.

2. Activity Draw a map or picture of Susanna's garden showing the various gates and other details that appear in the story.

3. Humanities Connection The painting on page 330 is one of many on the subject of Susanna and the Elders. Examine several of these paintings, looking first at how the artists present the factual details of the story, then determining what overall mood is expressed in each picture.

The Fiery Furnace

Another story from the period of the Babylonian Captivity concerns three young Jews who, like Daniel, were brought to the royal court to be educated. Their Hebrew names Hananiah, Mishael, and Azariah were changed to Shadrach, Meshach, and Abed-Nego.

cubit: about eighteen inches. The statue was about 90 feet tall.

satraps: regional governors.

magistrates: local judges.

languages: i.e., of every language.

lyre, zither: stringed instruments.

King Nebuchadnezzar had a golden statue made, sixty cubits high and six cubits wide, which he set upon the plain of Dura, in the province of Babylon. King Nebuchadnezzar then summoned the satraps, magistrates, governors, counsellors, treasurers, judges, lawyers, and all the provincial authorities to assemble and attend the dedication of the statue set up by King Nebuchadnezzar. Satraps, magistrates, governors, counsellors, treasurers, judges, lawyers and all the provincial authorities then assembled for the dedication of the statue set up by King Nebuchadnezzar and stood in front of the statue which King Nebuchadnezzar had set up. A herald then loudly proclaimed: "Peoples, nations, languages! Thus are you commanded: the moment you hear the sound of horn, pipe, lyre, zither, harp, bagpipe and every other kind of instrument, you will prostrate yourselves and worship the golden statue set up by King Nebuchadnezzar. Anyone who does not prostrate himself and worship will immediately be thrown into the burning fiery furnace." And so, the instant all the peoples heard the sound of horn, pipe, lyre, zither, harp, bagpipe and all the other instruments, all the peoples, nations and languages prostrated themselves and worshiped the statue set up by King Nebuchadnezzar.

Daniel 3: 1–8, 12–14, 15b–30 (New Jerusalem Bible).

Some Chaldaeans then came forward and maliciously accused the Jews. . . . "Now, there are certain Jews to whom you have entrusted the affairs of the province of Babylon: Shadrach, Meshach and Abed-Nego; these men have ignored your command, Your Majesty; they do not serve your gods, and refuse to worship the golden statue you have set up." Shaking with fury, Nebuchadnezzar sent for Shadrach, Meshach and Abed-Nego. The men were immediately brought before the king. Nebuchadnezzar addressed them, "Shadrach, Meshach and Abed-Nego, is it true that you do not serve my gods, and that you refuse to worship the golden statue I have set up? When you hear the sound of horn, pipe, lyre, zither, harp, bagpipe and every other kind of instrument, are you prepared to prostrate yourselves and worship the statue I have made? If you refuse to worship it, you will be thrown forthwith into the burning fiery furnace; then which of the gods could save you from my power?" Shadrach, Meshach and Abed-Nego replied to King Nebuchadnezzar, "Your question needs no answer from us: if our God, the one we serve, is able to save us from the burning fiery furnace and from your power, Your Majesty, he will save us; and even if he does not, then you must know, O king, that we will not serve your god or worship the statue you have set up." This infuriated King Nebuchadnezzar; his expression was changed now as he looked at Shadrach, Meshach and Abed-Nego. He gave orders for the furnace to be made seven times hotter than usual and commanded certain stalwarts from his army to bind Shadrach, Meshach, and Abed-Nego and throw them into the burning fiery furnace. They were then bound in their cloaks, trousers, headgear and other garments, and thrown into the burning fiery furnace. The king's command was so urgent and the heat of the furnace was so fierce, that the men carrying Shadrach, Meshach and Abed-Nego were burnt to death by the flames from the fire; the three men, Shadrach, Meshach and Abed-Nego fell, bound, into the burning fiery furnace.

King Nebuchadnezzar sprang to his feet in amazement. He said to his advisers, "Did we not have these three men thrown bound into the fire?" They answered the king, "Certainly, Your Majesty." "But,"

Chaldaeans: native Babylonians.

forthwith: immediately.

stalwarts: strong men.

he went on, "I can see four men walking free in the heart of the fire and quite unharmed! And the fourth looks like a child of the gods!" Nebuchadnezzar approached the mouth of the burning fiery furnace and said, "Shadrach, Meshach and Abed-Nego, servants of God Most High, come out, come here!" And from the heart of the fire out came Shadrach, Meshach and Abed-Nego. The satraps, magistrates, governors, and advisers of the king crowded round the three men to examine them: the fire had had no effect on their bodies: not a hair of their heads had been singed, their cloaks were not scorched, no smell of burning hung about them. Nebuchadnezzar said, "Blessed be the God of Shadrach, Meshach and Abed-Nego: he has sent his angel to rescue his servants who, putting their trust in him, defied the order of the king, and preferred to forfeit their bodies rather than serve or worship any god but their God. I therefore decree as follows, 'Peoples, nations, and languages! Let any of you speak disrespectfully of the God of Shadrach, Meshach, and Abed-Nego, and I shall have him torn limb from limb and his house turned into a dunghill; for there is no other god who can save like this.'"

The king then showered favors on Shadrach, Meshach and Abed-Nego in the province of Babylon.

FOR CLOSE READING

1. How do Shadrach, Meshach, and Abed-Nego answer when questioned by King Nebuchadnezzar?

2. What details in the story emphasize the king's power? the king's anger at the young Jews?

3. What does the king see when he looks in the furnace?

FOR THOUGHT AND DISCUSSION

4. Why do you think the power and fury of the king are described in such detail?

5. What is the effect of the repetition of certain phrases in the story?

6. How does the story increase the tension, drama, and impact of the young men's survival in the furnace?

7. Reread the king's last words. To what extent has he changed? To what extent is he won over to the God of Israel?

RESPONDING

1. Writing Imagine that you are one of the accusers of Shadrach, Meshach, and Abed-Nego. Write your diary entries for the week, beginning before you go to the king and ending after the three men have been promoted.

2. Activity Make a clay model of the furnace or portray the fiery furnace episode in some other art medium.

3. Activity With musical accompaniment and in your own words, retell the story of Shadrach, Meshach, and Abed-Nego.

Belshazzar's Feast

Belshazzar (bel shaz′ ər).

vessels: sacred cups and plates.

sanctuary: temple.

soothsayers ... exorcists: specialists in foretelling the future or controlling spirits.

purple: the royal color.

King Belshazzar gave a great banquet for his noblemen, a thousand of them, and, in the presence of this thousand, he drank his wine. Having tasted the wine, Belshazzar gave orders for the gold and silver vessels to be brought which his father Nebuchadnezzar had taken from the sanctuary in Jerusalem, so that the king, his noblemen, his wives and the women who sang for him could drink out of them. . . . They drank their wine and praised their idols of gold and silver, of bronze and iron, of wood and stone. Suddenly, the fingers of a human hand appeared and began to write on the plaster of the palace wall, directly behind the lamp-stand; and the king could see the hand as it wrote. The king turned pale with alarm: his hip-joints went slack and his knees began to knock. He shouted for his soothsayers, Chaldaeans, and exorcists. And the king said to the Babylonian sages, "Anyone who can read this writing and tell me what it means shall be dressed in purple, and have a chain of gold put round his neck, and be one of the three men who govern the kingdom." The king's sages all crowded forward, but they could neither read the writing nor explain to the king what it meant. Greatly alarmed, King Belshazzar turned even paler, and his noblemen were equally disturbed. . . .

Daniel was brought into the king's presence; the king said to Daniel, "Are you the Daniel who was one of the Judaean exiles brought by my father the king from Judah? I am told that the spirit of the gods lives in you, and that you are known for your perception, intelligence, and marvellous wisdom . . . so if you can

Daniel 5: 1–2, 4–9, 13–14, 16b–18, 20, 22–30 (New Jerusalem Bible).

read the writing and tell me what it means, you shall be dressed in purple, and have a chain of gold put round your neck, and be one of the three men who govern the kingdom."

Then Daniel spoke up in the presence of the king. "Keep your gifts for yourself, " he said, "and give your rewards to others! I can certainly read the writing to the king and tell him what it means. Your Majesty, the Most High God gave Nebuchadnezzar your father sovereignty, greatness, majesty and glory.... But because his heart grew swollen with pride, and his spirit stiff with arrogance, he was deposed from his sovereign throne and stripped of his glory.... But you, Belshazzar, who are his son, you have not humbled your heart, in spite of knowing all this. You have defied the Lord of heaven, you have had the vessels from his temple brought to you, and you, your noblemen, your wives and the women singing for you have drunk your wine out of them. You have praised gods of gold and silver, of bronze and iron, of wood and stone, which can neither see, hear nor understand; but you have given no glory to the God in whose hands are your breath itself and all your fortunes. That is why he has sent the hand which has written these words. The writing reads: *mene, mene, tekel* and *parsin*. The meaning of the words is this: *mene*: God has *measured* your sovereignty and put an end to it; *tekel*: you have been *weighed* in the balance and found wanting; *parsin*: your kingdom has been *divided* and given to the Medes and the *Persians*."

At Belshazzar's order Daniel was dressed in purple, a chain of gold was put round his neck and he was proclaimed as one of the three men who governed the kingdom.

That same night, the Chaldaean king Belshazzar was murdered, and Darius the Mede received the kingdom ....

deposed: removed.

mene (mē´nē) mene, tekel, and parsin: count, count, weigh, divide; Aramaic words. Parsin (Peres) is the same as "Persian."

wanting: lacking.

Darius (də rī´əs): king of Persia.

FOR CLOSE READING

1. The writing hand appears "suddenly," as if in response to something. What in the preceding lines might have caused this abrupt appearance?

2. What is Daniel's response when told of the reward he will receive for interpreting the writing?

3. What are the three charges that Daniel reports against Belshazzar?

FOR THOUGHT AND DISCUSSION

4. What are your feelings about Belshazzar's fate? Why?

5. What hints in the story prepare us for the news of Belshazzar's downfall? How does the story keep that outcome in suspense?

6. Belshazzar honors Daniel even though Daniel predicts that Belshazzar will lose his kingdom. Why do you suppose he does so? What would you have done?

7. You have probably read other stories that have a theme of "pride goes before a fall." Choose one and compare it with the story of Belshazzar. What other Bible stories have this theme?

RESPONDING

1. Activity The words that appear on the wall have been given various other explanations. Research these explanations in a reference book and write a report.

2. Activity Using clay or plaster of Paris, create a replica of the handwriting on the wall.

3. Humanities Connection Belshazzar's Feast is another biblical event that has fascinated artists for many centuries (see page 332 for one example). Find and examine other paintings on the Belshazzar theme. What different attitudes toward Belshazzar seem to be expressed?

In a Den of Lions

I t pleased Darius to appoint a hundred and twenty
satraps over his kingdom for the various parts, and
over them three presidents—of whom Daniel was
one—to whom the satraps were to be responsible.
This was to safeguard the king's interests. This
Daniel, by virtue of the marvellous spirit residing in
him, was so evidently superior to the other presidents
and satraps that the king considered appointing him
to rule the whole kingdom. The presidents and
satraps, in consequence, started hunting for some
affair of state by which they could discredit Daniel;
but they could find nothing to his discredit, and no
case of negligence; he was so punctilious that they
could not find a single instance of maladministration
or neglect. These men then thought, "We shall never
find a way of discrediting Daniel unless we try
something to do with the law of his God." The
presidents and satraps then went in a body to the
king. "King Darius," they said, "live for ever! We are
all agreed, presidents of the realm, magistrates,
satraps, councillors and governors, that the king
should issue an edict enforcing the following reg-
ulation: Whoever within the next thirty days prays to
anyone, divine or human, other than to yourself, Your
Majesty, is to be thrown into the lions' den. Your
Majesty, ratify the edict at once by signing this
document, making it unalterable, as befits the law of
the Medes and the Persians, which cannot be
revoked." King Darius accordingly signed the
document embodying the edict.

When Daniel heard that the document had been
signed, he retired to his house. The windows of his
upstairs room faced towards Jerusalem. Three times

satraps: regional governors.

punctilious: very careful; exact.

edict: royal command.

ratify: officially approve.

revoked: canceled.

Three times: i.e., according to Jewish law.

Daniel 6:1–28 (New Jerusalem Bible).

each day, he went down on his knees, praying and giving praise to God as he had always done. These men came along in a body and found Daniel praying and pleading with God. They then went to the king and reminded him of the royal edict, "Have you not signed an edict forbidding anyone for the next thirty days to pray to anyone, divine or human, other than to yourself, Your Majesty, on pain of being thrown into the lions' den?" "The decision stands," the king replied, "as befits the law of the Medes and the Persians, which cannot be revoked." They then said to the king, "Your Majesty, this man Daniel, one of the exiles from Judah, disregards both you and the edict which you have signed: he is at his prayers three times each day." When the king heard these words he was deeply distressed and determined to save Daniel; he racked his brains until sunset to find some way to save him. But the men kept pressing the king, "Your Majesty, remember that in conformity with the law of the Medes and the Persians, no edict or decree can be altered when once issued by the king."

The king then ordered Daniel to be brought and thrown into the lion pit. The king said to Daniel, "Your God, whom you have served so faithfully, will have to save you." A stone was then brought and laid over the mouth of the pit; and the king sealed it with his own signet and with that of his noblemen, so that there could be no going back on the original decision about Daniel. The king returned to his palace, spent the night in fasting and refused to receive any of his concubines. Sleep eluded him, and at the first sign of dawn he got up and hurried to the lion pit. As he approached the pit he called in anguished tones to Daniel, "Daniel, servant of the living God! Has your God, whom you serve so faithfully, been able to save you from the lions?" Daniel answered the king, "May Your Majesty live for ever! My God sent his angel who sealed the lions' jaws; they did me no harm, since in his sight I am blameless; neither have I ever done you any wrong, Your Majesty." The king was overjoyed and ordered Daniel to be released from the pit. Daniel was released from the pit and found to be quite unhurt, because he had trusted in his God. The king then sent for the men who had accused Daniel

signet: stamp, seal.

anguished: suffering.

and had them thrown into the lion pit, and their wives and children too; and before they reached the floor of the pit the lions had seized them and crushed their bones to pieces.

King Darius then wrote to all nations, peoples and languages dwelling throughout the world:

"May you prosper more and more! This is my decree: Throughout every dominion of my realm, let all tremble with fear before the God of Daniel:

dominion: territory.

He is the living God, he endures for ever,
his kingdom will never be destroyed
and his empire never come to an end.
He saves, sets free, and works signs and wonders
in the heavens and on earth;
he has saved Daniel from the power of the lions."

This Daniel flourished in the reign of Darius and the reign of Cyrus the Persian.

flourished: did well; thrived.

FOR CLOSE READING

1. How many times does the story mention that the law of Darius cannot be changed and the punishment must be carried out?

2. What details of the story show the king's concern for Daniel?

3. What happens to the people who accused Daniel?

FOR THOUGHT AND DISCUSSION

4. After Daniel is thrown into the lions' den, the story focuses completely on Darius. Why do you think the story does so?

5. What is Darius's attitude toward Daniel's God at the end? Compare his attitude with the attitudes of Nebuchadnezzar and Belshazzar when they acknowledged the power of the God of the Jews.

6. Daniel plays a part in three stories in this unit. What do you learn about Daniel's character and abilities in these stories? Describe Daniel in two sentences.

7. What similarities do you find among the stories from the Babylonian Captivity (Susanna, the fiery furnace, Belshazzar's feast, the lions' den)? For example, in several of the stories, Jews are put to a test of their faith in the God of Israel; often they must face a foreign king. What other similarities do you find? Try to make a general outline, or pattern for these stories.

8. Though the stories in this unit have grim settings of exile and danger, they often have moments of humor. What incidents struck you as humorous? Why?

RESPONDING

1. Writing The Bible summarizes what happened in the lions' den in only one sentence. Imagine and write a more detailed account from the viewpoint of Daniel—or perhaps from the viewpoint of a puzzled but talkative lion.

2. Activity With a group of classmates, create a picture book or a cartoon strip that would help you tell one of these Bible stories to young children.

3. Multicultural Connection Daniel's jealous enemies chose to attack him through his religion. Where else, in the Bible and in history, have Jews been in trouble because of their religion? What other people have suffered for similar reasons and "kept the faith"? Why do you think this happens? Research several of these stories and be prepared to report on the similarities and differences you find.

Judith with the Head of Holofernes, oil on wood by Lucas Cranach the Elder, c. 1530.
The Metropolitan Museum of Art, New York, Rogers Fund, 1911.

Susanna at the Bath, oil on wood by Albrecht Altdorfer, 1526. The Alte Pinakothek, Munich. Photograph, Joachim Blauel.

The Three Hebrews in the Fiery Furnace, painting in the Chamber of Velatio, Cemetery of Priscilla, Rome, mid-third century. Courtesy Benedittine Di Priscilla, Rome.

PAGE 332: *Belshazzar Sees the Writing on the Wall*, oil painting by Rembrandt Van Rijn. Reproduced by courtesy of the Trustees, The National Gallery, London.

Daniel, detail from a stained-glass window, twelfth century, Augsburg. Courtesy The Cathedral of Augsburg, Germany.

Esther

This story describes the experiences of Jews living in Persia during the reign of King Ahasuerus (ə haz⁄yü ėr⁄əs).

Esther Becomes Queen

It was in the days of Ahasuerus, the Ahasuerus whose empire stretched from India to Ethiopia and comprised one hundred and twenty-seven provinces. . . . For seven days the king gave a banquet for all the people living in the citadel of Susa, to high and low alike, on the esplanade in the gardens of the royal palace. . . .

citadel: walled stronghold within the city.

esplanade: open, level walking space.

Queen Vashti, for her part, gave a banquet for the women in the royal palace of King Ahasuerus. On the seventh day, when the king was merry with wine, he commanded Mehuman, Biztha, Harbona, Bigtha, Abagtha, Zethar and Carkas, the seven eunuchs in attendance on the person of King Ahasuerus, to bring Queen Vashti before the king, crowned with her royal diadem, in order to display her beauty to the people and the officers-of-state, since she was very beautiful. But Queen Vashti refused to come at the king's command delivered by the eunuchs. The king was very angry at this and his rage grew hot. Addressing himself to the wise men who were versed in the law . . . "According to law," he said, "what is to be done to Queen Vashti for not obeying the command of King Ahasuerus delivered by the eunuchs?" In the presence of the king and the officers-of-state, Memucan replied, "Queen Vashti has wronged not only the king but also all the officers-of-state and all the peoples inhabiting the provinces of King Ahasuerus. The queen's conduct will soon

eunuchs: male servants.

diadem: crown.

Esther 1:1, 3b, 9–13, 15–17a, 19a, 19c–21; 2:2, 4–5a, 7–8c, 10–11, 16a, 17, 21–23a; 3:1a, 2, 5–6, 8–11; 4:1, 4–7a, 8b–14; 5:1–4, 9–14; 6:1–7:10; 8:15–17 (New Jerusalem Bible).

become known to all the women, who will adopt a contemptuous attitude towards their own husbands.... If it is the king's pleasure, let him issue a royal edict ... that Vashti is never to appear again before King Ahasuerus, and let the king confer her royal dignity on a worthier woman. Let this edict issued by the king be proclaimed throughout his empire—which is great—and all the women will henceforth bow to the authority of their husbands, both high and low alike."

This speech pleased the king and the officers-of-state, and the king did as Memucan advised.... The king's gentlemen-in-waiting said, "A search should be made on the king's behalf for beautiful young virgins ... and the girl who pleases the king can take Vashti's place as queen." This advice pleased the king and he acted on it.

Now in the citadel of Susa there lived a Jew called Mordecai ... bringing up a certain Hadassah, otherwise called Esther, his uncle's daughter, who had lost both father and mother; the girl had a good figure and a beautiful face, and on the death of her parents Mordecai had adopted her as his daughter.

On the promulgation of the royal command and edict a great number of girls were brought to the citadel of Susa where they were entrusted to Hegai. Esther, too, was taken to the king's palace and entrusted to Hegai, the custodian of the women....

Esther had not divulged her race or parentage, since Mordecai had forbidden her to do so. Mordecai walked up and down in front of the courtyard of the

harem all day and every day, to learn how Esther was and how she was being treated....

Esther won the approval of all who saw her. She was brought to King Ahasuerus ... and the king liked Esther better than any of the other women; none of the other girls found so much favor and approval with him. So he set the royal diadem on her head and proclaimed her queen instead of Vashti....

At this time Mordecai was attached to the chancellery and two malcontents, Bigthan and Teresh, eunuchs in the king's service as guards of the threshold, plotted to assassinate King Ahasuerus. Mordecai came to hear of this and informed Queen Esther, who in turn, on Mordecai's authority, told the king. The matter was investigated and proved to be true. The two conspirators were sent to the gallows. . . .

Haman Plots Against Mordecai and the Jews

Shortly afterwards, King Ahasuerus singled out Haman son of Hammedatha, a native of Agag, for promotion . . . and all the royal officials employed at the chancellery used to bow low and prostrate themselves whenever Haman appeared—such was the king's command. Mordecai refused either to bow or to prostrate himself. . . . Haman could see for himself that Mordecai did not bow or prostrate himself in his presence; he became furiously angry. And, on being told what race Mordecai belonged to, he thought it beneath him merely to get rid of Mordecai, but made up his mind to wipe out all the members of Mordecai's race, the Jews, living in Ahasuerus' entire empire. . . .

Haman said to King Ahasuerus, "There is a certain unassimilated nation scattered among the other nations throughout the provinces of your realm; their laws are different from those of all other nations, and the royal laws they ignore; hence it is not in the king's interests to tolerate them. If their destruction be signed, so please the king, I am ready to pay ten thousand talents of silver to the king's receivers, to be credited to the royal treasury."

unassimilated nation: foreigners who remain separate or different.

The king then took his signet ring off his hand and gave it to Haman son of Hammedatha, the persecutor of the Jews. "Keep the money," he said, "and you can have the people too; do what you like with them."

When Mordecai learned what had happened, he tore his garments and put on sackcloth and ashes. Then he walked into the center of the city, wailing loudly and bitterly. . . .

When Queen Esther's maids and eunuchs came and told her, she was overcome with grief. She sent clothes for Mordecai to put on instead of his sackcloth, but he refused them. Esther then summoned Hathach, a eunuch whom the king had appointed to wait on her, and ordered him to go to Mordecai and inquire what the matter was and why he was acting in this way.

Hathach went out to Mordecai in the city square

implore: beg.

in front of the chancellery, and Mordecai told him what had happened to him . . . to show Esther for her information, with the message that she was to go to the king and implore his favor and plead with him for the race to which she belonged.

Hathach came back and told Esther what Mordecai had said; and she replied with the following message for Mordecai, "Royal officials and people living in the provinces alike all know that for anyone, man or woman, who approaches the king in the private apartments without having been summoned there, there is only one law: he must die, unless the

scepter: rod or staff symbolizing the king's power.

king, by pointing his golden scepter towards him, grants him his life. And I have not been summoned to the king for the last thirty days."

These words of Esther were reported to Mordecai, who sent back the following reply, "Do not suppose that, because you are in the king's palace, you are going to be the one Jew to escape. No, if you persist in remaining silent at such a time, relief and deliverance will come to the Jews from another quarter, but both you and your father's whole family will perish. Who knows? Perhaps you have come to the throne for just such a time as this." . . .

Esther Plots Against Haman

Three days later Esther put on her royal apparel and presented herself in the inner court of the palace, which was in front of the king's apartments. He was seated on the royal throne in the royal hall, facing the door. No sooner had he seen Queen Esther standing in the court than she won his favor and he held out to her the golden scepter he had in his hand. Esther approached and touched the end of it. "What is the matter, Queen Esther?" the king said. "Tell me what you want; even if it is half my kingdom, I grant it you." "Would it please the king," Esther replied, "to come with Haman today to the banquet I have prepared for him?" . . .

Haman left full of joy and high spirits that day; but when he saw Mordecai at the chancellery, neither standing up nor stirring at his approach, he felt a gust of anger. He restrained himself, however. Returning home, he sent for his friends and Zeresh his wife and held forth to them about his dazzling wealth, his

held forth: made a speech.

many children, how the king had raised him to a position of honor and promoted him over the heads of the king's officers-of-state and ministers. "What is more," he added, "Queen Esther has just invited me and the king—no one else except me—to a banquet she was giving, and better still she has invited me and the king again tomorrow. But what do I care about all this when all the while I see Mordecai the Jew sitting there at the chancellery?" "Have a fifty-cubit gallows run up," said Zeresh his wife and all his friends, "and in the morning ask the king to have Mordecai hanged on it. Then you can go with the king to the banquet, without a care in the world!" Delighted with this advice, Haman had the gallows erected.

That night the king could not sleep; he called for the record book, or annals, to be brought and read to him. They contained an account of how Mordecai had denounced Bigthan and Teresh, two of the king's eunuchs serving as Guards of the Threshold, who had plotted to assassinate King Ahasuerus. "And what honor and dignity," the king asked, "was conferred on Mordecai for this?" "Nothing has been done for him," the gentlemen-in-waiting replied. The king then said, "Who is outside in the antechamber?" Haman had, that very moment, entered the outer antechamber of the private apartments, to ask the king to have Mordecai hanged on the gallows which he had just put up for the purpose. So the king's gentlemen-in-waiting replied, "It is Haman out in the antechamber." "Bring him in," the king said, and as soon as Haman came in, went on to ask, "What is the right way to treat a man whom the king wishes to honor?" "Whom," thought Haman, "would the king wish to honor, if not me?" So he replied, "If the king wishes to honor someone, royal robes should be brought from the king's wardrobe, and a horse from the king's stable, sporting a royal diadem on its head. The robes and horse should be entrusted to one of the noblest of the king's officers-of-state, who should then array the man whom the king wishes to honor and lead him on horseback through the city square, proclaiming before him: 'This is the way a man shall be treated whom the king wishes to honor.'" "Hurry," the king said to Haman, "take the robes and the horse, and do everything you have just said to

antechamber: waiting room.

array: dress in rich clothes.

Mordecai the Jew, who works at the chancellery. On no account leave anything out that you have mentioned."

So taking the robes and the horse, Haman arrayed Mordecai and led him on horseback through the city square, proclaiming before him: "This is the way a man shall be treated whom the king wishes to honor." After this Mordecai returned to the chancellery, while Haman went hurrying home in dejection and covering his face. He told his wife Zeresh and all his friends what had just happened. His wife Zeresh and his friends said, "You are beginning to fall, and Mordecai to rise; if he is Jewish, you will never get the better of him. With him against you, your fall is certain." While they were still talking, the king's eunuchs arrived in a hurry to escort Haman to the banquet that Esther was giving.

second day: at the first dinner the king asked what Esther wanted. She requested only another dinner the following day.

The king and Haman went to Queen Esther's banquet, and this second day, during the banquet, the king again said to Esther, "Tell me your request, Queen Esther. I grant it to you. Whatever you want; even if it is half my kingdom, it is yours for the asking." "If I have found favor in your eyes, O king," Queen Esther replied, "and if it please your majesty, grant me my life—that is my request; and the lives of my people—that is what I want. For we have been handed over, my people and I, to destruction, slaughter and annihilation; had we merely been sold as slaves and servant-girls, I should not have said anything; but in the present case, it will be beyond the persecutor's means to make good the loss that the king is about to sustain." King Ahasuerus interrupted Queen Esther, "Who is this man?" he exclaimed. "Where is the man who has thought of doing such a thing?" Esther replied, "The persecutor, the enemy? Why, this wretch Haman!" Haman quaked with terror in the presence of the king and queen. In a rage the king got up from the banquet and went into the palace garden; while Haman, realizing that the king was determined on his ruin, stayed behind to beg Queen Esther for his life.

annihilation: being completely wiped out.

When the king came back from the palace garden into the banqueting hall, he found Haman sprawled across the couch where Esther was reclining. "What!" the king exclaimed. "Is he going to rape the queen in my own palace?" The words were scarcely out of his mouth than a veil was thrown over Haman's face. In the royal presence, Harbona, one of the eunuchs, said, "There is that fifty-cubit gallows, too, which Haman ran up for Mordecai, who spoke up to the king's great advantage. It is all ready at his house." "Hang him on it," said the king. So Haman was hanged on the gallows which he had erected for Mordecai, and the king's wrath subsided. . . .

veil . . . face: this indicates that Haman has been condemned to die.

Mordecai left the royal presence in a princely gown of violet and white, with a great golden crown and a cloak of fine linen and purple. The city of Susa shouted for joy. For the Jews there was light and gladness, joy and honor. In every province and in every city, wherever the king's command and decree arrived, there was joy and gladness among the Jews, with feasting and holiday-making. Of the country's population many became Jews, since now the Jews were feared.

feared: i.e., respected.

FOR CLOSE READING

1. How many times in the story is Ahasuerus given advice? How many times does he act on this advice?

2. What arguments does Mordecai use to convince Esther to help the Jews?

FOR THOUGHT AND DISCUSSION

3. What is your opinion of Ahasuerus as a king? as a husband? Support your views with evidence.

4. Consider how Esther became queen. If these events happened in modern times, how might opinions of Queen Vashti be different? How might opinions about Esther be changed?

5. In what ways does Esther change or develop during the story?

6. The triumph of the underdog is one appealing feature of the story of Esther. What other things in the story make it popular and appealing to many people?

10

Jesus: Birth and Early Ministry

Where Is He Who Has Been Born King?

The New Testament begins with the story of Jesus as told in the Gospels of Matthew, Mark, Luke, and John. The Bible selections in Units 10 and 11 are taken from Gospel accounts of Jesus' birth, miracles, teachings, death, and resurrection.

The Annunciation

Now in the sixth month the angel Gabriel was sent by God to a city of Galilee named Nazareth, to a virgin betrothed to a man whose name was Joseph, of the house of David. The virgin's name was Mary. And having come in, the angel said to her, "Rejoice, highly favored one, the Lord is with you; blessed are you among women!" But when she saw him, she was troubled at his saying, and considered what manner of greeting this was. Then the angel said to her, "Do not be afraid, Mary, for you have found favor with God. And behold, you will conceive in your womb and bring forth a son, and shall call his name Jesus. He will be great, and will be called the Son of the Highest; and the Lord God will give him the throne of his father David. And he will reign over the house of Jacob forever, and of his kingdom there will be no end." Then Mary said to the angel, "How can this be, since I do not know a man?" And the angel answered and said to her, "The Holy Spirit will come upon you, and the power of the Highest will overshadow you;

Luke 1:26.

betrothed: engaged to be married.

I do not . . . man: i.e., "I am a virgin."

Luke 1:26–38; 2:1–21. Matthew 2:1–16, 19–23. From *The Holy Bible, The New King James Version*. Copyright © 1979, 1980, 1982, Thomas Nelson, Inc. Reprinted by permission of Thomas Nelson, Inc., Publishers.
LEFT: *The Annunciation*, c. 1450. The Metropolitan Museum of Art, The Friedman Collection, Bequest of Michael Friedman, 1931 (32 . 100 . 35).

therefore, also, that holy one who is to be born will be called the Son of God. Now indeed, Elizabeth your relative has also conceived a son in her old age; and this is now the sixth month for her who was called barren. For with God nothing will be impossible." Then Mary said, "Behold the maidservant of the Lord! Let it be to me according to your word." And the angel departed from her. . . .

The Nativity

And it came to pass in those days that a decree went out from Caesar Augustus that all the world should be registered. This census took place while Quirinius was governing Syria. So all went to be registered, everyone to his own city. And Joseph also went up from Galilee, out of the city of Nazareth, into Judea, to the city of David, which is called Bethlehem, because he was of the house and lineage of David, to be registered with Mary, his betrothed wife, who was with child. So it was, that while they were there, the days were completed for her to be delivered. And she brought forth her firstborn son, and wrapped him in swaddling cloths, and laid him in a manger, because there was no room for them in the inn.

Now there were in the same country shepherds living out in the fields, keeping watch over their flock by night. And behold, an angel of the Lord stood before them, and the glory of the Lord shone around them, and they were greatly afraid. Then the angel said to them, "Do not be afraid, for behold, I bring you good tidings of great joy which will be to all people. For there is born to you this day in the city of David a savior, who is Christ the Lord. And this will be the sign to you: You will find a babe wrapped in swaddling cloths, lying in a manger." And suddenly there was with the angel a multitude of the heavenly host praising God and saying:

"Glory to God in the highest,
And on earth peace, good will toward men!"

So it was, when the angels had gone away from them into heaven, that the shepherds said to one another, "Let us now go to Bethlehem and see this thing that has come to pass, which the Lord has made

Caesar Augustus . . . registered: the Roman emperor ordered all people in the empire to return to their ancestral homes to register for taxation.

lineage: family.

swaddling cloths: long strips of cloth that are snugly wound around babies.

manger: place for food for animals.

Christ: literally, "anointed one"; the Greek translation of the Hebrew *mashiach* (messiah).

come to pass: happened.

known to us." And they came with haste and found Mary and Joseph, and the babe lying in a manger. Now when they had seen him, they made widely known the saying which was told them concerning this child. And all those who heard it marveled at those things which were told them by the shepherds. But Mary kept all these things and pondered them in her heart. Then the shepherds returned, glorifying and praising God for all the things that they had heard and seen, as it was told them.

pondered them: thought them over carefully.

And when eight days were completed for the circumcision of the child, his name was called Jesus, the name given by the angel before he was conceived in the womb. . . .

Wise Men from the East

Now after Jesus was born in Bethlehem of Judea in the days of Herod the king, behold, wise men from the East came to Jerusalem, saying, "Where is he who has been born king of the Jews? For we have seen his star in the East and have come to worship him." When Herod the king heard these things, he was troubled, and all Jerusalem with him. And when he had gathered all the chief priests and scribes of the people together, he inquired of them where the Christ was to be born. So they said to him, "In Bethlehem of Judea, for thus it is written by the prophet:

Matt. 2:1.

Herod: ruler of Judea, by authority of the Romans.

wise men: also called "magi" and "astrologers" in other translations.

scribes: professional experts in the laws of Moses.

'But you, Bethlehem, in the land of Judah,
Are not the least among the rulers of Judah;
For out of you shall come a ruler
Who will shepherd my people Israel.'"

Then Herod, when he had secretly called the wise men, determined from them what time the star appeared. And he sent them to Bethlehem and said, "Go and search diligently for the young child, and when you have found him, bring back word to me, that I may come and worship him also." When they heard the king, they departed; and behold, the star which they had seen in the East went before them, till it came and stood over where the young child was. When they saw the star, they rejoiced with exceedingly great joy. And when they had come into the house, they saw the young child with Mary his

diligently: thoroughly.

mother, and fell down and worshiped him. And when they had opened their treasures, they presented gifts to him: gold, frankincense, and myrrh. Then, being divinely warned in a dream that they should not return to Herod, they departed for their own country another way.

The Flight into Egypt

Now when they had departed, behold, an angel of the Lord appeared to Joseph in a dream, saying, "Arise, take the young child and his mother, flee to Egypt, and stay there until I bring you word; for Herod will seek the young child to destroy him." When he arose, he took the young child and his mother by night and departed for Egypt, and was there until the death of Herod, that it might be fulfilled which was spoken by the Lord through the prophet, saying, "Out of Egypt I called my son."

Then Herod, when he saw that he was deceived by the wise men, was exceedingly angry; and he sent forth and put to death all the male children who were in Bethlehem and in all its districts, from two years old and under, according to the time which he had determined from the wise men.

But when Herod was dead, behold, an angel of the Lord appeared in a dream to Joseph in Egypt, saying, "Arise, take the young child and his mother, and go to the land of Israel, for those who sought the young child's life are dead." Then he arose, took the young child and his mother, and came into the land of Israel. But when he heard that Archelaus was reigning over Judea instead of his father Herod, he was afraid to go there. And being warned by God in a dream, he turned aside into the region of Galilee. And he came and dwelt in a city called Nazareth, that it might be fulfilled which was spoken by the prophets, "He shall be called a Nazarene."

FOR CLOSE READING

1. Why do Mary and Joseph travel to Bethlehem?

2. In these passages, how does God communicate with people?

3. What two groups of visitors come to see the baby? How did they know that Jesus had been born? How are the two groups similar? How are they different?

4. How does King Herod react when he learns of the birth of "the king of the Jews"?

FOR THOUGHT AND DISCUSSION

5. Which part of the birth story of Jesus made the strongest impression on you? Why?

6. The Matthew section of the birth story (beginning on page 343) makes several references to what prophets had written. What do you think is the effect of these references?

7. Why do you think Herod reacts as he does to the news the wise men bring him?

8. What details of the birth story suggest lowliness, humbleness? What details suggest royalty, splendor? What details suggest danger, death? From what you know of Jesus' later life, what might these details foreshadow?

RESPONDING

1. **Writing** Imagine the events surrounding Jesus' birth from the viewpoint of a participant, Joseph, for example, or a shepherd, or a wise man. Express that person's thoughts in a letter, in journal entries, or as a reminiscence many years after the events.

2. **Activity** Of the four Gospels, only Matthew and Luke give detailed descriptions of Jesus' birth. Read and compare the complete birth stories in a Bible. What differences can you discover in the two accounts? How do these differences affect the

impression each story makes on the reader? Why do you think each story emphasizes different aspects of the Nativity? Compare the two accounts in some visual form—with illustrations or in a chart.

3. **Activity** The Matthew account never mentions how many wise men came to Bethlehem—yet tradition tells us there were three and even provides their names. With a group of classmates, investigate this tradition. Also, research what is known about astrologers in the ancient world, especially in Persia. What was their work? How were they trained? Share your information with the class.

4. **Multicultural Connection** The Nativity is celebrated in many countries with Christmas, a holiday that is associated with many religious and cultural traditions. By yourself or with a classmate, research the Christmas traditions of at least one country other than your own. Prepare a report for the class.

5. **Humanities Connection** The Nativity has been the source of many works of art and music. Find works of art that focus on a particular aspect of the Nativity: Mary and Jesus; Mary, Joseph, and the baby; the shepherds (the Annunciation to the Shepherds, the Adoration of the Shepherds); the wise men or magi (Journey of the Magi, Adoration of the Magi). You may wish to combine a visual presentation of these works with selected carols, spirituals, and other music that focus on these events.

Journey of the Magi

"A cold coming we had of it,
Just the worst time of the year
For a journey, and such a long journey:
The ways deep and the weather sharp,
5   The very dead of winter."
And the camels galled, sore-footed, refractory,
Lying down in the melting snow.
There were times we regretted
The summer palaces on slopes, the terraces,
10   And the silken girls bringing sherbet.
Then the camel men cursing and grumbling
And running away, and wanting their liquor and
     women,
And the night-fires going out, and the lack of shelters,
And the cities hostile and the towns unfriendly
15   And the villages dirty and charging high prices:
A hard time we had of it.
At the end we preferred to travel all night,
Sleeping in snatches,
With the voices singing in our ears, saying
20   That this was all folly.

Then at dawn we came down to a temperate valley,
Wet, below the snow line, smelling of vegetation;
With a running stream and a water mill beating the
     darkness,
And three trees on the low sky,
25   And an old white horse galloped away in the
     meadow.
Then we came to a tavern with vine-leaves over
     the lintel,
Six hands at an open door dicing for pieces of
     silver,

Lines 1–5 are adapted
from a 17th-century
Nativity sermon by
Lancelot Andrews.

galled: i.e., their skin had
sores from the rubbing of
packs or straps.

refractory: stubborn.

lintel: horizontal beam
over a door.

And feet kicking the empty wineskins.
But there was no information, and so we
    continued
30 And arrived at evening, not a moment too soon
Finding the place; it was (you may say) satisfactory.

All this was a long time ago, I remember,
And I would do it again, but set down
This set down
35 This: were we led all that way for
Birth or Death? There was a Birth, certainly,
We had evidence and no doubt. I had seen birth
    and death,
But had thought they were different; this Birth was
Hard and bitter agony for us, like Death, our death.
40 We returned to our places, these Kingdoms,
But no longer at ease here, in the old dispensation,
With an alien people clutching their gods.
I should be glad of another death.

dispensation: i.e.,
religious system.

FOR THOUGHT AND DISCUSSION

1. Who is speaking in this poem? How do you think
the speaker feels about the journey in each of the
stanzas?

2. What impressions do you have of the wise men or
magi in the Bible story? How do those impressions
compare with the impressions given by this poem?

3. What references to Jesus' later life can you find in
the second stanza? What is the effect of linking
these references to the Nativity?

4. What different meanings do the words "birth" and
"death" seem to have in the last stanza? Why do
you suppose the speaker links thoughts of birth
and death?

5. Why do you think the narrator is "no longer at
ease" (line 41)?

Nativity

Within a native hut, ere stirred the dawn,
Unto the Pure One was an infant born
Wrapped in blue lappah that his mother dyed.
Laid on his father's home-tanned deer-skin hide
5 The babe still slept by all things glorified.
Spirits of black bards burst their bonds and sang,
"Peace upon earth" until the heavens rang.
All the black babies who from earth had fled,
Peeped through the clouds, then gathered round his
     head.
10 Telling of things a baby needs to do,
When first he opens his eyes on wonders new;
Telling him that to sleep was sweeter rest,
All comfort came from his black mother's breast.
Their gifts were of love caught from the springing
     sod,
15 Whilst tears and laughter were the gifts of God.
Then all the wise men of the past stood forth
Filling the air East, West, and South and North;
And told him of the joys that wisdom brings
To mortals in their earthly wanderings.
20 The children of the past shook down each bough,
Wreathed frangipani blossoms for his brow;
They put pink lilies in his mother's hand,
And heaped for both the first fruits of the land.
His father cut some palm fronds that the air
Be coaxed to zephyrs while he rested there.
Birds trilled their hallelujahs; and the dew
25 Trembled with laughter till the babe laughed too.
All the black women brought their love so wise,
And kissed their motherhood into his mother's eyes.

lappah: a rectangular cloth tied around the waist to form a skirt.

bards: singer-poets.

sod: grass.

frangipani: a tropical flower, also known as red jasmine.

that: so that.
zephyrs: soft breezes.

FOR CLOSE READING

1. Where does this Nativity take place?

2. Who sings "Peace upon earth"?

3. What were the gifts of God?

FOR THOUGHT AND DISCUSSION

4. What impression did this poem have on you? What details in the poem contribute most to that impression?

5. List the details in this poem that are taken from the Bible. List the details that are different. Choose one or two of the differences and say what part they play in the story.

6. The poet is a woman of the Fanti tribe in the Gold Coast of Africa. What effects has she achieved by setting the Nativity where she does?

To Jesus on His Birthday

For this your mother sweated in the cold,
For this you bled upon the bitter tree: **tree:** a traditional
A yard of tinsel ribbon bought and sold;   reference to Jesus' cross.
A paper wreath; a day at home for me.
5   The merry bells ring out, the people kneel;
Up goes the man of God before the crowd;
With voice of honey and with eyes of steel
He drones your humble gospel to the proud.
Nobody listens. Less than the wind that blows
10   Are all your words to us you died to save.
O Prince of Peace! O Sharon's dewy Rose!   **Sharon's dewy Rose:** see
How mute you lie within your vaulted grave.   page 263.
The stone the angel rolled away with tears   **mute:** silent.
Is back upon your mouth these thousand years.

FOR THOUGHT AND DISCUSSION

1. What are your feelings after reading the poem by Millay? What details had the strongest effect on you? Why?

2. In the opening lines of the Millay poem, to what does "this" refer?

3. The Millay poem makes several ironic contrasts. For example, the efforts and sufferings of Mary and Jesus are contrasted with such trivial things as "a yard of tinsel ribbon." What other contrasts can you find in this poem?

4. What do you think is meant by the last two lines of the Millay poem?

WILLIAM SHAKESPEARE

Some say that ever 'gainst that season comes

'gainst: just before.

Some say that ever 'gainst that season comes
Wherein our Savior's birth is celebrated,
The bird of dawning singeth all night long:
And then, they say, no spirit dare stir abroad;
5 The nights are wholesome; then no planets strike,
No fairy takes, nor witch hath power to charm,

hallow'd: holy.

So hallow'd and so gracious is the time.

Hamlet, Act 1, Scene 1

FOR THOUGHT AND DISCUSSION

1. How does the mood or feeling of this passage
compare with the emotions of the Millay poem on
the preceding page?

2. Shakespeare wrote the "Some Say . . ." passage
before most of our present-day Christmas customs
began. According to this passage, how is the
Christmas season made special?

3. If you were to write a similar passage about the
Christmas season in the present day, what details
would you mention?

Is This Not the Carpenter?

The Baptism of Jesus

John came baptizing in the wilderness and preaching a baptism of repentance for the remission of sins. And all the land of Judea, and those from Jerusalem, went out to him and were all baptized by him in the Jordan River, confessing their sins. Now John was clothed with camel's hair and with a leather belt around his waist, and he ate locusts and wild honey. And he preached, saying, "There comes one after me who is mightier than I, whose sandal strap I am not worthy to stoop down and loose. I indeed baptized you with water, but he will baptize you with the Holy Spirit."

It came to pass in those days that Jesus came from Nazareth of Galilee, and was baptized by John in the Jordan. And immediately, coming up from the water, he saw the heavens parting and the Spirit descending upon him like a dove. Then a voice came from heaven, "You are my beloved son, in whom I am well pleased."

Mark 1:4.

John: the son of Elizabeth (see page 342), known as John the Baptist.

baptism . . . sins: ceremony using water to symbolize washing away what is impure.

Temptation in the Wilderness

And immediately the Spirit drove him into the wilderness. And he was there in the wilderness forty days, tempted by Satan, and was with the wild beasts; and the angels ministered to him. Now after John was put in prison, Jesus came to Galilee, preaching the gospel of the kingdom of God, and saying, "The time is fulfilled, and the kingdom of God is at hand. Repent, and believe in the gospel." . . .

gospel: message of good news.

[*Jesus called certain men to be his personal followers. Accompanied by these disciples (also called apostles) he spoke to a large crowd beside the Sea of Galilee and performed several miracles of healing.*]

"Peace, Be Still!"

On the same day, when evening had come, he said to them, "Let us cross over to the other side." Now when they had left the multitude, they took him along in the boat as he was. And other little boats were also with him. And a great windstorm arose, and the waves beat into the boat, so that it was already filling. But he was in the stern, asleep on a pillow. And they awoke him and said to him, "Teacher, do you not care that we are perishing?" Then he arose and rebuked the wind, and said to the sea, "Peace, be still!" And the wind ceased and there was a great calm. But he said to them, "Why are you so fearful? How is it that you have no faith?" And they feared exceedingly, and said to one another, "Who can this be, that even the wind and the sea obey him!"

rebuked: scolded.

The Gadarene Swine

Then they came to the other side of the sea, to the country of the Gadarenes. And when he had come out of the boat, immediately there met him out of the tombs a man with an unclean spirit, who had his dwelling among the tombs; and no one could bind him, not even with chains, because he had often been bound with shackles and chains. And the chains had been pulled apart by him, and the shackles broken in pieces; neither could anyone tame him. And always, night and day, he was in the mountains and in the tombs, crying out and cutting himself with stones. But when he saw Jesus from afar, he ran and worshiped him. And he cried out with a loud voice and said, "What have I to do with you, Jesus, Son of the Most High God? I implore you by God that you do not torment me." For he said to him, "Come out of the man, unclean spirit!" Then he asked him, "What is your name?" And he answered, saying, "My name is Legion; for we are many." And he begged him earnestly that he would not send them out of the

Gadarenes: also known as *Gerasenes*.

tombs: usually caves.

with an unclean spirit: possessed by demons; insane.

implore: beg.

my name is Legion: i.e., there is a legion, an army of us.

country. Now a large herd of swine was feeding there near the mountains. And all the demons begged him, saying, "Send us to the swine, that we may enter them." And at once Jesus gave them permission. Then the unclean spirits went out and entered the swine (there were about two thousand); and the herd ran violently down the steep place into the sea, and drowned in the sea.

swine: pigs.

Now those who fed the swine fled, and they told it in the city and in the country. And they went out to see what it was that had happened. Then they came to Jesus, and saw the one who had been demon-possessed and had the legion, sitting and clothed and in his right mind. And they were afraid. And those who saw it told them how it happened to him who had been demon-possessed, and about the swine. Then they began to plead with him to depart from their region. . . .

A Suffering Woman, a Dying Girl

Now when Jesus had crossed over again by boat to the other side, a great multitude gathered to him; and he was by the sea. And behold, one of the rulers of the synagogue came, Jairus by name. And when he saw him, he fell at his feet and begged him earnestly, saying, "My little daughter lies at the point of death. Come and lay your hands on her that she may be healed, and she will live."

synagogue: place of worship and religious study.

So Jesus went with him, and a great multitude followed him and thronged him. Now a certain woman had a flow of blood for twelve years, and had suffered many things from many physicians. She had spent all that she had and was not better, but rather grew worse. When she heard about Jesus, she came behind him in the crowd and touched his garment; for she said, "If only I may touch his clothes, I shall be made well." Immediately the fountain of her blood was dried up, and she felt in her body that she was healed of the affliction. And Jesus, immediately knowing in himself that power had gone out of him, turned around in the crowd and said, "Who touched my clothes?" But his disciples said to him, "You see the multitude thronging you, and you say, 'Who touched me?'" And he looked around to see her who had done this thing. But the woman, fearing and trembling, knowing what had happened to her, came and fell down before him and told him the whole truth. And he said to her, "Daughter, your faith has made you well. Go in peace, and be healed of your affliction."

While he was still speaking, some came from the ruler of the synagogue's house who said, "Your daughter is dead. Why trouble the teacher any further?" As soon as Jesus heard the word that was spoken, he said to the ruler of the synagogue, "Do not be afraid; only believe." And he permitted no one to follow him except Peter, James, and John the brother of James. Then he came to the house of the ruler of the synagogue, and saw a tumult and those who wept and wailed loudly. When he came in, he said to them, "Why make this commotion and weep? The child is not dead, but sleeping." And they laughed him to scorn. But when he had put them all out, he took the father and the mother of the child, and those who were with him, and entered where the child was lying. Then he took the child by the hand, and said to her, "Talitha, cumi," which is translated, "Little girl, I say to you, arise." Immediately the girl arose and walked, for she was twelve years of age. And they were overcome with great amazement. But he commanded them strictly that no one should know it, and said that something should be given her to eat.

Peter and James and John: Jesus' closest disciples.

tumult: noisy commotion.

A Prophet Without Honor

Then he went out from there and came to his own country, and his disciples followed him. And when the Sabbath had come, he began to teach in the synagogue. And many hearing him were astonished, saying, "Where did this man get these things? And what wisdom is this which is given to him, that such mighty works are performed by his hands! Is this not the carpenter, the son of Mary, and brother of James, Joses, Judas, and Simon? And are not his sisters here with us?" And they were offended at him. But Jesus said to them, "A prophet is not without honor except in his own country, among his own relatives, and in his own house." Now he could do no mighty work there, except that he laid his hands on a few sick people and healed them. And he marveled because of their unbelief. Then he went about the villages in a circuit, teaching. . . .

The Death of John the Baptist

Now King Herod heard of him, for his name had become well-known. And he said, "John the Baptist is risen from the dead, and therefore these powers are at work in him." Others said, "It is Elijah." And others said, "It is the prophet, or like one of the prophets." But when Herod heard, he said, "This is John, whom I beheaded; he has been raised from the dead!" For Herod himself had sent and laid hold of John, and bound him in prison for the sake of Herodias, his brother Philip's wife; for he had married her. For John had said to Herod, "It is not lawful for you to have your brother's wife." Therefore Herodias held it against him and wanted to kill him, but she could not; for Herod feared John, knowing that he was a just and holy man, and he protected him. And when he heard him, he did many things, and heard him gladly. Then an opportune day came when Herod on his birthday gave a feast for his nobles, the high officers, and the chief men of Galilee. And when Herodias' daughter herself came in and danced, and pleased Herod and those who sat with him, the king said to the girl, "Ask me whatever you want, and I will give it to you." He also swore to her, "Whatever you ask me, I will give you, up to half of my kingdom." So she went out and said to her mother, "What shall I ask?" And she said, "The head of John the Baptist." Immediately she came in with haste to the king and asked, saying, "I want you to give me at once the head of John the Baptist on a platter." And the king was exceedingly sorry; yet, because of the oaths and because of those who sat with him, he did not want to refuse her. And immediately the king sent an executioner and commanded his head to be brought. And he went and beheaded him in prison, brought his head on a platter, and gave it to the girl; and the girl gave it to her mother. And when his disciples heard of it, they came and took away his corpse and laid it in a tomb.

Herod: ruler of Galilee; son of Herod the Great (mentioned in the story of Jesus' birth).

opportune: convenient.

daughter: by her first husband. The daughter's name is Salome.

Feeding the Multitude

Then the apostles gathered to Jesus and told him all things, both what they had done and what they had taught. And he said to them, "Come aside by yourselves to a deserted place and rest a while." For there were many coming and going, and they did

told . . . things: earlier, Jesus had sent out his disciples to preach and heal.

not even have time to eat. So they departed to a deserted place in the boat by themselves. But the multitudes saw them departing, and many knew him and ran there on foot from all the cities. They arrived before them and came together to him. And Jesus, when he came out, saw a great multitude and was moved with compassion for them, because they were like sheep not having a shepherd. So he began to teach them many things. And when the day was now far spent, his disciples came to him and said, "This is a deserted place, and already the hour is late. Send them away, that they may go into the surrounding country and villages and buy themselves bread, for they have nothing to eat."

But he answered and said to them, "You give them something to eat." And they said to him, "Shall we go and buy two hundred denarii worth of bread and give them something to eat?" But he said to them, "How many loaves do you have? Go and see." And when they found out they said, "Five, and two fish." Then he commanded them to make them all sit down in groups on the green grass. So they sat down in ranks, in hundreds and in fifties. And when he had taken the five loaves and the two fish, he looked up to the heaven, blessed and broke the loaves, and gave them to his disciples to set before them; and the two fish he divided among them all. So they all ate and were filled. And they took up twelve baskets full of fragments and of the fish. Now those who had eaten the loaves were about five thousand men.

Walking on the Sea

Immediately he made his disciples get into the boat and go before him to the other side, to Bethsaida, while he sent the multitude away. And when he had sent them away, he departed to the mountains to pray. Now when evening came, the boat was in the middle of the sea; and he was alone on the land. Then he saw them straining at rowing, for the wind was against them. And about the fourth watch of the night he came to them, walking on the sea, and would have passed them by. But when they saw him walking on the sea, they supposed it was a ghost, and cried out; for they all saw him and were troubled. And immediately he talked with them and said to them,

compassion: sympathy.

denarii (di ner′ē i): Roman silver coins, each equal to a day's wages in Jesus' time.

ranks: rows.

fourth watch: a period of the night beginning at 3 A.M.

"Be of good cheer! It is I; do not be afraid." Then he went up into the boat to them, and the wind ceased. And they were greatly amazed in themselves beyond measure, and marveled. For they had not understood about the loaves, because their heart was hardened. . . .

The Bread of Life

And when they found him on the other side of the sea, they said to him, "Rabbi, when did you come here?" Jesus answered them and said, "Most assuredly, I say to you, you seek me, not because you saw the signs, but because you ate of the loaves and were filled. Do not labor for the food which perishes, but for the food which endures to everlasting life, which the Son of Man will give you, because God the Father has set his seal on him." Then they said to him, "What shall we do, that we may work the works of God?" Jesus answered and said to them, "This is the work of God, that you believe in him whom he sent." Therefore they said to him, "What sign will you perform then, that we may see it and believe you? What work will you do? Our fathers ate the manna in the desert; as it is written, 'He gave them bread from heaven to eat.'" Then Jesus said to them, "Most assuredly, I say to you, Moses did not give you the bread from heaven, but my Father gives you the true bread from heaven. For the bread of God is he who comes down from heaven and gives life to the world. Then they said to him, "Lord, give us this bread always."

And Jesus said to them, "I am the bread of life. He who comes to me shall never hunger, and he who believes in me shall never thirst. But I said to you that you have seen me and yet do not believe. All that the Father gives me will come to me, and the one who comes to me I will by no means cast out. For I have come down from heaven, not to do my own will, but the will of him who sent me. This is the will of the Father who sent me, that of all he has given me I should lose nothing, but should raise it up at the last day. And this is the will of him who sent me, that everyone who sees the Son and believes in him may have everlasting life; and I will raise him up at the last day."

John 6:25.

they: part of the crowd that had been fed the day before.

rabbi: teacher.

signs: miracles.

seal: sign (of authority or approval).

FOR CLOSE READING

1. Both John the Baptist and Jesus announce what is coming. What is the difference between their messages?

2. What miracles does Jesus perform in these passages?

3. What words and phrases are used to describe how various people react to Jesus and what he does?

FOR THOUGHT AND DISCUSSION

4. There are many connections between the lives of John and Jesus, beginning with the angelic foretelling of their births (page 342). What other connections can you find? How is the death of John related to the story of Jesus? Why do you suppose Mark withholds the details of John's death until later in the story?

5. Compare the three miracles of healing in these passages. What similarities and differences do you find?

6. Why do you think Jesus could do "no mighty work" in his own country?

7. Twice the disciples are caught in a storm at sea. What might these two stories tell about the disciples and their relationship to Jesus?

8. What pattern do you find in the ways people respond to Jesus in these stories? Support your answer with examples.

RESPONDING

Writing Review these passages as if you had never before heard of Jesus. What are you learning about his work and family? What personal traits does he seem to have? Where are these traits most clearly revealed? Write about your "discoveries."

The Jesus Infection

Jesus is with me
on the Blue Grass Parkway going eastbound.
He is with me
on the Old Harrodsburg Road coming home.
5 I am listening
to country gospel music
in the borrowed Subaru.
The gas pedal
and the words
10 leap to the music.
Oh throw out the lifeline!
Someone is drifting away.

Flags fly up in my mind
without my knowing
15 where they've been lying furled
and I am happy
living in the sunlight
where Jesus is near.
A man is driving his polled Herefords
20 across the gleanings of a cornfield
while I am bound for the kingdom of the free.
At the little trestle bridge that has no railing
I see that I won't have to cross Jordan alone.

Signposts every mile exhort me
25 to Get Right With God
and I move over.
There's a neon message blazing
at the crossroad
catty-corner to the Burger Queen:
30 Ye Come With Me.
Is it well with my soul, Jesus?
It sounds so easy

Blue Grass Parkway: a
highway in Kentucky.

polled Herefords: a
breed of cattle.

to be happy after the sunrise,
to be washed in the crimson flood.

35 Now I am tailgating
and I read the bumper sticker

Poland China: a breed of
hogs.

on a Ford truck full of Poland Chinas.
It says: Honk If You Know Jesus
and I do it.

40 My sound blats out for miles
behind the pigsqueal
and it's catching in the front end,
in the axle,
in the universal joint,

contagion: the spreading
of anything from one to
another.

45 this rich contagion.

We are going down the valley on a hairpin turn,
the swine and me, we're breakneck in,
we're leaning on
the everlasting arms.

FOR THOUGHT AND DISCUSSION

1. The speaker is listening to gospel music and
reading roadside signs. How might the words of
the religious songs and signs influence the
speaker's choice of images in the poem?

2. In line 13, what might the "flags" be? How might
they affect the speaker?

3. What seems to be the speaker's mood? Choose one
or two words to describe the speaker's feelings and
support your choice with details from the poem.

4. Think back to some moment in your own life when
you felt a similar mood and try to write about it
using specific objects and scenes the way the
speaker does.

from A Life of Jesus

The Japanese novelist Shusaku Endo begins
his study of the life of Jesus with the following
observations.

We have never seen his face. We have never heard his voice.

We do not really know what he looked like—the man called Jesus, of whom I propose to speak. Countless pictures of Jesus have been painted from imagination in accord with a conventional formula: long hair falling to the shoulders, the trimmed beard, the lean face with high cheekbones. Most artists have followed for centuries this traditional recipe in constructing their portraits of Jesus, each of them going on from there to suffuse the facial features of Jesus with the ideals of piety peculiar to the artist's own historical milieu.

Still, in the first days of the church the face of Jesus was never fashioned to the mold. The early Christians had a certain hesitant reserve about trying to depict the faces of holy persons. Consequently, the craftsmen of that era did not address themselves to picturing the face of Jesus in realistic fashion. They portrayed "the Lord" by means of symbols—a fish or a lamb, a shock of wheat or a tendril of grape. In the age of the catacombs Jesus appears in the guise of a young man, fashioned in the Greek style, with the beardless face of an adolescent, quite different from the conventional modern image. After some years, however, beginning in the fifth century, the influence of Byzantine art determined the model of the face of Jesus which has persisted into our own day. By studying these portraits we can learn how

suffuse: overspread; cover.

milieu (mil yǔ'): surroundings; environment.

the church: organized Christianity.

catacombs: underground tunnels and rooms usually used for burial. In a time of persecution, many early Christians survived by hiding in catacombs in and near Rome.

guise: form.

Byzantine art: (on page 363) the Byzantine or Eastern Roman empire survived the fall of Rome and developed its own distinctive style of art and architecture.

physiognomy (fiz′ē og′ nə mē): face.

Stauffer: possibly Ethelbert Stauffer, a 20th-century biblical scholar.

surmise: guess, imagine.

second coat: this is recorded in Mark 6:9.

Jesus . . . Jeshouah: Jesus is the Greek form of the Hebrew *Yeshua* (in English, Joshua). The name means "the Lord is salvation."

Josephus: an important first-century source of information about Jewish life in Palestine.

mankind through its long spiritual history has come to visualize in the highest degree of purity and beauty the physiognomy of the holiest person who ever lived.

No one has actually seen the face and form of Jesus except for the people who lived with him, the people whose lives he crossed. Even the New Testament in narrating the life of Jesus gives hardly a hint concerning his physical appearance. Yet by reading the Gospels we are able to bring to our own mind's eye a lively impression of Jesus, thanks to the people who did get to know him and then were unable to forget him the rest of their lives.

Since the New Testament tells us next to nothing about the face of Jesus, we are left with no other choice but to rummage our own imaginations. According to Stauffer, the Jewish religion of that time required of any man who preached the word of God that he be "a person tall in stature and well put together." Stauffer claims that a man falling short of this description would not be warmly received but would become an object of criticism. If Stauffer's explanation is correct—and since the Gospel record nowhere indicates that people ever condemned Jesus for his external appearance—then Jesus very likely was a man of normal stature for a Jew. From there we go on to think of him as looking like other Jews of ancient Palestine, parting his dark hair in the middle and letting it fall to the shoulders, growing a full beard and mustache, with the customary beard, the customary hair style, and his clothing probably the worse for wear, as we surmise from the Gospel of Mark where Jesus allows his disciples to possess only the usual "sandals, but not a second coat." So much for the outward figure of Jesus, as far as painstaking imagination can piece it together.

The name Jesus—more precisely Jeshouah—was a common name found everywhere. According to the Jewish historian Josephus, author of the *Jewish Antiquities*, so many men bore this name that it came to lack all individuality. During his brief span of life, therefore, Jesus had nothing in his name or in his looks to distinguish him. He was ordinary, appearing in no way different from the mass of men who had to sweat for a living.

ABOVE: *The Flight into Egypt*, serigraph by Sadao Watanabe, Japan, 1970. Lee Boltin.
PAGE 365: *The Annunciation*, painting by Romare Bearden, 1942. Courtesy of Mrs. Nanette Bearden.
The Adoration of the Magi, detail from a tempera on wood painting by Gentile da Fabriano, 1423.
SCALA/Art Resource.

The Baptism of Christ, detail from the Baptistry doors (south side), Florence. Bronze gilt relief by Andrea Pisano, c. 1330. SCALA/Art Resource.

ABOVE: *The Miracle of the Loaves and the Fishes*, lithograph by Jean Heiberg, USA, contemporary. Lee Boltin.
RIGHT: *The Good Samaritan* (after Delacroix), oil painting by Vincent Van Gogh, 1890. The Rijksmuseum, Kröller-Müller, Otterlo, The Netherlands.

ABOVE: *The Return of the Prodigal Son* by L. Bernardo. National Museum of Art, Bucarest, Romania. Cameraphoto/Art Resource.
RIGHT: *Christ with the Crown of Thorns*, wood, Africa, twentieth century. Lee Boltin.
BELOW: *The Last Supper*, mural by Richard West. Courtesy of Richard West.

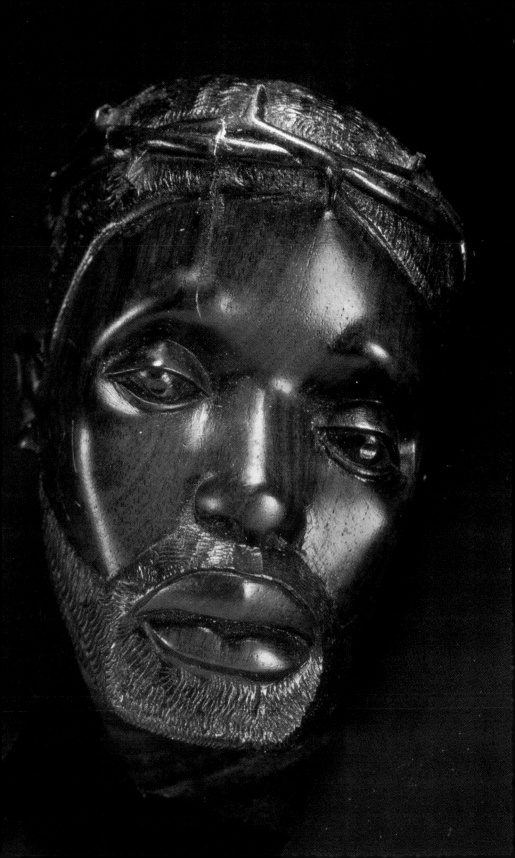

Georgia O'Keeffe, American, 1887-1986, *Black Cross, New Mexico,* oil on canvas, 1929, 99x77.2 cm, Art Institute Purchase Fund, 1943.95, photograph © 1994, The Art Institute of Chicago. All Rights Reserved.

(See "A Life of Jesus" on pages 363–364).

FOR CLOSE READING

1. According to Endo, how did Christians represent Jesus "in the first days of the church"?

2. What did the historian Josephus report about the name "Jesus"?

3. In his last sentence, how does Endo describe Jesus?

FOR THOUGHT AND DISCUSSION

4. In your opinion, how important is it to know what Jesus actually looked like?

5. How does Endo arrive at his conclusions about Jesus' appearance? How reasonable are these conclusions?

6. Consider the symbols that early Christians used to represent Jesus. Why do you think they chose those symbols?

7. You have probably seen many different images of Jesus—in paintings, sculpture, even portrayals in films. Which particular image or portrayal has made the strongest impression on you? How does this image compare with Endo's suggestions about Jesus' appearance?

11

Jesus: Teachings, Death, and Resurrection

The Sermon on the Mount

The Beatitudes

And seeing the multitudes, he went up on a mountain, and when he was seated his disciples came to him. Then he opened his mouth and taught them, saying:

> "Blessed are the poor in spirit
>> For theirs is the kingdom of heaven.
> Blessed are those who mourn,
>> For they shall be comforted.
> Blessed are the meek,
>> For they shall inherit the earth.
> Blessed are those who hunger and thirst for
>> righteousness,
>> For they shall be filled.
> Blessed are the merciful,
>> For they shall obtain mercy.
> Blessed are the pure in heart,
>> For they shall see God.
> Blessed are the peacemakers,
>> For they shall be called sons of God.
> Blessed are those who are persecuted for
>> righteousness' sake,
>> For theirs is the kingdom of heaven." . . .

for righteousness' sake: for doing right.

"But I Say to You"

You have heard that it was said to those of old, 'You shall not murder,' and whoever murders will be in danger of the judgment. But I say to you that whoever is angry with his brother without a cause shall be in danger of the judgment. . . .

be reconciled to: make up with.

Therefore if you bring your gift to the altar, and there remember that your brother has something against you, leave your gift there before the altar, and go your way. First be reconciled to your brother, and then come and offer your gift. . . .

"You have heard that it was said to those of old, 'You shall not commit adultery.' But I say to you that whoever looks at a woman to lust for her has already committed adultery with her in his heart. And if your right eye causes you to sin, pluck it out and cast it from you; for it is more profitable for you that one of your members perish, than for your whole body to be cast into hell. . . .

members: body parts.

"You have heard that it was said, 'An eye for an eye and a tooth for a tooth.' But I tell you not to resist an evil person. But whoever slaps you on your right cheek, turn the other to him also. If anyone wants to sue you and take away your tunic, let him have your cloak also. And whoever compels you to go one mile, go with him two.

tunic: shirt.

"You have heard that it was said, 'You shall love your neighbor and hate your enemy.' But I say to you, love your enemies, bless those who curse you, do good to those who hate you, and pray for those who spitefully use you and persecute you, that you may be sons of your Father in heaven; for he makes his sun rise on the evil and on the good, and sends rain on the just and on the unjust. . . .

"Take heed that you do not do your charitable deeds before men, to be seen by them. Otherwise you have no reward from your Father in heaven.

before: in front of.

"Therefore, when you do a charitable deed, do not sound a trumpet before you as the hypocrites do in the synagogues and in the streets, that they may have glory from men. Assuredly, I say to you, they have their reward. But when you do a charitable deed, do not let your left hand know what your right hand is doing, that your charitable deed may be in secret; and your Father who sees in secret will himself reward you openly." . . .

hypocrites: persons who only pretend to be good or religious.

The Lord's Prayer: Our Father

vain: useless.

But when you pray, do not use vain repetitions as the heathen do. For they think that they will be heard for their many words. Therefore do not be like them. For your Father knows the things you have need of before you ask him. In this manner, therefore, pray:

Our Father in heaven,
Hallowed be your name.
Your kingdom come.
Your will be done
On earth as it is in heaven.
Give us this day our daily bread,
And forgive us our debts,
As we forgive our debtors.
And do not lead us into temptation,
But deliver us from the evil one.
For yours is the kingdom and the power
    and the glory forever. Amen."

hallowed: sacred, holy.

debts: In other versions, "trespasses"; i.e., sins.

debtors: In other versions, "those who trespass against us."

Treasure

Do not lay up for yourselves treasures on earth, where moth and rust destroy and where thieves break in and steal; but lay up for yourselves treasures in heaven, where neither moth nor rust destroys and where thieves do not break in and steal. For where your treasure is, there your heart will be also." . . .

The Lilies of the Field

No one can serve two masters; for either he will hate the one and love the other, or else he will be loyal to the one and despise the other. You cannot serve God and mammon.

mammon: money, riches.

"Therefore I say to you, do not worry about your life, what you will eat or what you will drink; nor about your body, what you will put on. Is not life more than food and the body more than clothing? Look at the birds of the air, for they neither sow nor reap nor gather into barns; yet your heavenly Father feeds them. Are you not of more value than they? Which of you by worrying can add one cubit to his stature? So why do you worry about clothing? Consider the lilies of the field, how they grow: they neither toil nor spin; and yet I say to you that even Solomon in all his glory was not arrayed like one of these. Now if God so clothes the grass of the field, which today is, and tomorrow is thrown into the oven, will he not much more clothe you, O you of

stature: height.

arrayed: richly clothed.

little faith? Therefore do not worry, saying, 'What shall we eat?' or "What shall we drink?' or 'What shall we wear?' For after all these things the gentiles seek. For your heavenly Father knows that you need all these things. But seek first the kingdom of God and his righteousness, and all these things shall be added to you.

"Therefore do not worry about tomorrow, for tomorrow will worry about its own things. Sufficient for the day is its own trouble."

sufficient: enough.

Judge Not

Judge not, that you be not judged. For with what judgment you judge, you will be judged; and with the same measure you use, it will be measured back to you. And why do you look at the speck in your brother's eye, but do not consider the plank in your own eye?" . . .

measure: quantity.

A Solid Foundation

Therefore whoever hears these sayings of mine, and does them, I will liken him to a wise man who built his house on the rock: and the rain descended, the floods came, and the winds blew and beat on that house; and it did not fall, for it was founded on the rock. Now everyone who hears these sayings of mine, and does not do them, will be like a foolish man who built his house on the sand: and the rain descended, the floods came, and the winds blew and beat on that house; and it fell. And great was its fall."

And so it was, when Jesus had ended these sayings, that the people were astonished at his teaching, for he taught them as one having authority, and not as the scribes.

scribes: professional experts in the laws of Moses.

FOR CLOSE READING

1. To whom is Jesus speaking in this sermon? How do they respond to his message?

2. What patterns can you find in Jesus' speaking style throughout the sermon?

3. According to Jesus' sermon, what should people's attitude be toward such things as food and clothing?

FOR THOUGHT AND DISCUSSION

4. What statement in Jesus' sermon impressed you the most? surprised you the most? Why?

5. What would you say is the overall message or basic theme of the Beatitudes?

6. What would you say is the basic theme of the "But I Say to You" section?

7. Jesus presents many examples of how people should act toward each other. If everyone followed these examples, how might our society be affected? Do you think a society based on these principles is possible? Explain.

8. Jesus concludes his sermon with a parable, a short story with a moral. How may this story about two foundations be related to the sermon that precedes it?

RESPONDING

1. **Activity** Many phrases from the Sermon on the Mount have become well-known sayings. Select one of these sayings that particularly interests you and prepare a brief talk for your classmates, illustrating the saying with examples from your reading or experience.

2. **Activity** Create a collage of pictures from magazines or newspapers to illustrate one of the points in Jesus' sermon. Do not say which point, and see whether your classmates can identify it.

3. **Humanities Connection** Select or compose music to accompany an oral reading or singing of the Beatitudes.

JOHN CIARDI

In Place of a Curse

At the next vacancy for God, if I am elected,
I shall forgive last the delicately wounded
who, having been slugged no harder than anyone
      else,
never got up again, neither to fight back,
5   nor to finger their jaws in painful admiration.

They who are wholly broken, and they in whom
mercy is understanding, I shall embrace at once
and lead to pillows in heaven. But they who are

baiting: annoying,
tormenting.
      the meek by trade, baiting the best of their betters
10   with the extortions of a mock-helplessness

I shall take last to love, and never wholly.
Let them all into Heaven—I abolish Hell—
but let it be read over them as they enter:
"Beware the calculations of the meek, who gambled
      nothing,
15   gave nothing, and could never receive enough."

FOR THOUGHT AND DISCUSSION

1. A song entitled "If I Ruled the World" was once a
popular hit. What one thing would you do if you
ruled the world?

2. What two types of people does the speaker
mention? Which type would the speaker "forgive
last" and "take last to love"? Why?

3. How is it possible to extort (obtain) something by
pretending to be helpless (line 10)? Can you think
of an example?

Parables

During his teaching ministry, Jesus told many parables, brief stories that express truths or moral lessons. Some of the best known of his parables are included below.

The Good Samaritan

And behold, a certain lawyer stood up and tested him, saying, "Teacher, what shall I do to inherit eternal life?" He said to him, "What is written in the law? What is your reading of it?" So he answered and said, "'You shall love the Lord your God with all your heart, with all your soul, with all your strength, and with all your mind,' and 'your neighbor as yourself.'" And he said to him, "You have answered rightly; do this and you will live."

But he, wanting to justify himself, said to Jesus, "And who is my neighbor?" Then Jesus answered and said: "A certain man went down from Jerusalem to Jericho, and fell among thieves, who stripped him of his clothing, wounded him, and departed, leaving him half dead. Now by chance a certain priest came down that road. And when he saw him, he passed by on the other side. Likewise a Levite, when he arrived at the place, came and looked, and passed by on the other side. But a certain Samaritan, as he journeyed, came where he was. And when he saw him, he had compassion on him, and went to him and bandaged his wounds, pouring on oil and wine; and he set him on his own animal, brought him to an inn, and took care of him. On the next day, when he departed, he

Luke 10:25.

law: the Hebrew word is Torah (law, teaching), found in the first five books of the Bible.

justify himself: free himself from guilt.

Levite: assistant to a priest.

Samaritan: In Jesus' time, Jews and Samaritans disliked one another, though they were distantly related.

---

denarii (di ner/ē ī):
Roman silver coins, each
equal to a day's wages in
Jesus' time.

took out two denarii, gave them to the innkeeper, and
said to him, 'Take care of him; and whatever more
you spend, when I come again, I will repay you.' So
which of these three do you think was neighbor to
him who fell among the thieves?" And he said, "He
who showed mercy on him." Then Jesus said to him,
"Go and do likewise."

The Unforgiving Servant

Matt. 18:23.

Therefore the kingdom of heaven is like a certain
king who wanted to settle accounts with his
servants. And when he had begun to settle accounts,
one was brought to him who owed him ten thousand
talents. But as he was not able to pay, his master
commanded that he be sold, with his wife and
children and all that he had, and that payment be
made. The servant therefore fell down before him,
saying, 'Master, have patience with me, and I will pay
you all.' Then the master of that servant was moved
with compassion, released him, and forgave him the
debt. But that servant went out and found one of his
fellow servants who owed him a hundred denarii;
and he laid hands on him and took him by the throat,
saying, 'Pay me what you owe!' So his fellow servant
fell down at his feet and begged him, saying, 'Have
patience with me, and I will pay you all.' And he
would not, but went and threw him into prison till he
should pay the debt. So when his fellow servants saw
what had been done, they were very grieved, and
came and told their master all that had been done.
Then his master, after he had called him, said to him,
'You wicked servant! I forgave you all that debt
because you begged me. Should you not also have
had compassion on your fellow servant, just as I had
pity on you?' And his master was angry, and
delivered him to the torturers until he should pay all
that was due to him. So my heavenly Father also will
do to you if each of you, from his heart, does not
forgive his brother his trespasses."

talent: originally a unit of
weight, about seventy-
five pounds. That weight
of silver would be worth
a great deal today, as it
was then.

The Pharisee and the Tax Collector

Luke 18:9.

Also he spoke this parable to some who trusted in
themselves that they were righteous and
despised others: "Two men went up to the temple to

pray, one a Pharisee and the other a tax collector. The Pharisee stood and prayed thus with himself, 'God, I thank you that I am not like other men—extortioners, unjust, adulterers, or even as this tax collector. I fast twice a week; I give tithes of all that I possess.' And the tax collector, standing afar off, would not so much as raise his eyes to heaven, but beat his breast, saying, 'God be merciful to me a sinner!' I tell you, this man went down to his house justified rather than the other; for everyone who exalts himself will be abased, and he who humbles himself will be exalted."

Pharisee: a member of a religious party whose main goal (like that of Jesus) was to make the laws of Moses more relevant to the Jewish community. Pharisees are portrayed unfavorably in the New Testament.

tithes: a tenth of one's income.

The Kingdom of Heaven

Again, the kingdom of heaven is like treasure hidden in a field, which a man found and hid; and for joy over it he goes and sells all that he has and buys that field.

"Again, the kingdom of heaven is like a merchant seeking beautiful pearls, who, when he had found one pearl of great price, went and sold all that he had and bought it."

Matt. 13:44.

The Great Supper

Then he said to him, "A certain man gave a great supper and invited many, and sent his servant at supper time to say to those who were invited, 'Come, for all things are now ready.' But they all with one accord began to make excuses. The first said to him, 'I have bought a piece of ground, and I must go and see it. I ask you to have me excused.' And another said, 'I have bought five yoke of oxen, and I am going to test them. I ask you to have me excused.' Still another said, 'I have married a wife, and therefore I cannot come.' So that servant came and reported these things to his master. Then the master of the house, being angry, said to his servant, 'Go out quickly into the streets and lanes of the city, and bring in here the poor and the maimed and the lame and the blind.' And the servant said, 'Master, it is done as you commanded, and still there is room.' Then the master said to the servant, 'Go out into the highways and hedges, and compel them to come in, that my house may be filled. For I say to you that none of those men who were invited shall taste my supper.'"

Luke 14:16.

yoke: pair.

married: according to Jewish law, a newly married man was free of certain duties.

maimed: seriously injured.

compel: force.

The Lost Sheep

Luke 15:1.

tax collectors: hated because they paid the Romans for the job and were free to get and keep whatever amount they could from citizens.

Then all the tax collectors and the sinners drew near to him to hear him. And the Pharisees and scribes murmured, saying, "This man receives sinners and eats with them."

So he spoke this parable to them, saying: "What man of you, having a hundred sheep, if he loses one of them, does not leave the ninety-nine in the wilderness, and go after the one which is lost until he finds it? And when he has found it, he lays it on his shoulders, rejoicing. And when he comes home, he calls together his friends and neighbors, saying to them, 'Rejoice with me, for I have found my sheep which was lost!' I say to you that likewise there will be more joy in heaven over one sinner who repents than over ninety-nine just persons who need no repentance."

The Lost Coin

Luke 15:8.

diligently: carefully and continuously.

Or what woman, having ten silver coins, if she loses one coin, does not light a lamp, sweep the house, and seek diligently until she finds it? And when she has found it, she calls her friends and neighbors together, saying, 'Rejoice with me, for I have found the piece which I lost!' Likewise, I say to you, there is joy in the presence of the angels of God over one sinner who repents."

The Prodigal Son

Luke 15:11.

livelihood: estate, assets.

prodigal living: reckless spending, loose living.

pods: grain husks.

Then he said: "A certain man had two sons. And the younger of them said to his father, 'Father, give me the portion of goods that falls to me.' So he divided to them his livelihood. And not many days after, the younger son gathered all together, journeyed to a far country, and there wasted his possessions with prodigal living. But when he had spent all, there arose a severe famine in that land, and he began to be in want. Then he went and joined himself to a citizen of that country, and he sent him into his fields to feed swine. And he would gladly have filled his stomach with the pods that the swine ate, and no one gave him anything. But when he came to himself, he said, 'How many of my father's hired servants have bread enough and to spare, and I perish with hunger! I will arise and go to my father, and will say to him, "Father, I have sinned against heaven and before you, and I am no longer worthy to be called your son. Make me like one of your hired servants.'" And he arose and came to his father. But when he was still a great way off, his father saw him and had compassion, and ran and fell on his neck and kissed him. And the son said to him, 'Father, I have sinned against heaven and in your sight, and am no longer worthy to be called your son.' But the father said to his servants, 'Bring out the best robe and put it on him, and put a ring on his hand and sandals on his feet. And bring the fatted calf here and kill it, and let us eat and be merry; for this my son was dead and is alive again; he was lost and is found.' And they began to be merry.

fatted: fattened for a feast.

"Now his older son was in the field. And as he came and drew near to the house, he heard music and dancing. So he called one of the servants and asked what these things meant. And he said to him, 'Your brother has come, and because he has received him safe and sound, your father has killed the fatted calf.' But he was angry and would not go in. Therefore his father came out and pleaded with him. So he answered and said to his father, 'Lo, these many years I have been serving you; I never transgressed your commandment at any time; and yet you never gave me a young goat, that I might make merry with my friends. But as soon as this son of yours came, who has devoured your livelihood with harlots, you killed the fatted calf for him.' And he said to him, 'Son, you are always with me, and all that I have is yours. It was right that we should make merry and be glad, for your brother was dead and is alive again, and was lost and is found.'"

transgressed: disobeyed.

harlots: prostitutes.

FOR CLOSE READING

1. How does Jesus answer the lawyer's question about eternal life?

2. Which of these parables end with an explanation? Which do not?

FOR THOUGHT AND DISCUSSION

3. Several of these parables show a lowly or despised person doing the right thing, or gaining something, in contrast to the actions of "better" people. Which parables fit that pattern? Why do you suppose Jesus emphasizes this kind of teaching?

4. In "The Prodigal Son," how is the personality of each character revealed? Does the father seem to love one son more than the other? Whose story is being told: the father's? the older son's? the younger son's? Why do you think so?

5. What common themes do you find in the parables of the lost sheep, coin, and son? How would you summarize these themes?

6. Which parables seem to illustrate teachings from Jesus' Sermon on the Mount? In each case, what does the parable add to the point made in the sermon? In general, which method of teaching—sermon or parables—do you prefer? Why?

7. When "tested" by people opposed to his teachings, Jesus usually responds with parables. Why do you think Jesus used this teaching method in these challenging situations?

RESPONDING

1. Writing Whether you realize it or not, you know a good deal about teaching and teachers. Apply your knowledge to the Sermon on the Mount and the parables. What kind of teacher was Jesus? What methods did he use? Write a short essay expressing your views.

2. Writing The parables in this book are given their traditional titles. Create new titles for each, then share your choices with classmates.

3. Writing Tell the story of one of these parables in the first-person viewpoint of one of the participants: the shepherd, the woman who lost a coin, the man helped by the Samaritan.

The Prodigal Son

You are not merry, brother. Why not laugh,
As I do, and acclaim the fatted calf?
For, unless ways are changing here at home,
You might not have it if I had not come.
5   And were I not a thing for you and me
To execrate in anguish, you would be   **execrate:** curse.
As indigent a stranger to surprise,   **indigent:** poor, needy.
I fear, as I was once, and as unwise.
Brother, believe, as I do, it is best
10 For you that I'm again in the old nest—
Draggled, I grant you, but your brother still,
Full of good wine, good viands, and good will.   **viands:** food.
You will thank God, some day, that I returned,
And may be singing for what you have learned,
15 Some other day; and one day you may find
Yourself a little nearer to mankind.
And having hated me till you are tired
You will begin to see, as if inspired,
It was fate's way of educating us.
20 Remembering then when you were venomous,   **venomous:** poisonous;
You will be glad enough that I am gone,   i.e., hateful.
But you will know more of what's going on;
For you will see more of what makes it go,
And in more ways than are for you to know.
25 We are so different when we are dead,   **lentils:** plant of the pea
That you, alive, may weep for what you said;   family. This is a reference
And I, the ghost of one you could not save,   to the Jacob-Esau story
May find you planting lentils on my grave.   (see page 85).

FOR THOUGHT AND DISCUSSION

1. According to the speaker, how has the brother who
stayed home benefited from the prodigal's actions?

2. Which brother do you favor? Why?

Last Days in Jerusalem

*Accompanied by his twelve disciples,
Jesus made his way to Jerusalem.*

Entry into Jerusalem

Luke 19:29.

Olivet: also known as the
Mount of Olives.

And it came to pass, when he came near to
Bethphage and Bethany, at the mountain called
Olivet, that he sent two of his disciples, saying, "Go
into the village opposite you, where as you enter you
will find a colt tied, on which no one has ever sat.
Loose him and bring him here. And if anyone asks
you, 'Why are you loosing him?' thus you shall say to
him, 'Because the Lord has need of him.'" . . . Then
they brought him to Jesus. And they threw their own
garments on the colt, and they set Jesus on him. And
as he went, they spread their clothes on the road.
Then, as he was now drawing near the descent of the
Mount of Olives, the whole multitude of the disciples
began to rejoice and praise God with a loud voice for
all the mighty works they had seen, saying:

multitude: many others
have joined the original
twelve disciples.

> "'Blessed is the king who comes in the name
>   of the Lord!'
> Peace in heaven and glory in the highest!"

And some of the Pharisees called to him from the
crowd, "Teacher, rebuke your disciples." But he
answered and said to them, "I tell you that if these
should keep silent, the stones would immediately cry
out." . . .

temple: this event is
known as The Cleansing
of the Temple.

bought and sold: i.e.,
birds and animals for
temple sacrifice.

Then he went into the temple and began to drive
out those who bought and sold in it, saying to them,
"It is written, 'My house is a house of prayer,' but you
have made it a 'den of thieves.'"

Judas Plots

Now the Feast of the Unleavened Bread drew near, which is called Passover. And the chief priests and the scribes sought how they might kill him, for they feared the people.

Then Satan entered Judas, surnamed Iscariot, who was numbered among the twelve. So he went his way and conferred with the chief priests and captains, how he might betray him to them. And they were glad, and agreed to give him money. Then he promised and sought opportunity to betray him to them in the absence of the multitude.

The Last Supper

Then came the Day of Unleavened Bread, when the passover must be killed. And he sent Peter and John, saying, "Go and prepare the passover for us, that we may eat." So they said to him, "Where do you want us to prepare?" And he said to them, "Behold, when you have entered the city, a man will meet you carrying a pitcher of water; follow him into the house which he enters. Then you shall say to the master of the house, 'The teacher says to you, "Where is the guest room in which I may eat the passover with my disciples?"' Then he will show you a large, furnished upper room; there make ready." So they went and found it as he had said to them, and they prepared the passover.

And when the hour had come, he sat down, and the twelve apostles with him. Then he said to them, "With fervent desire I have desired to eat this passover with you before I suffer; for I say to you, I will no longer eat of it until it is fulfilled in the kingdom of God." Then he took the cup, and gave thanks, and said, "Take this and divide it among yourselves; for I say to you, I will not drink of the fruit of the vine until the kingdom of God comes." And he took bread, gave thanks and broke it, and gave it to them, saying, "This is my body which is given for you; do this in remembrance of me." Likewise he also took the cup after supper, saying, "This cup is the new covenant in my blood, which is shed for you. But behold, the hand of my betrayer is with me on the table. And truly the Son of Man goes as it has been determined, but woe to that man by whom he is betrayed!"....

Unleavened Bread: bread or cakes baked without yeast; eaten at Passover in remembrance of Israel's escape from Egypt.

conferred: discussed.

passover . . . killed: i.e., the passover lamb, whose blood would be smeared on doorposts as at the original Passover in Egypt.

covenant: agreement.

woe to: death and damnation upon.

But Peter said to him, "Even if all are made to stumble, yet I will not be." And Jesus said to him, "Assuredly, I say to you that today, even this night, before the rooster crows twice, you will deny me three times." But he spoke more vehemently, "If I have to die with you, I will not deny you!" And they all said likewise.

Praying in Gethsemane

And coming out, he went to the Mount of Olives, as he was accustomed, and his disciples also followed him. When he came to the place, he said to them, "Pray that you may not enter into temptation." And he was withdrawn from them about a stone's throw, and he knelt down and prayed, saying, "Father, if it is your will, remove this cup from me; nevertheless not my will, but yours, be done." . . . When he rose up from prayer, and had come to his disciples, he found them sleeping from sorrow. Then he said to them, "Why do you sleep? Rise and pray, lest you enter into temptation."

And while he was still speaking, behold, a multitude; and he who was called Judas, one of the twelve, went before them and drew near to Jesus to kiss him. But Jesus said to him, "Judas, are you betraying the Son of Man with a kiss?"

Peter's Denial

Then, having arrested him, they led him and brought him into the high priest's house. And Peter followed at a distance. Now when they had kindled a fire in the midst of the courtyard and sat down together, Peter sat among them. And a certain servant girl, seeing him as he sat by the fire, looked intently at him and said, "This man was also with him." But he denied him, saying, "Woman, I do not know him." And after a little while another saw him and said, "You also are of them." But Peter said, "Man, I am not!" Then after about an hour had passed, another confidently affirmed, saying, "Surely this fellow also was with him, for he is a Galilean." But Peter said, "Man, I do not know what you are saying!" And immediately, while he was still speaking, the rooster crowed. And the Lord turned and looked at Peter. And Peter remembered the word of the Lord, how he had said to him, "Before the rooter crows, you will deny me three times." Then Peter went out and wept bitterly.

Before the Council

Now the men who held Jesus mocked him and beat him. And having blindfolded him, they struck him on the face and asked him, saying, "Prophesy! Who is it that struck you?" And many other things they blasphemously spoke against him. As soon as it was day, the elders of the people, both chief priests and scribes, came together and led him into their council, saying, "If you are the Christ, tell us." But he said to them, "If I tell you, you will by no means believe. And if I also ask you, you will by no means answer me or let me go. Hereafter the Son of Man will sit on the right hand of the power of God." Then they all said, "Are you then the Son of God?" And he said to them, "You rightly say that I am." And they said, "What further testimony do we need? For we have heard it ourselves from his own mouth.

blasphemously: with irreverent scorn.

council: also called the Sanhedrin, this assembly had the power to make judgments under Jewish law. Only the Roman government, however, could pronounce and carry out the death penalty.

Judas's Remorse

Then Judas, his betrayer, seeing that he had been condemned, was remorseful and brought back the thirty pieces of silver to the chief priests and elders, saying, "I have sinned by betraying innocent blood." And they said, "What is that to us? You see to it!" Then he threw down the pieces of silver in the temple and departed, and went and hanged himself. But the chief priests took the silver pieces and said, "It is not lawful to put them into the treasury, because they are the price of blood." And they took counsel and bought with them the potter's field, to bury strangers in. Therefore that field has been called the Field of Blood to this day.

Before Pilate

Then the whole multitude of them arose and led him to Pilate. And they began to accuse him, saying, "We found this fellow perverting the nation, and forbidding to pay taxes to Caesar, saying that he himself is Christ, a king." So Pilate asked him, saying, "Are you the king of the Jews?" And he answered him and said, "It is as you say." Then Pilate said to the chief priests and the crowd, "I find no fault in this man." But they were the more fierce, saying, "He stirs

Pilate: Roman governor over Judea.

Christ: Greek translation of the Hebrew *mashiach* (messiah).

up the people, teaching throughout all Judea, beginning from Galilee to this place."

Before Herod

When Pilate heard of Galilee, he asked if the man were a Galilean. And as soon as he knew that he belonged to Herod's jurisdiction, he sent him to Herod, who was also in Jerusalem at that time. Now when Herod saw Jesus, he was exceedingly glad; for he had desired for a long time to see him, because he had heard many things about him, and he hoped to see some miracle done by him. Then he questioned him with many words, but he answered him nothing. And the chief priests and scribes stood and vehemently accused him. Then Herod, with his men of war, treated him with contempt and mocked him, arrayed him in a gorgeous robe, and sent him back to Pilate. That very day Pilate and Herod became friends with each other, for before that they had been at enmity with each other.

"Release to Us Barabbas"

Then Pilate, when he had called together the chief priests, the rulers, and the people, said to them, "You have brought this man to me, as one who misleads the people. And indeed, having examined him in your presence, I have found no fault in this man concerning those things of which you accuse him; no, neither did Herod, for I sent you back to him, and indeed nothing worthy of death has been done by him. I will therefore chastise him and release him." . . .

Now at the feast he was accustomed to releasing one prisoner to them, whomever they requested. And there was one named Barabbas, who was chained with his fellow insurrectionists; they had committed murder in the insurrection. Then the multitude, crying aloud, began to ask him to do just as he had always done for them. But Pilate answered them, saying, "Do you want me to release to you the king of the Jews?" For he knew that the chief priests had handed him over because of envy. But the chief priests stirred up the crowd, so that he should rather release Barabbas to them. And Pilate answered and said to them again, "What then do you want me to do

Herod: see page 357.

vehemently: heatedly, with strong feeling.

gorgeous robe: clothing fit for a king—mocking Jesus' "royal" status.

chastise him: punish him physically.

Mark 15:6.

insurrection: revolt.

with him you call the king of the Jews?" So they cried out again, "Crucify him!" Then Pilate said to them, "Why, what evil has he done?" And they cried out more exceedingly, "Crucify him!" So Pilate, wanting to gratify the crowd, released Barabbas to them; and he delivered Jesus, after he had scourged him, to be crucified.

gratify: please.

scourged: whipped.

The Crucifixion

Then the soldiers led him away into the hall called Praetorium, and they called together the whole garrison. And they clothed him with purple; and they twisted a crown of thorns, put it on his head, and began to salute him, "Hail, king of the Jews!" Then they struck him on the head with a reed and spat on him; and bowing the knee, they worshiped him. And when they had mocked him, they took the purple off him, put his own clothes on him, and led him out to crucify him.

Praetorium (prē tôr′ē əm): local headquarters of the Roman government.

garrison: soldiers stationed at the headquarters.

Now they compelled a certain man, Simon a Cyrenian, the father of Alexander and Rufus, as he was coming out of the country and passing by, to bear his cross. . . .

There were also two others, criminals, led with him to be put to death. And when they had come to the place called Calvary, there they crucified him, and the criminals, one on the right hand and the other on the left. Then Jesus said, "Father, forgive them, for they do not know what they do." And they divided his garments and cast lots. And the people stood looking on. But even the rulers with them sneered, saying, "He saved others; let him save himself if he is the Christ, the chosen of God." And the soldiers also mocked him, coming and offering him sour wine, and saying, "If you are the king of the Jews, save yourself." And an inscription also was written over him in letters of Greek, Latin, and Hebrew:

Luke 23:32.

Calvary: also called Golgotha.

cast lots: method of selecting by chance, probably by using marked stones.

inscription: sign.

THIS IS THE KING OF THE JEWS

Then one of the criminals who were hanged blasphemed him, saying, "If you are the Christ, save yourself and us." But the other, answering, rebuked him, saying, "Do you not even fear God, seeing you are under the same condemnation? And we indeed justly, for we receive the due reward of our deeds; but

blasphemed: scorned.

condemnation: death sentence.

sixth hour: noon.

veil: a heavy fabric
shield protecting the
most holy area of the
temple.

Matt. 27:46.

Elijah: a biblical prophet
(see page 211). It was
thought his return would
signal God's reign on
earth.

Luke 23:46.
commend: entrust.

centurion: Roman
officer.

counsel: decision
(regarding Jesus).

day ... preparation: i.e.,
for the Sabbath, which
began at sundown on
Friday.

this man has done nothing wrong." Then he said to Jesus, "Lord, remember me when you come into your kingdom." And Jesus said to him, "Assuredly, I say to you, today you will be with me in paradise."

And it was about the sixth hour, and there was darkness over all the earth until the ninth hour. Then the sun was darkened, and the veil of the temple was torn in two. . . .

And about the ninth hour Jesus cried out with a loud voice, saying, "Eli, Eli, lama sabachthani?" that is, "My God, my God, why have you forsaken me?" Some of those who stood there, when they heard that, said, "This man is calling for Elijah!" Immediately one of them ran and took a sponge, filled it with sour wine and put it on a reed, and gave it to him to drink. The rest said, "Let him alone; let us see if Elijah will come to save Him." . . .

And when Jesus had cried out with a loud voice, he said, "Father, 'into your hands I commend my spirit.'" And having said this, he breathed his last. Now when the centurion saw what had happened, he glorified God, saying, "Certainly this was a righteous man!" And the whole crowd who came together to that sight, seeing what had been done, beat their breasts and returned. But all his acquaintances, and the women who followed him from Galilee, stood at a distance, watching these things.

The Burial of Jesus

And behold, there was a man named Joseph, a council member, a good and just man. He had not consented to their counsel and deed. He was from Arimathea, a city of the Jews, who himself was also waiting for the kingdom of God. This man went to Pilate and asked for the body of Jesus. Then he took it down, wrapped it in linen, and laid it in a tomb that was hewn out of the rock, where no one had ever lain before. That day was the preparation, and the Sabbath drew near. And the women who had come with him from Galilee followed after, and they observed the tomb and how his body was laid. Then they returned and prepared spices and fragrant oils. And they rested on the Sabbath according to the commandment.

FOR CLOSE READING

1. Jesus appears before the council, Pilate, and Herod. He is asked: "Are you the Son of God?" and "Are you the king of the Jews?" How does he respond to these questions? How do Jesus' accusers interpret his answers?

2. Of what crime is Jesus accused? For what crime is Barabbas imprisoned?

3. In what ways is Jesus mocked?

4. What unusual events occur while Jesus is on the cross?

FOR THOUGHT AND DISCUSSION

5. Jesus is shown in many different situations that reveal many aspects of his character. Write down five words that you feel describe Jesus, and support your choices with evidence from these biblical passages.

6. Jesus' last week is filled with many contrasting scenes. For example, his triumphant entrance into Jerusalem is in sharp contrast to the procession leading to his execution. What other contrasts can you find in these passages?

7. What details in the story emphasize: *(a)* Jesus' isolation and aloneness? *(b)* his humiliation? *(c)* his physical suffering?

8. When Jesus enters Jerusalem, a multitude greets him joyously, and we are told that his enemies "feared the people." Only a few days later a mob is demanding Jesus' death. Which details in these passages might prepare the reader for this turnabout? Explain.

9. Why do you think the people asked Pilate to release Barabbas rather than Jesus?

10. Now that you have read the crucifixion story, reconsider the earlier events of Jesus' life. What similarities, foreshadowings, hints of things to come do you find in the earlier stories in Unit 10? For example, what similarities do you see between Jesus' birth and his entry into Jerusalem? Where in an earlier story do you find a ruler reluctant to execute an innocent man? What is the effect of these similarities?

RESPONDING

1. **Writing** Describe some part of the crucifixion story from the viewpoint of a participant— Barabbas, Simon of Cyrene, or Joseph of Arimathea. What were your thoughts and feelings as you became involved? Research some of the traditions surrounding the person you chose. (For example, according to tradition Simon of Cyrene was an African.)

2. **Activity** Listen to a recording of *Jesus Christ, Superstar* with your classmates. What differences do you find between the musical and the biblical story? What do you feel is the effect of the musical's changes?

3. **Humanities Connection** Identify and collect passages of music that express the mood or feeling at various points of Jesus' last days in Jerusalem—from the joyous entry into the city to the crucifixion and burial. If possible, tape-record your sequence of music to make a "tone poem" of the events.

Saint Judas

When I went out to kill myself, I caught
A pack of hoodlums beating up a man.
Running to spare his suffering, I forgot
My name, my number, how my day began,
5 How soldiers milled around the garden stone
And sang amusing songs; how all that day
Their javelins measured crowds; how I alone   **javelins:** spears.
Bargained the proper coins, and slipped away.
Banished from heaven, I found this victim beaten,
10 Stripped, kneed, and left to cry. Dropping my
    rope   **rope:** according to
Aside, I ran, ignored the uniforms: Matthew, Judas hanged
Then I remembered bread my flesh had eaten.   himself after Jesus was
The kiss that ate my flesh. Flayed without hope,   condemned.
I held the man for nothing in my arms.   **flayed:** i.e., stripped; laid
                                                     open.

FOR THOUGHT AND DISCUSSION

1. What impressions come to mind when you hear the
name "Judas"? What were your feelings after
reading this poem?

2. What events are referred to by "bread my flesh had
eaten" and "the kiss that ate my flesh"?

3. What do you think the last line means?

LEONID ANDREYEV

Ben Tobit

Golgotha: a place of
execution outside
Jerusalem; also called
Calvary.

ominous: threatening.

racking: i.e., torturing.

excruciating: causing
extreme suffering.

On the dread day of that monstrous injustice, when Jesus Christ was crucified among the thieves on Golgotha—on that day, Ben Tobit, a merchant in Jerusalem, had been suffering from an unbearable toothache since the early hours of the morning. It had started the night before; his right jaw had begun to hurt, and one tooth, the one in front of the wisdom tooth, seemed to have risen a little and it hurt when he touched his tongue to it. But after supper the pain disappeared, and Ben Tobit promptly forgot all about it. In fact, he had that very day traded his old donkey advantageously for a young, strong one, and so he was in rather high spirits and totally unconcerned about the ominous symptom.

That night he slept very well and very soundly, but just before dawn something began to bother him, as if someone were calling him on matters of great importance, and when Ben Tobit awakened with annoyance, he found that the toothache had returned, a direct and racking one that assailed him with the full force of sharp, stabbing pain. But now he could not tell whether it was the same tooth that had hurt him the night before, or whether other teeth were involved as well; his mouth and his head were filled with excruciating pain, as if he were being forced to chew a thousand sharp, red-hot nails. He filled his mouth with cool water from an earthen jug, and the fury of the pain subsided for a moment; his mouth began to twitch and throb, and this sensation was almost pleasant compared to the previous one. Ben Tobit lay back on his bed. He thought about his new donkey and he thought of how fortunate he would be if it were not for his teeth.

He tried to fall asleep again, but the water became warm, and in five minutes the pain was back, more savage than before. Ben Tobit sat up in his bed, and

398   JESUS: TEACHINGS, DEATH, AND RESURRECTION

soon his body swayed back and forth like a pendulum. His whole face was pulled together and puckered about a big nose, and on that nose, turned white with agony, a drop of cold sweat gathered. Thus it was that, swaying back and forth and moaning in pain, he beheld the first rays of the sun that was destined to see Golgotha with its three crosses and to grow dim with horror and sorrow.

Ben Tobit was a kind and good man who disliked injustice, but when his wife awakened, he had barely opened his mouth before he began to say a great many unpleasant things to her, complaining repeatedly that he was left alone, like a jackal, to howl and to writhe in agony. His wife listened patiently to the undeserved reproaches, for she knew it was not a mean heart that made him say such things, and she brought him many fine remedies: cleansed dung of rats to be applied to the cheek, a strong tincture obtained from a scorpion, and an authentic sliver of the stone tablets that had been smashed to bits by Moses. The rat dung helped a little, but not for long, as did also the tincture and the sliver, but each respite was followed by a violent onslaught of even greater pain. During the brief periods of relief, Ben Tobit comforted himself by thinking of his little donkey and day-dreaming about him; but when he felt worse, he moaned, scolded his wife, and threatened to dash his head against a rock if the pain did not subside. And he kept pacing all the time from one corner of the flat roof of his house to the other, ashamed to get too close to its outer edge because the kerchief he had tied around his head made him look like a woman.

Several times children came running to him to tell him hastily about Jesus of Nazareth. Ben Tobit would stop for a moment to listen to them; then he would contract his face and, stamping his foot angrily, would send them on their way. He was a kind man and fond of children, but now it irritated him to be pestered with all sorts of silly things.

He was also irritated because many people in the street and on neighboring roofs seemed to have nothing better to do than to stare in curiosity at him with his head wrapped in a kerchief like a woman's. He was just about to go downstairs when his wife called to him:

jackal: wild dog.

tincture (tingk′chər): solution of medicine in alcohol.

respite: period of relief.

"Look, there are the thieves! This might interest you!"

"Leave me alone, please. Don't you see how I'm suffering?" Ben Tobit answered angrily.

But his wife's words gave him a slight feeling that his toothache might be lessening. So he reluctantly went to the edge of the roof. With his head tilted to one side, one eye closed, his cheek in the palm of a hand, his face peevish and tearful, he looked down.

A huge, turbulently milling crowd, shrouded in dust, incessantly shouting, was moving up the steep, narrow street. Surrounded by the crowd, the criminals moved along with bodies bent low under the heavy burdens of the crosses, the whips of the Roman soldiers writhing like black snakes above them. One of them—the one who had long, fair hair and who was wearing a torn, blood-stained robe—stumbled on a stone someone had thrown at his feet and fell. The shouting grew louder and the crowd, like a many-colored sea, seemed to close over the fallen man. Ben Tobit suddenly winced with pain, as if someone had stabbed a red-hot needle into his tooth and twisted it there. He moaned, "Oh—oh—oh," and walked away from the edge of the roof, petulantly preoccupied and full of resentment.

"How they yell!" he said enviously, visualizing wide-open mouths with strong, never-aching teeth and thinking how he himself would be shouting if he were well. This mental image brought on another savage attack of pain. He kept shaking his kerchief-wrapped head, lowing, "M—moo—oo . . . "

"They say he healed the blind," said his wife, who had remained at the edge of the roof and had thrown a small stone at the place where Jesus, brought to his feet by the whips, moved along slowly.

"Yes, of course! Let him heal my toothache!" Ben Tobit retorted mockingly. "What a dust they kick up! Like a herd! They ought to be dispersed with a cane!" he added peevishly, in bitterness. "Help me down, Sarah!"

His wife was right; the spectacle did somewhat divert Ben Tobit, or perhaps it was the rat dung that helped him at last, and he managed to fall asleep.

When he awakened, the pain was almost gone; there was only a small swelling on his right jaw, so small it was hardly noticeable. His wife said it was completely unnoticeable, but Ben Tobit smiled knowingly: he knew well what a good wife he had and how much she loved to say pleasant things. His neighbor Samuel, the tanner, came to visit, and Ben Tobit took him to see his little donkey; he listened with pride while Samuel praised him and the animal enthusiastically.

Then, to satisfy Sarah's insistent curiosity, the three of them went to see the men crucified on Golgotha. On the way, Ben Tobit told Samuel the whole story from the beginning, how he had felt an ache in his right jaw the previous evening and how he was wakened by an excruciating pain during the night. For greater effect, he put on the air of a martyr, closed his eyes, shook his head and groaned, while the gray-bearded Samuel nodded sympathetically and said, "Oh, oh, oh—how painful!"

Ben Tobit enjoyed the sympathy and repeated the story, going back to the remote past when he had first had a tooth go bad, down on the left side. So it was, in animated conversation, that they came to Golgotha. The sun that was destined to shine upon the world on this dread day had already set behind the far hills, and in the west a crimson strip like a bloody mark, stretched across the sky. Against this background the crosses stood dark and indistinct, while white-clad figures knelt at the foot of the middle cross.

animated: lively.

The crowd had dispersed long before; it was growing cold, and, with a brief glance at the crucified men, Ben Tobit took Samuel's arm and gently turned him homeward. He felt particularly eloquent; he wanted to say more about the toothache. And so they walked away, Ben Tobit resuming the air of a martyr, shaking his head and groaning artfully, while Samuel nodded and exclaimed sympathetically. Black night was rising from the dark, deep gorges and from the distant, burned plains—as though it were trying to hide the enormous misdeed of the earth from the eyes of heaven.

dispersed: scattered.

FOR CLOSE READING

1. What details in the story emphasize Ben Tobit's suffering? What details refer to the sufferings of Jesus?

2. How is Ben Tobit affected by watching the procession to Golgotha? by seeing the crucified men?

FOR THOUGHT AND DISCUSSION

3. Briefly describe your first reactions to this story. What do you think caused those reactions?

4. "Ben Tobit was a kind and good man who disliked injustice . . . ." What evidence do you find that either supports or contradicts this description?

5. What effects does the writer achieve by linking toothache and crucifixion? by describing the crucifixion from the viewpoint of Ben Tobit?

The Making of the Cross

Rough fir, hauled from the hills. And the tree it
   had been,
Lithe-limbed, wherein the wren had nested,
Whereon the red hawk and the grey
Rested from flight, and the raw-head vulture
5 Shouldered to his feed—that tree went over
Bladed down with a double-bitted axe; was snaked
   with winches;
The wedge split it; hewn with the adze
It lay to season toward its use.

So too with the nails: milleniums under the earth,
10 Pure ore; chunked out with picks; the nail-shape
Struck in the pelt-lunged forge; tonged to a cask
And the wait against that work.

Even the thorn-bush flourished from afar,
As do the flourishing generations of its kind,
15 Filling the shallow soil no one wants;
Wind-sown, it cuts the cattle and the wild horse;
It tears the cloth of man, and hurts his hand.

Just as in life the good things of the earth
Are patiently assembled: some from here, some
   from there;
20 Wine from the hill and wheat from the valley;
Rain that comes blue-bellied out of the sopping
   sea.
Snow that keeps its drift on the gooseberry ridge,
Will melt with May, go down, take the egg of
   the salmon,
Serve the traffic of otters and fishes,
25 Be ditched to orchards . . .

lithe-limbed: having flexible branches.

adze: an axlike tool for shaping timber.

milleniums: thousands of years.

pelt-lunged: a reference to leather bellows, used to blow air into the forge's fire.

tonged: carried with tongs.

So too are gathered up the possibles of evil.

And when the Cross was joined, quartered,
As is the earth; spoked, as is the Universal Wheel—

unregenerate: wicked.
Those radials that led all unregenerate act
30 Inward to innocence—it met the thorn-wove
    Crown;

scourges: whips.
It found the Scourges and the Dice;
The Nail was given and the reed-lifted Sponge;
The Curse caught forward out of the heart corrupt;

excoriate: i.e.,
denouncement.
The excoriate Foul, stoned with the thunder and
    the hail—
35 All these made up that miscellaneous wrath

assumed: taken on.
And were assumed.

The evil and the wastage and the woe,

cyst (sist): i.e., diseased
growth.
As if the earth's old cyst, back down the slough
To Adam's sin-burnt calcinated bones

slough: a swampy place.
40 Rushed out of time and clotted on the Cross.

calcinated: burned to
ashes.

Off there the cougar
Coughed in passion when the sun went out;
    the rattler
Filmed his glinty eye, and found his hole.

FOR CLOSE READING

1. List the things of the earth that are used in the
crucifixion and tell how each one is used.

2. According to lines 37–40, what clotted on the cross?

3. What living creatures are mentioned in the poem?

FOR THOUGHT AND DISCUSSION

4. What different effects are achieved by the
references to various creatures throughout the
poem?

5. Complete the following sentence: "The Making of
the Cross" is about . . . . List as many possibilities as
you can. Support at least two of your responses
with evidence from the poem.

Mouth of Hell, anonymous woodcut.

ABOVE: *Jigo Soshi* (Hell Scroll), paper, early Kamakura Period, c. 1200. Tokyo National Museum.
RIGHT: *Shepherd and Flock with Prancing Deer*, detail from a needlework chair back, American, c. 1725. The Metropolitan Museum of Art, New York, Gift of Mrs. J. Insley Blair, 1950.

The Peaceable Kingdom by Edward Hicks. The Brooklyn Museum, Dick S. Ramsay Fund.

Simon the Cyrenian Speaks

He never spoke a word to me,
And yet He called my name;
He never gave a sign to me,
And yet I knew and came.

5 At first I said, "I will not bear
His cross upon my back;
He only seeks to place it there
Because my skin is black."

But He was dying for a dream,
10 And He was very meek,
And in His eyes there shone a gleam
Men journey far to seek.

It was Himself my pity bought;
I did for Christ alone
15 What all of Rome could not have wrought
With bruise of lash or stone.

FOR THOUGHT AND DISCUSSION

1. According to tradition, Simon the Cyrenian was a
black man. How does the poem make reference to
that tradition?

2. Why does the speaker at first refuse to carry the
cross? What changes the speaker's mind?

PÄR LAGERKVIST

from Barabbas

Translated by Alan Blair

This is the first chapter of a novel about the man who was released instead of Jesus.

Everyone knows how they hung there on the crosses, and who they were that stood gathered around him: Mary his mother and Mary Magdalene, Veronica, Simon of Cyrene, who carried the cross, and Joseph of Arimathea, who shrouded him. But a little further down the slope, rather to one side, a man was standing with his eyes riveted on the dying man in the middle, watching his death-throes from the first moment to the last. His name was Barabbas. . . .

He was about thirty, powerfully built, with a sallow complexion, a reddish beard and black hair. His eyebrows also were black, his eyes too deep-set, as though they wanted to hide. Under one of them he had a deep scar that was lost to sight in his beard. But a man's appearance is of little consequence.

He had followed the mob through the streets all the way from the governor's palace, but at a distance, somewhat behind the others. When the exhausted rabbi had collapsed beneath his cross, he had stopped and stood still for a while to avoid catching up with the cross, and then they had got hold of that man Simon and forced him to carry it instead. There were not many men in the crowd, except the Roman soldiers of course; they were mostly women following the condemned man and a flock of urchins who were always there when anyone was led out along their

Veronica: according to tradition, the woman who wiped Jesus' brow as he carried the cross.

sallow: yellowish, sickly.

urchins: young children.

street to be crucified—it made a change for them. But they soon tired and went back to their games, pausing a moment to glance at the man with the long scar down his cheek who was walking behind the others.

Now he was standing up here on the gallows-hill looking at the man on the middle cross, unable to tear his eyes away. Actually he had not wanted to come up here at all, for everything was unclean, full of contagion; if a man set foot in this potent and accursed place part of him would surely remain, and he could be forced back there, never to leave it again. Skulls and bones lay scattered about everywhere, together with fallen, half-mouldering crosses, no longer of any use but left to lie there all the same, because no one would touch anything. Why was he standing here? He did not know this man, had nothing to do with him. What was he doing at Golgotha, he who had been released?

The crucified man's head hung down and he was breathing heavily; it would not be long now. There was nothing vigorous about the fellow. His body was lean and spindly, the arms slender as though they had never been put to any use. A queer man. The beard was sparse and the chest quite hairless, like a boy's. He did not like him.

From the first moment Barabbas had seen him in the courtyard of the palace, he had felt there was something odd about him. What it was he could not say; it was just something he felt. He didn't remember ever having seen anyone like him before. Though it must have been because he came straight from the dungeon and his eyes were still unused to the glare. That is why at first glance the man seemed to be surrounded by a dazzling light. Soon afterwards the light vanished, of course, and his sight grew normal again and took in other things besides the figure standing out there alone in the courtyard. But he still thought there was something very strange about him and that he was not like anyone else. It seemed quite incredible that he was a prisoner and had been condemned to death, just as he himself had been. He could not grasp it. Not that it concerned him—but how could they pass a sentence like that? It was obvious he was innocent.

unclean: according to Jewish law, contact with dead bodies made one religiously impure, requiring a cleansing ritual.

vigorous: energetic, lively.

Then the man had been led out to be crucified—and he himself had been unshackled and told he was free. It was none of his doing. It was their business. They were quite at liberty to choose whomever they liked, and it just turned out that way. They had both been sentenced to death, but one of them was to be released. He was amazed himself at their choice. As they were freeing him from his chains, he had seen the other man between the soldiers disappear through the archway, with the cross already on his back.

He had remained standing, looking out through the empty arch. Then the guard had given him a push and bellowed at him:—What are you standing there gaping for, get out of here, you're free! And he had awakened and gone out through the same archway, and when he saw the other dragging his cross down the street he had followed behind him. Why, he did not know. Nor why he had stood here hour after hour watching the crucifixion and the long death agony, though it was nothing whatever to do with him.

Those standing around the cross up there surely need not have been here? Not unless they had wanted to. Nothing was forcing them to come along and defile themselves with uncleanness. But they were no doubt relations and close friends. Odd that they didn't seem to mind being made unclean.

That woman must be his mother. Though she was not like him. But who could be like him? She looked like a peasant woman, stern and morose, and she kept wiping the back of her hand across her mouth and nose, which was running because she was on the brink of tears. But she did not cry. She did not grieve in the same way as the others, nor did she look at him in the same way as they did. So it was evidently his mother. She probably felt far more sorry for him than they did, but even so she seemed to reproach him for hanging there, for having let himself be crucified. He must have done something to let himself in for it, however pure and innocent he was, and she just could not approve of it. She knew he was innocent because she was his mother. Whatever he had done she would have thought so.

He himself had no mother. And no father either, for that matter; he had never even heard one mentioned. And he had no relatives, as far as he

defile: i.e., stain, make impure.

morose (mə rōs′): gloomy.

knew. So if he had been the one to be crucified there would not have been many tears shed. Not like this. They were beating their breasts and carrying on as though they had never known the like of such grief, and there was an awful weeping and wailing the whole time.

He knew the one on the right-hand cross quite well. If by any chance the fellow saw him standing down here, he probably thought it was because of him, in order to see him suffer well and truly. He wasn't, he was not here because of that at all. But he had nothing against seeing him crucified. If anyone deserved to die, it was that scoundrel. Though not because of what he had been sentenced for, but because of something quite different.

But why was he looking at him and not at the one in the middle, who was hanging there in his stead? It was because of him he had come. This man had forced him up here, he had a strange power over him. Power? If anyone looked powerless, he did. Surely no one could look more wretched hanging on a cross. The other two didn't look a bit like that and didn't seem to be suffering as much as he was. They obviously had more strength left. He hadn't even the strength to hold his head up; it had flopped right down.

stead: place.

Now he did raise it a bit, all the same; the lean, hairless chest heaved with panting, and his tongue licked his parched lips. He groaned something about being thirsty. The soldiers who were sprawled over a game of dice a little further down the slope, bored because the men hanging there took so long to die, did not hear. But one of the relatives went down and told them. A soldier got up reluctantly and dipped a sponge in a pitcher, passing it up to him on a stick, but when he tasted the fusty, tainted liquid offered him he did not want it. The wretch just stood there grinning, and when he rejoined his companions they all lay grinning at what had happened. . . .

fusty: stale-smelling.

The relatives or whoever they were looked despairingly up at the crucified man, who was panting and panting; it was clear that he would soon give up the ghost. And just as well if the end came soon, Barabbas thought, so that the poor man would not have to suffer any more. If only the end would come! As soon as the end came he would hurry away and never think of this again. . . .

But all at once the whole hill grew dark, as though the light had gone out of the sun; it was almost pitch-dark, and in the darkness above, the crucified man cried out in a loud voice:

—My God, my God, why hast thou forsaken me?

It sounded horrible. Whatever did he mean? And why had it grown dark? It was the middle of the day. It was quite unaccountable. The three crosses were just faintly visible up there. It looked weird. Something terrible was surely going to happen. The soldiers had leapt to their feet and grabbed their weapons; whatever happened they always rushed for their weapons. They stood there around the crosses with their lances, and he heard them whispering together in alarm. Now they were frightened! Now they were not grinning any longer! They were superstitious, of course.

He was afraid himself. And glad when it began to get light and everything became a little more normal. It got light slowly, as it does at dawn. The daylight spread across the hill and the olive trees around about, and the birds that had been silent started twittering again. It was just like dawn.

The relatives up there were standing so still. There was no longer any sound of weeping and lamentation from them. They just stood looking up at the man on the cross; even the soldiers did so. Everything had grown so still.

Now he could go whenever he liked. For it was all over now, and the sun shone again and everything was just as usual. It had only been dark for a while because the man had died.

Yes, he would go now. Of course he would. He had nothing to stay for, not now that he, that other one, was dead. There was no longer any reason. They took him down from the cross, he saw before he went. The two men wrapped him in a clean linen cloth, he noticed. The body was quite white and they handled it so carefully, as if they were afraid they might hurt it, however slightly, or cause it pain of any kind. They behaved so strangely. After all, he was crucified and everything. They were queer people, to be sure. But the mother stood with dry eyes looking at what had been her son, and the rough, dark-complexioned face seemed unable to express her sorrow, only the fact that she could not grasp what had happened and would never be able to forgive it. He understood her better.

As the sorry procession moved past some little distance from him, the men carrying the shrouded body and the women walking behind, one of the women whispered to the mother—pointing to Barabbas. She stopped short and gave him such a helpless and reproachful look that he knew he could never forget it. They went on down towards the Golgotha road and then turned off to the left.

reproachful: full of blame or disapproval.

He followed far enough behind for them not to notice him. In a garden a short distance away they laid the dead man in a tomb that was hewn out of the rock. And when they had prayed by the tomb they rolled a large stone in front of the entrance and went away.

He walked up to the tomb and stood there for a while. But he did not pray, for he was an evil-doer and his prayer would not have been accepted, especially as his crime was not expiated. Besides, he did not know the dead man. He stood there for a moment, all the same.

not expiated: i.e., he had not paid the penalty.

Then he too went in towards Jerusalem.

FOR THOUGHT AND DISCUSSION

1. What is your impression of Barabbas after reading this passage? Support your view with details from the story.

2. Why do you think Barabbas was on the hill?

3. What feelings about Jesus does Barabbas express in this passage?

4. Both Barabbas and Ben Tobit (page 398) witness the crucifixion of Jesus. What similarities and what differences do you find between the reactions of the two men? How were you affected by these two viewpoints of the crucifixion?

The Tomb Is Empty

first day of the week: Sunday.

they: the women from Galilee who had followed Jesus.

He Is Not Here

Now on the first day of the week, very early in the morning, they, and certain other women with them, came to the tomb bringing the spices which they had prepared. But they found the stone rolled away from the tomb. Then they went in and did not find the body of the Lord Jesus. And it happened, as they were greatly perplexed about this, that behold, two men stood by them in shining garments. Then, as they were afraid and bowed their faces to the earth, they said to them, "Why do you seek the living among the dead? He is not here, but is risen! Remember how he spoke to you when he was still in Galilee, saying, 'The Son of Man must be delivered into the hands of sinful men, and be crucified, and the third day rise again.'" And they remembered his words. Then they returned from the tomb and told all these things to the eleven and to all the rest. It was Mary Magdalene, Joanna, Mary the mother of James, and the other women with them, who told these things to the apostles. And their words seemed to them like idle tales, and they did not believe them. . . .

the eleven: the original disciples minus Judas, who had committed suicide.

On the Road to Emmaus

Now behold, two of them were traveling that same day to a village called Emmaus, which was about seven miles from Jerusalem. And they talked together of all these things which had happened. So it was, while they conversed and reasoned, that Jesus himself drew near and went with them. But their eyes were restrained, so that they did not know him. And he said to them, "What kind of conversation is this that you have with one another as you walk and are sad?"

restrained: limited, darkened.

Luke 24: 1–11, 13–37, 44–53. From *The Holy Bible, The New King James Version.* Copyright © 1979, 1980, 1982, Thomas Nelson, Inc. Reprinted by permission of Thomas Nelson, Inc., Publishers.

Then the one whose name was Cleopas answered and said to him, "Are you the only stranger in Jerusalem, and have you not known the things which happened there in these days?" And he said to them, "What things?" And they said to him, "The things concerning Jesus of Nazareth, who was a prophet mighty in deed and word before God and all the people, and how the chief priests and our rulers delivered him to be condemned to death, and crucified him. But we were hoping that it was he who was going to redeem Israel. Indeed, besides all this, today is the third day since these things happened. Yes, and certain women of our company, who arrived at the tomb early, astonished us. When they did not find his body, they came saying that they had also seen a vision of angels who said he was alive. And certain of those who were with us went to the tomb and found it just as the women had said; but him they did not see." Then he said to them, "O foolish ones, and slow of heart to believe in all that the prophets have spoken! Ought not the Christ to have suffered these things and to enter into his glory?" And beginning at Moses and all the prophets, he expounded to them in all the scriptures the things concerning himself.

Then they drew near to the village where they were going, and he indicated that he would have gone farther. But they constrained him, saying, "Abide with us, for it is toward evening, and the day is far spent." And he went in to stay with them.

redeem: rescue, save; literally, to protect the rights of a kinsman, as when God redeemed Israel, his first-born son, from slavery in Egypt.

expounded . . . himself: i.e., explained that the Hebrew Bible had foretold his appearance.

constrained him: held him back.

Jesus Reveals Himself

Now it came to pass, as he sat at the table with them, that he took bread, blessed and broke it, and gave it to them. Then their eyes were opened and they knew him; and he vanished from their sight. And they said to one another, "Did not our heart burn within us while he talked with us on the road, and while he opened the scriptures to us?" So they rose up that very hour and returned to Jerusalem, and found the eleven and those who were with them gathered together, saying, "The Lord is risen indeed, and has appeared to Simon!" And they told about the things that had happened on the road, and how he was known to them in the breaking of bread.

Now as they said these things, Jesus himself stood in the midst of them, and said to them, "Peace to you." But they were terrified and frightened, and supposed they had seen a spirit. . . .

spirit: ghost.

The Ascension

Then he said to them, "These are the words which I spoke to you while I was still with you, that all things must be fulfilled which were written in the law of Moses and the prophets and the psalms concerning me." And he opened their understanding, that they might comprehend the scriptures. Then he said to them, "Thus it is written, and thus it was necessary for the Christ to suffer and to rise from the dead the third day, and that repentance and remission of sins should be preached in his name to all nations, beginning at Jerusalem. And you are witnesses of these things. Behold, I send the promise of my Father upon you; but tarry in the city of Jerusalem until you are endued with power from on high."

comprehend: understand.

remission: forgiveness.

tarry: wait.
endued with: given.

And he led them out as far as Bethany, and he lifted up his hands and blessed them. Now it came to pass, while he blessed them, that he was parted from them and carried up into heaven. And they worshiped him, and returned to Jerusalem with great joy, and were continually in the temple praising and blessing God.

FOR CLOSE READING

1. How do the disciples respond to the news the women bring?

2. At what point do Cleopas and his companion recognize Jesus?

3. When Jesus "stood in the midst of them," the disciples are frightened and think he is a ghost. When has this happened to the disciples before?

4. What final instructions does Jesus give to his followers?

FOR THOUGHT AND DISCUSSION

5. Examine the series of events by which Jesus' resurrection is revealed. How do you think the story would have been affected if Jesus had suddenly appeared in a public display of glory?

6. Jesus explains the meaning of his life "beginning with Moses." What similarities and connections can you find between the lives of Jesus and Moses? Why is it significant that Jesus links himself with Moses?

7. Why do you think Jesus' followers are "slow of heart to believe"? When they finally realize that Jesus is with them again, which of the following feelings do you think is strongest: surprise, guilt, joy, fear, or confusion? Give reasons for your choice.

RESPONDING

1. Writing Read the Gospel of Luke, giving special attention to the roles played by women. Write a brief report of your findings.

2. Humanities Connection With a group of class-mates find several works of art that depict one of the events from these Bible passages: the discovery of the empty tomb, on the road to Emmaus, the Ascension. What different details does each painting emphasize? What differences in mood or feeling do you notice?

3. Multicultural Connection The annual celebration of Jesus' resurrection—Easter—involves many traditional symbols and practices, not all of which are based on the Bible story. List as many of these symbols and practices as you can, then choose one and try to trace the origin of the symbol or practice.

12

In the End
of Days

The Earth Is Broken

Certain biblical writings focus on "the end of days" or apocalypse. These prophetic passages are vivid, spectacular visions of world upheaval, final judgment, and God's total victory over evil.

This unit contains four groups of these visions, including passages from the books of Isaiah, Daniel, and Revelation. Questions and activities appear after "A New Heaven, A New Earth."

The earth dries up and withers,
    the world languishes and withers;
    the heavens languish together with the earth.
The earth lies polluted
    under its inhabitants;
for they have transgressed laws,
    violated the statutes,
    broken the everlasting covenant.
Therefore a curse devours the earth,
    and its inhabitants suffer for their guilt;
therefore the inhabitants of the earth dwindled
    and few people are left. . . .

Desolation is left in the city,
    the gates are battered into ruins.
For thus it shall be on the earth
    and among the nations,
as when an olive tree is beaten,
    as at the gleaning when the grape harvest is ended.

Isa. 24:4.
languishes: becomes weak.

transgressed: disobeyed.

covenant: agreement.

Isaiah 24:4–6, 12–13, 17–23 (New Revised Standard Version).
LEFT: *The Last Judgment*, detail from the west tympanum of the cathedral of Saint-Lazare, Autun, France. Carved by Gislebertus before 1135. Bulloz.

Terror, and the pit, and the snare
    are upon you, O inhabitant of the earth!
Whoever flees at the sound of the terror
    shall fall into the pit;
and whoever climbs out of the pit
    shall be caught in the snare.
For the windows of heaven are opened,
    and the foundations of the earth tremble.
The earth is utterly broken,
    the earth is torn asunder,
    the earth is violently shaken.
The earth staggers like a drunkard,
    it sways like a hut;
its transgression lies heavy upon it,
    and it falls, and will not rise again.

On that day the Lord will punish
    the host of heaven in heaven,
    and on earth the kings of the earth.
They will be gathered together
    like prisoners in a pit;
they will be shut up in a prison,
    and after many days they will be punished.
Then the moon will be abashed,
    and the sun ashamed;
for the Lord of hosts will reign
    on Mount Zion and in Jerusalem,
and before his elders he will manifest his glory.

snare: trap.

asunder: apart.

host of heaven: heavenly beings.

abashed: confused, perplexed.

Marvelous Visions

Revelation (also known as The Apocalypse in some versions of the Bible) is the last book of the New Testament. Revelation is written as a letter by John on the island of Patmos and tells of his visions of the end of days.
The Book of Daniel also includes visions of the end.

The Throne in Heaven

After this I looked, and there in heaven a door stood open! And the first voice, which I had heard speaking to me like a trumpet, said, "Come up here, and I will show you what must take place after this." At once I was in the spirit, and there in heaven stood a throne, with one seated on the throne. And the one seated there looks like jasper and carnelian, and around the throne is a rainbow that looks like an emerald. Around the throne are twenty-four thrones, and seated on the thrones are twenty-four elders, dressed in white robes, with golden crowns on their heads. Coming from the throne are flashes of lightning, and rumblings and peals of thunder, and in front of the throne burn seven flaming torches, which are the seven spirits of God; and in front of the throne there is something like a sea of glass, like crystal.

Around the throne, and on each side of the throne, are four living creatures, full of eyes in front and behind: the first living creature like a lion, the second living creature like an ox, the third living creature with a face like a human face, and the fourth living creature like a flying eagle. And the four living

Rev. 4:1.

jasper ... carnelian: semi-precious stones.

Revelation 4: 1–11. Daniel 7:2–7, 9–14 (New Revised Standard Version).

creatures, each of them with six wings, are full of eyes all around and inside. Day and night without ceasing they sing,

> "Holy, holy, holy,
> the Lord God the Almighty,
>   who was and is and is to come."

And whenever the living creatures give glory and honor and thanks to the one who is seated on the throne, who lives forever and ever, the twenty-four elders fall before the one who is seated on the throne and worship the one who lives forever and ever; they cast their crowns before the throne, singing,

> "You are worthy, our Lord and God.
>   to receive glory and honor and power,
> for you created all things,
>   and by your will they existed and were created."

Daniel's Dream of the Great Beasts

Dan. 7:2.

I Daniel, saw in my vision by night the four winds of heaven stirring up the great sea, and four great beasts came up out of the sea, different from one another. The first was like a lion and had eagles' wings. Then, as I watched, its wings were plucked off, and it was lifted up from the ground and made to stand on two feet like a human being; and a human mind was given to it. Another beast appeared, a second one, that looked like a bear. It was raised up on one side, had three tusks in its mouth among its teeth and was told, "Arise, devour many bodies!" After this, as I watched, another appeared, like a leopard. The beast had four wings of a bird on its back and four heads; and dominion was given to it. After this I saw in the visions by night a fourth beast, terrifying and dreadful and exceedingly strong. It had great iron teeth and was devouring, breaking in pieces, and stamping what was left with its feet. It was different from all the beasts that preceded it, and it had ten horns. . . .

dominion: the power to rule.

As I watched,
thrones were set in place,
    and an Ancient One took his throne,
his clothing was white as snow,
    and the hair of his head like pure wool;
his throne was fiery flames,
    and its wheels were burning fire.
A stream of fire issued
    and flowed out from his presence.
A thousand thousands served him,
    and ten thousand times ten thousand stood
        attending him.
The court sat in judgment,
    and the books were opened.

Ancient One: God. In some versions, Ancient of Days.

I watched then because of the noise of the arrogant words that the horn was speaking. And as I watched, the beast was put to death, and its body destroyed and given over to be burned with fire. As for the rest of the beasts, their dominion was taken away, but their lives were prolonged for a season and a time. As I watched in the night visions,

I saw one like a human being
    coming with the clouds of heaven.
And he came to the Ancient One
    and was presented before him.
To him was given dominion
    and glory and kingship,
that all peoples, nations, and languages
    should serve him.
His dominion is an everlasting dominion
    that shall not pass away,
and his kingship is one
    that shall never be destroyed.

Scenes from the Final Judgment

Michael: archangel (a chief angel) who protected Israel.

Satan Is Thrown Down

And war broke out in heaven; Michael and his angels fought against the dragon. The dragon and his angels fought back, but they were defeated, and there was no longer any place for them in heaven. The great dragon was thrown down, that ancient serpent, who is called the Devil and Satan, the deceiver of the whole world—he was thrown down to the earth, and his angels were thrown down with him. . . .

The Bowls of Wrath

Then I heard a loud voice from the temple telling the seven angels, "Go and pour out on the earth the seven bowls of the wrath of God."

So the first angel went and poured his bowl on the earth, and a foul and painful sore came on those who had the mark of the beast and who worshiped its image.

The second angel poured his bowl into the sea, and it became like the blood of a corpse, and every living thing in the sea died.

The third angel poured his bowl into the rivers and the springs of water, and they became blood. . . .

The fourth angel poured his bowl on the sun, and it was allowed to scorch them with fire; they were scorched by the fierce heat, but they cursed the name of God, who had authority over these plagues, and they did not repent and give him glory.

The fifth angel poured his bowl on the throne of the beast, and its kingdom was plunged into darkness; people gnawed their tongues in agony, and

---

Revelation 12:7–9; 16:1–4, 8–14, 16–20; 20:1–3, 7–15 (New Revised Standard Version).

cursed the God of heaven because of their pains and sores, and they did not repent of their deeds.

The sixth angel poured his bowl on the great river Euphrates, and its water was dried up in order to prepare the way for the kings from the east. And I saw three foul spirits like frogs coming from the mouth of the dragon, from the mouth of the beast, and from the mouth of the false prophet. These are demonic spirits, performing signs, who go abroad to the kings of the whole world, to assemble them for battle on the great day of God the Almighty. . . . And they assembled them at the place that in Hebrew is called Harmagedon.

signs: miracles.

The seventh angel poured his bowl into the air, and a loud voice came out of the temple, from the throne, saying, "It is done!" And there came flashes of lightning, rumblings, peals of thunder, and a violent earthquake such as had not occurred since people were upon the earth, so violent was that earthquake. The great city was split into three parts, and the cities of the nations fell. God remembered great Babylon and gave her the wine-cup of the fury of his wrath. And every island fled away, and no mountains were to be found . . . .

Harmagedon (här′mə ged′n): Also, Armageddon. Place of the final battle between the forces of good and evil.

The Thousand Years

Then I saw an angel coming down from heaven, holding in his hand the key to the bottomless pit and a great chain. He seized the dragon, that ancient serpent, who is the Devil and Satan, and bound him for a thousand years, and threw him into the pit, and locked and sealed it over him, so that he would deceive the nations no more, until the thousand years were ended. After that he must be let out for a little while. . . .

thousand years: also called the millennium.

When the thousand years are ended, Satan will be released from his prison and will come out to deceive the nations at the four corners of the earth, Gog and Magog, in order to gather them for battle; they are as numerous as the sands of the sea. They marched up over the breadth of the earth and surrounded the camp of the saints and the beloved city. And fire came down from heaven and consumed them. And the devil who had deceived them was thrown into the lake of fire and sulfur, where the beast and the false prophet were, and they will be tormented day and night forever and ever.

The Last Judgment

Then I saw a great white throne and the one who sat on it; the earth and the heaven fled from his presence, and no place was found for them. And I saw the dead, great and small, standing before the throne, and books were opened. Also another book was opened, the book of life. And the dead were judged according to their works, as recorded in the books. And the sea gave up the dead that were in it, Death and Hades gave up the dead that were in them, and all were judged according to what they had done. Then Death and Hades were thrown into the lake of fire. This is the second death, the lake of fire; and anyone whose name was not found written in the book of life was thrown into the lake of fire.

book of life: book containing the names of all the righteous.

works: deeds, actions.

Hades (hā′dēz′): place of the dead.

A New Heaven, a New Earth

Then I saw a new heaven and a new earth; for the first heaven and the first earth had passed away, and the sea was no more. And I saw the holy city, the new Jerusalem, coming down out of heaven from God, prepared as a bride adorned for her husband. And I heard a loud voice from the throne saying,

Rev. 21:1.

"See, the home of God is among mortals.
He will dwell with them as their God;
they will be his peoples,
and God himself will be with them;
he will wipe every tear from their eyes.
Death will be no more;
mourning and crying and pain will be no more,
for the first things have passed away."

mortals: human beings.

And the one who was seated on the throne said, "See, I am making all things new." Also he said, "Write this, for these words are trustworthy and true." Then he said to me, "It is done! I am the Alpha and the Omega, the beginning and the end. To the thirsty I will give water as a gift from the spring of the water of life. Those who conquer will inherit these things, and I will be their God and they will be my children. But as for the cowardly, the faithless, the polluted, the murderers, the fornicators, the sorcerers, the idolaters, and all liars, their place will be in the lake that burns with fire and sulfur, which is the second death." . . .

Alpha . . . Omega: the first and last letters of the Greek alphabet.

Revelation 21:1–11, 18, 21; 22:1–5. Isaiah 2: 2–4 (New Revised Standard Version).

The New Jerusalem

Then one of the seven angels who had the seven bowls full of the seven last plagues came and said to me, "Come, I will show you the bride, the wife of the lamb." And in the spirit he carried me away to a great, high mountain and showed me the holy city Jerusalem coming down out of heaven from God. It has the glory of God and a radiance like a very rare jewel, like jasper, clear as crystal. . . . The wall is built of jasper, while the city is pure gold, clear as glass. . . . And the twelve gates are twelve pearls, each of the gates is a single pearl, and the street of the city is pure gold, transparent as glass. . . .

Then the angel showed me the river of the water of life, bright as crystal, flowing from the throne of God and of the lamb through the middle of the street of the city. On either side of the river is the tree of life with its twelve kinds of fruit, producing its fruit each month; and the leaves of the tree are for the healing of the nations. Nothing accursed will be found there any more. But the throne of God and of the lamb will be in it, and his servants will worship him, they will see his face, and his name will be on their foreheads. And there will be no more night; they need no light of lamp or sun, for the Lord God will be their light, and they will reign forever and ever.

In days to come
    the mountain of the Lord's house
shall be established as the highest of the mountains,
    and shall be raised above the hills;
all the nations shall stream to it.
    Many peoples shall come and say,
"Come, let us go up to the mountain of the Lord,
    to the house of the God of Jacob;
that he may teach us his ways
    and that we may walk in his paths."
For out of Zion shall go forth instruction,
    and the word of the Lord from Jerusalem.
He shall judge between the nations,
    and shall arbitrate for many peoples;
they shall beat their swords into plowshares,
    and their spears into pruning hooks;
nation shall not lift up sword against nation,
    neither shall they learn war any more.

---

lamb: Jesus.

Rev. 22:1.

Isa. 2:2.

Zion: Jerusalem.

arbitrate: make decisions.

pruning hooks: curved blades on poles for trimming branches and vines.

FOR CLOSE READING

1. In "The Earth Is Broken" section, what images are used to describe the condition of the earth? According to this passage, why are the earth's inhabitants being punished?

2. In "Marvelous Visions," eight creatures are described. What differences are there between the four "living creatures" and the four "beasts" from the sea?

3. In "Scenes from the Final Judgment," what is "the second death"?

FOR THOUGHT AND DISCUSSION

4. Which passage made the strongest impression on you? Why?

5. What would you say is the main mood or feeling expressed in each of the four sections?

6. Thrones are mentioned throughout these passages. What is the effect of that repetition? Fire is also mentioned many times. What does fire seem to represent in these passages?

7. Angels pour out on the earth the "seven bowls of the wrath of God." Do any of the resulting disasters recall incidents from other Bible stories you have read? Explain.

8. What episodes in these visions show the locking up or the destruction of a terrible creature? What is the effect of this repeated pattern?

9. Throughout these passages, events and conditions on earth are related to events and conditions in heaven and vice versa. What is the effect of this connection?

10. What three details in these passages seem most horrible to you? What three details seem most comforting and pleasant? Why?

RESPONDING

1. **Activity** With a group of classmates, make a collage of photographs showing the earth lying "polluted under its inhabitants."

2. **Activity** In clay or some other medium, create a sculpture of one of the beasts described in "Marvelous Visions." Do not label it, and see whether your classmates can recognize the creature.

3. **Humanities Connection** Select music appropriate for each of the four passages. Prepare a reading of these passages to your musical accompaniment.

4. **Humanities Connection** Images of "the end of days"—both horrible and heavenly—have inspired many works of art over the centuries (see pages 405–408 for some examples). Examine a number of paintings on the subject. What details of the paintings seem to connect most directly to Bible passages you have read?

5. **Multicultural Connection** There are many scientific theories and popularly expressed ideas about how the world will end. Religious traditions in many cultures also include visions of the end. With a group of classmates, generate a list of these theories, ideas, and traditions, then choose one or more for further research. Prepare a report of your findings.

Epistle to Be Left in the Earth

epistle: letter.

. . . It is colder now,
            there are many stars,
                      we are drifting
North by the Great Bear,
                 the leaves are falling,
The water is stone in the scooped rocks,
                   to southward
Red sun grey air:
            the crows are
Slow on their crooked wings,
              the jays have left us:

Great Bear: group of stars forming the rough shape of a bear.

Long since we passed the flares of Orion.
Each man believes in his heart he will die.
Many have written last thoughts and last letters.
None know if our deaths are now or forever:
None know if this wandering earth will be found.
We lie down and the snow covers our garments.

Orion (ō ri′ən): a group of stars forming the rough shape of a man, named for a hunter in Greek myth.

I pray you,
        you (if any open this writing)
Make in your mouths the words that were our names.

I will tell you all we have learned,
                   I will tell you everything:
The earth is round,
           there are springs under the orchards,
The loam cuts with a blunt knife,
                beware of
Elms in thunder,
           the lights in the sky are stars—
We think they do not see,
              we think also

loam: rich, fertile soil.

The trees do not know nor the leaves of the grasses
    hear us:
The birds too are ignorant.
                                    Do not listen.
35 Do not stand at dark in the open windows.
We before you have heard this:
                            they are voices:
They are not words at all but the wind rising.
Also none among us has seen God.
40 (. . . We have thought often
The flaws of sun in the late and driving weather
Pointed to one tree but it was not so.)
As for the nights I warn you the nights are dangerous:
The wind changes at night and the dreams come.

45 It is very cold,
                    there are strange stars near Arcturus,

Voices are crying an unknown name in the sky

FOR THOUGHT AND DISCUSSION

1. What main impression did this poem have on you?
What details in the poem contribute most to this
feeling?

2. There are various theories about how our world
will end. Which theory seems evident in this poem?

3. What can you tell about the speaker from the list of
"all we have learned" (beginning with line 23)?

4. What do you think is the "tree" mentioned in line
42? What might be the "unknown name" mentioned
in the last line? Why do you think so?

5. Suppose you could put a letter in a time capsule to
be found by future generations or in an unmanned
space probe to be sent deep into space. What would
you say?

The Masque of the Red Death

The Red Death had long devastated the country. No pestilence had ever been so fatal, or so hideous. Blood was its avatar and its seal—the redness and the horror of blood. There were sharp pains, and sudden dizziness, and then profuse bleeding at the pores, with dissolution. The scarlet stains upon the body and especially upon the face of the victim were the pest ban which shut him out from the aid and from the sympathy of his fellow men. And the whole seizure, progress, and termination of the disease were the incidents of half an hour.

pestilence: plague; disease.

avatar (av́ə täŕ): i.e., sign.

dissolution: i.e., death.

But the Prince Prospero was happy and dauntless and sagacious. When his dominions were half depopulated, he summoned to his presence a thousand hale and light-hearted friends from among the knights and dames of his court, and with these retired to the deep seclusion of one of his castellated abbeys. This was an extensive and magnificent structure, the creation of the Prince's own eccentric yet august taste. A strong and lofty wall girdled it in. This wall had gates of iron. The courtiers, having entered, brought furnaces and massy hammers and welded the bolts. They resolved to leave means neither of ingress nor egress to the sudden impulses of despair or of frenzy from within. The abbey was amply provisioned. With such precautions the courtiers might bid defiance to contagion. The external world could take care of itself. In the meantime it was folly to grieve, or to think. The Prince had provided all the appliances of pleasure. There were buffoons, there were *improvvisatori*, there were ballet dancers, there were musicians, there was Beauty, there was wine. All these and security were within. Without was the Red Death.

dauntless: brave.

sagacious: shrewd, intelligent.

castellated: built like a castle.

august: grand.

ingress or egress: entering or leaving.

improvvisatori (ēḿ prôv vḗzä tôŕē): those who compose, recite, or sing on the spur of the moment.

without: outside.

It was toward the close of the fifth or sixth month of his seclusion, and while the pestilence raged most furiously abroad, that the Prince Prospero entertained his thousand friends at a masked ball of the most unusual magnificence.

It was a voluptuous scene, that masquerade. But first let me tell of the rooms in which it was held. There were seven—an imperial suite. In many palaces, however, such suites form a long and straight vista, while the folding doors slide back nearly to the walls on either hand, so that the view of the whole extent is scarcely impeded. Here the case was very different, as might have been expected from the Prince's love of the bizarre. The apartments were so irregularly disposed that the vision embraced but little more than one at a time. There was a sharp turn at every twenty or thirty yards, and at each turn a novel effect. To the right and left, in the middle of each wall, a tall and narrow Gothic window looked out upon a closed corridor which pursued the windings of the suite. These windows were of stained glass whose color varied in accordance with the prevailing hue of the decorations of the chamber into which it opened. That at the eastern extremity was hung, for example, in blue—and vividly blue were its windows. The second chamber was purple in its ornaments and tapestries, and here the panes were purple. The third was green throughout and so were the casements. The fourth was furnished and lighted with orange, the fifth with white, the sixth with violet. The seventh apartment was closely shrouded in black velvet tapestries that hung all over the ceiling and down the walls, falling in heavy folds upon a carpet of the same material and hue. But in this chamber only, the color of the windows failed to correspond with the decorations. The panes here were scarlet— a deep blood-color. Now in no one of the seven apartments was there any lamp or candelabrum, amid the profusion of golden ornaments that lay scattered to and fro or depended from the roof. There was no light of any kind emanating from lamp or candle within the suite of chambers. But in the corridors that followed the suite there stood, opposite to each window, a heavy tripod, bearing a brazier of fire, that projected its rays through the tinted glass and so glaringly illumined the room. And thus were

voluptuous: pleasing to the senses.

impeded: blocked.

disposed: arranged.

casements: windows.

depended: hung down.

brazier: heavy pan for burning coals or oil.

produced a multitude of gaudy and fantastic appearances. But in the western or black chamber the effect of the firelight that streamed upon the dark hangings through the blood-tinted panes was ghastly in the extreme, and produced so wild a look upon the countenances of those who entered that there were few of the company bold enough to set foot within its precincts at all.

countenances: faces.

precincts: areas.

It was in this apartment, also, that there stood against the western wall a gigantic clock of ebony. Its pendulum swung to and fro with a dull, heavy, monotonous clang; and when the minute hand made the circuit of the face, and the hour was to be stricken, there came from the brazen lungs of the clock a sound which was clear and loud and deep and exceedingly musical, but of so peculiar a note and emphasis that, at each lapse of an hour, the musicians of the orchestra were constrained to pause, momentarily, in their performance, to hearken to the sound; and thus the waltzers perforce ceased their evolutions; and there was a brief disconcert of the whole gay company; and, while the chimes of the clock yet rang, it was observed that the giddiest grew pale, and the more aged and sedate passed their hands over their brows as if in confused revery or meditation. But when the echoes had fully ceased, a light laughter at once pervaded the assembly; the musicians looked at each other and smiled as if at their own nervousness and folly, and made whispering vows, each to the other, that the next chiming of the clock should produce in them no similar emotion; and then, after the lapse of sixty minutes (which embrace three thousand and six hundred seconds of the Time that flies) there came yet another chiming of the clock, and then were the same disconcert and tremulousness and meditation as before.

brazen: brass.

disconcert: confusion.

pervaded: spread throughout.

tremulousness: trembling.

But in spite of these things, it was a gay and magnificent revel. The tastes of the Prince were peculiar. He had a fine eye for colors and effects. He disregarded the *decora* of mere fashion. His plans were bold and fiery, and his conceptions glowed with barbaric luster. There are some who would have thought him mad. His followers felt that he was not. It was necessary to hear and see and touch him to be *sure* that he was not.

revel: party.

decora: i.e., decorative arrangements.

He had directed, in great part, the movable

embellishments of the seven chambers, upon occasion of this great fete; and it was his own guiding taste which had given character to the masqueraders. Be sure they were grotesque. There were much glare and glitter and piquancy and phantasm—much of what has been since seen in *Hernani*. There were arabesque figures with unsuited limbs and appointments. There were delirious fancies such as the madman fashions. There was much of the beautiful, much of the wanton, much of the bizarre, something of the terrible, and not a little of that which might have excited disgust. To and fro in the seven chambers there stalked, in fact, a multitude of dreams. And these—the dreams— writhed in and about, taking hue from the rooms, and causing the wild music of the orchestra to seem as the echo of their steps. And, anon, there strikes the ebony clock which stands in the hall of the velvet. And then, for a moment, all is still, and all is silent save the voice of the clock. The dreams are stiff frozen as they stand. But the echoes of the chime die away—they have endured but an instant—and a light, half-subdued laughter floats after them as they depart. And now again the music swells, and the dreams live, and write to and fro more merrily than ever, taking hue from the many tinted windows through which stream the rays from the tripods. But to the chamber which lies most westwardly of the seven, there are now none of the maskers who venture; for the night is waning away, and there flows a ruddier light through the blood-colored panes; and the blackness of the sable drapery appalls; and to him whose foot falls upon the sable carpet, there comes from the near clock of ebony a muffled peal more solemnly emphatic than any which reaches *their* ears who indulge in the more remote gaieties of the other apartments.

But these other apartments were densely crowded, and in them beat feverishly the heart of life. And the revel went whirlingly on, until at length there commenced the sounding of midnight upon the clock. And then the music ceased, as I have told; and the evolutions of the waltzers were quieted; and there was an uneasy cessation of all things as before. But now there were twelve strokes to be sounded by the bell of the clock; and thus it happened, perhaps, that more of thought crept, with more of time, into the meditations of the thoughtful among those who reveled. And thus, too, it happened, perhaps, that before the last echoes of the last chime had utterly sunk into silence, there were many individuals in the crowd who had found leisure to become aware of the presence of a masked figure which had arrested the attention of no single individual before. And the rumor of this new presence having spread itself whisperingly around, there arose at length from the whole company a buzz, or murmur, expressive of disapprobation and surprise—then, finally, of terror, of horror, and of disgust.

In an assembly of phantasms such as I have painted, it may well be supposed that no ordinary appearance could have excited such sensation. In truth the masquerade license of the night was nearly unlimited; but the figure in question had out-Heroded Herod, and gone beyond the bounds of even the Prince's indefinite decorum. There are chords in the hearts of the most reckless which cannot be touched without emotion. Even with the utterly lost, to whom life and death are equally jests, there are matters of which no jest can be made. The whole company, indeed, seemed now deeply to feel that in the costume and bearing of the stranger neither wit nor propriety existed. The figure was tall and gaunt, and shrouded from head to foot in the habiliments of the grave. The mask which concealed the visage was made so nearly to resemble the countenance of a stiffened corpse that the closest scrutiny must have had difficulty in detecting the cheat. And yet all this might have been endured, if not approved, by the mad revelers around. But the mummer had gone so far as to assume the type of the Red Death. His vesture was dabbled in *blood*—and his broad brow, with all the features of the face, was besprinkled with the scarlet horror.

When the eyes of Prince Prospero fell upon this spectral image (which, with a slow and solemn movement, as if more fully to sustain its role, stalked to and fro among the waltzers) he was seen to be convulsed, in the first moment with a strong shudder either of terror or distaste; but, in the next, his brow reddened with rage.

"Who dares?" he demanded hoarsely of the

disapprobation: disapproval.

license: freedom.

out-Heroded Herod: i.e., gone beyond the extremes of the masquerade. This is a quotation from Shakespeare's *Hamlet*.

habiliments: clothing.
visage: face.

mummer: costumed person.
vesture: clothing.

spectral: ghostly.

blasphemous: unholy.

battlements: tower walls.

courtiers who stood near him—"who dares insult us with this blasphemous mockery? Seize him and unmask him—that we may know whom we have to hang at sunrise, from the battlements!"

It was in the eastern or blue chamber in which stood the Prince Prospero as he uttered these words. They rang throughout the seven rooms loudly and clearly—for the Prince was a bold and robust man, and the music had become hushed at the waving of his hand.

It was in the blue room where stood the Prince, with a group of pale courtiers by his side. At first, as he spoke, there was a slight rushing movement of this group in the direction of the intruder, who at the moment was also near at hand, and now, with deliberate and stately step, made closer approach to the speaker. But from a certain nameless awe with which the mad assumptions of the mummer had inspired the whole party, there were found none who put forth hand to seize him; so that, unimpeded, he passed within a yard of the Prince's person; and while the vast assembly, as if with one impulse, shrank from the centers of the rooms to the walls, he made his way uninterruptedly, but with the same solemn and measured step which had distinguished him from the first, through the blue chamber to the purple—through the purple to the green—through the green to the orange—through this again to the white—and even thence to the violet, ere a decided movement had been made to arrest him. It was then, however, that the Prince Prospero, maddening with rage and the shame of his own momentary cowardice, rushed hurriedly through the six chambers, while none followed him on account of a deadly terror that had seized upon all. He bore aloft a drawn dagger, and had approached, in rapid impetuosity, to within three or four feet of the retreating figure, when the latter, having attained the extremity of the velvet apartment, turned suddenly and confronted his pursuer. There was a sharp cry—and the dagger dropped gleaming upon the sable carpet, upon which, instantly afterward, fell prostrate in death the Prince Prospero. Then, summoning the wild courage of despair, a throng of the revelers at once threw themselves into the black apartment, and, seizing the

impetuousity: rushing force.

prostrate: face down.

mummer, whose tall figure stood erect and motionless within the shadow of the ebony clock, gasped in unutterable horror at finding the grave cerements and corpselike mask, which they handled with so violent a rudeness, untenanted by any tangible form.

cerements: burial shroud.

And now was acknowledged the presence of the Red Death. He had come like a thief in the night. And one by one dropped the revelers in the blood-bedewed halls of their revel, and died each in the despairing posture of his fall. And the life of the ebony clock went out with that of the last of the gay. And the flames of the tripods expired. And Darkness and Decay and the Red Death held illimitable dominion over all.

illimitable dominion: complete rule.

FOR CLOSE READING

1. Briefly describe the rooms in which the masquerade takes place.

2. How do the party-goers react to the chiming of the clock?

3. What do the party-goers discover when they seize and unmask the strange figure?

FOR THOUGHT AND DISCUSSION

4. In your opinion, which seems most important in this story: plot, setting, or characterization? Why do you think so?

5. How would the story be changed if there had been no clock?

6. Compare "The Masque of the Red Death" with the Bible passages in this unit. What similarities do you find? Which of the four biblical sections seems most similar to "Red Death" in imagery and mood? Give reasons for your choice.

Rise and Shine

ribbed architrave: i.e., the trunk of the body.

fastidiously don: i.e., carefully put on.

cankered: decayed.

griffin: mythical creature that is half eagle, half lion.

At the big trumpet, we must all put on
our dentures, tie old strings to knees, adjust
shank upon socket, wig to cranium, bust
on ribbed architrave, fastidiously don
5   our properties, and blink to face the sun.
Farewell, dream image, cankered in our dust,
and sweets shrunk in the brain, farewell, we trust.
Uprise, O fragment brethren! We have won—
For, hallelujah, these dry graves are torn!
10   Thin bugles crash the valley of our bones
to rock the vultures wide away and scare
the griffin from his precipice as, worn
and damp, we crawl like grubs from under stones
to scarf our loves in paradisial air.

FOR THOUGHT AND DISCUSSION

1. To whom is the speaker referring by "we" in line 1?

2. Death and decay are often regarded as gruesome or frightening. What seem to be the speaker's feelings about these things?

3. The speaker says, "We have won" in line 8. What victory do you think the poem proclaims?

Appendix

A Brief History of the Bible

[Note: the following information represents a consensus of critical scholarship; the views of some religious traditions may vary. The designations B.C.E. ("Before the Common Era") and C.E. ("Common Era") are used in place of B.C. and A.D.]

The Hebrew Bible

How did the Bible become the Bible? The Bible itself offers clues to the process. In 622 B.C.E. a scroll was found in a storage room of the temple in Jerusalem. When the scroll was read to Josiah, the king of Judah, he was so impressed that he proclaimed the laws in that document to be the law of the land. Most critical scholars agree that the scroll was a major part of the Book of Deuteronomy, and this event—recorded in 2 Kings 22-23—marks the first stage of gathering Hebrew writings and oral traditions into a book that would be authoritative for the everyday lives and religious activities of Jewish people.

Nehemiah 8 describes a later major event around 400 B.C.E. Ezra read "the book of the law of Moses" to all the people of Jerusalem who had gathered in the great square by the Water Gate. This document, most scholars believe, was the first five books of the Bible, covering the creation of the world to the death of Moses, just before Israel entered the land of Canaan. These books (Genesis, Exodus, Leviticus, Numbers, and Deuteronomy) are known as the **Pentateuch** ("five scrolls") or **Torah** ("teaching" or "law").

By Ezra's time other documents had been gathered together into collections that were also being regarded as sacred literature by the Jewish community. The **Former Prophets** (Joshua, Judges, 1 and 2 Samuel, 1 and 2 Kings) continue Israel's story from the entry into Canaan—around 1225 B.C.E.—until the exile of the Jewish people to Babylonia some 650 years later. A major theme of this continuation of Israel's history was that Israel was either blessed or punished depending on its obedience to or disobedience of God's laws. In this collection we have stories that describe the activities of some of the early prophets of Israel (Deborah, Samuel, Nathan, Elijah, and many others) as they interacted with the rulers of Israel and tried to guide their people.

Beginning about 750 B.C.E. and extending to the time of Ezra, the oracles of some prophets were written down and preserved in separate scrolls. A major theme of these prophets was the coming of divine judgment on Israel for having neglected God's laws. When the Babylonians sacked Jerusalem in 587 B.C.E., the people realized that these prophets had spoken truly. Thus the **Latter Prophets** collection (Isaiah, Jeremiah, Ezekiel, and the twelve "Minor Prophets") gradually took shape. From Ezra's time on, "the law and the prophets" would be authoritative religious texts for the Jewish people.

One term for the Hebrew Bible is **TaNaK,** a word indicating that the Hebrew Bible is divided into three parts. The "T" is the first letter of Torah, the first five books. The "N" is the first letter of the Hebrew word for "prophets," including both the Former and Latter Prophets. The "K" is the first letter of the Hebrew word for **Writings,** covering all the other books. Books like Job and Psalms give some indication that the Jewish community had produced many other religious writings over the centuries. It was not until shortly after Jerusalem fell to the Romans in 70 C.E., however, that it was determined which of these works would be included in the Writings section of the Bible. In all, 39 books were accepted into the Tanak.

Targum

Virtually all of the Tanak was originally written in Hebrew. After the exile of 587 B.C.E., most Jews were cut off from their homeland and home language. Aramaic, a sister language of Hebrew, became the everyday language of Jews living throughout the Middle East and would remain so for a thousand years. Aramaic translations of the Hebrew text allowed many exiled Jews to continue to use scripture for study and worship. Scholars have discovered at least one Aramaic translation, or **Targum,** for every Hebrew book except Daniel, Ezra, and Nehemiah—the three books that originally contained passages of Aramaic.

The Septuagint

Translation of the text into a more familiar language became a repeated pattern in Bible history. After the conquests of Alexander the Great around 330 B.C.E., Greek became the most commonly used language throughout large parts of the ancient world. Some time in the third century B.C.E., a Greek translation of the Hebrew Bible, the **Septuagint,** was produced in Alexandria, Egypt. ("Septuagint" is the Latin word for "seventy." According to tradition, seventy-two elders, working in pairs, began the translation, and each pair miraculously produced exactly the same translation as the other thirty-five pairs.) Because this translation was completed at least three hundred years before a Jewish community settled on the final 39 books of the Hebrew Bible, the Septuagint contains additional writings. Sometimes called the **Apocrypha** (from the Greek for "hidden"), these additional works include traditions about such biblical figures as Solomon, Manasseh, Jeremiah, Esther, Ezra, and Daniel; other books contain the religious teachings or heroic actions of figures such as Judith and the Maccabee brothers.

The Christian Bible

Most early Christians readily accepted the Hebrew scriptures, following the example of Jesus, who referred frequently to the "law and the prophets" in his teachings. As Christianity spread through the Greek-speaking world of the Mediterranean, the Septuagint became the earliest Bible for Christians. It was not long, however, before Christians began to produce additional religious literature, most of it written in Greek. The apostle Paul traveled through much of the Mediterranean world, writing to churches that he either had founded or was trying to help. Though each **letter**, or **epistle**, was addressed to the unique concerns of a specific church, Christian leaders recognized that his teachings and advice would be valuable to all the early churches. Paul's epistles were soon collected and shared.

Stories of the life, teachings, death, and resurrection of Jesus, called **gospels** ("good news"), began to circulate. As the Christian message spread throughout much of the Roman empire, many different gospel stories arose in various regions, each church relying on the gospel that had gained acceptance in its region. Though an early Christian leader tried to combine these many gospels into one, the Christian community finally decided to accept four separate Gospels—Matthew, Mark, Luke, and John.

Additional writings were being circulated, including *(1)* epistles by other writers (1 Peter and 1 John were particularly favored); *(2)* the Acts of the Apostles, the second half of Luke's work that describes the history of early Christians and Paul's journeys; and *(3)* Revelation, which describes events ending the world. The letters of Paul, the four Gospels (including Acts), 1 Peter, and 1 John were accepted as authoritative scripture fairly early, but it took more than three hundred years to reach a consensus about the final contents of what came to be known as the **New Testament**. A number of early Christian apocryphal writings, among them the Gospel of Thomas, the Apocalypse of Peter, and the Acts of Paul, are not included in the New Testament.

Early Christians added the New Testament to the end of the Hebrew Bible, which they renamed the **Old Testament.** They also rearranged the Old Testament, putting the prophets at the end in order to show the relationship they saw between prophecy and the life and teachings of Jesus recorded in the New Testament.

The Vulgate

Christians now had both Testaments in the Greek language—but Latin was the common language of the Roman empire. In the late fourth century the Roman pope commissioned a scholar, Jerome, to translate the entire Bible into Latin. Jerome noticed the many differences between the Greek Septuagint and the Hebrew Bible, and he decided to base his translation on the Hebrew text. He did include the Septuagint's books of Apocrypha, however; these he placed in a separate section having secondary status. Jerome completed his Latin translation, known as the **Vulgate** (from the Latin for "common" or "popular" language), around 405 C.E. The Vulgate was the official Bible of western Christianity for more than one thousand years.

English Translations

In 14th-century England, Latin was neither common nor popular. Virtually the only people who could read the Bible were the clergy. The first sustained effort to translate the whole Bible from Latin into English was made in the 1380s by John Wycliffe, an English priest. Over the next 150 years a host of factors—including the invention of the printing press, Renaissance interest in ancient languages and learning, the rise of national feeling, and the Protestant Reformation—brought new momentum to the translation movement.

The most influential English figure in this process was William Tyndale, who had been influenced in turn by the Protestant Reformation and Martin Luther's translation of the Bible into German. Tyndale's vigorous translations of the New Testament, the Pentateuch, the Psalms, and Jonah had a major influence on the style and language of English versions that followed. Much of Tyndale's work was included in the first printed English translation of the Bible, produced by Myles Coverdale.

In Tyndale's time, translating the Bible was secret, dangerous work performed against the wishes of kings and clergy; Tyndale was executed before he could complete his translation. Within two generations the political climate had changed completely, and the king of England himself authorized scholars to prepare an English version of the Bible. Published in 1611, this **King James Version,** or **Authorized Version**, has had a powerful and lingering effect on the language, literature, culture, and imagination of the English-speaking world.

English Roman Catholics working in France completed an English translation of the Vulgate in 1610. Known as the **Douay** or the **Rheims-Douay Version** (after the French cities in which it was first published), this translation served as the authoritative English version for Roman Catholics for several centuries.

Other translations appeared over the centuries without lasting effect (though in the 19th century, many Protestant editions began to omit what they considered Apocrypha). In the years after World War II, however, an array of new translations has appeared, acknowledging changes in our language and aided by recent archeological discoveries and advances in biblical scholarship. Some of these new translations attempt to keep the style, language, and cadence of the King James Bible; others deliberately express the Bible's meaning in new language and a more modern style. For a comparative sampling of some of these translations, see pages 453-455.

Timeline of Bible Events

The timeline shown on pages 448–449 emphasizes events described in *The Bible as/in Literature* (including information from "A Brief History of the Bible," page 444). Biblical people and events are shown on the right; other historical people and events are shown on the left. This timeline represents a consensus of critical scholarship; some datings may vary according to religious traditions. The designations B.C.E. ("Before the Common Era") and C.E. ("Common Era") are used in place of B.C. and A.D. History, of course, does not begin in 1300 B.C.E. Pyramids were being

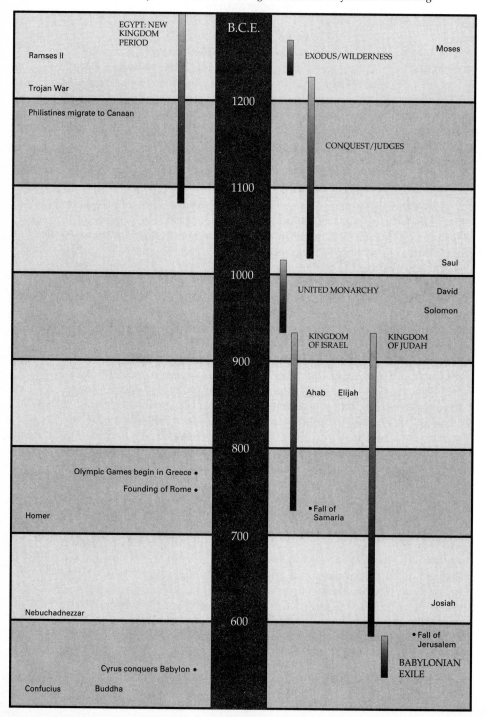

built in Egypt twelve hundred years before Moses. A few centuries later law codes were being written in the Tigris-Euphrates valley (now modern Iraq). The best known of these, the Code of Hammurabi, appeared about the time of Abraham and Sarah. They began a journey from the Tigris-Euphrates region to Canaan, the Promised Land. Several generations later, their descendants would become slaves in Egypt. Subsequent events are shown in the timeline.

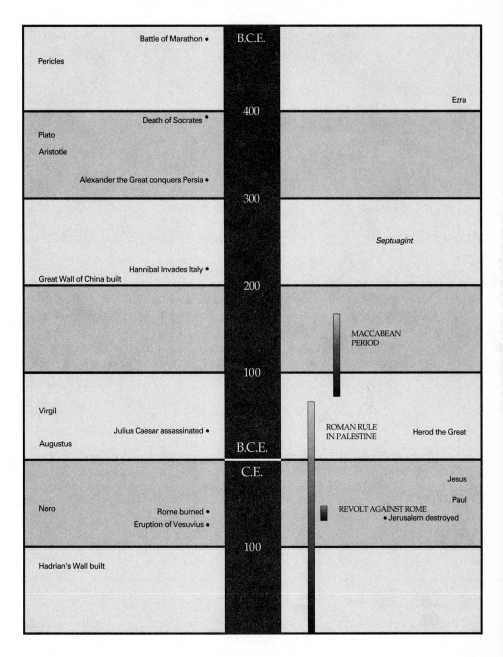

Egypt to Canaan in Biblical Times

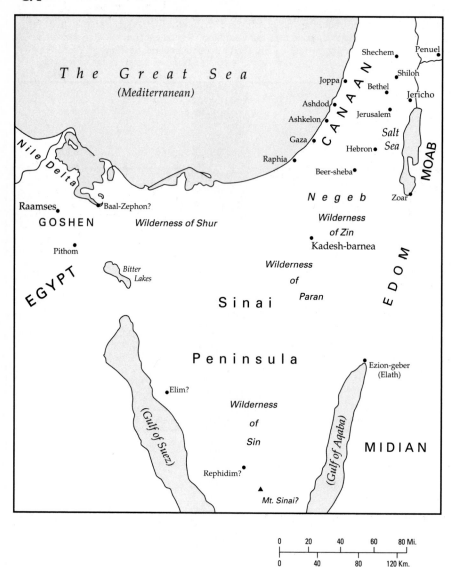

The Great Sea
(Mediterranean)

Shechem
Penuel
Joppa
Shiloh
Bethel
Ashdod
Jericho
Ashkelon
Jerusalem
C A N A A N
Gaza
Salt
Hebron
Sea
Raphia
MOAB
Beer-sheba
Nile Delta
Raamses
Baal-Zephon?
N e g e b
Zoar
GOSHEN
Wilderness of Shur
Wilderness
of Zin
Pithom
Kadesh-barnea
EGYPT
Bitter
Lakes
Wilderness
of
EDOM
S i n a i
Paran
P e n i n s u l a
Ezion-geber
(Elath)
Elim?
Wilderness
of
Sin
MIDIAN
Rephidim?
Mt. Sinai?
(Gulf of Suez)
(Gulf of Aqaba)

0   20   40   60   80 Mi.

0   40   80   120 Km.

Note: The maps on pages 450-452 emphasize locations mentioned in the biblical passages of *The Bible as/in Literature.*

The Kingdoms of Israel and Judah

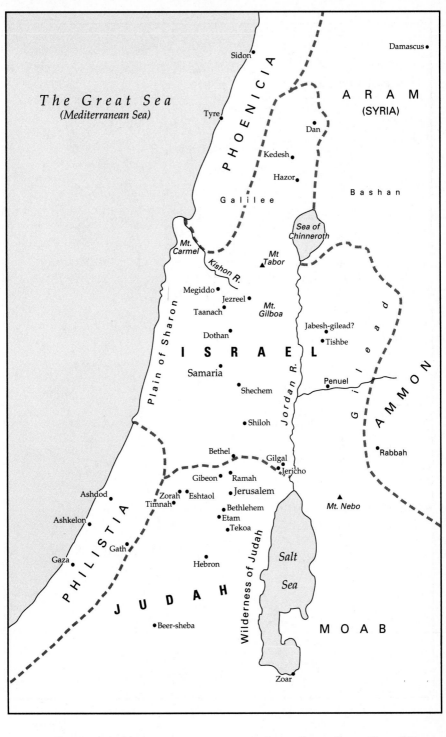

Palestine in the Time of Jesus

(Mediterranean Sea)

PHOENICIA

GAULANITIS

GALILEE

• Bethsaida

Cana •

Capernaum

Sea
of
Galilee

Mt. Carmel

Nazareth •

Mt.
▲ Tabor

• Gadara

Plain
of
Esdraelon

DECAPOLIS

• Caesarea

Plain of Sharon

SAMARIA

Sabaste •
(Samaria)

Gerasa
•

▲ Mt. Ebal

Mt. Gerizim ▲

Jordan R.

Jabbok R.

• Arimathea?

PEREA

JUDEA

Jericho •

• Emmaus?

Jerusalem •

• Bethany

Bethlehem •

• Qumran

(Dead
Sea)

| 0 | 10 | 20 | 30 | 40 Mi. |
| 0 | 20 | 40 | 60 Km. |

A Sampler of Bible Translations

This sampler displays eight different translations of the first six verses of Psalm 8. Dates are given for the King James and Douay versions; the others are current twentieth-century translations.

DOUAY BIBLE (1610)

O Lord, our Lord, how admirable is thy name in the whole earth! For thy magnificence is elevated above the heavens.

Out of the mouth of infants and of sucklings thou hast perfected praise, because of thy enemies, that thou mayst destroy the enemy and the avenger.

For I will behold thy heavens, the works of thy fingers: the moon and the stars which thou hast founded.

What is man that thou art mindful of him? or the son of man that thou visitest him?

Thou hast made him a little less than the angels, thou hast crowned him with glory and honor . . . .

KING JAMES VERSION (1611)

O Lord our Lord, how excellent is thy name in all the earth! who hast set thy glory above the heavens.

Out of the mouth of babes and sucklings hast thou ordained strength because of thine enemies, that thou mightest still the enemy and the avenger.

When I consider thy heavens, the work of thy fingers, the moon and the stars, which thou hast ordained;

What is man, that thou art mindful of him? and the son of man, that thou visitest him?

For thou hast made him a little lower than the angels, and hast crowned him with glory and honor. . . .

NEW AMERICAN BIBLE

O Lord, our Lord,
how glorious is your name over all the earth!

You have exalted your majesty above the heavens.
Out of the mouths of babes and sucklings
   you have fashioned praise because of your foes,
   to silence the hostile and the vengeful.
When I behold your heavens, the work of your fingers,
   the moon and the stars which you set in place–
What is man that you should be mindful of him,
   or the son of man that you should care for him?

You have made him little less than the angels,
   and crowned him with glory and honor. . . .

NEW INTERNATIONAL VERSION

O Lord, our Lord,
   how majestic is your name in all the earth!

You have set your glory
   above the heavens
From the lips of children and infants
   you have ordained praise
because of your enemies,
   to silence the foe and the avenger.

When I consider your heavens,
   the work of your fingers,
the moon and the stars,
   which you have set in place,
what is man that you are mindful of him,
   the son of man that you care for him?
You made him a little lower than the heavenly beings,
   and crowned him with glory and honor. . . .

NEW JERUSALEM BIBLE

Yahweh our Lord,
how majestic is your name throughout the world!

Whoever keeps singing of your majesty higher than the heavens,
even through the mouths of children, or babes in arms,
you make him a fortress, firm against your foes,
to subdue the enemy and the rebel.

I look up at your heavens, shaped by your fingers,
at the moon and the stars you set firm–
what are human beings that you spare a thought for them,
or the child of Adam that you care for him?

Yet you have made him little less than a god,
you have crowned him with glory and beauty . . .

NEW JEWISH PUBLICATION SOCIETY TRANSLATION

O Lord, our Lord,
How majestic is your name throughout the earth,
You who have covered the heavens with your splendor!
From the mouths of infants and sucklings
You have founded strength on account of your foes,
to put an end to enemy and avenger.
When I behold your heavens, the work of your fingers,
the moon and the stars that you set in place,
what is man that you have been mindful of him,
mortal man that you have taken note of him,
that you have made him little less than divine,
and adorned him with glory and majesty . . .

NEW REVISED STANDARD VERSION

O Lord, our Sovereign,
how majestic is your name in all the earth!

You have set your glory above the heavens.
Out of the mouths of babes and infants
you have founded a bulwark because of your foes
to silence the enemy and the avenger.

When I look at your heavens, the work of your fingers,
the moon and the stars that you have established;
what are human beings that you are mindful of them,
mortals that you care for them?

Yet you have made them a little lower than God,
and crowned them with glory and honor. . . .

REVISED ENGLISH BIBLE

Lord our sovereign,
how glorious is your name throughout the world!
Your majesty is praised as high as the heavens,
from the mouths of babes and infants at the breast.
You have established a bulwark against your adversaries
to restrain the enemy and the avenger.

When I look up at your heavens, the work of your fingers,
at the moon and the stars you have set in place,
what is a frail mortal, that you should be mindful of him?
a human being, that you should take notice of him?

Yet you have made him little less than a god,
crowning his head with glory and honor. . . .

Handbook of Bible Stories and Biblical Expressions

This reference summarizes the people, events, and key terms included in The Bible as/in Literature. *It also highlights words and phrases from the Bible that continue to echo through literature, others arts, and ordinary conversation. Quotations are given in the* King James Version, *the one most commonly quoted in literary allusions. Wording may vary slightly from the translations used within this book.*

Abraham
T̶ father, or ancestor, of both Jews and Arabs through his sons I̶ c and **Ishmael**. God made a **covenant** or agreement with A̶ raham **"to make of thee a great nation."** Abraham's obedience to God brought him to Canaan, **the Promised Land.** His wife, **Sarah**, gave birth to Isaac miraculously late in their lives. Later, Abraham's obedience brought him to the point of agreeing to a **sacrifice of Isaac**; an angel's voice stopped him, and **a ram caught in a thicket** was sacrificed instead. [Genesis 12–22.]

Adam and Eve
The first man and woman, parents of the human race. God formed Adam from **the dust of the ground, breathed into his nostrils the breath of life** , and put him in the **Garden of Eden.** Seeing that **"It is not good that the man should be alone,"** God created a **help meet** for him, making Eve from **Adam's rib.** Adam said, **"This is now bone of my bones, and flesh of my flesh."** The two **"were both naked . . . and were not ashamed."** [Genesis 1–2.]

Amos
A migrant worker and prophet from the Southern Kingdom who spoke out against social injustice in Israel, the Northern Kingdom. Amos first condemned Israel's enemies (**"For three transgressions . . . and for four, I will not turn away the punishment"**), then shocked Israel by condemning their own treatment of the poor (**"they sold the righteous for silver, and the poor for a pair of shoes"**). [Amos.]

Ark

Three Bible meanings: (1) **Noah**'s vessel, in which he and the animals survived the **Flood.** (2) The same Hebrew word is used for the basket in which the infant **Moses** was set afloat by his mother to survive Pharaoh's murderous campaign against male Hebrew babies. (3) The **Ark of the Covenant,** the sacred chest containing special objects, probably including the tablets of the law given to Moses. The ark was regarded as the seat on which God sat invisibly enthroned.

Armageddon

The great and final battle between good and evil forces at the end of the world. (Also, **Harmagedon.**) The term is often used to describe any earth-shaking, potentially earth-ending conflict. [Revelation 16.]

Babel

When the whole earth had **one language** and **one speech,** people began to build a city and a tower to the heavens **"to make us a name."** The Lord came down to **confound their language** and **scatter them abroad upon the face of all the earth.** Babel is associated with human ambition and the dispersion and various languages of the human race. [Genesis 11:1-9.]

Babylonian Captivity

A period of **exile** for Jews following the conquest of Jerusalem by **Nebuchadnezzar.** Many Jews were taken to Babylonia to serve Nebuchadnezzar and his son **Belshazzar** until Babylonia in turn was conquered by the Medes and the Persians. The stories of **Daniel** and **Esther** take place during this period. For biblical prophets, the Babylonian Captivity represented a judgment of God, requiring repentance and a return to God in order to be restored to Jerusalem. For biblical poets, the Captivity produced a literature of lament (**"By the rivers of Babylon, there we sat down, yea, we wept when we remembered Zion."**).

Belshazzar's Feast

A profane party given by a careless king, Belshazzar's Feast was suddenly interrupted by **handwriting on the wall.** Daniel was brought in to reveal that the words **Mene, Mene, Tekel, and Parsin** meant that Belshazzar's feast, reign, and life were at an end because he had been **weighed and found wanting.** [Daniel 5.]

Cain and Abel

Adam and Eve's first sons. Cain was a farmer; Abel was a shepherd. Cain resented his younger brother, whose sacrifice had been chosen by God over Cain's. Cain killed Abel (the first murder) and cynically answered God, **"Am I my brother's keeper?"** Cain dreaded being **a fugitive and vagabond in the earth.** The Lord put a mark—the **mark of Cain**—upon him to protect him. Cain moved **east of Eden** to the **land of Nod,** where he founded the first city. [Genesis 4.]

Covenant
An agreement describing the terms of a relationship between individuals, between people and a ruler, or between people and God. Covenants mentioned in the Bible include those that God made with **Noah,** with **Abraham,** and with the **Israelites** (through **Moses and the Ten Commandments**). Jesus announced a new covenant to his disciples at the **Last Supper** before he was crucified.

Creation
God's acts of making the universe and all forms of life. Genesis 1:1–2:4a describes God's creative work in six days, from **"Let there be light"** on the first day to creating human beings on the sixth day: **"in the image of God created he him; male and female created he them." "God saw every thing that he had made, and, behold, it was very good";** he rested on the **seventh day.**

Genesis 2: 4b–25 describes God forming Adam from the **dust of the ground,** creating a **garden in Eden,** making wild animals and birds for Adam to name, and finally creating **Eve.**

Daniel
One of the young Jews taken into captivity in Babylon. There he displayed courage, faith, and gifts of prophecy. Among the best known events in his life are his intervention in the trial of **Susanna**, who was falsely accused by two lustful elders; his interpretation of the handwriting on the wall at **Belshazzar's Feast,** and his miraculous survival **in a den of lions** (where he had been thrown for his faithfulness to God). [Daniel.]

David
Israel's greatest king. The Bible offers many different pictures of David: shepherd boy; stone-slinging victor over the giant Philistine, **Goliath**; eloquent mourner for the slain Saul and Jonathan (**"How are the mighty fallen!"**); charismatic, conquering king; murderous adulterer with **Bathsheba;** aged father grieving for his dead rebel son (**"O my son Absalom, my son, my son Absalom!"**). In all phases of his life, a major characteristic is David's devotion to God. [1 and 2 Samuel.]

Deborah

A judge of Israel, the only prophet and only woman to be given that God-supported role. Deborah joined with the Israelite leader **Barak** to lead the Israelites to victory over the iron chariots of the Canaanite army. The fleeing Canaanite general, **Sisera,** took refuge in the tent of a woman, **Jael,** who killed him with a tent peg as he slept. **The Song of Deborah and Barak** celebrates God's victory and the downfall of Sisera: **"the stars in their courses fought against Sisera."** [Judges 4–5.]

Eden

The garden created by God as a home for Adam. Eden is associated with a natural perfection, peace, and innocence—paradise. But Adam and Eve, tempted by the **serpent,** ate the **forbidden fruit** of the **tree of knowledge.** This first disobedience—often referred to as the **Original Sin** or the **Fall**—brought guilt, shame, and God's judgment on Adam (**"In the sweat of thy face shalt thou eat bread, till thou return unto the ground . . . for dust thou art, and unto dust shalt thou return"**); on Eve (**"I will greatly multiply thy sorrow . . . in sorrow thou shalt bring forth children"**); and on the serpent (**"upon thy belly shalt thou go"**). Adam and Eve were then expelled from Eden. [Genesis 2-3.]

Elijah

A prophet in the Northern Kingdom, **Israel,** during the reign of **Ahab.** Though he believed himself isolated—**"I, even I only, remain a prophet of the Lord"**—Elijah challenged Ahab, his foreign wife **Jezebel,** and other followers of the Canaanite god, **Baal.** These confrontations included Elijah's foretelling of **drought** to Ahab; his triumph over **four hundred fifty prophets of Baal** in a sacrificial **contest on Mount Carmel;** his jubilant **running before Ahab's chariot** to Jezreel in the drought-ending rainstorm; his flight to Mount Horeb, where he heard **"the still, small voice"** of God. After Jezebel arranged the murderous theft of **Naboth's vineyard** to cheer up her husband, Elijah foretold a gruesome fate for Jezebel, Ahab, and his family. At various times Elijah was miraculously fed by **ravens,** by **angels,** by a widow's inexhaustible **handful of meal** and **cruse of oil.** [1 Kings 17–22.]

Esther

A Jewish maiden who lived in exile in Persia, adopted by **Mordecai** after the death of her parents. Esther won a beauty contest to replace **Queen Vashti** as wife of **King Ahasuerus.** When **Haman,** the Persian prime minister, plotted to destroy Mordecai and all Jews living in Persia, Mordecai turned to

Esther for help. Esther risked her life to approach the king and revealed Haman's plot. In a stunning turnabout, Haman was hanged on the very gallows he had prepared for Mordecai. [Esther.]

Garden of Gethsemane

Site of Jesus' **Agony in the Garden,** just before his arrest and trial. After the **Last Supper,** Jesus went there with his disciples to pray. While his disciples slept, Jesus prayed, "**Father, if thou be willing, remove this cup from me: nevertheless not my will, but thine, be done.**" Then Judas entered the garden to betray his master with a kiss.

Ishmael

Son of **Abraham,** born to **Sarah**'s Egyptian maid, **Hagar.** After Sarah gave birth to her own son, **Isaac,** she forced Abraham to expel Hagar and Ishmael. Hagar expected death in the wilderness, but God assured her (as he had assured Abraham) that he would make of Ishmael a great nation. Many Arabs trace their descent from Abraham through Ishmael, and stories of **Ibrahim, Hajar,** and **Ismail** (Arabic versions) are important Islamic traditions. [Genesis 16, 21.]

Jacob

God-favored son of Isaac. Key events of his life include buying his older twin's birthright (a hungry **Esau sold his birthright for a mess of pottage**); stealing Esau's blessing by tricking their aged father; experiencing the vision of **Jacob's ladder** reaching into heaven; cheerfully working **seven years** as a labor of love to marry his uncle Laban's daughters **Rachel** and **Leah**; and wrestling for a blessing at Peniel, after which God gave Jacob a new name, **Israel.** Jacob's twelve sons became founders of the **twelve tribes of Israel.** [Genesis 25-33.]

Jesus

See **Nativity, Sermon on the Mount, Miracles, Parables, Passion, Garden of Gethsemane, Resurrection.**

Job

The **"upright"** and **patient** (i.e., suffering) man whose terrible torments raise the question of **why the righteous suffer. Job's comforters** tried to justify God's actions, while Job demanded that God justify himself. God ended the exchange with a series of powerful questions that brought Job to his knees. Well-known quotations from Job include **"Let the day perish wherein I was born"**; **"No doubt but ye are the people, and wisdom shall die with you"**; **"Man that is born of a woman is of few days, and full of trouble"**; **"I know that my redeemer liveth"**; **"I was eyes to the blind and feet . . . to the lame"**; **"Canst thou draw out leviathan with a hook?"** [Job.]

John the Baptist
A cousin and forerunner of Jesus, John preached and baptized in the wilderness of Judea, where he lived on **locusts and wild honey.** At the beginning of Jesus' ministry, John baptized him in the Jordan River; the **Spirit** descended **like a dove** and a voice said, **"Thou art my beloved son, in whom I am well pleased."** Later, John was imprisoned by King Herod and finally beheaded at the demand of Salome, as a reward for **Salome's dance** before the king.

Jonah
The reluctant prophet who at first fled from God's assignment to preach to the evil city of Nineveh. Jonah's presence on board nearly caused a ship to sink (ever after, a "Jonah" is one who brings bad luck, especially to a voyage). Jonah survived three days **in the belly of a fish** (or **whale,** according to tradition) before grudgingly proclaiming God's message to Nineveh, bringing that great city to its knees in repentance. [Jonah.]

Joseph
Favored son of Jacob. Key features of Joseph's life include his special robe (or **coat of many colors)** and boyhood dreams of supremacy that provoked his brothers to **cast him into a pit** and **sell him into Egypt.** God gave Joseph success in Egypt despite the false accusations of **Potiphar's wife** and imprisonment. Joseph's abilities (particularly in the **interpretation of dreams**) caused **Pharaoh** to make him governor over Egypt. A great famine brought his brothers to Egypt, and Joseph was reunited and reconciled with all his family. Later, a Pharaoh who **knew not Joseph** would oppress and enslave their descendants, the **children of Israel.** [Genesis 37–50.]

Judas Iscariot
The disciple who **betrayed Jesus** to his enemies **with a kiss** for **thirty pieces of silver.** After Judas hanged himself in remorse, the **blood money** was used to purchase a **potter's field** for the burial of strangers.

Judith

A devout widow who lived in Bethulia. When the Assyrians marched against Israel in overwhelming force, Judith put on all her finery and, with her maid, went to the Assyrian camp. The Assyrian leader, **Holofernes,** was intoxicated by her beauty and later became drunk with wine. Judith killed the unconscious general, cut off his head, and returned to Bethulia. The Israelites promptly routed the Assyrians and celebrated Judith's deed in a triumphal procession. [Judith; in the Apocrypha in some Bibles.]

Kingdom of Israel

The monarchy founded when **Samuel** anointed **Saul** king. Under Saul and his successor, **David**, the tribal groupings of Israel were forged into a united kingdom; David established **Jerusalem** as the capital. Under David's son **Solomon,** the kingdom achieved its peak of power and wealth. After Solomon's death Israel split into two kingdoms. The **Northern Kingdom** kept the name Israel, and **Samaria** was eventually built as its capital. The **Southern Kingdom, Judah,** retained Jersualem as capital. Israel survived about two centuries before falling to the Assyrians. Judah endured some one hundred fifty years longer, falling to the Babylonians under Nebuchadnezzar.

Last Supper

Jesus' last meal with his twelve disciples before his crucifixion, set in an **upper room.** Jesus told his disciples of his coming betrayal, suffering, and death. He broke bread, saying, **"This is my body which is broken for you,"** and took wine, saying, **"This cup is the new covenant in my blood, which is shed for you."** After Jesus noted the presence of his betrayer, Peter proclaimed his loyalty. Jesus foretold Peter's triple denial that night before the cock would crow. Afterwards, Jesus led the disciples to the **Garden of Gethsemane** to pray.

Miracles

Supernatural events, signs of God's power. The Bible describes many miracles, including a number associated with **Moses** and the journey of the Israelites from Egypt to the **Promised Land** (the **burning bush,** the **ten plagues,** the **parting of the sea, manna from heaven,** the **tumbling walls of Jericho**). **Elijah's** prayers revived **the widow's son** from the dead and later called down **the fire of the Lord** to consume **the sacrifice at Mount Carmel.** During the Babylonian Captivity, three young Jews survived in a **fiery furnace; Daniel** read handwriting on the wall at **Belshazzar's Feast** and later survived in a **den of lions. Jesus'** ministry included many miracles, including **healings, raising**

Jairus's daughter from the dead, feeding thousands with only **five loaves and two fishes, walking on the sea, calming a storm,** and **rising from the grave** three days after his crucifixion.

Moses
Leader and lawgiver, Moses led the people of Israel in their **Exodus** from Egypt. Among the key features of his life: as an infant he was concealed from the Egyptians in a floating **basket made of bulrushes**; he was found and raised by Pharaoh's daughter; he killed an Egyptian who was beating a Hebrew and fled into exile. God called him through a **burning bush** to tell Pharaoh, **"Let my people go."** With the help of his brother **Aaron**, Moses confronted Pharaoh. After a series of **ten plagues,** the climactic one being the **slaying of the first-born,** Pharaoh released the Israelites. **The parting of the sea** (by tradition, the **Red Sea)** miraculously allowed them to escape Egyptian pursuit. In the Wilderness, many began to **long for the flesh pots of Egypt;** God then provided **manna from heaven.** At Mount Sinai Moses received the stone tablets of **the Ten Commandments,** while below his impatient people worshiped a **golden calf.** The people of Israel spent **forty years wandering in the Wilderness.** Moses died shortly before his people, led by **Joshua, crossed the Jordan River** to a land **flowing with milk and honey,** the **Promised Land.**

Nativity
The birth of Jesus, described in the Gospels of Matthew and Luke. In the **Annunciation** as reported by Luke, the angel **Gabriel** appeared in Nazareth to a virgin, **Mary ("Hail, thou that art highly favored, the Lord is with thee: blessed art thou among women")**, instructing her that she would miraculously give birth to a son, to be named **Jesus,** who would be called **"Son of the Highest . . . and of his kingdom there shall be no end."** Mary accompanied her betrothed husband, **Joseph**, to Bethlehem, **the city of David,** and while there gave birth to her first-born son, laying him **in a manger, because there was no room for them in the inn.** Shepherds nearby were told by an angel the **"good tidings of great joy"** and heavenly hosts said, **"Glory to God in the highest, and on earth peace, good will toward men."** Matthew describes the arrival in Jerusalem of **wise men from the east** asking where is **he that is born king of the Jews** because they had **seen his star in the east** and had come to worship him. King Herod directed the wise men to Bethlehem, hoping to find this potential rival. The wise men rejoiced to find the child and gave him **gifts of gold, frankincense, and myrrh.** Having been warned by a dream, they

did not report back to Herod. Joseph, also dream-warned, took Mary and Jesus out of the country (a journey known as the **Flight into Egypt**). They escaped the murderous Herod, who ordered the killing of all male babies in the vicinity of Bethlehem (an atrocity known as **the Slaughter of the Innocents**). After the death of Herod, Joseph (again guided by dreams) brought his family to Nazareth.

Noah
A righteous man in an evil generation. Noah obeyed God's instructions to build an **ark** and to **bring two of every living thing** aboard. Only those on the ark survived the **Flood** after it rained **forty days and forty nights**. A **dove** carrying an **olive branch** was Noah's first sign that the waters had receded. Later God set the **rainbow** as the sign of a new **covenant,** or agreement, with Noah and with every living creature. [Genesis 6–9.]

Parables
Brief stories that teach a truth or moral. The prophet **Nathan** told a parable to accuse **King David** of his sins with **Bathsheba**: **"Thou art the man."** Jesus, in particular, told many parables, including ones about a **good Samaritan, a great banquet, a good shepherd, a pearl of great price, a prodigal son.**

Passion
The sufferings and death of **Jesus. Passion Week** began with Jesus' triumphal entry into Jerusalem on a colt, his followers loudly praising God. Jesus then drove out those who sold in the temple (the **Cleansing of the Temple**). Later Jesus ate a **Last Supper** with his twelve disciples, then led them to the **Garden of Gethsemane** to pray. There Jesus was betrayed by Judas and arrested. He was brought before the Jewish **council,** then to **Pilate**, to **Herod**, and back to Pilate, who finally delivered him to be crucified. Soldiers whipped Jesus, **mocked him** with a royal robe, **crowned him with thorns,** and led him to **Calvary**, making **Simon the Cyrenian** carry the cross. Among the words of Jesus while dying on the cross between two criminals: **"Father, forgive them, for they know not what they do"; "My God, my God, why hast thou forsaken me?"; "Father, into thy hands I commend my spirit."** The sun was darkened and the veil of the temple was torn in two. **Joseph of Arimathea** cared for the body of Jesus and laid it in a tomb.

Pilate
The Roman governor of Judea at the time of Jesus' crucifixion. Though he could find no crime worthy of death, Pilate gave

Jesus up to be crucified, first releasing the criminal **Barabbas** to **gratify the crowd.**

Resurrection
The rising of Jesus from death, first discovered by the women who, on Sunday morning, found an empty tomb and two men in shining garments who asked, **"Why seek ye the living among the dead? He is not here, but is risen."** In one of his first post-resurrection encounters, Jesus walked and talked unrecognized with two of his followers **on the road to Emmaus.** He revealed himself to them and later to the eleven disciples, continuing to explain and instruct. Finally, Jesus led his followers to Bethany; and, as he blessed them, he parted from them and was carried up into heaven—the **Ascension.**

Ruth
A Moabite woman, daughter-in-law of Naomi. After both their husbands died, Ruth accompanied Naomi to Bethlehem, saying,"**. . . thy people shall be my people, and thy God my God."** Ruth **gleaned in the fields** for grain; there she attracted the notice of **Boaz,** a kinsman of Naomi's. He married Ruth; their son Obed was the grandfather of **King David.** [Ruth.]

Samson
A judge of Israel. Under special vows as a Nazirite, Samson drew **great strength** from his uncut hair. Samson fell into a deadly cycle of revenge with the Philistines, once killing a thousand men with **the jawbone of an ass.** The Philistines hired a woman, **Delilah,** to discover the source of Samson's strength. Once she learned the secret, Samson was quickly shaved, captured, blinded, and imprisoned. While the Philistines mocked him, Samson called to the Lord; he was able to topple the main pillars of the building, killing himself and thousands of Philistines. [Judges 13–16.]

Samuel
The prophet of God who anointed **Saul** king of Israel. After God rejected Saul, Samuel anointed the youth **David** as Saul's eventual successor. Before his rejection, Saul relied on Samuel as a source of God's guidance. Even after Samuel's death Saul sought him out, causing the medium or **witch of Endor** to call up Samuel's spirit on the eve of Saul's last battle. [1 Samuel.]

Saul
The first king of Israel, anointed by **Samuel** and acclaimed as king by the people at Gilgal. A commanding presence—**higher than any of the people**—Saul proved a capable military leader.

After Saul's incomplete obedience to God after victory over the Amalekites, however, Samuel informed him that God "**hath rejected thee from being king.**" For the rest of his life and reign, Saul was haunted by his rejection and tormented by the rise of the God-favored **David**. Saul and his sons died on the battlefield against the Philistines. [1 Samuel 9–31.]

Sermon on the Mount
A vital message of Jesus' teaching ministry, recorded in Matthew. The Sermon includes **Beatitudes** ("**Blessed are the meek, for they shall inherit the earth**"), a prayer ("**Our Father which art in heaven**"), and many sayings, among them "**Love your enemies**"; "**Turn the other cheek**"; "**No man can serve two masters**"; "**You cannot serve God and mammon**"; "**Where your treasure is, there will your heart be also**"; "**Consider the lilies of the field**"; "**Judge not, that ye be not judged.**" [Matthew 5–7.]

Shadrach, Meshach, and Abed-Nego
Three young men of Israel who were brought to King Nebuchadnezzar's court during the **Babylonian Captivity.** Faithful to their God, they refused to bow to a golden image and were thrown into a **burning fiery furnace.** They emerged unharmed, winning the king's awed respect. [Daniel 3.]

Susanna
A God-fearing woman of great beauty who lived in Babylon during the **Captivity.** She spurned the sexual advances of two lustful elders, and they falsely accused her of adultery. Susanna was condemned to death on the testimony of the elders, but a young boy, **Daniel,** intervened. By questioning the elders separately, Daniel exposed their lies. Susanna's innocent life was saved; the two elders were put to death. [Daniel; in the Apocrypha in some Bibles.]

Acknowledgments

(Continued from page ii.)

Selections

10 "The Creation" by James Weldon Johnson from *God's Trombones* by James Weldon Johnson. Copyright 1927 by The Viking Press, Inc., renewed © 1955 by Grace Nail Johnson. Used by permission of Viking Penguin, a division of Penguin Books USA Inc.

13 "Heaven and Earth in Jest" from *Pilgrim at Tinker Creek* by Annie Dillard, pages 5-9. Copyright © 1974 by Annie Dillard. Reprinted by permission of HarperCollins Publishers, Inc. and Blanche C. Gregory, Inc.

22 "Original Sequence" by Philip Booth from *Letter from a Distant Land* by Philip Booth. Copyright © 1957 by Philip Booth. Used by permission of Viking Penguin, a division of Penguin Books USA Inc.

24 "Eden is that old-fashioned House" by Emily Dickinson from *The Poems of Emily Dickinson*, Thomas H. Johnson, ed., Cambridge, Mass.: The Belknap Press of Harvard University Press. Copyright © 1951, 1955, 1979, 1983 by the President and Fellows of Harvard College. Reprinted by permission of the publishers and the Trustees of Amherst College.

36 "New World" from *Collected Poems 1948–1984* by Derek Walcott. Copyright © 1986 by Derek Walcott. Reprinted by permission of Farrar, Straus & Giroux, Inc. and Faber & Faber, Ltd.

41 "Cain" by Howard Nemerov from *The Next Room of the Dream* by Howard Nemerov. Copyright © 1962 by Howard Nemerov. Reprinted by permission of The Estate of Howard Nemerov.

66 "Noah's Prayer" by Carmen Bernos de Gasztold from *Prayers from the Ark* by Carmen Bernos de Gasztold, illustrated by Jean Primrose, translated by Rumer Godden. Translation copyright © 1962 by Rumer Godden. Original copyright 1947, © 1955, 1956 by Editions du Cloitre. Used by permission of Viking Penguin, a division of Penguin Books USA Inc. and Curtis Brown Ltd.

67 "Noah" by David Ignatow from *Say Pardon* by David Ignatow. Copyright © 1961 by David Ignatow. Wesleyan University Press by permission of University Press of New England.

78 "Sarah" by Delmore Schwartz from *Summer Knowledge* by Delmore Schwartz. Copyright © 1959 by Delmore Schwartz. Reprinted by permission of Robert Phillips, Literary Executor for The Estate of Delmore Schwartz.

79 "The Parable of the Old Men and the Young" by Wilfred Owen from *Collected Poems of Wilfred Owen* by Wilfred Owen. Copyright © 1963 by Chatto & Windus, Ltd. Reprinted by permission of New Directions Publishing Corporation.

80 "The Father" from *The Bridal March and Other Stories* by Björnstjerne Björnson. Translated from the Norse by Rasmus B. Anderson. First published 1882.

91 "The Jacob's Ladder" from *Poems 1960-1967* by Denise Levertov. Copyright © 1960 by Denise Levertov Goodman. Reprinted by permission of New Directions Publishing Corporation and Laurence Pollinger Limited.

124 Lucille Clifton. "moses" copyright © 1987, by Lucille Clifton. Reprinted from *Good Woman: Poems and a Memoir 1969-1980*, by Lucille Clifton, with the permission of BOA Editions, Ltd., 92 Park Ave., Brockport, NY 14420.

125 "Runagate Runagate" by Robert Hayden from *Selected Poems*. Copyright © 1966 by Robert Hayden. Reprinted by permission of October House Inc.

143 "The Murder of Moses" by Karl Shapiro from *Selected Poems* by Karl Shapiro. Copyright 1944 by Karl Shapiro. Reprinted by permission of Wieser and Wieser.

146 Chapter 18 from *The Tables of the Law* by Thomas Mann, translated by H.T. Lowe-Porter. Copyright 1945 and renewed © 1973 by Alfred A. Knopf, Inc. Reprinted by permission of Alfred A. Knopf, Inc.

160 "Sisera" by Muriel Spark from *Collected Poems: I*. Reprinted by permission of Harold Ober Associates Incorporated. Copyright © 1968 by Muriel Spark.

169 Vachel Lindsay, *Collected Poems*, New York, N.Y.: Macmillan Publishing Company, Inc., 1917, 1945.

179 "Women" by Louise Bogan from *The Blue Estuaries* by Louise Bogan. Copyright © 1968 by Louise Bogan. Reprinted by permission of Farrar, Straus & Giroux, Inc.

& Brothers; copyright renewed 1953 by Ida M. Cullen. Reprinted by permission of GRM Associates, Inc., Agents for the Estate of Ida M. Cullen.
410 From *Barabbas* by Pär Lagerkvist, translated by Alan Blair. Copyright 1951 by Random House, Inc. Reprinted by permission of Random House, Inc. and Chatto and Windus Ltd.
433 "Epistle to Be Left in the Earth" by Archibald MacLeish from *Collected Poems 1917-1982* by Archibald MacLeish. Copyright © 1985 by the Estate of Archibald MacLeish. Reprinted by permission of Houghton Mifflin Company. All rights reserved.
442 "Rise and Shine" by Richmond Lattimore from *Poems from Three Decades* by Richmond Lattimore. (First appeared in *The New Yorker*, April 6, 1957). Copyright © 1957 by Richmond Lattimore. Reprinted by permission.

Pronunciation Key

The letters and signs used are pronounced as in the words below. The mark ′ is placed after a syllable with primary or heavy accent, as in **ab bre vi ate** (ə brē′ vē āt). The mark ′ after a syllable shows a secondary or lighter accent, as in **ab bre vi a tion** (ə brē′ vē ā′ shən).

a	hat, cap	j	jam, enjoy	u	cup, butter
ā	age, face	k	kind, seek	u̇	full, put
ä	father, far	l	land, coal	ü	rule, move
		m	me, am		
b	bad, rob	n	no, in	v	very, save
ch	child, much	ng	long, bring	w	will, woman
d	did, red			y	young, yet
		o	hot, rock	z	zero, breeze
e	let, best	ō	open, go	zh	measure, seizure
ē	equal, be	ô	order, all		
ėr	term, learn	oi	oil, voice	ə	represents:
		ou	house, out		a in about
f	fat, if				e in taken
g	go, bag	p	paper, cup		i in pencil
h	he, how	r	run, try		o in lemon
		s	say, yes		u in circus
i	it, pin	sh	she, rush		
ī	ice, five	t	tell, it		
		th	thin, both		
		ŧ͟ħ	then, smooth		

The pronunication key is from the *Scott, Foresman Advanced Dictionary,* copyright © 1993 by Scott, Foresman and Company. All Rights Reserved.

Index